AVRO AIRCRAFT
& COLD WAR AVIATION

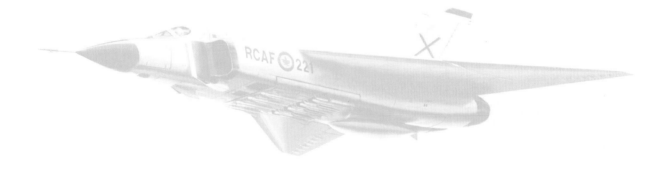

Randall Whitcomb

Vanwell Publishing Limited
St. Catharines, Ontario

Vanwell Publishing acknowledges the financial support of the Government of Canada through the Book Publishing Industry Development Program for our publishing activities.

Design: Linda Moroz-Irvine
Cover Illustration: Randall Whitcomb

Vanwell Publishing Limited
1 Northrup Crescent
P.O. Box 2131
St. Catharines, Ontario L2R 7S2
sales@vanwell.com
phone 905-937-3100
fax 905-937-1760

Howell Press
1713-2D Allied Lane
Charlottesville, VA 22903
USA
phone 804-977-4006
fax 804-971-7204
www.howellpress.com

Printed in Canada

National Library of Canada Cataloguing in Publication Data

Whitcomb, Randall, 1964-
        Avro Aircraft and Cold War aviation

1st ed.
Includes bibliographical references and index.
ISBN 1-55125-082-9

1. A.V. Roe Canada—History. 2. Aeronautics, Military—Canada--History. 3. Aeronautics, Military—Great Britain—History. 4. Aeronautics, Military—United States—History. 5. Cold War. 6. Aircraft industry—Canada—History. 7. Aircraft industry—Great Britain—History. 8. Aircraft industry—United States—History. I. Title.

TL686.A9W48 2001   338.4'7623746'0971   C2001-903665-5

Table of Contents

Preface

SINCE THE CANCELLATION OF THE ARROW PROJECT IN 1959 an emotional debate has raged over the company, the politics and the products of A.V. Roe Canada Ltd. This debate has been intensified by the broad gulf separating the opinions of the "pro-government" and "pro-Avro" extremes. This book began as a critical examination of the products of the company in an attempt to come to a less emotional conclusion. It became clear to me however, during a CF-18 Hornet simulator flight in 1991 that Avro's Arrow, at least, was more than competitive. Subsequent research in gathering material for this book showed Avro's engineering to be visionary, not merely competitive.

Most of the other works on Avro Canada and some of the more searching books on British Cold War aviation also raise the possibility of possible US pressure over some of the more important armament developments in the geo-political sphere. I have taken the view that the corporate, political, military and financial elites, not to mention their intelligence services, had a strategy regarding the aerospace race and the products, companies and nations in competition. Early on in researching this book it became clear that these areas have not been fully explored, let alone put into context. As a result, the scope of this book grew from that of a technical analysis to an attempt to portray the Cold War aerospace arena on a more geo-political level.

The pro-government side of the Avro argument goes to lengths to prove that the United States was supportive of the Arrow project in particular. The evidence seemed to show that this blanket view is simplistic. Just as some in the RCAF were against the Arrow (as an example), some in the USAF and other American institutions were supportive of Avro and their efforts. The pro-government faction also tends to dismiss CIA and intelligence community interest and intrigue surrounding the Arrow and even the Jetliner, CF-100, Avro flying saucers the company, and indeed British aviation as a whole. This book is an effort to build on the excellent work of Kay and George Shaw, Palmiro Campagna and Murray Peden in exploring this arena. Former Canadian finance minister Walter Lockhart Gordon also provided a rather unique and compelling description of some of the geo-political events of the era in his books.

The pro-Avro group however has a wildly divergent view of the products and events surrounding the story and many insist that the record was expunged of pro-Avro documentation after Black Friday, February 20, 1959. It is hard to dismiss this claim considering it is public knowledge that the Diefenbaker Conservatives ordered the destruction of all data and information on the Arrow after Black Friday. This led me to a critical analysis of the statements of various governments and experts involved at the time with some of the performance documentation that survives regarding Avro's products and those of the competition. When seeking the true breakthroughs and "firsts" in aviation, I discovered very early on that the record appears to be somewhat biased, perhaps due to the nearness of the United States with its enormous media output. This book has been, if nothing else, a sincere effort to give credit where credit is due. Unfortunately, this has at times involved dismantling some of the conventional wisdoms.

Over the many years of investigation my opinion has shifted regarding Avro and its products, beginning as an air cadet, in the "anti-Avro, pro-American aircraft" camp and ending firmly entrenched with the "pro-Avro" group. For this, I make no apologies. After all, that opinion was arrived at honestly through over ten years of work.

Virtually all works on Avro Canada have not, in my opinion, given due emphasis to Avro Canada's unique position in being a world-class company with access to both American and British technology. Others have universally failed to see the size and power of the Hawker Siddeley Group of companies, of which A.V. Roe Canada was a part. An important sub-plot of American vs. British aerospace competition emerges. Indeed, there was serious competition within the Hawker Siddeley Group companies themselves. This competitive environment has relevance to the modern day battles of Boeing and Airbus Industries. An effort has been made to show the history and products of these companies in context with Avro Canada and their competitors.

While a great deal of space is devoted to it, this book is not just about the Avro Arrow. It is about a company producing advanced products in a very competitive, and politically charged, time. The Avro company history, from its roots in Britain, is explored as is the evolution of aircraft technology worldwide.

Most of all however, this book is about the human genius behind creativity, and the hottest, sleekest examples of the aviation state-of-the-art made by minds and hands. May the reader find some value in the exploration of some little-known facets of our historical mosaic and find some of the supersonic hardware and Cold War intrigue entertaining if not informative.

Randall Whitcomb
Owen Sound,
November 2001

Acknowledgements

In an effort to put the Avro Canada story into proper perspective it was necessary to try and portray the events in light of the times, i.e., the height of the Cold War with all its intrigues, and indeed at the height of the aerospace race. For information and opinions in these areas, sources in addition to the normal Canadian government documents and works on Avro were consulted. Some of these sources are cited in the bibliography.

Excellent information on some of the corporate coups and defeats of the Cold War, was provided by Evan Mayerle and Joe Baugher. Mr. Mayerle has a wealth of experience in aerospace engineering for US corporations such as Pratt & Whitney, Boeing Rocketdyne (missile) Division, Northrop on the B-2 project, and currently Raytheon. His early guidance answered many questions about US equipment and corporate wrangling, with of course, a view of the political landscapes surrounding events of the Cold War. Having himself worked at Pratt & Whitney Florida on the F-401 engine that was to have gone into the F-14 Tomcat, his expert analysis and "thumbs up" regarding the Orenda Iroquois engine were welcome. He was also instrumental in pointing out the major advances in turbo-jet-engine design, hence his enthusiasm for the Iroquois. His input and patient debates have added greatly to the depth of this book.

Special thanks is due to Paul McDonell who created several images especially for this book. These and other examples of his artwork can be found on his excellent website, www.mach3graphics.com.

Touring with my aviation art put me in contact with literally hundreds of ex-Avroites and their children. These shows also allowed me to meet hundreds of veterans who helped put the human aspect to aircraft development and operations. Shows at airports also put me in touch with current commercial airline pilots. All of these sources certainly increased my familiarity with the subject, and I thank all those who cared to share their experiences and opinions.

My short stint in Canadian Forces pilot training was an excellent introduction to some of the basic aerospace sciences, with the people at hand to put things into perspective. To all the CF pilots, such as Travis Brassington, G.C.P., Paul Frigault, John Laidler, Dave Jurkowski and others who took the time to share their insights I extend my appreciation.

One of the most dogged pursuers of the Avro story since the Arrow was cancelled on Black Friday is the late Les Wilkinson. His contribution cannot underestimated. It is largely due to his determination and work that we have the range of published images and information on Avro Canada. Similarly, Vern Morse and Hugh McKechnie are pivotal for having taken most of the Avro photos in this and other books on the subject. Author Palmiro Campagna, himself a defence scientist in Canada, was gracious in allowing use of the materials in his book and for sharing his thoughts as were Peter Zuuring, Grieg Stewart, Bill Zuk, and Murray Peden.

A special debt of thanks is owed the incomparable Jan Zurakowski for having taken so much time, at various points through the past several years, to share material from his collection, his written remarks, and for enduring a long, wide-ranging interview in March 1997. Aside from his importance in the story itself as the first test pilot to fly the Arrow and as an important CF-100 development pilot, his insights into some of the political aspects led to a deeper appreciation for the feelings of some of those on the chopping block on Black Friday, February 20, 1959. I also thank George and Kay Shaw for having had the courage to put those feelings onto paper while employed at Avro after Black Friday.

Don Rogers, Avro's Chief Test Pilot is thanked for taking the time to meet with me at his impressive lecture on Avro to the Professional Engineers of Ontario and for speaking with me earlier while I was touring as an artist. He was also kind enough to loan his original Avro model of the Arrow (adapted on the cover) which helped in creating the painting for the Arrow design chapter. Don is an important part of the Avro story since he was a test-pilot at Victory Aircraft on the Canadian-built Lancasters. His love-affair with the Avro Jetliner has been a long one as has the list of his accomplishments as a test pilot for de Havilland Canada.

Most important of all, however, from the standpoint of contributions to both the history of Avro Canada, and as a primary source of information for this book, is Jim Floyd. As a young man, Jim Floyd was already designing at Avro in England when the Anson and Lancaster were laid out and some of the credit is his. He is widely considered the father of the Avro Jetliner and of the Avro Arrow and has an outstanding record of development projects. Floyd took the time to talk with me shortly after I left the CF, when I was promoting a painting of the Arrow. Repeatedly Mr. Floyd has loaned period documents and taken the time to go through the manuscript and revisions to ensure accuracy on some of the key Avro projects, organisation and decisions. Indeed Jim Floyd was gracious enough to lend his own research material on the fate of the Avro talent after Black Friday. His loan of personal and Avro documents, formerly Secret, on advanced Arrows and Avro's aerospace plane, on Hawker Siddeley, Avro Canada's SST design studies and so much more were an unexpected bonus and are of historical importance. This material probably provides the most new information on the Avro story contained in this book. His patience, friendship and amazing generosity have been most inspiring. However, everyone I have met who worked somewhat intimately with Jim Floyd describes him as a genius for design and for inspiring others through example. May his trust, as shown by his contribution, be proven well-placed. The opinions and errors, however, are the responsibility of the author.

To the creators, who through genius and sweat take up tools
and make real those things that before were only dreams.

ALLIOTT VERDON ROE was an early aviation pioneer. Born in Manchester England in 1877, he actually lived in Canada as a teenager for two years until 1894, when the family returned to England. He left home at the age of seventeen to secure work as an apprentice at a locomotive works. He obviously didn't like to be "land-locked" and he left this work to study marine engineering at King's College in London. He then joined the merchant navy and during one voyage became fascinated by the flight of a lone Albatross that had been following his ship and looking for an easy meal. Thereafter Roe became, as so many young men do, obsessed with flight. His particular obsession became the "ludicrous" idea of building a manned flying machine.

The Roe 1 biplane.

In 1907 Roe entered a model airplane competition and defeated two hundred other entrants to receive the £75 prize. He used this money to build a full size version of his model and on 8 June 1908, proceeded to fly it at the Brooklands race track. He thus became the first Englishman to fly a heavier-than-air craft. Roe wrote a letter to the London Times urging Britons to take a more active interest in aviation. The Times published his letter with the following disclaimer:

> It is not to be supposed that we in any way adopt the writer's estimate of his undertaking, being of the opinion, that all attempts at artificial aviation on the basis he describes are not only dangerous to human life, but foredoomed to failure.

By 1910 A.V. Roe Company was registered and operating out of a rented hanger at Brooklands in England. An interesting early advertisement guaranteed his machines to fly five miles. An early design, the A.V. Roe model G, was evaluated by the British War Office in August 1912 and three derivatives were ordered for the nascent Central Flying School (CFS). This design was far ahead of its time and evolved into the famous Avro 504, which was a standard flying trainer for the British Empire for several decades, and right up to World War II. This

CHAPTER ONE

A.V. Roe Canada Origins

From Humble Beginnings

The secrets of flight will not be mastered within our lifetime... not within a thousand years.

—Wilbur Wright, 1901

visionary prewar design looked much like the best designs to emerge at the end of the first global conflict and was the standard trainer at Canada's only military flying training base, Camp Borden, until 1929. The base was commanded for a time by Canada's second greatest ace of the Great War, the intrepid William Barker V.C.

The Avro Type E, which led to the famous Avro 504. For 1912 it was an exceptionally advanced design.

Roy Chadwick, a prime figure in both the history of A.V. Roe and indeed the British war effort in both World Wars, joined A.V. Roe in 1911 as a draftsman. His exceptional talent earned him a place as the chief designer and he was largely responsible for the design of the superb Avro 504, the Avro Anson, and notably the Avro Lancaster. He remained chief designer until his tragic death in 1947, sadly in an aircraft of his own design, an Avro Tudor transport aircraft.

Roy Chadwick.
(Jim Floyd collection)

Another key person at A.V. Roe at this time was Roy Dobson. He was raised in the wilderness of the northern moors of Yorkshire, England, later home to most RCAF bomber squadrons of the Second World War. He is described by Jim Floyd as "one of the Bulldog breed" and in fairness, if one compares his visage with that of Winston Churchill, one would think they were brothers. Surely the similarities between these men were more than superficial.

Roy Hardy Dobson joined A.V. Roe in 1914 as a mechanic after having apprenticed as an engineer in Manchester. He was undoubtedly attracted to hands-on pioneering work in what was surely considered a wild and dangerous area of human endeavour. Certainly, the consensus among cooler heads in those days was that had man been meant to fly, he would have been born with wings! Dobson's physical and intellectual courage and no-nonsense approach, coupled with his intellect, served him and the company well. He was knighted in 1945 for his contribution to the war effort, mainly for his tenacity and far-sightedness regarding the Lancaster bomber project. He probably did not mind his moniker, "Sir Dobbie," as it reflected what a determined and hardy individual could accomplish if he did not allow himself to be smothered by pomp, naysayers and red-tape.

In 1928 Roe sold his interest in the company bearing his name and purchased an interest in S.E. Saunders Ltd., a boat-building company. Operating as Saunders-Roe Ltd., the company soon began producing flying boats. In the early 1950s Saunders-Roe (also known as Saro) would produce a turbojet and rocket powered experimental interceptor that would prove stiff competition to A.V. Roe's Avro 720 interceptor of the same concept.

Roy Dobson (via Jim Floyd)

The Hawker Siddeley Group

After the First World War, another British aviation firm, Sopwith, renamed itself Hawker Aircraft with Thomas Sopwith's blessing. This was due to their reverence for Harry Hawker, an Australian test pilot for Sopwith and a powerful proponent of the Sopwith Camel. In 1935 Hawker Aircraft became a founding member of the Hawker Siddeley Group.

Harry G. Hawker was an Australian of modest upbringing who was born in Melbourne in January 1889. He left school at the age of 12 to become an apprentice mechanic. At the age of 16 he attended one of the first aircraft displays in Australia and so caught the aviation bug. He left for England in 1911 and managed to get a job working for Thomas Sopwith as a mechanic at the Brooklands track, which was now becoming Britain's center of aviation. He spent all his wages on pilot training, gaining his certificate in 1912. He soon represented Sopwith aircraft at the races and air displays. With the huge orders for aircraft that accompanied the beginning of World War I, Sopwith Hawker found plenty to do. Perhaps his most notable contribution was test flying the Sopwith Camel, an aircraft that much impressed him. Anyone familiar with World War I history will know that the Camel made quite an impression on the Germans as well. The Canadian ace, William Barker VC, would be credited with 60 victories, most of them with the tricky Camel.

After so much production and fame in World War I, Sopwith Aircraft fell on hard times after the war and was liquidated in 1920. The company re-formed however, but took the name of their most famous test-pilot in the process. The "new" company was named H.G. Hawker Engineering Ltd. Hawker himself died in the 1921 Aerial Derby at only thirty-two years of age. T.O.M. Sopwith was still around though, and would be the Chairman of the Hawker Siddeley Group when the Arrow program was underway.

John Siddeley had been one of the founders of Britain's automotive industry. After founding his own company, the Siddeley Autocar Company, he joined first Wolseley Motor Company, then the Deasy Motor Car Company, adding his name to both. After World War I, the Armstong-Whitworth company, another automaker, and Siddeley-Deasy merged to form Armstrong-Siddeley Motors. Due to a "re-organization" of the automotive industry, similar to one in the aviation industry which will be discussed briefly much later, the company stopped producing cars in 1960. In 1935 however, Hawker Aircraft, A.V. Roe Ltd., Armstrong-Siddeley, Armstrong Whitworth and Gloster merged to form the Hawker Siddeley Group, with each component company retaining their names.

Roy Dobson had become the managing director of Avro aircraft in 1941. Later, in 1958, Sir Frank Spriggs decided to retire from the management of the Hawker Siddeley

Canadian ace Bill Barker in his Sopwith Camel. The Camel is credited with more enemy aircraft destroyed than any other allied pursuit aircraft. After it was liquidated in 1920, the Sopwith company was reformed immediately with the name of the company's greatest test pilot and advocate of the Camel, Harry G. Hawker.
(Public Archives of Canada via Larry Milberry)

Group and, although Dobson was in the running to take over his position, he was not the favourite. By this time Crawford Gordon Jr. was running A.V. Roe Canada and—although he hadn't been Dobson's first choice to replace Walter Deisher at the helm of the Canadian operation—Gordon gave Dobson's cause a real boost. According to Greig Stewart in *Shutting Down the National Dream*, Gordon asked for, and received, the written resignations of many of his top executives at Avro Canada and threatened to make those resignations official if Dobson was not granted the top job in the Hawker Siddeley Group. This heavy-handed gambit paid off and Dobson got the job. Unfortunately Dobson would be at the helm when various political and government intrigues seriously weakened the Hawker Siddeley Group as an independent corporation, some time after the Avro Arrow, Avro Canada and Crawford Gordon Jr. were similarly destroyed.

James Charles Floyd

Jim Floyd was certainly one of the most important and influential long-term executives of Avro Canada. As a teenager growing up near the Newton-Heath plant of A.V. Roe in North Manchester, with a keen imagination and intellect, he could not help but notice the amazing strides going on worldwide in the glamorous field of aviation. Those were the days of Charles Lindbergh, Amelia Earhart and so many others, and a great many headlines were being generated by the hometown heroes at A.V. Roe, with Bert Hinkley flying an Avro Avian solo to Australia. In keeping with Dobson's personal path to success and his belief that people with a genuine passion for aviation, common sense, and real initiative were at least as good as many formally trained university graduates, Dobson instituted a far-sighted apprenticeship program for A.V. Roe. In 1930

Floyd heard that a schoolboy could, with luck, join the company and if he was deemed valuable, have his university-standard education paid for by the company. Through a relative who had invented a propeller-making machine for the company, an overawed and timid fifteen-year-old named Jimmy Floyd got an interview with the hard-nosed Roy Dobson, who was then works manager.

Apparently, and likely to his surprise, Floyd passed his audition in the lion's den and was allowed to begin at a capstan lathe turning out thousands of bolts (while being soaked in whale-oil) for A.V. Roe Aircraft for, as Jim later put it, "the princely sum" of about a dollar a week. After hiring him Dobson warned Floyd to pull his weight and stated that "From here on, I don't know you." The bolts produced at the smelly, hot lathe must have been good ones however, as Jim was soon inducted into the special apprenticeship scheme. As the depression hit in 1930, Floyd was laid off for a time, securing alternate work in an automobile junkyard. Luckily the lay-off was short and once back Floyd began working on real airplanes—installing wiring and fuel lines into Avro Tutor trainers from a diagram written on a postcard! All special apprentices were expected to work and learn in every department and aspect of aircraft production and were often lent out to other components of the Hawker Siddeley Group. Floyd remembered working in the Bedford wind-tunnel facilities and elsewhere, as well as a tool and die maker and every other job to gain experience. This and further advancement upward while going to the Manchester College of Technology one day a week, studying most evenings and without doubt, a rigorous program of self-study (snooping about the place) led to a solid understanding of all the facets involved in aircraft manufacture. It also seemed to imbue him with an ability to empathise and communicate effectively with anyone. This last is something that would hold him in good stead while communing with many of the leading lights of Western aviation.

As Floyd wrote of this period: "The best part of my apprenticeship was a nine-month stint at the company's airfield at Weedford, where I was assigned as a 'pilot's slave' to the Assistant Chief Test Pilot Billy Thorn, a wonderful person who taught me to fly. During the time I was with him, we had some really hair-raising experiences. I joined Roy Chadwick's design team in 1934, in the days of the Anson and later worked on the Lancaster, York, Lincoln and Tudor projects. Sadly, Billy Thorn and Roy

A National Steel Car-built Avro Anson in service with the British Commonwealth Air Training Plan (BCATP) in Canada.
(image by R.L. Whitcomb)

Chadwick were both killed in the crash of a Tudor on August 23, 1947."

Floyd now characterizes much of his early experience at Avro as "glamorous slavery" but speaks with real affection for these early years. Floyd obviously didn't mind getting his hands dirty, perhaps to his mother's ire as she was sometimes confronted by Jim's motorcycle engines disemboweled across her kitchen table. At a mere nineteen years of age he was allowed to design much of the fuel system and the elegant tail of the Avro Anson. This aircraft served in many roles from passenger transport to coastal reconnaissance to light bomber, and most notably perhaps, as a standard multi-engine aircrew trainer for the Second World War British Commonwealth Air Training Program (BCATP) centered in Canada. Some 11,000 examples were built of this simple yet robust design. Its reliability and rugged construction earned the airplane the moniker "Faithful Annie."

Floyd is an extremely modest individual and it is difficult to induce him to speak about his personal contributions to any of the aircraft he was involved with. The reply to questions is invariably "well... I was only a small part

of a large team..." and the inquisitor is quickly deflected to the contributions of others. Floyd was deeply involved in the design of the Avro Lancaster, the ultimate mainstay and saviour of Sir Arthur Harris's night-bombing offensive against the Third Reich. He was largely responsible for the tail design of the Manchester Bomber which later developed into the superb Lancaster. Much later in life Floyd toured one of the two flying Lancasters in the world, at the Canadian Warplane Heritage Museum in Mount Hope, Ontario. An elderly Jim Floyd, of small stature himself, is reported as having remarked upon reaching the cockpit area of the Lanc: "Heavens.... I had no idea we had designed it so small!" But then, the Lancaster was designed for spry, 20-year-old airmen of similar build—not retired gentlemen! The Lancaster was an incredibly efficient design, and much of its success can be attributed to the single-minded approach of eliminating all the "frills" in order to maximize its function: efficient bomb delivery to Hitler's Reich. As has been pointed out in numerous treatments of the Lancaster story, this aircraft, in competition with the much later Boeing B-29, set a speed record for a 22,000 lb. bomb load, and this using engines of

A Victory Aircraft Ltd. Lancaster, the "Mynarski" 419 Squadron RCAF aircraft from the painting *For Right, King & Country*. (painting by R.L. Whitcomb)

about half the power! Considering the fact that the Lancaster wasn't even flush-riveted, this was quite a feat.

It was during his time working on the Manchester and Lancaster designs that Floyd met his wife-to-be, Irene, who was drafting in the design office at A.V. Roe. After being noticed spending an inordinate amount of his time leaning over her drafting table, they were married in July 1940 during the Battle of Britain as Churchill was delivering his immortal "We shall NEVER surrender!" speech.

The Lancaster Bomber

The Lancaster began as the Avro Manchester to suit a—rapidly changing—specification from the British War Ministry in 1938. The continual changes to the specifications should be no surprise considering how fast Hitler's war industry had advanced the state of the art, largely with the help of international banking and corporate investment, and technology transfer. Nazi Germany decided they could afford a massive military industrial complex because they came to realize that money is *a* tool, not the *only* tool, and that there are many ways to employ it. For example,

rather than beginning war production using monies lent by the banks at interest to finance the venture, money was put in under interest-free direct-investment with benefits resulting from reduced overheads and the elimination of financing charges. In Canada, similar government-created firms were established for war production purposes. This method of putting money in the front without interest nearly doubled the size of the Canadian economy during the Second World War, no mean feat and a remarkable demonstration of the potential of "pump-priming" economics and direct government investment. Canada followed a unique and extremely effective monetary and economic policy during the war years and for about a decade afterward. How else can one explain Canada having successfully absorbed all the unemployed when the war ended? Today such monumental accomplishments are branded impossible.

Floyd was lent to Hawkers to work on the design of the Hotspur fighter, itself a variation of the Hurricane design, from 1935 to 1937 even while the legendary Sydney Camm perfected the Hurricane derivation of the Fury

Saviour of the world? Sydney Camm
and Stuart Davies' prototype Hurricane.
Teamed with Reginald Mitchell's
Spitfire, this aircraft would defeat the
Luftwaffe in the Battle of Britain.
(Hawker Aircraft)

bi-plane, with Stuart Davies running the project design. Davies followed Jim Floyd back to Avro, arriving in 1938, to assume duties as Avro's assistant chief designer, working under Roy Chadwick. Jim Floyd became "Dave" Davies' assistant toiling thereafter in Davies' office within the "special security" design office.

Amazingly, the initial heavy-bomber design specification prescribed an aircraft with a take-off weight of approximately 20,000 pounds, while the Lancaster eventually carried a single bomb that weighed more! This is an excellent example of the need for a designer to leave plenty of room for growth in a design and this was something Jim Floyd would remember later during projects such as the C-102 Jetliner and CF-105 Arrow. The 1938 Avro heavy-bomber program, which resulted in the Type 679 or Manchester, was initially restricted to using two Rolls-Royce Vulture compound engines designed to produce 1,760 horsepower (hp). This engine was essentially two Rolls-Royce Kestrel, V-12 engines joined at the crankshaft with the second series of twelve cylinders being inverted.

Interestingly, the Messerschmitt Bf-109 (often incorrectly called the Me-109) and Heinkel He-111 "Blitz Bomber" would initially fly with the Kestrel engine since the German engine manufacturers were, in the mid 1930s, behind the British in high-performance engine design. So were American designers; in fact the Americans would never produce an inline, liquid-cooled engine to match British wartime designs. Other than the rather late Bristol Centaurus, however, the US led in air-cooled radials. Dobson did not like the idea of designing an unproven airframe around an unproven engine in the Manchester program. This premonition proved correct and the lesson stayed with Jim Floyd—with good reason—throughout his long career. There are echoes of this throughout Avro Canada's forcibly abbreviated history. By this time another special apprentice scheme enrollee, Bob Lindley, had persuaded Floyd to ask Chadwick about letting him into the "special security" section of the Avro design office. Floyd thought this odd, especially considering the fact that Lindley rode to work daily with Chadwick; nevertheless he put in the word and a very youthful Lindley was allowed into the "holy of holies."

Perhaps predictably, the Avro Manchester was plagued with problems stemming mostly from the engine's poor performance, unreliability and a tendency to catch fire in flight! Even when the engines held together, they didn't put out "as advertised" and had to be operated at too high a throttle setting to last. (High power settings, when required for normal cruise flight, wear engines out quickly and result in a higher rate of catastrophic failures.) The aircraft was such a disaster that the War Ministry tried to have it cancelled and relegate Avro to producing Handley-Page Halifax bombers under license. Dobson and Chadwick however had wisely (and surreptitiously) anticipated the Manchester's problems and had already enlisted Davies, Floyd and two other engineers to produce general layout and performance calculations for Manchester variants using Bristol Centaurus or Napier Sabre 2,500 horsepower-class engines. These engines were some years down the road in the reliability department circa 1940 however. Studies showed that an extended wing Manchester with a slightly revised tail and four Rolls-Royce Merlins, at roughly 1,000 hp each, held significant performance advantages over the Vulture powered variant and indeed over the Merlin-engined and flush-riveted Halifax bomber.

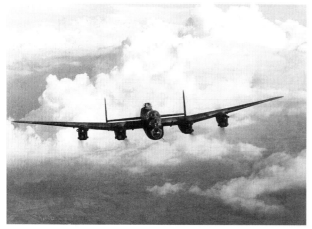

An Avro Lancaster. This view shows the relatively small frontal area of the Lancaster compared to any of the Allied heavy bombers and explains, in part, its excellent performance.

It is a little known fact that it was Jim Floyd who produced the first Type 683 Merlin-engine Manchester arrangement drawings. When Dobson saw the performance projections for this version he was elated. Somehow, despite every Merlin engine being desperately needed at that time for fighters, Dobson managed to receive assurance from Rolls-Royce's Lord Hives for provision of these scarce engines, complete with Beaufighter mountings and nacelles, for the Type 683 aircraft. He then managed to get a stay of execution from the Ministry of Aircraft Production (MAP). Stuart Davies, now Avro's experimental manager, received a note demanding that he have the modified aircraft ready to fly by 31 December 1940 — "OR ELSE!" The team was nine days late.

In an effort to ensure they met this timetable, the designers and engineers had their desks moved to the floor of the plant around the growing Lancaster prototype and almost lived on the floor until it was done. A similar tactic was employed later in Canada on the first passenger jet to fly in North America. Dobson's hard-headed approach saved Avro's heavy bomber program from disaster, but not without antagonizing the "bean-counters" and politicians with his "damn the torpedoes" and "to hell with the bureaucrats" method. The simple fact was that to re-tool the factory to produce the Halifax would have taken longer than producing a superior four-engined Manchester, or Lancaster as it was renamed. Certainly Mr. (later Sir) Frederick Handley Page was non-plussed by this development and thereafter lost the initiative in aircraft production to A.V. Roe and the Hawker Siddeley Group.

The first flight of the re-engined and re-named heavy bomber shattered the performance records achieved by competing designs and (almost) silenced the critics. At one demonstration a lightly loaded Lancaster outran a Hawker Hurricane fighter in level flight at over 300 miles per hour (mph) sustained speed. Britain needed a serious offensive war machine, and she now had one.

Since there was a shooting war going on at this time, Floyd understandably tried to enlist in the RAF. His first attempt was refused on medical grounds and his second was pre-empted by Avro's insistence on his higher value in designing war-winning aircraft rather than "enjoying himself" in the RAF! Floyd was probably somewhat frustrated at having to fly a desk but his immediate boss, Harold Rogerson, understood his feelings and ensured that he was able to fly as much as was practical on Avro test flights. Those were days when time was of the essence and normal pre-flight testing procedures were deemed an unaffordable luxury. Floyd recalls several stomach-emptying and hair-raising experiences brought on by pilots whose daring sometimes exceeded their skill, or at least the comfort margin of their fellow crew! Additional excitement was provided by sometimes less

National Steel Car's first Lysander. (via Larry Milberry)

The Hampden bomber. It was not successful against the Luftwaffe. (Public Archives of Canada)

than adequate parts and systems under test. On one of these flights, a cover over a door system under test in an Avro York transport blew out, and Floyd, tape measure in hand, found himself dangling in the slipstream over Cheshire, England. Luckily another manoeuvre and slipstream buffet placed him dazed and confused (but no doubt relieved) at the back of the fuselage.

The demand for the Lancaster, as a result of its having the lowest average loss rate and also the highest speed and bomb load of virtually all Allied heavy bombers in the European theatre, soon outstripped the capacity of the scores of British plants involved in production. According to decorated members of the RCAF serving in Lancasters and Halifaxes, (such as F/O Jack Dundas) the Lancaster cruised to the target 45 mph faster than a Boeing B-17 Flying Fortress and returned 75 mph faster. The radial-engined Halifax III was not far behind the Lancaster in speed, indeed the Mk. 6, with developed but problematic Bristol Hercules engines, was even faster than the Merlin-Lancaster and had superior altitude performance. Both British machines carried four times the bomb load to Berlin as the Boeing B-17.

National Steel Car and Victory Aircraft

In 1938, with the storm clouds of war rising in Europe, a rapid expansion of the munitions industry was undertaken by the western soon-to-be allies. A part of this response was the establishment of the National Steel Car plant at Malton, Ontario, Canada in 1938 as an addition to National's wheeled-vehicle operations. The first aviation contract for the firm was the short take-off and landing, (STOL) army co-operation aircraft, the Westland Lysander. The first Canadian-produced Lysander flew on 17 August 1939, just over a month before the Nazi invasion of Poland that started World War II. The Lysander would distinguish itself as a staff "hack" aircraft, an observation platform during the desert war against Erwin Rommel's Afrika Korps, and as a covert operations "O", or Moon Squadron, aircraft dropping supplies and spies to the resistance movement in Hitler's occupied Fortress Europe.

As National Steel Car's expertise and experience grew new projects quickly came their way. Soon the company was heavily involved in producing Avro Ansons for the BCATP as well as the Handley-Page Hampden bomber. Hawker

Hurricane airframes were at the same time being produced at Fairchild's plant in Thunder Bay while Canadian Vickers would produce the Catalina flying boat. Noorduyn was building scores of Harvard trainers and many other companies were involved in similar production projects.

Under the guidance of C.D. Howe, the all-powerful minister of munitions and supply, National Steel Car soon looked to greater challenges and in anticipation of receiving a contract to produce the Martin B-26 Marauder medium bomber, they undertook a major expansion of the Malton facility. Due to the Marauder's teething problems, (most noticeably a very high-wing-loading and center-of-gravity problem which resulted in under-trained wartime pilots killing their crews and themselves in landing accidents), this program never came to fruition. A tale from Ireland, of a row of houses at the approach end of a Marauder training base, provides a clue. Apparently this row of houses became constantly shorter as aircraft stalled and flick-rolled into the housing on approach for landing. The rate of row-shortening increased dramatically when the Marauders appeared.

The Americans would persist with the Marauder despite it being a bomber which naturally requires a low wing loading for a decent bomb load to keep the induced drag down. It was fast on the deck however, and needed to be. Around this time National Steel Car's founder passed away and the remaining company management became decidedly hostile to the company's aviation pursuits. At this time Fred Smye was the 27-year-old National Director of Aircraft Production. Smye, C.D. Howe and the government became concerned about the new attitude at National Steel Car and opted to nationalize the plant, renaming the new Crown-owned company Victory Aircraft. The plant's surplus floor space, and Britain's constant shortage of aircraft, presented an opportunity for both parties.

During the re-organization of National Steel Car into Victory Aircraft, the former management was replaced by a number of Howe's "bright boys." The new President was J.P. Bickell, a senior executive of the Canadian Imperial Bank of Commerce, with Dave Boyd as General Manager.

Victory Aircraft, guided by such brash, confident upstarts (inspired by perhaps an even more illustrious leader in the form of Howe), began trumpeting the potentials of Victory Aircraft with its new facilities, and of Canadian industry in general to the hard-pressed British. Wild claims of being able to produce a Lancaster faster and better than its own designers were heard in England, and the bluff was called.

By January 1942 Victory had a contract to produce one of the largest, most complex and advanced aircraft in the world, the Lancaster long range heavy bomber.

Despite enormous difficulties and frustrations, Victory rolled out its first pseudo-complete Lancaster in August 1943. Dobson, hearing the boasts about the superior quality of the Canadian Lancaster and other mixtures of fact and fancy, decided to visit Canada and see for himself the roll-out of the first Victory Lancaster. Apparently, he arrived a little late as the plant outperformed his expectations and delivered its first offspring early. His comments upon seeing the Canadian operation are well documented and according to *Jet Age* by Scott Young, his words were to the effect: "It opened my eyes, I'll tell you. If these so and so's can do this during a war, what can't they do after?" Dobson was so confident in the future of the North American branch that he predicted Canada would become the center of aircraft production for the British Commonwealth within a decade. Howe is on record in that year as saying "Never again will there be any doubt that Canada can manufacture anything that can be manufactured elsewhere." Unfortunately many Canadians today don't seem to believe this, despite Avro and their subcontractors having proven it time and again in the forties and fifties, often too early for their genius to be recognized.

Victory would go on to produce 430 Lancasters during the war, and produce them at the one-a-day rate as promised in the initial boasts to the British. Most of these aircraft would equip RCAF squadrons operating from Dobson's home turf in Yorkshire, England, against German industrial targets. Towards the end of the conflict, Victory Aircraft would tool up and produce one example of the Lancaster's successor, the Lincoln bomber. This was a stretched Lancaster with advanced Merlins and more modern on-board systems.

When the war ended, some 10,000 employees were released without notice, leaving an enormous pool of unused human talent, not to mention a world-class facility sitting virtually idle at Malton.

A.V. Roe Canada Limited

The turmoil of thousands of troops returning home to Canada, coupled with the lay-off of thousands of workers involved in armament production, left difficult issues on the employment front. Here was a country, according to British author/historian Len Deighton in his phenomenal book *Blood Tears and Folly*, that had committed a higher percentage of her population to wartime uniformed military service than *any* of the combatants, with the added distinction of this mass of manpower being comprised largely of volunteers. Deighton goes on to show that Canada had also yielded the highest per capita industrial output dedicated to the war effort once again of *any* of the combatants —yet had begun the conflict with relatively little of her own indigenous industry. Howe and his bright boys had sought to change all of that and had succeeded beyond all expectations. It was once common knowledge that Canada had ended the war with the third largest navy, the fourth largest air force, and the fifth largest army of any of the wartime players. (These rankings were described in the Canadian Forces' [CF] Air Force Indoctrination Course [AFIC] for many years.) Post-war Canada, flush with hard-won confidence, sought to maintain her global position. A newly-knighted Roy Dobson also felt justified to continue Avro involvement in this emerging, postwar world. To the hardy and determined, a setback is seen as an opportunity. Such was the case with the unemployed youth and brainpower of Canada, and the idle plant at Malton.

Fred Smye, A.V. Roe Canada's first employee. (Avro Canada)

Again, a young Fred Smye enters the picture. Smye's ability and enthusiasm, along with Dobson's appreciation of Victory Aircraft's achievements and Canada's potential, would combine to produce a sum that was greater than the parts. Britain's economy and human resource pool were devastated by the Second World War and Britannia was essentially bankrupt. Dobson saw clearly that the future lay in the New World, backed up by the simple fact that the power base of the post-war world lay in the United States, and so did the money. It is no secret that US corporations had made huge fortunes during the conflict. In short, North America

was where the money and action was and would be for the foreseeable future. Avro was the only company with the level of first-hand experience in Canada that the production of the Lancaster demanded and was thus in a position to act on Canada's need for a postwar "mission" if you will.

Eventually, despite grave monetary, corporate and political misgivings in Britain over the decision to support an overseas operation adjacent to the largest aircraft industry on the planet (that of the United States), Dobson and Howe, through Smye, came to a rent-to-own agreement. Avro, under the Hawker Siddeley Group, would take over the Malton facility and begin producing an aircraft, any aircraft, in Canada. A.V. Roe Canada Ltd. was established on 1 December 1945, and took over the Victory Aircraft facility in Malton. Its only employee at this time was a youthful Canadian named Fred Smye. He would proudly boast later about his identification card's number: ONE. Smye was probably the most important person in A.V. Roe Canada management, at least as far as the aircraft side goes, of anyone who ever worked in the company— Crawford Gordon Jr. included. Ex-Avro officials point out his confidence, enthusiasm and ability as being crucial to the company from the first day.

Jim Floyd wrote in an article discussing the formation of Avro Canada that, at the time, the Hawker Siddeley Group was the largest and most flexible aerospace company on earth. Whether this company and its parents future problems were due to inability and bad decisions or external influences is open to interpretation. At the time however, Canada was very sensitive to her lack of high-tech industry, lack of design capabilities, and lack of an armaments industry that could be counted on to serve Canada *first*. It is interesting that the Hawker Siddeley Group was, at the time, the ideal company to provide all of those things and more. After all, how many other industrial alliances could boast planes, trains, automobiles, engines and more?

Canada's experience as a secondary power subservient to the Great Powers during two conflicts, and having had to suffer the inadequacies of equipment and command that this naturally entailed, was understandably sensitive about her lack of an indigenous defence industry. Her excellence in air power, demonstrated by Deighton's assertion that Canada always produced the world's best fighter pilots and backed up by our out of proportion contribution to air power in both conflicts, suggested that aerospace was a natural pursuit for this newly confident land. Canada was then aware that it had the largest land and sea area to defend in the free world and recognized the nation's responsibility to do just that. The feeling in the RCAF and government at the close of World War II, undoubtedly spurred on by the likes of Air Marshal Wilf Curtis and Smye, was that Canada should develop and produce her own fighter aircraft of especially long endurance, range and potency. In fact, work had already begun to this end in the government establishment of Turbo Research, a crown corporation investigating jet engine design during the war. C.D. Howe was at this time advised by Crawford Gordon Jr., then Director of Defence Production, that Avro should be encouraged to take over Turbo Research if they were interested.

Turbo Research Limited

During the war, the progress and performance promised by Sir Frank Whittle's jet engine designs, along with the rumours coming from behind the veil of the Third Reich, (rumours that all too soon for the Allies turned to reality in the form of the Me-262 jet fighter) demonstrated to the Canadians the need to get involved on the ground floor of this new technology.

In early 1943 Paul Dilworth and Ken Tupper, research engineers with Canada's National Research Council (NRC), were sent to Britain for five months to study the progress of Whittle's engine program. Thus, all available research and theoretical information, most of which was handed over gladly by the British, was gathered and, by 4 January 1944 a Whittle jet was running in Winnipeg, conducting cold weather research at a new Canadian facility. Turbo Research Canada was officially established in July 1944 as a Crown corporation.

Design studies were conducted on various centrifugal compressor type jets suitable for military fighter aircraft. These were largely similar to the Whittle designs, with the exception being the TR-4 axial-flow design masterminded

Harry Keast, jet engine aerodynamicist extraordinaire.
(Orenda Engines Ltd. via *Jet Age*)

by Winnett Boyd, Turbo Research's chief design engineer. With the end of the Second World War the urgency pushing the development of jets vanished, and with it government support. The Manchester had suffered from Avro's inability to direct engine development and allocation in the past, and a golden opportunity presented itself with the Canadian government's zeal to divest itself of its interests in the field of turbojet engine development.

The initial requirements set forth by the RCAF and the government relating to the engine type to be built by Turbo Research/Avro Gas Turbines naturally reflected both the rapid advances in jet propulsion theory and the turmoil caused by the cessation of hostilities in Europe. The conservative side of the argument (including Whittle himself) supported a centrifugal-type compressor, while the more adventurous pointed out the future advantages of the axial-flow concept. Firmly in the cutting edge camp was the visionary Winnett Boyd. Many specifications were bandied about based on the mass airflow and size limitations which translated into a certain nacelle size being recognized as *the* factor determining an engine's performance possibilities. This convention is still normal today. Finally, a specification for an axial flow design to fit a 32 inch nacelle was accepted and by the end of 1945, Paul Dilworth and Winnett Boyd had a couple of preliminary designs roughed out on paper. One would eventually become the TR-4 Chinook. All that was lacking was a gifted aerodynamicist.

In 1942, despite war-torn England's manpower shortages, Harry Keast, young engineer, was unemployed. He

The TR-4 Chinook turbojet. (A.V. Roe Canada Ltd.)

received an offer from Whittle's top secret Power Jets company but was initially sceptical. All visionaries like Whittle are initially considered eccentric at best, or more usually as lunatics with crazy ideas. Keast got over his reservations and would become one of those visionaries with his own "crazy" ideas. With the end of the war, Whittle's government-funded, secret enterprise largely evaporated due to Whittle's resignation over the cancellation of the Miles M.52 supersonic research aircraft. Keast, now a convert with, suddenly, much less exciting prospects on the horizon, heard of Winnett Boyd's search for a competent aerodynamicist. Keast was especially intrigued by Turbo Research's bold leap into the future embodied by their commitment to axial-flow design. At this point axial-flow compressors were developing significantly lower compression numbers as compared with their centrifugal cousins. Keast arrived in Canada in August 1946 to help in the design of the TR-4 engine.

A pilot trainee who had studied at Toronto's Ryerson Polytechnic under Harry Keast described him as an excellent and inspiring professor who often pointed out the systems and problem solving techniques of Avro/Orenda. In fact, when the US farmed out design aspects of the National Aerospace Plane (a Hypersonic+ aerospace plane) in the late 1980s, Ryerson and Keast were reportedly asked to design, with the assistance of the students, aspects of the intake. The intake design was for up to

Mach 8 and apparently under Keast's inspiration, the old "breadboard" approach was used to great effect. This concept uses a system of small, performance development steps gradually narrowing in focus to the "right" design. I was told Ryerson's solution was very effective and the end users were very surprised at the low cost.

Consider what an advanced engine the Chinook was. While most of the world's manufacturers were struggling to get centrifugal compressor engines to work, the Canadians were charging ahead with an axial-flow design. The essential difference between a centrifugal-flow engine and an axial-flow design relates to how the air taken in through the intake is compressed to give a good charge for mixing with fuel for burning. The more air (oxygen) you can compress into a small volume, the more fuel you can then mix with it and burn. More air/fuel mixture to burn means more thrust (power) issuing from the jet pipe. A centrifugal-flow engine takes air in the center and a ribbed spinning disc flings it centrifugally outward into a smaller volume section (thereby compressing it) that leads to the combustion chambers (combustors), requiring essentially four ninety-degree changes of direction. An axial-flow design sucks the air past sets of compressor (fan) blades of progressively smaller diameter (thereby compressing it) resulting in a straight-through design. The theoretical compression ratio attainable by a centrifugal flow design is around 7 to 1, while axial flow designs have achieved

The Messerschmitt Me-262 "Swallow" jet fighter.

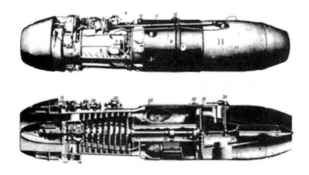

The first jet engine in combat, the Junker's Jumo axial-flow design.

over three times that ratio. The problem was, and still is, to figure out the aerodynamics, mechanics and materials for an axial-flow design that will allow the utmost efficiency in the smallest package.

The Junkers Jumo 004 design that powered the Me-262 German jet fighter at the end of the war was an axial-flow design of approximately 2000 lbs thrust. Its arrival certainly shocked the Allies. Had it not been for Hitler's interference and the delays that resulted, this engine and aircraft might have seriously prolonged or even changed the outcome of the war. In the course of one attack by a Squadron of Me-262s, thirty of a force of thirty-six B-17 Flying Fortresses were shot down. By later standards however, the Jumo's entry into service was premature. The engine suffered from problems relating to aerodynamics, materials, control systems and production quality. Some examples displayed, at the worst possible moments, a very short lifespan and the design was prone to fires and catastrophic failures in flight. Many Me-262s were shot down by Spitfires, Mustangs and other Allied fighters while limping along on one engine.

Before the end of the war Lockheed P-80 Shooting Stars (forerunner of the T-33 Silver Star) were already stationed in Europe, flying with Whittle-derivative Allison centrifugal-flow jet engines and suffering from terrible fuel control system problems and engine fires. It would have been a most interesting match-up had the P-80 ever gone into combat with the Me-262. For the record, the Rolls-Royce

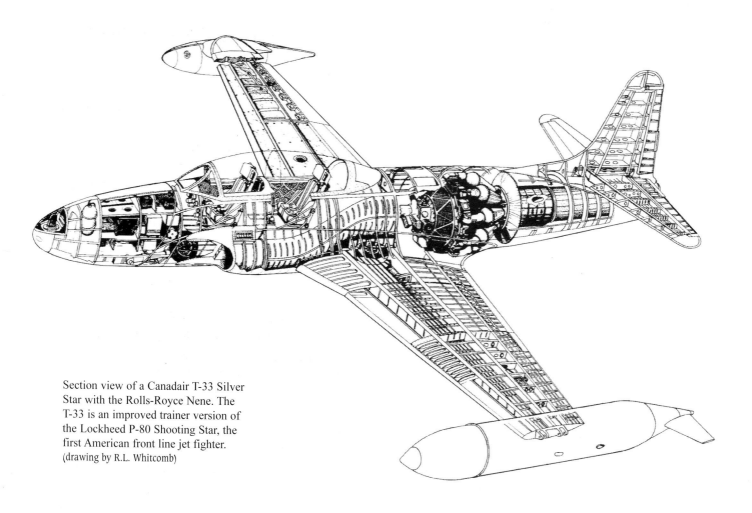

Section view of a Canadair T-33 Silver Star with the Rolls-Royce Nene. The T-33 is an improved trainer version of the Lockheed P-80 Shooting Star, the first American front line jet fighter. (drawing by R.L. Whitcomb)

The Avro Gas Turbine's TR-4
Chinook on the test stand.
(Orenda newsmagazine)

Nene 10, still in use in Canada's T-33, is still likely the most bullet-proof jet engine flying today. Ingestion of items (like small birds) through the intake which would literally cause an axial flow design to vaporize into millions of tiny and highly airframe-unfriendly parts barely cause the Nene to waver in rpm. Indeed CF pilots on leave have been rumoured to stuff pairs of skis into the intakes of T-33s before flying off to the slopes!

Within months of Keast's arrival the first Canadian-designed gas-turbine engine sprang to life. It first ran on 17 March 1948 and was a resounding success. It produced a reliable 2,600 lb. thrust from what was at the time a very small package. Fred Smye stated that the Chinook was A.V. Roe's first success and that this small band of 40 bright minds had beaten both mighty engine corporations, Rolls-Royce and General Electric, in overcoming the aerodynamic, fuel control and material challenges the axial-flow design presented. Considering the still relatively modern configuration of this engine, and the ones of similar thrust to follow, it is a wonder no applications were found for the Chinook. But then, the world was just beginning to wake up to the possibilities of jet propulsion and many piston-engine aircraft would be designed after this success. The Chinook had plenty of development potential but Avro Gas Turbine Division was interested in producing larger more powerful engines for military and civilian applications. The RCAF and government also favoured a higher

thrust engine and they were the ones putting up the money at that time.

The First Big Step: A Jet Passenger Aircraft

By the fall of 1944 Dobson saw the need to look ahead, past the cessation of hostilities and consider the company's long-term prospects and optimum design path. Avro's Yeadon (UK) plant had built a camouflaged underground production and office facility called "the mine." Here Davies was sequestered with some key staff to lead Avro's "think-tank." Jim Floyd again appeared as Davies' (his nickname was Dave), project engineer. Certainly a few turbine-powered transport and bomber concepts were tossed around here. Avro UK would soon be fully occupied producing a new delta-winged jet bomber as well—the legendary Vulcan. A couple of transport designs from Yeadon helped open discussions with the Canadian government representatives for Avro's Canadian operation.

In 1945 Dobson's prospective crown jewel had, at the time of its inception, plenty of dreams and no product. Dobson had taken over the entire facility and the enormous floor space was ominously silent. The bays were still crammed with Lancaster and Lincoln parts with equipment and tools lying where they had been at war's end. Dobson's faith and guts, and the good will of his Canadian partners were in serious need of more than the always-free verbal support and encouragement. A.V. Roe Canada Ltd. needed contracts. Discussions with Trans Canada Airlines

Rolls-Royce Merlins being overhauled at Bristol's facility in Montreal. (via *Canadian Geographical Journal*)

(today Air Canada) and the RCAF had shown potential in two areas. One possible requirement was a modern indigenous fighter suited to defending Canada's enormous territory. The other possibility seemed to come in the form of a high-speed airliner to speedily service the nation's huge landmass while still being able to operate from rather short and undeveloped airfields. These two prospective projects were initially begun only with verbal support from the RCAF, the Canadian Government and TCA.

It had seemed to Davies' Yeadon team that, due to the wartime halt to commercial aircraft manufacturing and with the interim wear imposed on the airframes in service, a commercial airliner replacement would be one good bet for the future. Several designs were looked at including small DC-3 replacements, turbo-prop designs and even pure jet aircraft, all based on the Yeadon team's work. At about this time Dobson was in discussion with Howe about the possibility of his proposed Canadian company developing aircraft in Canada tailored particularly to Canadian needs. One idea was for a commercial aircraft for Canada's flagship carrier Trans Canada Air Lines. Howe was generally favourable provided TCA was interested, and a viable design was agreed upon. As such A.V. Roe's top technical man, Stuart Davies, met with TCA's Chief Engineer, Jack Dyment, and they discussed design ideas with Davies recommending a very economical turboprop aircraft. Davies also met with the remaining Victory Aircraft senior engineers, on a visit at this time, and worked over some configurations and specifications. Among this group of originals were Bill Shaw, Mario Pesando, Jack Millie and Ken Barnes. One promising design consisted of a 30-passenger aircraft using Armstrong-Siddeley's new "Z" engine, which became the successful Mamba turboprop engine. This configuration

would later show its potential via the success of the Vickers Viscount, purchased later by TCA, and so many others. In this case, the Hawker Siddeley Group would have been able to direct both the airframe and engine development since Armstrong-Siddeley was a group member.

Jim Bain, another highly placed TCA technical man, after meeting with Rolls-Royce executives, became wildly enthusiastic about an engine under development at Rolls, the axial-flow Avon, and insisted that the new aircraft be fitted with this pure jet engine. That this engine was only in the early design stages and might well fail, or be reserved for top secret military programs did not seem to occur to Bain, partially due undoubtedly to excellent salesmanship by Rolls-Royce's managing director, Lord Hives. One should bear in mind that Rolls-Royce and indeed all of British industry were desperate for contracts after the war since they too had an unemployment problem; in fact their economy was in a shambles after the long fight against Hitler. Rolls-Royce was likewise extremely pleased with Canada since its first ever commercial engine project was an adaptation of the Rolls-Royce Merlin engine for the Canadair North Star airliner, soon to enter service with TCA. Thus, it was the Canadians who had allowed Rolls-Royce to enter the commercial aero-engine field in which they now are one of the "Big Three" players. Rolls was understandably grateful and enthusiastic about dealing with Canada and TCA.

In reality Rolls-Royce experienced serious difficulties with the Avon engine, and the British government was also refusing to release it for any commercial use for security reasons. For just these reasons, Avro had initially protested this engine choice to TCA and Howe. The development of the Avon took so long that by the time it was an effective engine, the Chinook had already run and solved for the Canadians most of the problems of axial-flow design. Indeed the Avon would have to compete with a second Winnett Boyd design in the form of Avro Gas Turbine Division's fabulous Orenda engine! It was clear that the jet transport team could not count on getting Avons and a substitute in the form of four Rolls-Royce Derwent centrifugal-flow engines was adopted in the interim. Interestingly, an excellent engine installation for the Jetliner would have been commercially rated TR-5 "Orenda" engines; however, this engine was far from being a sure thing when the engine installations were being designed for the Jetliner.

Nevertheless, Avro UK's Stuart Davies returned from his discussions with Dyment and Bain bubbling with enthusiasm for the project. From the rough aircraft requirement a feasibility study was begun in England with Jim Floyd, once again, heavily involved. A team was assembled to emigrate to Canada and get A.V. Roe Canada Limited rolling. A Canadian, Walter Deisher, was installed as president, with Fred Smye as his right-hand man. Edgar Atkin was appointed as chief designer of the new company with Stan Harper as his administrative assistant. These two individuals were about to leave for Canada when Jim Floyd was approached and asked if he wanted to pursue the jet project in Canada. He had by this time accepted a job offer from Chrislea Aircraft in the hallowed position of chief designer. Apparently Davies had a fit and asked Floyd if he had completely and utterly lost his mind! After all, not many people get an opportunity to direct the development of what could very well be the first jet passenger aircraft in the world. Floyd duly arrived in Malton to what was likely his first taste of real snow during a storm in February 1946. It took him some five days to make the trip due to weather concerns aircraft and airport servicing problems. This same trip takes about eight hours in a 747 while the Concorde, another aircraft Floyd became involved with, takes about three and a half hours. This is an illustration of the state of the art for commercial passenger service in the 1940s. Needless to say, the Jetliner design would have been a giant improvement.

On his arrival Floyd discovered that there was still a tiny but excellent team of engineers who had agreed to remain at Victory until such time as the ultimate fate of the facility was decided. Atkin would be heading up all projects as Avro Canada's chief designer with Floyd as his chief technical officer. Bill Shaw and Stanley Harper, formerly Victory Aircraft's chief engineer now Atkin's administrative assistant, hired Jim Chamberlin, a Canadian wartime engineer from Noorduyn. Fred Smye would say that Robert Noorduyn himself, aware his company was dying, recommended Chamberlin. It was a decision Smye certainly never regretted. Noorduyn had been busy during the war cranking out hundreds of Harvard trainers for the BCATP and other customers. These Harvards would be replaced, starting in 1964, by the Canadair Tutor Jet trainer, which won a competition with Avro during the dying days (literally) of the Arrow program. Also from Noorduyn came Carl Lindow. These last two engineers would be two of the linch-pins in the Avro operation to the end, especially where the Arrow project was concerned. Another was Mario Pesando, who had been Victory's chief aerodynamicist. This individual would eventually run the Avro Project Research Group which produced some truly revolutionary and visionary concepts such as a hypersonic aerospace-plane. All three gentlemen would be very important to the American space race after Avro was destroyed.

Pesando accompanied Floyd to TCA's Winnipeg headquarters for more formal discussion of the airline's requirements. They left with a firmer design designated the Avro C-102. TCA's president H.J. Symington followed up with a letter of intent to Avro to purchase thirty such aircraft if they met the carrier's specification. The program was now officially underway and Avro quickly built up its engineering staff to about 100 people, with design progressing rapidly under Atkin and Floyd. Avro Canada was going to take its first big step and as its very first project produce the first jet passenger aircraft in North America, if not the world.

The Next Big Step: Jet Fighters For the RCAF

As mentioned earlier, Canada had suffered from a lack of nationally-owned defence industries in two world wars. Canadian servicemen had been forced to make do with what was offered and arguably this cost lives. An example of this dilemma was the very real threat to the West Coast posed by the Japanese invasion of the Aleutian Islands. At this time, Hurricane fighters were sorely needed to defend this area but were earmarked for delivery to Russia, despite having been built in Canada. This event played very much in the mind of RCAF Air Vice Marshal (AVM)

Wilf Curtis at the time and would stay with him while he was Chief of the Air Staff. Canada had acquired a new confidence in her abilities, hard won during the war, and a new determination to stand on her own, provide for her own defence with her own equipment, and play a more active role on the world stage to help prevent another catastrophic conflict. Since air power was a natural specialty and represented the most logical way to defend the nation's huge area, this was rightly seen as the best area in which to specialize.

The early steps, however, were quite timid. Following the cessation of hostilities with the Axis powers, the RCAF "reverse engineered" its air defence plan by looking at what was out there and deciding what they thought could be done with it, and by looking at the air defence plans of Britain, knowledge of which Canada had gained from wartime experience. The RCAF, Department of Defense Production (involving Crawford Gordon Jr.), Defense Research Board (DRB), and National Aeronautical Establishment (NAE), which operated under the National Research Council (NRC), collaborated and a specification was drawn up for a modest, single-seat, single-engine jet fighter, with an air defence plan built around it. They envisioned usage of an engine of about 5,000 lb. of thrust using the axial-flow concept. No matter where they went however, they could not find an engine of this performance other than the larger, heavier, centrifugal-flow compressor types such as the Rolls-Royce Nene, then about the most performant emerging jet powerplant in the world. This would force unacceptable compromises in aircraft size, weight, drag, fuel and weapons load, and range. The RCAF looked within Canada to Turbo Research and suggested they look at the design of a 5,000 lb thrust, axial-flow engine to meet the specification, which ruled out their emerging Chinook of just over half that output. This was the beginning of the TR-5 Orenda engine which was such

The Gloster Meteor, state of the art in 1947.   (Hawker Siddeley)

A de Havilland Canada-built Mosquito constructed for purchase by the USAAF, the Mosquito was probably the best multi-role aircraft of World War II. (Peter M. Bowers)

a success that Turbo Research would be re-named Avro Gas Turbines division and then named again, the last time after this engine.

In September 1945, before A.V. Roe Canada was established, a meeting was held in Ottawa to discuss the RCAF's requirement and to assure the government of Dobson and Avro UK's commitment to establish their Canadian subsidiary. Representatives included Fred Smye, three RCAF air vice marshals including Wilf Curtis, three engineers from Turbo Research including Paul Dilworth and Winnett Boyd, and some Hawker Siddeley *alumnii eruditus*. The three Hawker Siddeley Group representatives were some of the best aviation minds in Britain. Davies, now chief designer at Avro's Yorkshire plant, W.H. Lindsay from Armstrong Siddeley engines and W.W.W. Downing from Gloster Aircraft came over with Fred Smye to discuss the government and TCA's needs for a fighter, an airliner and jet engines. While Stuart Davies was concentrating his efforts on TCA and the engineering staff remaining at Malton, Lindsay was concentrating on consulting with Turbo Research, with Downing focusing on the RCAF's fighter requirements.

On viewing the RCAF plan and the specification for the light fighter, one of Hawker Siddeley's representatives, W.W.W. Downing, was mortified. He adamantly argued that such an aircraft might be suitable for Britain with the short ranges involved there, but insisted such an aircraft was totally inadequate for Canada considering the size of the nation, the harsh weather and long distances between air bases. He insisted that Canada needed an aircraft with two engines of significantly higher thrust than the single one being proposed, and a crew of two to handle the chores of managing such a sophisticated aircraft over long flight durations and distances.

With Downing's words of wisdom undoubtedly ringing in their ears, AVM Curtis and the others abandoned their specification and devised an air defence plan that could actually defend the country. From this emerged an idea of the kind of aircraft required. They were forced to take a sober look and adopt a "best-of-the-best" approach. They needed a long-range, day-or-night, all-weather aircraft to take on and defeat alone, any likely threat coming over the top of the world from the Soviet Union. They envisaged a long-range jet interceptor using sophisticated radar and weaponry, a crew of two to handle the tasks of long-range navigation, target acquisition and the necessarily sophisticated aircraft systems which would allow it to operate semi-autonomously. Two engines were also specified for reliability during these long missions. They also specified a very high rate of climb and relatively short-field take-off and landing characteristics.

This was late 1945 and one might bear in mind that the state-of-the-art aircraft then in service which came closest to these requirements was the superlative de Havilland

Mosquito radar-equipped night-fighter. It still didn't satisfy the RCAF's very tall order, and a team left Canada in 1946 to explore all the manufacturers in the free world to see if a suitable aircraft was under development—*anywhere*. Canada was not naive enough to think that she could afford to spend this kind of money only to duplicate something that was going to happen elsewhere anyway, especially considering the rapid advances in the state of the art and the risks associated with the development of such an aircraft, propulsion and weapons systems. The team arrived home empty-handed. Curtis was on the record as asserting that such an aircraft did not exist anywhere, nor was one in the design phase or even being planned.

Thus, in 1946 the RCAF issued the revised plan under the title "Air-7-1-Issue 2." Its requirements were staggering. The specification contained a requirement for an aircraft corresponding to the following:

> A two-seat all-metal aircraft powered by two gas turbine (jet) engines with a required operational combat ceiling of at least 50,000 feet requiring a highly pressurized cabin.

Effective operations in Canada's climate demanded it function in temperatures from -57 to +45 degrees Celsius.

The mission profile:

- start, run-up and taxi of four minutes followed by one minute take-off,
- climb to 40,000 feet with an initial climb rate of not less than 10,000 feet per minute,
- cruise out to its combat radius of 650 nm (nautical miles, one nautical mile equalling approx. 1.15 statute miles)
- engage in combat for 15 minutes at 490 knots at this altitude,
- return the 650 nm, followed by a 10-minute descent and a 7-minute approach for landing.

This involved a flight time of about three and a half hours. By contrast, a combat mission of a current F-18 Hornet is just over one hour even though the average speed of the missions is, in reality, quite similar. The maximum level-flight airspeed was to be not less than 490 knots (over 560 mph). Compare this specification to the performance of the Spitfire, itself designed as an interceptor. The Spitfire Mk. 9 took over seven minutes to climb to 25,000 feet, had a combat speed of about 300 mph and a radius of action of about 150 miles.

Wilf Curtis was the major RCAF crusader who was working to get the specification approved and to have A.V. Roe Canada entrusted with the job of building the world-beating airframe and engine. His reputation was very much on the line over this rare gamble of giving an unproven company such enormous, expensive and risky tasks. He is on record as saying he never regretted his confidence in the company. Since he worked well with both the company and the government, Curtis later took on a directorship of A.V. Roe Canada Ltd. (This seemed to be viewed by the later Conservative government not as an exploitation of a talented honest-broker but nearly as some form of bribery-after-the-fact—although it is standard practice today.)

Roy Dobson's upstart Canadian company now had a very full plate. They were undertaking to build an aircraft with performance no one else in the world seemed prepared to attempt, along with the first jet passenger aircraft, *and* a revolutionary axial-flow engine of about the highest thrust anywhere. Shocking considering these were the infant company's first designs! A.V. Roe Canada seemed determined to fly before it had demonstrated it could crawl! At the time, other than the Avro Vulcan and the Gloster Javelin developments, the XC-100 fighter, C-102 Jetliner and TR-5 Orenda engine projects were the most prestigious undertakings going on within the Hawker Siddeley Group.

Under Avro Canada's chief designer Edgar Atkin's leadership were two teams: Military Projects for the Avro XC-100 experimental jet interceptor (soon to be taken over by John Frost of de Havilland UK), and Transports, under Jim Floyd as chief design engineer for the Jetliner project.

First Success: The TR-4 Chinook

Avro was facing severe difficulties in several areas by the spring of 1948. TCA was becoming increasingly troublesome with their tactics toward the Jetliner program and Avro as a whole. This was translating into a good deal of rumour-mongering which filtered into government and other spheres of influence. Rolls-Royce was certainly not helpful in the engine department. Millions of taxpayers' dollars were pouring into the company with no success to date. Every year the government was faced with the decision to either continue the funding of Avro or cut them off.

Avro needed to produce a success quickly to justify their continued existence.

Axial-flow jet engine design was still in its infancy. Everyone else in the industry expected the first start-up of Avro Gas Turbine's Chinook to either not take at all or only happen with a great deal of flame, compressor surges and probably a good deal of smoke and noise. This was because, with the axial-flow design, it was difficult to correctly match the several compressor discs to allow smooth and consistent airflow over the rpm range from start to running rpm. Designing a fuel control system that would inject the correct amount of fuel at all rpm and load factors was another problem area. Winnett Boyd felt the British were still designing engines with a trial and error "suck it and see" method while he felt very confident that the Canadian team could predict and thus design the compressor sections according to mathematical models. This would allow them to not only predict the performance of an engine (which they had successfully done in critiquing the Rolls-Royce Avon design) but also to design from the drawing board an engine which would meet the performance goals they set for it.

They had such confidence that they invited a great number of people and politicians, some with the power to kill Avro, to witness the *first* start of the Chinook engine. No fudging or unofficial starts were done to make sure the team had a bankable product. On 17 November 1948 a great number of dignitaries were invited into the Avro Gas Turbines test cell, probably to their unwitting peril. Without any fuss whatsoever a single start button was pressed on the Chinook and it lit in a very quick (for the day) 30 or so seconds, didn't spew flame at all and ran smoothly. It was a very remarkable achievement indeed! Fred Smye would relate later:

> ...the small band of some forty young Canadian Engineers....beat both Rolls-Royce and General Electric in accomplishing basic specification performance for their engines."

The Avro Jetliner over Manhattan on the first jet transport flight in the United States, 18 April 1950. From the painting and limited edition series "New World Debutante."   (image by R.L. Whitcomb 2002)

THE DESIGN FOR A TCA PASSENGER AIRCRAFT with capacity for about thirty passengers originated with two "paper airplane" inter-city proposals (brochures with basic lay-out drawings). One was turboprop powered (like today's Dash-8) and one was a pure jet design (like today's Regional Jet). Upon presentation of the designs to TCA's chief engineer in late March 1946, it became obvious that the pure jet was far and away the favourite. The initial design specifications produced at this consultation between the engineers of both companies was as follows:

- Payload capacity of 10,000 pounds including 30 passengers.

- A still-air range of 1,200 miles.

- Full-load range of 500 miles against a 20-mph headwind with standard fuel reserves.

- A cruising speed of at least 400 mph.

- Runway requirement not to exceed 4,000 feet under standard conditions.

- Approach, landing, take-off and stall speeds to be comparable to contemporary piston-engine designs.

- Reliability and maintainability to be state of the art.

- Operating costs to be competitive with existing designs.

This passenger aircraft was to have a loaded cruising speed better than the maximum speeds attained by fighter aircraft such as the Spitfires and Bf-109s during the Battle of Britain only six years earlier. It was to cruise over 200 mph faster than TCA's brand new DC-3s. These specifications led TCA President H.J. Symington to issue an official letter of intent to purchase the Jetliner, provided the aircraft lived up to the agreed figures.

Right from the beginning the design team decided to work to a higher performance specification than those above in order to leave room in the design for future development. They increased the target cruising speed to 425-450 mph and the still-air range to 1,500 miles, while the passenger capacity was expanded to forty with allowances being made to further raise this if required.

The initial general arrangement was that of a low-straight-wing aircraft powered by two Rolls-Royce Avon turbojets. The wing inboard of the engines would

CHAPTER TWO

First to Fly

The C-102 Jetliner

Whatever the future holds for us, let's pursue it and stick together and go forward. The future will only belong to Canada if Canada, the people of Canada, have faith in the destiny of Canada and work like blazes to make that destiny come true.

—Sir Roy Dobson, speaking at the tenth anniversary of the establishment of A.V. Roe Canada Ltd.

A Jetliner center section. The thick wing meant it could be made very light, and very strong. (Avro Canada)

have no dihedral, with the outboard sections having dihedral added *a la* Lancaster. The center straight area formed a very strong center section also like the Lancaster's with the overall wing dihedral arrangement resembling that of the Lancaster from the front.

Construction techniques and finishing were much different from those wartime methods employed in the dispersed-construction operation for the Lancaster design. New alloys of aluminum were used in the wing and fuselage structure and skins for the ultimate in strength, lightness and long-term durability. Since the fuselage had the ability to operate at higher altitudes than those of piston-engine aircraft, it had to employ some kind of advanced design to safely handle the high cabin pressurization such operation requires. Avro chose to design to a very high pressurization level to actually make the aircraft at least as "pressure-gradient" comfortable as the lower-altitude-cruising propliners of the noisy, bouncy "golden age" of air travel.

Avro simply decided to do the engineering to make it light, strong, and relatively simple to manufacture and maintain. Borrowing from Chadwick and Atkin's Tudor fuselage, they also devised one-piece circular fuselage formers made of 75ST, a high-strength aluminum alloy. Some of Avro UK's Tudor drawings for the Tudor's construction and production equipment were sent to Avro Canada. These helped the new team save time and money, not to mention solve problems. To maintain its temper and

strength characteristics these rings had to be machined while immersed in a hot oil bath. With a few trial runs and likely some ugly messes, Avro's "Men From Mars" with their protective gear began producing acceptable formers. These formers and the stringer attachment system that went with them were quite advanced. The fuselage was designed to be adaptable to different wings, tails, engines and lengths in an Avro-typical modular approach. It was of significant diameter, was very light, strong and aerodynamically *very* smooth. To beef it up Avro could either add stringers or make some of the existing ones of a stronger material.

Also unlike the Lancaster, the XC-102 design used flush-riveting. In fact, Avro Canada developed and patented a system and hardware to install the rivets with a self-centering, floating grinder that would smooth the rivet to the surface of the skin perfectly, without weakening the skin itself. At the same time another development effort for the Jetliner resulted in "Skydrol" fire-resistant hydraulic fluid, today the absolute standard for commercial use.

One other high-tech installation was a transparent, electrically-heated laminate in the windshield's glass. It eliminated the rather inelegant external and internal heater blowers which often robbed engine power excessively, especially if fed by compressor bleed air from a turbine engine. Don Rogers, Avro's chief test pilot, relates some hair raising experiences proving the Jetliner's impressive anti-icing arrangement while trying to get into icing, a

Painting of a TCA North Star over Tampa Bay Florida titled *Canadair's First Lady*. (painting by R.L. Whitcomb, collection of Fred Moffatt)

most abnormal thing for any *sane* pilot to do. This system used an aerodynamically clean, electrically heated, rebated boot similar in appearance to the boots on some wartime aircraft that were simply blown up to crack off ice. Those old-style systems were "blown up" by compressed air and were normally not rebated (recessed) to match the airfoil surface, but applied over a normal leading edge. It was not nearly as aerodynamically advantageous to allow ice to build before breaking it off, nor was the airfoil the proper shape while this was being done. The C-102, like her CF-100 stablemate, was very much advanced in terms of anti-icing capability and helped develop the art. The RCAF and NRC also had a series of icing research aircraft called the "Rockcliffe Ice Wagon." At the speeds the later Arrow was to achieve, no anti-icing was required, aside from the intake and canopy for low-speed safety, since skin friction would prevent its formation. Don Rogers described some exciting "St. Elmo's Fire" dancing along the wet leading edge when the boots, under development in cooperation with the manufacturer, shorted out and burned away on

one test flight. The system was quickly perfected to everyone's satisfaction.

Problems Beyond Their Control

By this time, however, TCA was clearly and inexplicably losing its stomach for the Jetliner project. The only area in which the Jetliner had slipped in performance expectations (with the loss of the Avon engine) was in fuel economy. TCA seemed reluctant to admit that their choice of the Avon had been very wishful thinking and used the fuel efficiency discrepancy between the early projections with an unavailable engine, and the realities of a Derwent-powered version, as a tool to distance themselves from the project. The follow-up letter of intent in the spring of 1946 contained so many hedges and demands that it has been described by James Dow (a former CF officer and author of the book *The Arrow*) as "an invitation to commit financial suicide." It demanded a fixed price of $350,000 per aircraft yet refused to specify if they wanted one or 100 copies! They also demanded that Avro not sell Jetliners or modified versions of the aircraft to any other carrier for three full years after TCA purchased their own. Furthermore, TCA demanded that, if the Jetliner failed to meet any of the performance estimates in the original specification, that Avro would refund any initial payments made to the company for the aircraft.

When it became clear that TCA was not willing to specify any quantity of aircraft to be ordered, it also became obvious that Avro would be foolish to agree to these kinds of terms. Avro also knew that in a gallon per seat-mile comparison, which TCA seemed inclined to pursue, even an Avon Jetliner would be at a disadvantage. TCA and even Transport Canada seemed intent on saddling an aircraft that was realistically projected to be one of the cheapest, fastest and simplest aircraft to fuel, service, fix and turn-around, with fuel reserve penalties, and operational speed and altitude restrictions which adversely affected the Jetliner's economics. It is worth pointing out that a price of $350,000 per aircraft for Jetliners was just over one-half the projected price of the slow, noisy and decidedly old-tech Canadair North Star according to 1945 TCA projections. This price did not include engines however since those quotations came before the engine had been agreed upon, especially since the Avon had been withdrawn, and because Avro was proposing a number of engines as alternatives to the Derwents. Other writers have criticised Avro for this bizarre chain of events, implying they were dishonest in quoting without engines hoping to add that cost later. This just isn't the case and is a misinterpretation of the facts. The comparatively older North Star, using largely new-old-stock Merlin engines, was priced at $670,000 per copy yet TCA purchased many, according to Larry Milberry in his first book *The Canadair North Star*.

For all intents and purposes TCA was out of the picture. Howe became involved when TCA asked him to allow them to back away from their original letter of intent to purchase Jetliners. TCA wanted to issue a stop-work order and Howe actually advised Avro to stop work pending a consultation with Dobson in the spring of 1947. Dobson duly arrived and went through the project with a fine-toothed comb. He was magnificently experienced in aircraft design and development and nothing escaped his attention. By this time over one third of the detailed drawings had been released to the production department. He wrote Howe that he was "quite satisfied" as to the soundness of the design but was worried over the "go-slow" policy of the government of Canada who had been funding development thus far. Dobson even offered to have the Hawker Siddeley Group chip in funds to ensure the design was completed and ready to fly in early 1949.

This offer was a real statement of confidence on the part of Dobson when one considers the nasty pill his company had had to swallow due to a similar BOAC and government created fiasco regarding the British Avro Tudor transport. Two had been lost, one in the Bermuda Triangle, although in both cases the aircraft itself could not be blamed since the wreckages weren't found. Nevertheless, BOAC did everything in their power to ensure they wouldn't receive the plane, while criticizing the aircraft and manufacturer, and enlisting the British government to allow them to back away. This was also due to the Rolls-Royce Merlin not being an ideal commercial engine and the fact that the Tutor was partially based on the Lancaster design (it used the Lancaster wing) and was therefore somewhat heavier than American commercial designs. The relatively poor fuel economy of the Merlin was a factor that would be a problem for TCA with their North Stars.

Jan Zurakowski related to the author in 1996 the reason why the Merlins didn't deliver particularly good fuel economy. "Zura" claimed Rolls-Royce had designed the Merlin in much the same way they designed automotive engines. He said they used a much longer stroke (distance the piston travels up and down) than the bore (diameter of the piston). As a result there was too much operating friction from the piston and its rings travelling a relatively farther distance than other competing designs. Pumps for liquid cooling and the mechanical supercharger design (rather than exhaust-driven turbocharging) also didn't help although liquid-cooled engines are potentially more efficient than air-cooled ones.

This kind of meddling and backpedaling would characterize many dealings between Avro and governments on both sides of the Atlantic. Without question Avro was losing its stomach for politicians of every stripe and this distaste would be reflected, despite all efforts, in their evolving attitudes. In Canada, at the end, Avro would be accused of arrogance and inflexibility. Seeming ignorance, duplicity and incompetence in government and government-owned airline circles had the potential to result in polarizations that could threaten Avro's very existence. Avro always knew it skated a thin line between pleasing and angering its greatest sponsor, the government. Avro also counted on the government to bargain in good faith.

Certainly, some would start having doubts on both sides of the fence, one from lack of faith and due to external pressures, with both suffering as a consequence.

At this point fate intervened with Smye informing Floyd by telephone from England that Rolls-Royce's managing director, Lord Hives, had informed him that the Avon engine would not be certified for civilian use "for many years." In reality, they had run into so many problems with the design that it would not be ready for *any* kind of use for some time. Keast and Dilworth of the Avro Gas Turbine Division were not surprised by the withdrawal of the Avon. Dilworth commented in *Shutting Down the National Dream* that he had advised against the Avon from the outset since axial-flow designs were facing severe developmental problems and that a civilian passenger aircraft—especially the first one—should have proven reliable engines. Keast knew that the Avon was simply a terrible design with a bad compressor and that the "many years" would be spent pouring money into a *"rotten engine."*

A Rolls-Royce Avon turbojet.

Unfortunately, Jim Bain of TCA had been sold heavily on the Avon by Rolls-Royce and had thus also sold TCA management on the unproven engine. He must have faced some searching questions about the viability of the entire pure-jet concept from his masters at TCA over the loss of the engine he had sold so hard. It seems this was likely the final nail in the coffin as far as TCA's attitude was concerned. By this time Avro Gas Turbines had experienced success with their own axial-flow Chinook and were embarking on the Orenda axial design, which would prove to be one of the most powerful and reliable engines in its class within a few years' time. For some reason they couldn't comprehend the Jetliner really being built with an upgradable engine nacelle design, which would allow substitution to something like the Avon or even the Orenda

engine with minimal expense down the road. In reality Bain seemed to get cold feet over the loss of his beloved Avons while TCA got a new boss, one who didn't want his carrier to be the first to offer jet passenger service.

Rolls-Royce did do Smye the honour of compiling data and producing a suggested installation design for four centrifugal-flow Derwents for the first Jetliner prototype and pointed out that their calculations showed it to be a viable, if somewhat less performant, alternative. Smye took the results back to Floyd at Malton. At first Floyd was understandably disappointed, especially in view of the fact that the design was well along on the twin-Avon prototype. He soon realised however, that despite the small increase in weight and fuel consumption, there were advantages in the new installation such as much simpler landing gear design requirements, and increased overall thrust. Reliability and safety using four engines with a bullet-proof track record were also factors any airline would find attractive for the world's first medium-range jet passenger plane.

Floyd and his team produced a new engine and nacelle layout that not only left the wing's main spar untouched but also allowed for simple substitution of engines should they ever desire to take advantage of higher-technology power plants once they became available. Since they had already done some work on the Avon installation, they had that as a back-up design to offer as a future twin-engine option even while the four-engine Derwent-powered first prototype proved the entire jet travel concept. Avro also had a very smooth and strong high-altitude fuselage design to serve as the core of other variants, civilian or military.

When the design of the Avro Jetliner was commenced in 1946, it was the first jet passenger aircraft development to receive approval in North America. The de Havilland Comet jet was being designed at the same time but was to be a long range intercontinental aircraft and thus was suited for a much smaller market segment. The Avro Jetliner was designed for inter-city and continental service and would remain the only medium-range design of its kind for a very long time. British thought on the ideal routes for a jet airliner concentrated on long-range routes to tie the far-flung remnants of the British Empire (now Commonwealth) together. In North America it was felt, initially, that the best usage of a jet transport would be on the inter-city medium-range routes. Coincidentally the larger Comet gained much of its range advantage over the Jetliner by sacrificing passenger load for fuel. Its payload was approx-

One of two RCAF Comets. The RCAF would be the first air force to use a pure jet transport. Unfortunately, it was not the Canadian Jetliner. (Public Archives of Canada)

imately 7,000 lbs while the Jetliner's was 10,000. In reality the Comet and Jetliner were both well suited to the markets of their countries of origin. There was also a much larger global market for a medium-range design. Avro knew they were one of two out of the gates early. One or the other might stumble, and there was a massive US aviation industry that had done startling things in the past to short time scales.

The Comet 1 would prove to be a fatally flawed design, however, and would require a very expensive and time-consuming redesign. The windows on the Comet 1 were a sharp-cornered square design. Interestingly TCA had originally specified that the Jetliner have square windows since they were something of the fashion at the time. Floyd and others were also stress specialists, however, so both square and rounded designs were put in the mock-up to show that vision through a rounded window was just as good and, notably, structurally stronger considering the high cabin pressurization the high-altitude design would require. It was just this effect, that of the sharp corners in the Comet's windows serving as stress risers, which caused them to rip open in flight. Many lives were lost and aircraft damaged and destroyed before the flaw was understood and corrected. The Jetliner had no such defect and was pressure-tested extensively both on the ground and in flight. Apparently, one ingenious and inexpensive pressurization test of a Jetliner fuselage section was done by having an air-filled bladder in the section with a fork-lift truck pressing a cup on the protruding end of this bag up to the required pounds-per-square-inch (psi) pressure to see what happened to the fuselage. Mario Pesando relates being particularly shaky around this apparatus, considering the potential energy stored in that bag and restrained only by some light alloy structure!

TCA and Government Interference

By September 1947 the Avro design office produced the revised design and performance specifications. These figures quoted performance specifications that still exceeded those of the original TCA/Avro agreement, the clause regarding "comparable operating expenses in all respects" leaving a possible fuel-consumption loophole. At about this time TCA and the government decided to drive a truck through that hole.

Since the Canadian government was involved in funding the program, Howe insisted that TCA's engineering division be kept informed of the design if only to provide a second opinion as to the aircraft's commercial merits. This author feels it is still open to interpretation where the impetus behind that tactic lay, in TCA alone or with Howe now also against Jetliner development altogether. Whatever the case, the TCA engineers found ways to suggest that the Jetliner was unsuitable, such as bringing in factors never broached previously. These included the lack of Instrument Landing System (ILS) installations in Canadian airports. This was a *total* red-herring since Floyd and friends had intentionally designed the Jetliner to operate in the holding patterns, approach and landing phases at the same speeds (and in some cases lower) as the lumbering prop-liners. It had a stall speed of only 78 knots! This is comparable to modern, light piston-engine twins. TCA also inexplicably invented new higher reserve fuel requirements for the aircraft and then used these figures to conclude the aircraft would not meet their range requirements! They then issued further new specifications for a "suitable" aircraft suggesting a passenger load of forty with a cruising speed of 500 mph! Conveniently, no mention was made of the *original* TCA specification or whether the revised four-engine design met it. (It did.) Finally, it was added that, even if Avro were to modify the design to meet these higher criteria, TCA would not be interested in purchasing any! One can only imagine the frustration of A.V. Roe Canada and its designers. The new TCA president, Gordon McGregor, eventually admitted that he did not want his airline to be the first to initiate jet-passenger service on the continent. In the space of about a year TCA had gone from a company demanding a three-year monopoly on Jetliners to reneging on the project entirely. To add insult to injury McGregor would publicly pillory Avro. Jan Zurakowski tells of sharing the spotlight with McGregor during the 1959 ceremonies for the Fiftieth Anniversary of powered flight in Canada: "I was shocked when McGregor, Chairman of T.C.A., as guest speaker on the 50th anniversary of the first flight in Canada, spent most of his speech glorifying the DC-8 which he had just ordered."

Incidentally, neither TCA nor any other carrier *ever* used TCA's sudden, new reserve-fuel allowance, not even for transatlantic flights. On the Jetliner's record-breaking flight from Toronto to New York City on 18 April 1950, the new requirements would have demanded a fuel load of about 30,000 lb. while the trip itself only required 9,400 lb. TCA's new estimate, using this massive fuel reserve, showed the Jetliner with thirty-six passengers as having a range of only 300 miles. Later Trans-World Airlines' (TWA) detailed studies with full TWA fuel reserves and forty passengers put the aircraft range at 940 miles with the Derwent installation or 1,500 miles with two Rolls-Royce Nene engines. These figures are twice, and three times, the original TCA range specification. TWA stressed that the Jetliner could do all but one of their American (Los Angeles to New York City) routes non-stop. TWA would also prove that the Jetliner was far cheaper to operate than the thrashing props as well. After all, kerosene is cheap compared to high-octane Avgas with poisonous tetra-ethyl lead added to it.

Seemingly to the eternal wrath of Howe, Avro found a means to escape TCA's hostility and Transport Canada's restrictions while, at the same time, operating the aircraft

The Jetliner prototype takes shape in the Malton shops. A mutual fund company used this view and the spirit of the day for a recent series of television ads. (Avro Canada)

in the United States and proving route systems for jet passenger aircraft, while proving the excellent pedigree of the Jetliner to an enthusiastic crowd.

Jim Floyd's feeling was that all of the TCA assessments and suggestions were designed as a final attempt to have the program discredited, if not in Howe's eyes, than at least as far as any future TCA interest was concerned. Since TCA had decided not to introduce jet passenger service to the continent, they would not have wanted to face the prospect of being forced to compete against carriers that would. When Floyd was asked about the possibility of modifying the design to meet the 500-mph cruise speed and other escalations, he responded that it would be "easier to convert a cow to a crocodile!" He could have added that it should have been sufficient to be 200 mph faster than most of the competition without adding another 100 mph, which would have effectively doubled the speed of most airliners then in service!

By this time the Jetliner project had attracted the attention of a number of US and European carriers, who had a great deal more experience in working with a manufacturer during aircraft development while possessing the capacity for many more aircraft as well. Floyd felt that if Avro could maintain the backing of the Canadian government, despite TCA's running interference, "the world is our oyster!" This, and a predictably negative backlash from the government, are probably why Avro didn't sue TCA over their renege. They knew they could sell many more Jetliners in the US than TCA could possibly absorb, while the government might be expected to side with TCA in any legal proceedings!

In contrast to Floyd's enthusiasm as he expressed it to Dobson during the TCA/government intrigues, the industry

worldwide was facing difficulties with civilian aircraft designs. All the major US producers lost money in 1947 (today Boeing says they broke even), and in Britain the few manufacturers' attempts to produce viable commercial aircraft were beginning to develop into a full-scale disaster. The British would not have a viable and successful passenger design in service until the mid-1950s in the form of the Vickers Viscount, itself a turboprop design virtually identical to the original drawings presented to TCA as prepared by Floyd and the team in Yorkshire under Davies. Ironically, TCA bought many. Before this time, it was the Canadair North Star that had saved the British carriers from buying American.

These factors, and the problems BOAC and the British government were causing for Avro UK over the Tudor airliner, were in the mind of Sir Roy Dobson when he met with Jim Floyd privately in the spring of 1948. It was likely Floyd's undying enthusiasm for the project that saved it from the axe. As he was departing Dobson added "... you'd better make sure that when that 102 of yours flies it's going to be so damn good that we're going to have the airlines queuing up for the thing. I'm staking my reputation on that, so don't let me down. It's got to be perfect!"

The Jetliner Spreads Her Wings

The problem for Avro was that they had no contract or firm interest and, therefore, no real specification to meet for the production variant. It now became obvious that Avro would have to prove the soundness of the design through test flights in order to show off the aircraft to the airlines. At the same time they would be using the carrier's comments and suggestions to devise the specification for the second pre-production aircraft

The Jetliner strikes a pose on her maiden voyage. Photo taken from the Mitchell chase plane flown by Mike Cooper-Slipper. (via Jim Floyd)

and the subsequent production Jetliner. The name Jetliner was applied to the aircraft and *patented* at this time. This didn't stop Boeing, however, from using this proprietary name in their much-later advertising for the Boeing 707.

Once TCA backed away from "their" Jetliner, government funding for the program halted as well. TCA certainly, and Howe possibly, were hoping the Jetliner would die on the vine. It is a testament to the confidence Hawker Siddeley Group had in the design that they continued to fund the development. In any case, Howe later found a means to kill the project. The reasons for his change of heart over the Jetliner have never been satisfactorily explained. But then, according to author Palmira Campagna's findings, Howe's files on the Jetliner fiasco went missing long ago. Certainly, competing interests would use any lever they could find.

One should note that Howe stated that his most prized possession was a "fly anywhere for free" card from the airline. His loyalty to TCA, which he had helped to create, coupled with Canadair's civilian trans-

port business, mitigated against Avro once TCA had decided against the Jetliner. Add to these factors the pressure from various agencies in the US to keep the aircraft from smashing the US manufacturers and one comes up with a powerful scenario for what was going on behind the scenes.

By the spring of 1949, most of the engineering drawings had been released and the actual prototype was nearing completion. On 24 June 1949, the first engine runs were conducted and led to minor exhaust extractor and nacelle skin modifications. True to Dobson's demand that the aircraft be "perfect" Floyd and his team were very meticulous and spent whatever time was required to ensure all glitches were properly rectified before the first flight. It is without doubt that had they been a little less demanding, the Avro Jetliner would have been the first jet airliner to fly. Even so, Jim Floyd and many under his charge practically lived at the plant and sixteen-hour days were the norm. Testimony today suggests that it was a labour of love and that nobody minded their "killer" hours too much. After all, they were working to put Canada on top!

Elated crew after the first flight: Bill Baker, Jimmy Orrell and Don Rogers. Airmen seem to light-up after flying too.
(Avro Canada)

Jimmy Orrell, Avro UK's chief test pilot, was brought over for the first flight. Don Rogers, who had a great deal of wartime and subsequent test-flying experience, was Avro Canada's chief test pilot and was to be the co-pilot on the first flight. Bill Baker, with several thousand hours' military flying experience, was the flight engineer. He would go on to become a vice-president of McDonnell Douglas (in charge of the old Avro plant) after Avro folded; quite a position for a former Lancaster flight engineer! Mike Cooper-Slipper, a wartime Spitfire pilot, was Avro Canada's assistant chief test pilot and back-up co-pilot for the Jetliner's first flight. On 27 July, when the Jetliner was virtually finished all of the last-minute checks, it was announced that the de Havilland Comet had briefly skipped into the air. Transport Canada (one of C.D. Howe's portfolios) then tore up the main runways at Malton for resurfacing and further complicated things by forcing Avro to test on a short runway. The taxi and emergency braking tests that were conducted on this runway led to blown tires because there was not much runway available and because the anti-skid braking mechanisms were still in the hands of the manufacturer. Even when this now-standard piece of equipment was installed the Canadian Department of Transport would not allow Avro to activate it since the

Americans had not come out with guidelines for its usage! Another sad testament to a lack of leadership and an unwillingness to take responsibility.

Extreme temperatures in the 90 to 100 degree (F) range then complicated things. Jet engines are susceptible to high temperatures since hot air is less dense than cold. Thrust suffers as a result. During some early take-off attempts, Orrell decided that the aircraft was not going to be able to hop into the air and still stop on the short runway, and he applied the brakes while there was little weight on the main wheels. This again caused the tires to burst, but the aircraft proved easy to control despite having all main tires blown. Finally, it was decided that on 10 August they were going to take off on the short runway and be done with it. In a stiff crosswind the aircraft spooled up to full power and the brakes were released. After a short run the Jetliner lifted off cleanly and kept right on going. During a circuit of the airfield Orrell got a feel for the controls and liked what he felt. He then buzzed the group of engineers and climbed to 8,000 feet. Liking the control checks and instrument readings at this altitude he announced that they would climb higher and continue with tests scheduled for later flights. By the time the Jetliner was on approach to land, after a maiden flight of

The Jetliner beats up the Malton airport during Avro's annual Gala Day.
(Avro Canada)

over one hour, the crosswind had worsened to 35 knots at 50 degrees to the runway. This is a difficult crosswind component even in an aircraft with which one is experienced. The approach was flawless and Orrell made a very short landing, then taxied the Jetliner back to the shacks, thus completing the first jet transport flight in the Western Hemisphere. His comments after the debriefing described the flight as "a piece of cake" and that the Jetliner was the "perfect lady." Orrell added that there were no snags on the flight worth reporting. This stellar snag sheet would almost be equalled by the XC-100 and Arrow.

Baker, the flight engineer on the first flight and many others, provided some interesting comments for Floyd's impressive book *The Avro Canada C-102 Jetliner*:

> Fifteen years of flying had established in my mind that noise meant power, that more noise meant more power, and that power was essential for flight. The Jetliner in first flight configuration had minimal insulation or sound absorption material installed. When we gradually opened the throttles on [against] the brakes, we could certainly hear those Derwents. As we gained speed, the sound level was obviously dropping. When Jimmy pulled up, the noise seemed to disappear altogether and my heart stopped at the same time. It was hard to

accept the airspeed indicator winding up while the rate of climb was demonstrating fighter performance and no noise! What a thrill! Later in the first flight Mike Cooper-Slipper formed up on us with a Mitchell for picture-taking and we were able to advise him that his propellers were out of synchronization! Imagine hearing another aircraft in flight while flying in one yourself—awesome!

While the Comet flew thirteen days earlier and entered service in May 1952, due to a deadly, explosive decompression problem related to structural design, it was withdrawn in April 1954. During these first two years of service the Comet flew mainly medium-range routes rather than the long-range stages for which it had been designed. By the time the aircraft was re-designed and had re-emerged as the Comet 4, four years had passed and not much remained of the original fuselage. It wasn't until 1958 that the Comet 4 inaugurated transatlantic jet service, only about a year ahead of the Boeing 707.

Six days after that perfect first flight, the Jetliner was in the air again carrying out stall and other very demanding tests. During the stall testing, which caused natural buffet vibrations as the airflow separated and re-attached to the wings, the undercarriage locks moved to a position that would not allow their release. The fact that no method,

The Avro Jetliner circa 1949. (courtesy of George Laidlaw)

including the use of all three emergency gear-extension systems, would bring the wheels down understandably caused enormous anguish on board the aircraft. Baker discovered later that he had even broken some ribs pulling on an emergency release cable! Don Rogers related in a live presentation in 2001 the crew's colourful reaction to a Malton Airport authority suggestion to ditch Jetliner Number One in Lake Ontario. Orrell was faced with the requirement to belly land the pristine Jetliner which he did, across the grass and some hardtop, with astonishingly little damage. Don's aerial photos of the Jetliner sleek on the grass, nudged up nearly against the fence, are quite evocative. It took a few approaches, however, since the aircraft, lightly loaded, just didn't want to come out of ground effect and land. Needless to say, the lack of whirling propellers contributed to the low amount of damage done. The fact that the nose gear was down, as recommended by Avro's people via their control tower, ensured only the aft section of the engine nacelles, and perhaps some of the rear fuselage bottom, would be damaged. After simple

gear-lock modifications and testing, plus very minor repairs to the engine nacelles and the rear underside of the fuselage, the third test was conducted five weeks later on 20 September 1949. Intensive test flying then commenced with the aircraft undergoing stall and other performance and drag tests in all configurations and up to maximum weight. Orrell returned to England after the 16th flight, and Rogers and Cooper-Slipper took over the flying duties.

On 22 November the aircraft was slated to explore its maximum speed. Rogers climbed to 30,000 feet and incrementally increased speed until he felt the controls begin to stiffen slightly. This is the area that indicates the beginning of "compressibility" effects where the airflow over the wings begins to approach the speed of sound. Upon analysis it was found that the aircraft had exceeded 500 mph or Mach .73. At this time only the fastest operational fighters were reaching this speed which is in fact faster than the Vmax (do-not-exceed speed) of the Canadair Tutor Jet! Another record was thus broken by a large margin. This maximum speed rating was important since, at

A Nene powered T-33 Silver Star.   (image by R.L. Whitcomb)

the time, North American airline regulations only permitted a maximum cruise speed 15 percent less than the speed where compressibility or control force increases presented themselves. The cruise speed indicated by the level of Mach .73 indicated a cruise speed of 425 mph, right on the design goal and 25 mph above the original TCA spec. Avro was confident that the aircraft would demonstrate adequate handling at Mach .76, thus allowing a cruise speed of nearly 440 mph. They were also advised that the Americans were considering reducing the maximum cruise speed margin from 15 to 10 percent which would have given the Jetliner a max cruise speed of about 460 mph. On average this was 200 mph faster than the propeller driven aircraft in service and 150 mph faster than the fastest of them.

Shock to the US System!

On 10 March 1950, the Jetliner flew to Ottawa from Toronto along with the XC-100 prototype in 36 minutes—another record. TCA's scheduled service gave a flight time of 1 hour 40 minutes! On 18 April 1950 the Jetliner made what was probably the most publicised aircraft flight ever in the US or Canada, when it flew from Toronto to New York City in 59 minutes. Yet another record smashed! On board were Rogers, Cooper-Slipper, Baker, Smye, Floyd, Pesando and Gordon McGregor, President of TCA. Over 500 newspapers carried the story in concert with other media coverage. The Jetliner delegation was transported via motorcade on their rounds.

On 11 January 1951 the *Rochester Democrat* ran the following article under a photo of the Jetliner over New York:

A commercial jet airliner, built in Canada, has smashed all American speed records for aircraft of that type by flying from Chicago to New York in 1 hour and 42 minutes. Besides hurtling along at 459 miles an hour, the airliner set a new altitude record for transports.

This should give our nation a good healthful kick in its placidity. The fact that our massive but underpopulated good neighbor to the north has a mechanical product that licks anything of ours is just what the doctor ordered for our overdeveloped ego. The Canadian plane's feat accelerates a process already begun in this nation—a realization that Uncle Sam has no monopoly on genius.

That amazing flight of the Canadian plane serves another purpose — a fair and friendly warning that our neighbor is equipped to step into a competitive field. All in all, that record-breaking flight was pleasant to dwell upon, especially if the blast of the jet engines blew the cobwebs from some of our thinking.

Later, the August issue of the American *Air Trails* magazine published the following article with the headline "What Happened to the Great American Aircraft Industry?" emblazoned across a photo of the Jetliner over New York city:

This is a jet-powered airliner, the Avro "Jetliner" built by Avro Canada. It is the first transport plane in the Western Hemisphere to use turbo-jet engines. These are four Rolls-Royce Derwent V's of 3,200 pounds thrust each. The Jetliner can carry 40 to 60 passengers in a large, comfortable cabin which maintains sea level altitude up to 21,500 feet in contrast to American transports which are pressurized at 8,000 feet when flying at 21,500. The Jetliner flew 450 miles from Toronto to New York City in just under 1 hour; normal transports take 1 hour, 45 minutes.

This is New York City, business capital of America. Most Americans believe that their nation has the greatest aviation industry in the world—an industry which embraces the most progressive manufacturers and the best in aeronautical brains. How, then, could first honors for a jet-powered transport go to the Canadians instead of our own fabulous aircraft industry? In the race to get a jet liner into the air, Canada won hands down. United States designers had not passed the "doodling" stage when the Jetliner appeared. Our hats off to the Canadians.

In no time Avro received literally hundreds of invitations to demonstrate their new "Queen of the Skies." Avro chose the opportunities that would generate the maximum exposure for the Jetliner and crew while making sure that all major American carriers had an opportunity to see her. On one such flight Dan Beard, at this time American Airlines' chief test pilot and the pilot behind the development of the most successful medium range transport in history, the Douglas DC-3, commented:

"You've got a bloody good aircraft there, I reckon it could be the DC-3 of the jets!" This was the man who would know. In fact, at one point there was serious debate in the United States over who should get credit for the design of the incredibly successful DC-3; American Airlines, or Douglas Aircraft. Dan Beard had, by this time, been a major American Airlines influence on the Douglas DC-3 design. As for the DC-3/C-47 Dakota, General and later President Dwight D. Eisenhower stated that it was one of the top ten instruments for the Allied victory over Hitler. As for Beard's glowing appraisal of the Jetliner, Floyd heartily agreed—after all, they had designed it to be exactly that, a "good, safe workhorse with a promising future."

As the marketing effort in the United States took on a life of its own, another American Airlines visionary named Dixon Speas left his prestigious position as assistant to the President of American Airlines to head up international marketing of the Jetliner. He was (like C.D. Howe) a Massachusetts Institute of Technology (MIT) engineering graduate who knew, and was respected by, practically everyone in the business. It is safe to say he was wild with enthusiasm for the Jetliner and would not have taken the job otherwise.

Very soon Avro was scrambling to provide brochures on different engine installations and other information as every major airline in the US was approached (or approached Avro) and expressed keen interest. By June 1950, National Airlines was looking hard at the aircraft. G.T. Baker, National's president, sent two of his top executives to Avro forthwith to do a detailed analysis of the Jetliner and conduct flying tests. To quote Baker:

I send two of my most conservative men up to Canada for a couple of days to look at the C-102 Jetliner and they come back stark raving mad with enthusiasm for it!

A follow-up letter from Speas to Avro about the National discussions mentioned that National was "very much interested in purchasing a limited quantity of Jetliners ... In all conversations it was generally understood the limited number of aircraft would be expanded to a full fleet subject to the aircraft meeting all expectations."

By this time the basic modifications for the second prototype (to be incorporated into the production version) were decided upon. The fuselage would be stretched 24 inches to allow up to 60 passengers (double the TCA letter of intent requirement) in a revised seating arrangement. The split flaps were replaced with a double-slotted type allowing improved low speed characteristics at higher gross weights. Actual construction of the second prototype was well underway even while Avro explored a replacement engine installation. It is a tragedy of the first order

(for Canada at least) that this aircraft was prevented from being completed.

Various engines were investigated from both the US and Britain. At the time the Rolls-Royce Nene (similar to the Derwent only larger and more powerful) looked like the ideal choice and was tentatively slated for installation in the second prototype. The increase in range to over 1200 miles (1500 according to TWA reserves), improved payload, fuel economy and simplicity combined to form a truly impressive package. Indeed the Nene has stood the test of time for over 50 years and is still providing bullet-proof service in the CF's utility jet; the ancient T-33 Silver Star.

Despite TCA's earlier statements and tactics, once offered a hands-on look at the Jetliner at least one person in the company caught the "Jetliner bug." Ironically it was Jim Bain, the TCA technical man behind the airline's Avon enthusiasms. After a detailed evaluation he commented officially on the Jetliner's excellent pedigree in 1949 (as published in *Storms of Controversy*):

Further to my memo this date in regard to the experimental operation of the C-102, I can bring you up-to-date on my last talk to the Avro Company during a recent visit.... It was interesting to see the *evidence of interest shown by most of the major airlines on this continent.* In particular, Eastern Air Lines are serious enough in their discussions that the second prototype will be built with the double slotted flap which will meet Eastern's low landing speed requirement. A physical examination of the aircraft showed a quality of workmanship which I have never seen surpassed on a prototype aircraft nor indeed by many production aircraft. Taken by and large, the skinning and metal work is beautiful and far surpasses the quality achieved by Canadair in production North Stars. They appear also to have left very few ends untied and even in the prototype the general equipment installation design shows enough care and foresight to make the C-102 a really modern aircraft incorporating the best of present installation knowledge. [italics added]

This letter was dated 2 May 1949 and was addressed to W.F. English, vice president of operations for TCA. According to *Storms*, this was the last evaluation report TCA produced on the aircraft.

Even while the Jetliner program appeared ready to revolutionize the commercial airline market and secure Avro's place as a major producer of civilian aircraft, domestic and international events were taking place that would have enormous implications for the program.

Stop All Work

The Korean War erupted in June 1950 with Communist troops streaming over the 54th parallel into "free" Korea. The West was caught with its collective pants down, although a chronological examination of American activity in the months before this event would almost suggest that the US was inviting the Communists in. While Soviet troops remained in North Korea, all US troops were ordered out in 1948 by the State Depatment. In January 1950, Secretary of State Dean Acheson (member of the Council on Foreign Relations and former member of its predecessor, the Rockefeller Institute) declared that the Western defence perimeter of the United States stopped short of Korea! (This interesting "invasion invitation" was mirror-imaged by US diplomatic assertions to Iraq, that the US was entirely disinterested in Kuwait just before the Iraqis invaded the tiny fiefdom—which had been taken by force from "Iraq" by the British in the mid-1800s!)

By June 1950 the Avro XC-100 prototype had flown with Rolls-Royce Avon engines and the second aircraft was about a month away from its first flight. The Orenda engine to power the production CF-100 Canuck had not even flown by this time. The CF-100 was *far* from ready to enter production even had the airframe been perfect at this time, which it was not!

Despite this situation, and supposedly due to the Korean crisis, the XC-100 was placed on super-priority by the government and Howe embarked on what can only be described as a whipping spree against Avro to get the CF-100 into *mass* production. Smye was coerced by Howe to officially "put the brakes" on the Jetliner's production-standard, second prototype and move the main engineering effort to the CF-100 project.

The XC-100 project was, up to that time, only an experimental development and Avro had no contract for production and no assembly line or hard tooling with which to produce the airplane. This fact is an important one and has been neglected in every book on the subject the author is aware of, save one: Kay Shaw's *There Never Was an Arrow*. At that time, the XC-100 didn't have a radar or fire-control system and the ability to "drop one in" was not a foregone conclusion. According to Shaw:

> It was only in October of 1950 that the government suddenly decided that the CF-100 should be put

into full production at the rate of 25 per month. No such production rate had been previously suggested and no such production lines existed.

Further confirmation of this comes from the *Globe and Mail's* aviation correspondent James Hornick, in his column of 10 October 1951:

> Emphasis from the start was on design and development, not production. It was only in October of last year [1950] that Avro received the authorization to build production-line fighters for the RCAF. Originally, 10 pre-production models were to be completed on leisurely spaced delivery dates.
>
> The Defence Department subsequently asked for 124 aircraft, to be delivered at the rate of five a month. Then it changed its mind. Deliveries were to be at the rate of 20 a month, then 50, finally 100. [this last absurd demand for 100 was reduced to 25 per month.]
>
> Avro was totally unprepared for the assignment. It lacked forewarning, tooling and space. [They didn't lack space at all in fact.] But the decision was made in Ottawa.

It's interesting that the sudden switch from an experimental program, to a massive production order came about as soon as major and virtually universal interest in the Jetliner became evident in the USA. It is also interesting that Avro was expected to reach the same production rate as the wartime plant for Lancasters virtually overnight (the 100-per-month figure notwithstanding). The CF-100 design was far more demanding, especially since Avro would also be building the engines for this aircraft. Furthermore, by the production order date, the CF-100 had revealed itself as having major structural problems, ones that would delay production by at least a year. Avro's performance in turning this situation around, in design, tooling and actually finding subcontractors to make all the various components in quantity, was a struggle of titanic proportions. Full production of quality-revised CF-100s began in late 1952. In the course of this, Floyd was removed from the Jetliner program and was assigned as Avro's trouble-shooting works manager, handling the problems of mass production of the still-being-modified CF-100 on the shop floor. This reassignment lasted nine months and gave him an excellent overview of the detailed problems of production, even more so than had his special apprenticeship at Avro in England.

The real lunacy of Howe's inexplicable decision is that the Jetliner was performing flawlessly and was exceeding all expectations. The Mk. 1 was wholly acceptable as it was and could have entered production immediately. Even the USAF stated that the aircraft was excellent as it was and about the only thing they would have liked were larger cockpit side-windows! It is difficult to imagine that it never occurred to Howe that the Jetliner could have contributed more, sooner, to the Korean conflict than the CF-100 was likely to, all things considered. After all, the Americans had plenty of jet fighters but *nobody* had jet transport aircraft, or indeed jet refuellers. The C-102 would have made a superb aerial refueller and certainly could have been easily adapted for trans-oceanic flight simply by adding fuel cells in the wing or even in bladders in the fuselage. As a troop transport, cargo or medivac aircraft it would have been unrivalled. As it was, the RCAF's North Stars did the heavy hauling for Canada in this "police action" and were known to outperform the American aircraft in similar employment. S/L R. Brown relates hauling in North Stars during the Korean airlift and killing an engine, then swooping by kissing-cousin radial-powered Douglas C-54s, restarting and passing by without losing any airspeed while climbing back to their (superior) cruising altitude and speed.

Even the USAF and US Navy were interested in the Jetliner. In a letter from USAF HQ dated 20 December 1950, when the Korean War was in full swing, Major Jim Venable of the USAF wrote Dixon Speas, sales team leader for the Jetliner: "I was pleased to learn from you that A.V. Roe was preparing a military brochure which would be submitted to the Air Force. I personally feel that your airplane is a 'natural' for either short and medium range military light transport operation, as it could be used by the military itself. In case the military decided to take over a large portion of the airlines [sic] airplanes it should be a logical replacement aircraft for the airlines. It appears to me that the primary advantage of the jet liner is that to do a given transport job, fewer aircraft are required. This is a decided advantage in wartime when we are trying to get the most for our money and where rapid production transports is necessary."

Dixon Speas relates further in *The Avro Canada C-102 Jetliner*:

> Both the US Air Force and the US Navy showed great interest in the airplane, with the Air Force interest advancing to a "buy" decision.

Major-General Donald Putt flew the airplane on a very rainy day from and to Washington National Airport. Despite the inclement weather, or possibly because of the airplane's handling ... Putt expressed enthusiasm for the airplane and it was then invited to Wright Field for intensive tests and evaluation. We received verbal word that the USAF was budgeting $20 million to buy 20 of the aircraft...

In slightly over one year the marketing program of the Jetliner had led to the threshold of two orders, one from National Airlines for ten airplanes ... and another from the USAF for 20.

When news came that the Canadian government had decided to put the airplane on the shelf, it came as a deadening shock.

After this incredible stop work order, Avro received incredulous and very disappointed letters from many US airlines that were seriously pondering orders for the Jetliner.

Even after the stop-work order came down, Avro did not abandon all hope of selling the next generation air transport. In 1952 Hughes Aircraft was developing a new radar and fire-control system which would become the interim system for the F-102 Delta Dagger and the upgraded system for the CF-100 Mk. 4, the Hughes MG-2 system. Avro offered Hughes the use of the Jetliner to assist in some of the flight testing. The Jetliner was an excellent vehicle for this purpose but the real idea was to get the Jetliner down to the billionaire flight pioneer and owner of TWA and Hughes Aircraft, Howard Hughes himself. Hughes was so thrilled with the Jetliner when he flew it that he managed to kidnap the aircraft for six months (!) and flew it at every opportunity. TWA's engineers concluded that the operating costs of the Jetliner compared favourably to the airline's then current equipment—even while reducing the flight times by about one third! Fuel economies would stem from the vastly reduced flight time and from the fact that kerosene is much cheaper than highly refined, high-octane aviation gasoline (Avgas). Don Rogers' flight logs suggest the pounds of fuel consumed by the Derwent-powered Jetliner were comparable to a Lockheed Constellation on a similar range flight. The payload of the Jetliner in reality was also comparable to the Constellation in the Mk. 2 version, while other economies were substantial. It should further be noted that the Jetliner was tested under operating conditions favourable to the current piston-engine aircraft and that further operational economies would have been realized by "flying a jet like a jet," especially by taking advantage of the Jetliner's exceptional high-altitude characteristics.

Hughes and TWA tried to have Avro build them thirty aircraft although normally even whispers about the cancellation of an aircraft design will send potential buyers packing. It is quite a testament to how badly TWA wanted Jetliners that Hughes tried to place the order—and for the Mk. 2 version which had yet to be built, let alone flown! Even the USAF, normally hampered by a "buy American" restriction, was looking at up to 100 aircraft to use as transport and jet bomber navigation trainers. If there had ever been a time when the US government might have allowed the Jetliner to enter service, it was when US industry was at maximum expansion but still wanting more for Korea and its possible implications. Kay Shaw points out in her book that, due to this situation, there was no pressure against the CF-100 brought to bear by the American powers, both commericial and political. It is notable that the USAF has only purchased a very few foreign designs and did so because these aircraft were clearly so uniquely suited to their needs that they far exceeded the ability of US industry to produce them economically or in an acceptable time frame. An interesting coincidence was the USAF's purchase of the English Electric Canberra reconnaissance bomber around this time. This contract was won in a competition against Avro Canada's own CF-100! The Canberra is the only combat aircraft to have served for 50 years (and counting), providing the Americans with reliable spyplanes in Vietnam, while the CF-100 was retired in 1983 purely due to lack of spare parts. The USAF would not have a jet cargo aircraft until years after the Korean War ended.

Again the Canadian government interfered and means were found to ensure the Jetliner would not be built in Canada for TWA. Hughes was so desperate to get Jetliners built that arrangements were attempted with Convair, involving negotiations with Mr. Rockefeller from that firm, to have it license produced in the United States. This time the US government interfered by using a bill purportedly designed to ensure new production of aircraft in the US would be for the construction of warplanes for Korea. Of course, the Jetliner would have made a far superior cargo plane, troop transport and medevac aircraft, but this option was never pursued.

Meanwhile, anyone from Clausewitz to Tsun Tsu will admit that logistics are everything in time of war. Strangely, Truman's "Statement of Economic Principles" related to Canada that, in a defensive alliance, Canada and the United States would purchase defence equipment from one another where the products were the best available. The "Buy American Act" of 1954 certainly set that aside. This rather dualistic approach would be mirrored in bi-lateral programs between not only Canada and the US, but between Britain and America as well.

Once the Korean War ended, the US Congress swiftly passed the 1954 "Buy American Act," which forbade the purchase of foreign products for US government use. In cases where the foreign product was the only alternative, duties and penalties would be applied. (According to American government documents relating to a secret international incident (described later) over the cancellation of the Arrow and subsequent failure of Defence Production and Development Sharing (DPDS), the US granted Canada an exception to the act in 1958. This same document states that Canada cancelled the Arrow program to gain access to American defence contracts through DPDS.) As the ultimate in pugnacious hypocrisy, the Buy American Act even contains a clause which states that any foreign government passing a similar law would become the target of manda-

The Jetliner at Hughes's airfield in Culver City, California. Hughes was very covetous of this aircraft and retained it, and some Avro staff including Don Rogers, for some six months. CF-100s also went down to California for fire-control system work and development work with Douglas and the US Navy on the Sparrow missile for the CF-105. (courtesy Jim Floyd)

tory US trade sanctions. In reality, the paper exemption for Canada bore no fruit at all. This ugly charade was repeated during the run-up to the cancellation of the Arrow where the US promised DPDS to a complicit Diefenbaker who, only days after the Arrow cancellation, would find it wasn't worth the paper it was written on. Only three days after Black Friday the Diefenbaker government learned that their US "deal" to trade Convair F-106 Delta Darts for Canadair-built CL-44 Yukon transports had fallen through "because US manufacturers would not stand for it!"

Floyd to this day considers the cancellation of the Jetliner a possibly worse blow to Avro Canada than the cancellation of the CF-105 Arrow program. It is easy to see why. Avro was realistically projecting sales of *hundreds* of Jetliners while the projected sales potential of the later Arrow, although undeniable (yet still denied), was probably somewhat lower. Sales of the Jetliner would have provided dividends and continuity which would have allowed the development of follow-up, commercial jet passenger aircraft to keep them well ahead of the competition. Production of commercial airliners would have ensured the survival of Avro even in the event of the cancellation of military contracts such as the Arrow. Even so, Avro had many commercial concepts, many employing the basic Jetliner fuselage, on the boards by the time of the Arrow program; one in particular looking astonishingly similar to current Airbus designs. There were also business jets and prodigal supersonic transports under study. Indeed it seems both British and American designers had some difficulty keeping up with the regional and supersonic airline designs Floyd and his colleagues were, and would be, involved with. With an eight-year advantage over the competition, it seems quite possible that Avro Aircraft Canada Ltd., but for the interference of a few key people and some

rather ruthless politics, might today be one of, if not *the*, largest commercial aircraft companies in the world.

While the US government imposes sanctions upon foreign government funded programs, the Boeing 707 was itself the result of one. It was announced in September 1952, while the American press was bashing their aircraft industry for being left in the Jetliner (and Comet's) wake, that Boeing had commenced design of a civilian jet passenger aircraft. Boeing had of course spent years doing their own parametric studies into various payload, speed and propulsion possibilities. Their wing designs up to this point included slightly swept, high-mounted arrangements like the B-47 Stratojet (then emerging from development), plus some with engines mounted *above* the wings. The Boeing 367-80 (Dash 80), which was developed into the KC-135 tanker and the Boeing 707 jet airliner, was, if the 367 designator can be trusted, a jet-powered development of the Boeing 367 piston-engine "Stratotanker" and civilian "Stratoliner." Boeing today (on their website) states that this model number was chosen as a cover to protect their super-secret development from competing manufacturers. The Boeing 367 Stratoliner meanwhile, entered service in 1949 and acquired a reputation for being the "best three-engine airliner in service" due to its unreliable engines. Several of the classic American "propliners" would face various groundings for engine fires and other problems.

The Dash 80 was unveiled in 1954. The fuselage appeared to be entirely different to that of the Boeing 367, giving Boeing's cover story some credibility. However the fuselage shape and size would be changed twice after the Dash 80 first flew, slightly on the military KC-135, and significantly on the 707 passenger jet still four years away. The engine installations were, essentially, civilianized

The Boeing 367-80 prototype of 1954. Harold Hoekstra, chief engineer of the American Civil Aeronautics Administration (now FAA), mentioned in a recollection prepared for Jim Floyd's book *The Avro Canada C-102 Jetliner* that the original Dash 80 plans, "design 473" envisioned passenger capacity of 60 to 75 persons. (Boeing)

Jetliner on approach for one of its last landings. (via Jim Floyd)

B-52 Stratofortress engines on similar pylons. Boeing's new jet had only the first few rows of passenger windows and a different fuselage width than either the KC-135 or the civil 707 derivative. The USAF promptly ordered twenty nine KC-135s as air-to-air refuellers. There is no question that the 707 development that followed this flight was subsidized by profits from the government sales of KC-135 tankers. Boeing now states at their web site that this aircraft was designed in secret to give the company an advantage over their competitors. The Boeing announcement two years earlier of their jet airliner design's commencement, at the height of "Jetliner-mania," would certainly mean that Avro was included in their list of competitors. Today, Boeing unfortunately fails to mention the Avro Jetliner at its site, while it comments on the British Comet and the French Caravelle.

A Sad Ending for the Jetliner

As Kay Shaw relates in *There Never Was an Arrow*:

On a certain Saturday, early in 1957, after eight years of flying, the Jetliner had come in for a routine check and to have a new nose-wheel fitted.... When the staff came to work on Monday morning, they found it had been cut in two on Sunday night, in such a hurry that not even the equipment had been removed or the plane properly dismantled. No one knew who had ordered it, or why...

Well, it may be pure coincidence, but the *Saturday Evening Post* which appeared on the stands a few days later, carried a two-page colour centerfold that proudly advertised the new Boeing "Jetliner" the 707. It was described as "America's first Jetliner, the only American jet airliner flying today." Today?... when that ad went to press, the Canadian Jetliner had been flying for 8 years, was still flying and had a full flying schedule ahead of it. When the ad appeared on the newsstands, the... Jetliner no longer existed except as scrap.

In reality the Jetliner was cut up due to the worries of Transport Canada about corrosion inside the structure of the Jetliner, and the fact that nobody seemed willing to take it on to preserve it. Floyd had sent a letter to Parkin of the NAE asking if they could use it for research purposes but the response was not positive. By that time, Parkin was an Avro detractor having taken Avro to task for their perceived shortcomings on the Arrow design. This notwithstanding, the wording of Smye's "Private and Confidential" letter to Jim Floyd telling him to destroy his pride and joy used very unusual language: "In accordance with our conversation of today, the Jetliner is to be grounded immediately. In fact, with great regret I must say that the Jetliner is not to fly again, but rather is to be dismantled, in an appropriate fashion, as quickly and as quietly as can be done, every precaution being taken to attract as little attention as possible, with the avoidance of any fanfare." It is hard to explain the tone unless he was under some kind of pressure.

It is worth noting that it took Boeing nearly three years to re-unveil the commercial 707 after the Dash-80's first flight in 1954. This time it even had all the windows, seats and a *16-inch* wider fuselage! Further to this, its formerly classified B-52 engines were now cleared for commercial use. Boeing built their commercial aviation company into the largest on the planet on the back of the 707—an aircraft with arguably less sales potential than the Jetliner considering the runway strength and length the 707 required, not to mention its vastly higher price. All in all, it took Boeing about twice as long to produce their commercial 707, using many existing parts plus their expertise from their jet bombers, than it did Avro Canada to produce the original Jetliner.

Would the Jetliner have sold like hotcakes? Absolutely. Would it have been the DC-3 of the jets? Probably. We'll leave the final word in the form of TWA's 1952 flight assessment of the Jetliner, (from *There Never Was an Arrow*):

The direct operating cost per mile of the Jetliner compares very favorably with that of TWA's present equipment, yet reduces current trip times by as much as 30 percent between major centers of population.

Although this analysis was conducted on a conventional aircraft flight plan, which puts the jet transport at a decided economic disadvantage, the Jetliner compares exceptionally well with modern propeller-driven aircraft on a cost per seat-mile basis.

By making certain changes in the flight plan... the overall economic picture can be improved still further—without any sacrifice in safety.

The Avro Jetliner, powered by P&W (Pratt & Whitney) J-56 [sic] engines (license-built Rolls-Royce Nenes) can operate safely and efficiently over every TWA internal route except New York/Los Angeles, non-stop.

The Jetliner's high cruising speed enables it to cut present scheduled operating times by as much as 30 percent. This is undoubtedly the Jetliner's major contribution to air transportation.

The "Jet Power" aspect of the aircraft ensures consistently higher load factors through its passenger appeal. The absence of fatiguing propeller vibration, the smooth, swift flight and the initial novelty of jet travel collectively indicate an attractive and profitable operation.

Existing runways, even at minor airports, are in most cases more than adequate for scheduled Jetliner operation. The approach speed of the aircraft is entirely normal. The simplicity of flying and handling the aircraft reduces problems in pilot training to a minimum.

The numerous flights conducted to date demonstrated that the Jetliner does not present any severe traffic control problems which some anticipated for it. The fact that it can, if necessary, be operated in a conventional manner in the traffic and holding pattern and still show a profit is indicative of its versatility.

The only thing TWA's assessment team forgot to mention was the fact that the C-102 operated above the weather, and thus did not suffer as much from weather-related flight delays and had a much smoother ride. As Bill Baker said after the first flight, "Awesome!"

CF-100 Mk. 4Bs of 428 "Ghost" Squadron RCAF.   (Public Archives of Canada)

WITH THE END OF WORLD WAR II, and once a credible defence plan had been designed for Canada, an aircraft specification to meet the requirement was established. No such aircraft was found anywhere to meet the combined range, speed, weapons and weather requirements, neither in the design phase nor actual development, so Canada took on the enormous responsibility of designing its own.

The XC-100 project was begun under the direction of Edgar Atkin as chief designer. Atkin had been involved at A.V. Roe England with the Avro York and Tudor transports and before this with Boulton Paul Aircraft as a senior designer. In 1947, John Frost, formerly of de Havilland UK, arrived to add his expertise. This expertise was considerable since he had been deeply involved in the design of the DH.108 Swallow experimental, tailless, jet aircraft. He'd also been involved in the design of the Westland Whirlwind fighter and had designed the Slingsby Hengist military glider. The performance and general arrangement specifications of the experimental Canadian fighter were hammered out in late 1945–early 1946. The speed requirements were not a major advance but they were impressive for the time. The weapons, range, propulsion and especially the flight control, radar, altitude, climb rate and weather requirements, however, combined to make the fighter a very advanced and potent design.

Aerodynamics for the speeds specified were fairly well understood at this point, so the design team under Atkin (later assisted by Frost) played it safe in this respect and designed an aerodynamic shape which optimized the state of the art without overly pushing the envelope. The non-existent engines and radar/flight management systems were another story altogether. The combination, in one package, of an aircraft with the overall capabilities of the XC-100 were simply revolutionary (no matter what current historians might say in hindsight).

This was a package representing approximately double the propulsive power of the existing state of the art. This package provided a similar, concentrated, center-line firepower to that of the heavy hitting Mosquito fighter variant; yet it was specified to be over 100 knots faster (the CF-100 would prove nearly 300 knots faster in fact). Maximum level flight speeds were to be superior to that of the fighter version of the Messerschmitt Me-262 swept-wing jet design. The RCAF specification also demanded a bomb load equivalent to the Mosquito's normal bomber version. The design was also to incorporate a radar system superior to that carried on the Mosquito night-fighter variant.

CHAPTER THREE

The Mighty "Clunk"

The Avro Canada CF-100 Canuck

Heavier than air flying machines are impossible. Radio has no future. X-rays are a hoax.
—William Thomson, president of London's Royal Society (1895-1904)

Integration of all these singularly state-of-the-art systems would be one of the most demanding tasks. The CF-100 required flight control, navigation and weapons delivery system integration like no aircraft on the planet and a climb rate and maximum operating altitude that was above the operational altitude of many reconnaissance aircraft. When one adds to this string of peak performance characteristics the ability to operate in exteme icing conditions with long-range and the utmost endurance capabilities, one can see that the RCAF truly wanted to have its cake and be able to eat it, too—while having it all delivered in one nicely wrapped, shiny silver package! They wanted it all. The fact that, by 1954 (with delivery of the first Mk. 4s), they got it all probably influenced the radical specifications that led to the Arrow project.

As mentioned earlier, and contrary to popular belief, the original development contract made it clear that the project was of an experimental nature with no guarantee of future production. This is entirely understandable since Canada had never produced an original aircraft design even

approaching this order of sophistication. At the time, Avro Canada had not produced anything. As such, the original contract of October 1946 only called for the production of two prototypes and a static test airframe.

Enter John Frost

Now proceeding on two aircraft designs and hiring competent engineers from around the world, Avro decided to bring a separate XC-100 project manager on board. John Frost had worked at de Havilland Aircraft since 1942 and had been tagged by their management to turn the Vampire jet fighter design into a tailless configuration in order to prove the tailless concept, since the Comet airliner was originally designed in this configuration. He also was told to have the result in the air in eight months! The gorgeous DH.108 Swallow was the result and provided a great deal of aerodynamic data on the tailless configuration for the western powers. Unfortunately compressibility problems conspired to cause one of the examples to disintegrate in mid air during a practice for an assault on the

John Carver Frost with General Arthur Trudeau of the US Army Foreign Technology branch when Avro was contracted for flying saucer studies. Trudeau figures prominently in LCol Philip Corso's book *The Day After Roswell.* Corso also points out that the foreign technology branch acquired their technology through various means, including covert methods. Corso claims the UFO phenomenon is of alien origin while Frost apparently didn't think so. (Avro Canada via Bill Zuk)

The XC-100 mock-up under construction, apparently slightly after the arrival of John Frost at Avro. (Avro Canada)

sound barrier and world speed record. Testimony states that the Swallow did go supersonic, as evidenced by a sonic boom. Tragically, Geoffrey de Havilland, Jr., son of the company owner, was killed on this flight when the aircraft came apart in the dive. This occurred on 27 September 1946 yet on 9 September 1948, John Derry, another test pilot at de Havilland, claimed a remaining, modified Swallow briefly exceeded Mach 1 in an uncontrolled dive. The basic cause of the controllability problems was the fact that the West was putting undue faith in the designs developed by Lippisch and Horten, developed in Germany before and during the Second World War, while lacking their own test data to confirm the speed and aerodynamic limitations of the designs. Geoffrey de Havilland's fatal crash was largely the reason that Britain abandoned early efforts at breaking the sound barrier while also ensuring that the Comet was designed with a separate tailplane.

At this point it may be worthwhile to back up a little. The main reason for the phenomenal high-speed characteristics of the Spitfire was its thin wing. When the Hawker Typhoon, Gloster Meteor and Spitfire were test flown against each other in an effort to see which would be most effective against the V-1 "buzz-bombs" raining down on Britain in 1944, the authorities were quite surprised to find the older Spitfire was still the fastest aircraft at low altitude. Indeed the thick wing of the Typhoon, after many dangerous diving experiments in the capable hands of Roland Beamont, was dropped in favour of a wing much like that of the late Spitfires to gain airspeed potential. Meanwhile, the Typhoon wing—analyzed by itself in the tunnel—seemed quite capable of high speed. The basic Spitfire design of 1936 would eventually prove the airframe capable of a limiting Mach of .91 whereas the P-51

Mustang of 1941, designed for higher speeds but using a thicker wing and placing the cockpit canopy (bulge) too far forward, would be limited to Mach .85. These numbers were proven by very brave test pilots since the propellers were patently *not* suitable for these kinds of speeds and would be literally threatening the pilot's life hundreds of times per second due to vibrations caused by subsonic, transonic and supersonic flow all occurring across the length of the same propeller blades. Tony Martindale twice lost the propeller (with gearbox once) while diving the Spitfire past Mach .9. The Lippisch/Horten designs, although cutting-edge by being highly swept and based on the delta/tailless concept, were too thick and of the wrong profile for supersonic flight, and as such suffered enormously from the effects of Mach compressibility. Unpredictable and erratic pressure effects and shock-wave movement over the surface of a thick curved wing would prove destructive and make some early designs like the Swallow uncontrollable. The strong nose-down tendencies were caused by the shock-waves on the upper and lower surfaces of the wing being staggered rather than at the same position top and bottom, creating the "nose tuck." Later delta/tailless designs, such as Avro's visionary 1951-52 C-104 and C-105 designs, combined the thin wing/flat surface concept with the delta planform (the silhouette of the aircraft from top or bottom, like a plan view drawing) with astounding success.

Frost arrived at Malton in June 1947 to take over the growing XC-100 project. When he viewed the wooden mock-up that had been constructed corresponding to the basic design, he was horrified by what he saw. To him it was so crude that he termed it "monstrous." The vision he saw was a crude bumpy beast that appeared to be cobbled together by somewhat poor carpenters rather than professional aviation engineers. It had a semi-square fuselage arrangement with two large engine nacelles joined to the fuselage but sitting on top of the wing. The fuselage appeared too bulbous and not very sleek and, as Floyd could have attested from his stress work on the square fuselage of Atkin and Chadwick's York transport, Avro would face weight and design problems with this fuselage shape. Frost quickly set to work changing the fuselage into a circular section while pinching and lengthening it to make it sleeker. He moved the engines down and forward to reduce the frontal area. It quickly transformed into a slick, powerful-looking design somewhat reminiscent of German wartime aircraft according to some contemporary observers. Frost was also disappointed with the straight-wing design with his preference being for a swept wing. He came up with a drawing that incorporated a swept wing on the emerging design.

Avro management was probably somewhat leery of Frost's swept-wing designs due to the Swallow legacy. Edgar Atkin and Jim Chamberlin might have been slightly resentful, despite themselves, over Frost's sweeping changes to "their" design. With all the other changes adding a swept-wing would make the aircraft unrecognizable from the one they had worked out over 18 months' time. Due to a lack of reliable data and the fact that wind tunnel testing showed the straight-wing to be more than adequate as far as reaching the design speed was concerned, Frost's swept-wing version was not adopted. Avro had enough on its plate in developing and integrating the systems, engines, weapons and other components into the aircraft without adding yet another high-risk aspect to the design.

In hindsight, the volume occupied by the engine nacelles and the fuselage probably mitigated against any kind of radical improvement in the CF-100's speed, swept-wing or straight. This is based on a "Sears-Haack" or "area-rule" evaluation of the fuselage with these terms and their application being explored in more detail in chapter four. Simply put, the CF-100's center fuselage occupied too much volume compared to the aircraft length, even without considering the volume of the wings as well, for efficient transonic or supersonic operations, all other limiting factors notwithstanding.

Smye was worried by the original selection of the emerging General Electric (GE) J-47 axial-flow engine which he felt was questionable based on thrust, size and general design. He met with Lord Hives of Rolls-Royce who agreed to provide reduced thrust versions of the troublesome Avon engine for the XC-100 even while stating that the Avon would *not* be released for the C-102 Jetliner for several reasons—these relating to development problems and the British government having put the engine on the secret list. (Much later, putting the Rolls-Royce RB.545 engine on the secret list later meant Britain found no partners for its HOTOL space-shuttle development program of the late 1980s and early 1990s. This engine is a "turbo-rocket," a concept, like so many others, well known in the 1950s—making all the secrecy rather suspect. As a result the RB.545's designer, Alan Bond, set up Reaction Engines Ltd. in hopes of ensuring that his brain-child would see a productive life.)

At this time the TR-4 Chinook proof-of-concept engine had not yet run even though Avro Gas Turbines had also commenced design on a larger but very similar engine designated "TR-5," which would become the Orenda. Interestingly, Paul Dilworth is on record (in Greig Stewart's *Shutting Down the National Dream*) as stating that the XC-100 was designed around the Orenda engine right from the start. If this is the case, then Avro certainly had a lot of balls in the air. Considering the Chinook was still a year away from its first successful run, one must conclude that the Gas Turbine Division designers were a very confident bunch. They must have been very persuasive in convincing Avro management of their competence! They were, however, evolving designs that were at the forefront of axial-flow design. This is no surprise when one considers that the main engineers had all been among the very first proponents of the concept other than the German wartime designers. In fact, these fellows would exceed the successful World War II German BMW jet engine team of Hermann Oestrich and company, who had been "liberated" from internment camps by the French and put to work on what would become the French ATAR engines.

When one considers the state of engine progress at the time it seems apparent that the XC-100 was designed around nacelles which could take either the Avon, the Gas Turbine Division designers' emerging TR-5 design, or whatever else emerged between design commencement and first flight. The Avro Gas Turbine engineers' critical analysis of the Avon design (which proved correct) must have been encouraging as far as the management was concerned. Dilworth states that the Avon was slated for the first few aircraft only as a hedge since they expected the Orenda to take longer to develop than the XC-100 airframe. A very brash bunch, yet their projections were proven true.

The XC-100 development proceeded with little urgency along a relatively leisurely schedule in the beginning. By January 1948 the prototype, although far from finished where equipment installations were concerned, was ready for wind-tunnel testing. Frost left for England at this time to consult with various British manufacturers on the propulsion, ejection seat, landing gear and other issues. At this time, back in Canada, wind-tunnel tests seemed to suggest that the center of lift was too far forward as compared to the center of gravity so Chamberlin, with the approval of Atkin, produced a modification that moved the engines back. The engine was tapered and larger at the front so the movement required that the main spar be modified to dip under the engines once they were relocated. This weakened the spar somewhat and in the end would produce the most serious problem the aircraft development faced. Upon Frost's return it was decided the design had progressed so far in the interim that a further revision was impractical if not unnecessary. Frost was furious and pointed out that while moving the engines back would move the center of lift back, it would also move the center of gravity back. In other words, the aerodynamic lift movement would be negated by the weight movement and worst of all, the main spar would be "fouled" and weaken the wing. He was probably right on all counts and certainly on the spar strength issue.

Security concerns also arose during the development of the XC-100. *Aviation Week & Space Technology* (to this day called "Aviation LEAK" by many in military aviation circles) produced a November 1948 article on the aircraft including an embarrassingly accurate rendering of the jet. The article described the performance projections for the aircraft with similar accuracy and concluded that the aircraft had an impressive combination of speed, armament, range and fire-power. The RCAF and government were so angry that a Royal Canadian Mounted Police (RCMP) investigation was convened resulting in security policy changes with one Avro employee being terminated. This song would be re-sung virtually note for note during the Arrow program when *Flight* published section drawings of the Arrow and Avro was again lambasted, apparently with some American agents running up some red flags in Ottawa regarding Avro security.

The TR-5 Orenda Turbojet

The larger TR-5 was designed to a specification that, at the time, made it the most powerful engine ever produced.

(The Pratt & Whitney J-47 was in service by this time yet the Orenda was more powerful.) Less than a year after the first run of the Chinook the TR-5 Orenda sprang to life. As an example of the microscope under which the government and RCAF had placed Avro, the Orenda was not permitted to run before the first start-up in front of official witnesses. The Chinook invitation had resulted in the dignitaries inviting themselves to the next party! This is an unbelievable restriction on a company during the development of cutting-edge technology and one can only imagine the possible result of a failure before a crowd of the men handling the money. To say the Avro team was nervous on 10 February 1949 would be an understatement. But, once again the start switch was pressed and the engine lit without a hitch!

The high thrust and mechanical durability of the Orenda were so high right from the beginning that the RCAF delayed negotiations with the Americans over the purchase of GE J-47 powered F-86 Sabres. Winnett Boyd commented on the early tests:

> The first time on the test stand it ran for about 30 hours. Then it was stripped and inspected, and since it was in perfect condition, it was reassembled, put back on the stand, and run for 70 hours. During this run it exceeded its design thrust of 6,500 pounds by 200 pounds. After the above test, the Orenda was again inspected, and since it was still in perfect condition, it was reassembled.

With jet engines of that era, the first-running engine was often junked with any viable parts being removed and used in an improved redesign.

Fuel control has been mentioned by many involved in these early days of turbine engine development as a major design problem for the jet engineers. Many factors had to be taken into consideration to properly meter fuel to the combustors. These included air temperature and pressure, engine rpm and load, exhaust temperature, throttle position and others. Most jet engines at the time required that the pilot, under most circumstances, open the throttle painfully slowly to prevent compressor surge or flame-out, and backing off and trying again if the compressor did surge. Avro was the first to develop an easily manageable and efficient fuel control unit. The Orenda became famous not only for its high thrust and durability, but also for being easy to fly and forgiving of rapid throttle movements. This was no mean feat and much effort was required to perfect the system.

Again from *Shutting Down the National Dream:*

Early development running of the Orenda continued through 1949 and early 1950. However, the early success of the engine caught A.V. Roe's gas turbine engineers completely off guard since they suddenly realised that they had a flyable engine and nothing to fly it in.

Paul Dilworth didn't quite agree, feeling the Orenda was ready to be slipped into a North American Aviation (NAA) F-86 Sabre and flown. Dobson insisted it fly on a test-bed aircraft first however. A Lancaster Mark X (built in the same plant during the war) was quickly modified to accept two Orendas in the place of two of the four Rolls-Royce Merlins. It flew in July of 1950. The Lancaster was a very

Avro's Lancaster modified to be the Orenda test-bed aircraft. It later burned in a hanger fire at Avro. (Jet Age)

Orenda turbojets packaged for delivery. Those who used them were well satisfied. (courtesy Jim Floyd)

fast aircraft for its type with the Merlin engines during the war and, with two Orenda's supplementing the Merlins it was actually superior to the B-29s and B-50s of the USAF's Strategic Air Command (SAC). On at least one occasion this "Super-Lanc" buzzed the Air National Guard airfield near Buffalo, New York. The eyebrows of more than one P-47 Thunderbolt pilot were raised when, after they scrambled to intercept, they were effortlessly left in the Lancaster's wake.

The RCAF was instrumental in convincing NAA to modify a Sabre to accept the Orenda and this aircraft first flew in October of 1950. The take off and climb performance of the Sabre were greatly improved by the installation of the Orenda. One Orenda test-cell engineer related to the author that NAA felt there was no way to modify the intake duct to the requirements of the Orenda without sacrificing overall performance compared to the GE J-47 then in use in the aircraft. He commented that Orenda devised a flexible duct for test and placed hundreds of points where pitot tubes could be placed to compare air pressure (and thus flow characteristics) around and down the length of the duct to allow a "hard" design to be contrived. They were highly successful and did it with a minimum of fuss and hardship.

Jacqueline Cochrane, the American record-breaking aviatrix over several decades, set five world speed records in the early Orenda-powered Sabre. She described the Orenda as being "far smoother and finer in every way than the other three" jet engines she had flown with.

The Orenda engine was simply the finest and most powerful jet engine in its class for the day and it is a pity it was not allowed a successor. The Orenda powered both the CF-100 and Canadair Sabre and was adapted for industrial power applications. Canadair Sabres with the Orenda providing the power were sold to several nations including Great Britain, Germany and others. In Britain, on the military side, the Orenda Sabre was the equivalent of the civilian North Star. Both served Britain well when their own aircraft were delayed in design or found wanting. Clearly, spending at home was an important consideration for Britain, one that was apparently lost on Canadian politicians during the Arrow debacle even while it was a *requirement* for the CF-100 program. RCAF Sabres without question ruled the skies in the NATO European theatre during the 1950s and were easily superior to their USAF counterparts and many later designs as well. Several 1950s NATO CF-100 pilots have stated to the author that the *only* adversary that worried them in the skies over Europe, even sunlit skies, was the Orenda-powered CF-86 Sabre. Some insist this assessment extended to the superb Hawker Hunter, the supersonic F-100 Super Sabre and even the F-102 Delta Dagger. Jim Floyd points out that the CF-100 had a critical Mach number of .93 (despite the pilot's notes suggesting not to exceed Mach .85); and was thus potentially faster at altitude than either the Hunter or F-86.

The Chinook and Orenda were singular successes, and the engine side of A.V. Roe Canada's house soon had

The XC-100. The sleek and nimble look changed with the addition of the radar, weapons, and the changes to the nacelle shape due to the spar problem. (Jet Age)

another major project on the drawing boards—the phenomenal PS-13 Iroquois.

First Flight of the XC-100

Once the XC-100 design was crystallized, it had no major setbacks in production and the first flight date in January 1950 soon arrived. The prototype, without the add-ons and modifications of the later combat-ready versions, resplendent in black with a white lightning bolt down the fuselage, had the look of a revolutionary and graceful thoroughbred. The prototype aircraft, unencumbered by armament or the large nose radar and cowl modifications to come, was quite attractive. It shared basic shapes and configuration with the Jetliner and also had the same grace and economy of line as its Avro stable-mate. It differed in having the look, once angered, of a very serious and powerful adversary. With the later Mk. 4 at least, looks were not deceiving.

Once flying however, the XC-100 faced two major obstacles, one of which was the beginning of the Korean War, while the other was structural and was produced in-house by the aforementioned last-minute engine relocation.

The original interceptor contract was only for the development of an experimental aircraft, then designated the XC-100, with potential production being an option for later discussion. With the advent of the Korean War Avro was faced with sudden and unanticipated government demands for ever-increasing production numbers. Up to October 1950 Avro only had orders in hand for ten pre-production aircraft. This was suddenly and incrementally increased to a required production rate of 25 aircraft plus 100 engines per month. The Orenda engine, meanwhile, had first flown only four months earlier! The government had apparently decided that Avro's impressive achievements in design and engineering could be duplicated in production numbers, numbers that the company at the time simply lacked the infrastructure to achieve.

By the fall of 1949 the XC-100 was almost complete and minds turned to the rapidly approaching maiden flight. As with the Jetliner, the most competent pilot available was sought to undertake this groundbreaking flight of a fighter aircraft of unprecedented sophistication.

Bill Waterton, a Canadian from Alberta, had established quite a reputation in Britain as a Spitfire Squadron Leader in the RAF. During the war he had also logged a considerable amount of time in the West's first operational jet fighter, the Gloster Meteor. He also had quite a lot of test

flying time in other single and twin-engine jets in England and was familiar with the Rolls-Royce Avon engines fitted to the first prototype XC-100. He was simply the most experienced jet pilot in the Hawker Siddeley Group at the time. Although he was Canadian, he had to be called home from Britain. When Dobson asked him about going to Canada to fly the XC-100, Waterton apparently thought it was a joke and accepted in the same vein. His bluff was called and he was shipped "home" forthwith!

Duly arriving in Canada in December 1949, upon first inspection, Waterton was generally pleased with the design of the aircraft. Generally speaking, if an aircraft looks right, it flies right and the XC-100 looked good. Frost was involved in the painting of the prototype and consulted Dick Smallman-Tew, known at Avro for being artistic. He suggested that since expensive luxury cars are usually painted black so too should the XC-100. In addition to the black, Tew remarked "...because it is long and thin and wicked looking, give it a white lightning flash to show it off." This little "lightning flash" became the trademark (only in a double red stripe) of RCAF and CF aircraft into the 1980s.

The pressure was on to fly the new black beauty in late 1949, but Waterton was not entirely satisfied with the state of finish of the jet and apparently thought it would take about four more months to bring it up to his standard. He again underestimated Avro Canada and by 17 January 1950 sufficient progress had been made and he commenced taxi-trials.

This says something about Waterton's experience with British engineers. World War II Polish ace, Janusz Zurakowski, (Zura) would relate similar feelings about his experience in Britain. Waterton developed a deep respect for Chamberlin who, unlike some aerodynamic engineers in England, was quite up-front and invariably accurate about the design, capabilities and limitations of his team's product. Frost impressed him too by being very helpful and by accepting constructive criticism, and for flying on the eighth flight himself to investigate spar flexing. Thus, in the spirit of teamwork, they corrected the perceived deficiencies. All in all, Waterton stated that the taxi-trials went better on the XC-100 than on any other aircraft he was ever involved with.

Taxi-trials were completed in an incredible two days with the first flight being slated for 19 January. The entire plant was outside watching along with members of the press, RCAF, and government. Even local roads were jammed with cars to see history being made. Bill Waterton described the take-off:

> Acceleration was tremendous, and in less than 500 yards, we lifted cleanly from the runway. I throttled back, and at 140 Knots, climbed to 500 feet... I gently braked the wheels and pressed the up button to raise the undercarriage. But, as on all my first flights in prototypes, part of the machinery had gone wrong—the button did not want to be pressed home.

Unperturbed Waterton took the aircraft up to 5,000 feet and conducted tests at up to 180 Knots including checks on airbrakes, flaps, controllability and turns. He felt it handled quite well and came in "as steady as a rock, and touched down in the first 150 yards of runway. We stopped with smooth ease within 600 yards of the start of the runway. For a first flight I was well pleased."

The failure of the gear to retract was traced to the failure of a "weight-on-wheels" switch which prevented the pilot from selecting gear up while there was still weight on the landing gear. A very minor glitch. Avro's collection of first flight snag-sheets was still worthy of bragging rights to any aerospace company, especially considering their very first products were cutting-edge jets.

Dobson came to Canada at the end of January 1950 to witness the new jet in flight. Waterton decided to give him a show. He demonstrated some high-speed aerobatics with rolls, turns and a tight pull-up zoom. During a particularly hard "pull" the extra G force (acceleration against gravity) caused the main spar to flex at the area that had been cut away during the engine re-location. A nacelle former cracked with a loud BANG and the cowlings were bent out of shape as a result. The aircraft was quickly brought to earth and parked to the side with the cowlings opened to disguise the damage. Frost said:

> What I feared was happening—the center section spar with the bends [relief cuts] in the top boom made it locally very shallow and, therefore, more flexible at this point than the rest of the wing. This was also the point of highest (load) bending so local deflections were large.
>
> It wasn't a question of strength, just deflection.... The result was the fairing had to buckle. All prototype aircraft have some problems come to light during test flying, but this worried me, considerably.

No doubt! The main spar is called "main" for a good reason; it is the main structural load-bearing member in the aircraft. While Frost knew it was strong enough to support the aircraft in all design operating regimes (speeds, altitudes, weights, "G" loadings etc), it was obvious the flex could not be absorbed without the surrounding structure being deformed.

Doubler plates were attached to the weak area of the spar and other minor modifications were made in an effort to alleviate the problem. Waterton was initially satisfied with the changes. He would add that in the air, the XC-100 promised an excellent top performance. Happily, rates of climb, level speeds and Mach numbers all seemed to be above expectations. He also pointed out the XC-100 could fly rings around the smaller and lighter Vampire jet fighter. This is no minor point.

The Vampire was described to the author by Zurakowski as being a very manoeuvreable aircraft and an absolute pleasure to fly in aerobatics. As for performance in the climb, the XC-100 and later CF-100s would walk away from even an Orenda Sabre—a very key attribute for an interceptor. Superior climb performance also often gives the pilot greater latitude in deciding when, where, and how to fight. Perhaps even more importantly, it gives the fighter pilot the luxury of deciding, on his own terms, *if* he wants to join a fight at all. This same climb advantage was one key to the US Navy's success in fighting the Japanese Zero in World War II, which they could not touch in a manoeuvring fight. Canadian Hornet pilots to this day continue to gripe about how the USAF F-15 pilots regularly refuse to "come down and play" with the CF-18, where the Hornet has the advantage. (Had even the Arrow Mk. 1 been produced, USAF F-15 Eagle pilots would be complaining about the same thing, as performance curves in this book show.) Clearly, for the day the XC/CF-100 was a powerful adversary in regimes where it has routinely been denigrated.

The XC-100 was taken to Washington to be shown off in May 1950. In an effort to impress the Americans with the XC-100's take-off power and phenomenal climb performance Waterton requested take-off clearance for a runway considered too short for the American jets then in service. In Waterton's words "...the CF-100 did not need a long runway for take-off, and made them duck as it screamed over their heads to start a performance with which no American plane of its class could hope to compete."

During this spectacular and enthusiastic display, another nacelle former cracked. Waterton was so shaken this time that he refused to fly the jet home. It was loaded on a flat-bed truck, covered with tarp and hauled back to Canada.

During another enthusiastic display of the second prototype at the Canadian National Exhibition (CNE) Air Show in Toronto, another former cracked. It was now obvious that Avro had a serious problem in the nacelle area that had to be addressed by a major engineering effort rather than the band-aid solution of adding metal to the dip in the spar.

By this time it was felt by some at Avro that Waterton was over-protective of "his" aircraft and was holding up the problem-solving efforts. Some said he held up the program by six months and others saw him as a prima donna. This is probably somewhat unfair to Waterton who had obviously overcome his initial scepticism regarding the aerospace potential of his native land. Indeed Bill's perhaps over-enthusiastic exhibitions were diametrically opposed to his initial conservatism when he first viewed the design. His efforts to impress observers with the performance of the aircraft, to the point of breaking it in public are obviously far from being "overprotective." They are evidence of him being overconfident in his countrymen's product. On 7 February 1951 Waterton was boarding a plane to return to England. From Avro, only John Frost showed up to see him off. There are many sad performances in the Avro story, but this is one of the few the author can attribute to members of the company itself.

Delays imposed by the structural problem, compounded by the sudden change of status from an experimental development project to a full scale production program cost Avro over two years. Many other hurdles were encountered in tooling up for full-scale production, equipment standardization and *en masse* component sourcing, and contributed to the delays as well. One of the major problems was in standardizing the equipment being used on the CF-100. In keeping with the RCAF and government belief that the CF-100 was of strategic significance in the life of the nation, it was deemed important that as much of the equipment for the CF-100 as possible be designed and produced in Canada. In fact, Canadian independent production as national policy was one of the main reasons why the program began in the first place. Avro's Gas Turbine Division was also tooling up to mass-produce the Orenda engine, now suddenly in demand for a huge number of RCAF Sabres (and soon Canadair Sabres which were sold all over the world) as well as the CF-100s. The first two prototype XC-100s were over 50 percent foreign (mainly American and British) content. By the time the last CF-100 Mk 5M rolled off the line the Canadian content was over 90 percent. (Figures from Dow's *The Avro Arrow* and others.) A Canadian high tech industry of the first order grew from almost nothing to become one of the leading sectors in Canada thanks in large measure to Avro's programs.

The first disaster struck the XC-100/CF-100 program on 5 April 1951. Bruce Warren of the RCAF had taken the second prototype up with Avro employee Robert Ostrander in the back seat for a high altitude test flight. The aircraft was reportedly seen in a vertical dive by a TCA pilot. Indeed the aircraft plummeted into a marsh near London killing both on board. No cause was found for the crash until someone was looking through Warren's desk at Avro and found a tube from his oxygen mask in the drawer. Apparently he had cleaned his own mask and left out this tube. One can only imagine the horror of Ostrander being conscious as he realized the aircraft was going to crash with an unconscious pilot at the controls. Unfortunately for this unfortunate soul, at this time, the XC-100 was fitted with ejection controls that were operated from the front seat. This feature was normal for the day and was continued with other aircraft for a considerable time. Avro quickly changed the arrangement.

Those were not happy days at Avro. They had a Jetliner they were not allowed to build and had thus been forced to turn away customers. They had a CF-100 that was requiring a super-human effort to convert into an effective production fighter due to the spar problem and the unrealistic expectations of the government. Avro Gas Turbines was still facing, at this point, fuel control problems with the Orenda that were plaguing every other jet propulsion program. By now Winnett Boyd had suffered a nervous breakdown and had been shuffled out of the company. Now A.V. Roe's general manager, Walter Deisher, was suffering. He became increasingly reclusive and indecisive in the day to day operation of the company. There were murmurs about Avro having covered up the extent of the aircraft's spar problems as well. No doubt Avro was in damage control mode over this aspect while still promoting the successful Jetliner and Orenda with all the skill they could muster. When looking for a replacement for Deisher, Dobson suggested to Howe that Smye would be a good choice. Howe replied that the job would kill him as he was accepting far too much responsibility as it was. Howe suggested Crawford Gordon, his young but already very accomplished Director of Defence Production.

Enter Crawford Gordon, Jr.

Gordon was born in Winnipeg, on Boxing Day 1914, to a bank executive father and a mother who had survived

Captains of Industry, 1951. Left to right: Sir Frank Spriggs, Chairman of the Hawker Siddeley Group; Crawford Gordon Jr., new President at Avro; Sir Roy Dobson, "Boss of Everything"; C.D. Howe "Minister of Everything" on the occasion of the appointment of Gordon as President of A.V. Roe Canada Ltd. (courtesy Jim Floyd)

the sinking of the *Titanic*. Perhaps his mother impressed on her son the need to live life to the fullest from the tragedy in which she had lost her father and brother. His father moved the family, first to Jamaica, then to England and finally to Toronto. This point may also explain another of Gordon's character traits: fierce independence. He would grow into a man in a hurry who thought he could take on the world single-handedly and win! He also would not be a man to allow personal feelings to impede hard business decisions.

His first full-time job was with Canadian General Electric (CGE), where, after a two-year training course in New York State, he took up a position as a company auditor involved in research, costing, profits and strategic planning. When war exploded in Europe, Gordon asked CGE to lend him to C.D. Howe to work in the Department of Munitions and Supply. Gordon idolized Howe, a man known for straight, tough talk and for getting things done yesterday, a man he chose to emulate to a large degree. Thus Gordon, in his late twenties, became one of Howe's bright young "dollar-a-year" men. He worked as director general of organization and as assistant co-ordinator of defence production. These were tremendously challenging portfolios to fill, especially for someone of Gordon's youth. That Canada's per capita war production was higher than any of the other combatants, including Germany and the Soviet Union, is the best testimony to his talents one can give ... and this from a country that was not well industrialized before the conflict! Indeed the Canadian Gross

National Product (GNP) essentially doubled between 1939 and 1945. A graph in the November 1953 issue of *Canadian Geographic* shows that in 1938 Canada's total aviation production was less than $10 million. It rose to $425 million in 1942 and fell to less than $40 million again after the end of the war. After the war Howe referred to Gordon as one of his "towers of strength" and recommended Gordon for decoration. Gordon duly received the Order of the British Empire (OBE) in 1946. In England a grateful nation knighted gentlemen such as Roy Dobson, Sidney Camm, Thomas Pike (of the RAF) and many others.

At the end of the war it was Gordon who submitted the report to Howe on Turbo Research Ltd., stating essentially that the government would not be able to justify continuing the effort of financing the research establishment since it could not compete with large firms elsewhere. Gordon felt the best hope for a return on the effort already expended was to roll the enterprise into some corporation willing to locate and operate in Canada, namely A.V. Roe Ltd. of Great Britain. Turbo Research became Avro Canada's Gas Turbine Division shortly thereafter.

In a comment that would demonstrate Gordon's patriotism and ambition for Canada, he said of his wartime service that it gave him an opportunity to view wartime shortages and diversion of resources to outside powers "caused by our reliance on others for the basics of our aircraft and other industries." His tone was right in line with the feelings of the Canadian government and military after World War II. He seemed to have his mission in mind. Later, at the helm of A.V. Roe Canada Ltd., Gordon embarked on a one-man (or one-company?) crusade to repatriate the Canadian economy. This aspect of the Avro story has been largely ignored by every other commentator on the subject. It is this author's opinion that this is one reason why Avro had some powerful interests working (and networking) against the company and their products, although usually in secret.

After the transformation of Howe's Department of Munitions and Supply into the Department of Reconstruction, Gordon found himself as director general of this department and later became the director of defence production. In 1949 Canada joined the North Atlantic Treaty Organization (NATO) in a response to the increasingly belligerent activities of the Soviet Union. In 1950 war erupted in Korea. Gordon suddenly found himself in charge of a $5 billion defence budget. Probably his biggest problem was the development and production of Avro's CF-100.

The Chief Designers, members of the Hawker Siddeley Design Council. Left to right: Dr. L.W. Newman, Chief Engineer for armaments, Armstrong-Whitworth aircraft; Jim Floyd, Chief Engineer, Avro Canada; Sir Sydney Camm, Director and Chief Designer, Hawker Aircraft; R. Walker, Chief Designer, Gloster Aircraft; and Stuart Davies, Chief Designer, A.V. Roe England. Camm's enthusiasm for his Hunter is evident while Floyd may have felt slightly embarrassed holding the CF-100 since he didn't have much to do with its original design. (Jim Floyd collection)

Although the project had been commenced as a development program only, once the decision was made to push the aircraft into full production, Gordon, the government and the RCAF expected miracles. He was, in Dobson's words "rough as hell" on the company over the development problems encountered in turning the XC-100 into a reliable operational interceptor. A year after the production order for the CF-100, it was felt that Avro Canada needed a new man at the helm and Gordon stepped in, to the initial reservations of Dobson. Gordon described his challenges in characteristically succinct terms: "to organize, deputize and supervise. For nearly six years we've been designing, planning, testing and carrying on intricate research. We've achieved very ambitious objectives: two Canadian jet engines, a Jetliner, a Canadian jet fighter. The next step will be to produce them in quantity." It is clear from this statement that Gordon was aware of the engineering and design strengths of his new company and of its need to build up its manufacturing capability.

RCAF Service

On 18 October 1951, the first CF-100 Mk. 2 was delivered to the RCAF some four months after the first flight of the original Mk. 2 Orenda powered version. It had taken five years from design drawings to delivery, which is a fair-

ly good timeframe, especially when one considers the sophistication of the aircraft. The aircraft was not up to scratch, however, and this problem was mostly related to out-sourced equipment variables (many systems were tried for similar tasks and consistency was a problem, as Avro sorted out which out-sourced items were up to par, and which needed improvement or replacement) and the vexing spar problem. The engines, probably the RCAF's greatest worry, considering the move to jets, were, however a most pleasant surprise.

The early RCAF testing of the CF-100 Mk. 2 was a fiasco. Early test flying by RCAF test pilots, who flew the interceptor like a World War II dogfighter with little regard for smooth handling, again caused major cracking around the nacelle area. The Mk. 2 was rejected out of hand by the RCAF and the aircraft were returned to Avro. Avro's colossal efforts to turn an experimental aircraft into a production one, while fixing serious problems, were not receiving any consideration whatsoever from the RCAF. But then fighter pilots should be able to count on their aircraft since worrying about their "ride" killing them is highly distracting when they also have to worry about the enemy.

Much consternation was encountered by Avro in trying to devise an acceptable solution to the problem of spar flex. Stuart Davies from A.V. Roe England, an early booster of the Jetliner program, was brought over to review the aircraft. According to Stewart in *Shutting Down the National Dream*, Davies spent two weeks going over the design and the aircraft itself with a fine toothed comb and his recommendation to Fred Smye was *"burn it!"* Floyd, very experienced in working with Davies doubts if "Dave" (his nickname) made such an extreme remark, but it was obvious the design had problems. He was not overly impressed with the CF-100's structural design in more areas than just the main spar and felt the aircraft was also under-stressed in other areas.

Smye, for the sake of the company's survival, could not recommend to anyone the abandonment of the airframe project. Davies also evidently recommended that Atkin take a sideways transfer with Floyd being raised to overall head of engineering, with Frost also being moved outside the CF-100 program and allowed to research aerodynamic and propulsive theories applicable to disc-shaped aircraft (flying saucers). Bob Lindley, another Avro UK "special apprentice," was placed in charge of the "Blitz Group" with orders to "fix the 100". Lindley formed a team to address the worst problem; namely the flexing wing spar. The Polish stuctural specialist Waclaw Czerwinski had earlier joined Avro from de Havilland Canada and was internally re-assigned to the spar problem. His "Czerwinski joint" probably saved the whole CF-100 program. It strengthened the spar somewhat in the weak area, but more importantly it relieved the stress on the skin and structure at the wing/engine joint by including a hinge design that allowed the wing to flex under manoeuvring G forces without stressing the nacelle structure.

S/L Joe Shultz, a famous RCAF Mosquito intruder ace during World War II, was one of the RCAF test pilots intimately involved in the early CF-100 RCAF test flying. He personally returned the broken CF-100 to Malton:

> When I landed it at Malton it was an interesting sight; rivets and things were hanging on the bottom of the wings through the cracks. Engine nacelles were scratched because the wings flexed. Engine billets bent thirty degrees. Quite a mess.

Quite a testament to the effect of World War II pilots flying high-speed aircraft roughly; i.e.; with sudden "G" onsets and snap reversals. Taking an aircraft from a 1G dive to a 7.33G (CF-100 limit) climb in a snap-pitch change, will subject the wing to a *much* higher peak load than would a smooth transition to such a performance state. To do so in an aircraft of six times the weight and

power and twice the speed of a Spitfire subjects the aircraft wing to exponentially higher demands. Air Force Indoctrination Course (AFIC) content repeatedly stressed the massive aircraft loss rate, both of CF-86s and CF-100s that was wrought by wartime "retreads" pressed back into service around the time of the Korean war. These warriors just didn't understand the physics of high performance jet flight and, as a result, many killed themselves in otherwise serviceable aircraft. It is one thing to pull the stick of a 7,000 lb Spitfire at 250 knots until the relatively low power told you that you were asking too much, and quite another to ask a 38,000 lb aircraft with six times the power and well over twice the cruise speed to do the same thing. Wartime pilots didn't understand that Force equals One-Half Mass Times Velocity *Squared*. Expectations due to their experience were turning men and machines into smoking holes in the ground. Somewhat undeservedly, Avro was suffering from this RCAF training deficiency.

Guns, Guns, Guns: the business end of the CF-100 Mk. 3. Eight fifty-calibre machine guns on the centerline packed a great deal of concentrated firepower. (Avro Canada)

One by one, the problems were tackled. The most pressing concerns were addressed immediately and resulted in the CF-100 Mk. 3 variant becoming the first in RCAF service. The first eight-gun Mk. 3 was delivered to the RCAF in October 1952 just after Squadron Leader Joe Shultz did the CNE Air Show in a pre-production Mk. 3 trainer version. Screaming along at 500 knots on the deck he pulled hard into a vertical zoom. This time he exceeded the allowable "G" limit (pilot error) and bent the wings yet again. Once again he delivered a bent CF-100 to Malton. Even while this was going on, a more thorough re-design was being developed which would culminate in the most produced version, the excellent Mk. 4.

Avro's CF-100 development aircraft taking off with rocket-assist. It had excellent take-off performance even without such expedients.
(Hugh McKechnie and Avro Canada)

A 419 "Moose" Squadron CF-100 salvoeing its fifty-eight 2.75 inch folding fin rockets.   (Public Archives of Canada)

Virtually identical to the Mk. 3 in appearance, some 14,000 of the 15,000 or so parts were redesigned. Floyd, Lindley, Pesando and Lindow had taken charge and weren't hedging any bets.

Although the Mk. 3 was a vast improvement over the pre-production CF-100s, the author knows several ex-RCAF pilots who did not paint them in a very flattering light. Similar to stories of the much-later, first-production Canadair Challenger 600s, which the Canadian Air Force was forced to accept (whereas Avro was forced to halt the Jetliner while the RCAF purchased the de Havilland Comet!), the Mk. 3 was inconsistent from example to example. It seemed that instrument panels, wiring routes, equipment installations and the like were placed differently in each aircraft as if the production personnel were "feeling out" the best way to build the aircraft. One would not know whether a fuel pump, instrument or other item would be of US, British or Canadian manufacture with severe complications in servicing and reliability arising from these factors. Some of these problems could no doubt be traced to changes made "on the fly" to components developed to Mk. 2 specifications in the panic to get the aircraft operational and stop the bloodletting from Ottawa and the RCAF. Howe wanted CF-100s on the tarmac and he got them. Meanwhile Avro's Jetliner Number One was soaring through the heavens with the greatest of ease and demonstrating no vices whatsoever.

Annoying technical problems presented themselves. Shultz would joke that if the pilot reported successful gear retraction, then that would be the last transmission you would hear because the radio would certainly fail as a result! But then, the electronics of the CF-100 were not shock mounted, just like most aircraft of the day. In fact the Hughes MG-2 radar/fire control system, used in the CF-100 (and Convair F-102), was so vibration-sensitive that for training purposes all eight .50-calibre machine guns could not be fired at once. The ASTRA (Automatic Search & Track Radar) system, developed for the Arrow, was the world's first rack-mounted, shock-isolated, retractable radar/fire control system. It had a number of other surprising firsts as well, which are explained in Chapter Five.

Jan Zurakowski is on record as having experienced an unselected gear retraction on approach:

> I realised during my landing run that the under-carriage was retracting. Since my speed was too low to get airborne again, I switched off the engines and the aircraft skidded to a stop, damaging the flaps badly. After an investigation had been carried out in the hangar, it was determined that everything was in perfect order; lowering or raising of the undercarriage functioned properly and the indicators were correct. Conclusion: pilot error.

> I was called into the hangar to see for myself. I set all the controls and switches as I had during landing, operated the undercarriage several times, and, sure enough, everything was just fine. I was just getting out of the cockpit when the foreman said: "You see, that's a really good old aircraft"—and enthusiastically slapped the fuselage with his hand. That started it. All by itself, the undercarriage retracted.

Zura no doubt walked away without a word (and a dubious smirk) while the technician was probably scratching his head and contemplating a future with Canada Post.

Other problems were not of the aircraft's doing. The CF-100 was arguably the most sophisticated interceptor flying at the time. With those credentials came requirements in flight training and maintenance that were far beyond what was required by the mostly World War II-trained crews of the day. Air Commodore A.C. Hull, an RCAF Bomber Command veteran, remarked that, during

A Mk. 3 CF-100 at the gun butts at night. (DND)

Avro's Sabre Mk. 6 chaseplane. With the developed Orenda and a new wing design the Canadair Sabre 6 was the top day-fighter in the NATO European Theatre of Operations for several years. Licensed airframe production profited both Convair and North American Aviation. Avro's Mike Cooper-Slipper is believed to be the pilot in this photo, taken from a T-33. (Avro Canada)

the phasing into service, the CF-100 loss rate was about 10 percent. A frightening statistic. He noted:

> But as time went on, we realized we were losing them, not so much from the fact they weren't that great an aircraft, but because we weren't training our pilots properly in their use.

But then, World War II RCAF retreads were boring smoking holes in terra firma with the excellent CF-86 Sabres at a shocking rate as well.

Joe Morley, Avro's sales and service representative, summed up the problems caused by poor attitudes, inadequate training and unrealistic expectations for a new aircraft just entering service:

> Sure it had bugs and fixes were required. But our military were not prepared for this eventuality. They had always flown more or less tried and proven "old days" [aircraft]. If you think the 747s being delivered today are the same as Pan Am originally bought, you're off your rocker. The same can be said of the DC-4, the F-4, the F-15 Eagle. Any good airplane must have growth in it, otherwise it's a dud.

But there were those in the lower military ranks who just could not comprehend airplane development. [CF-100 operations were] mainly night and all weather, a real challenge for those who were used to clear skies day and night.

The day of the "seat-of-the-pants" flier were gone as far as military aviation was concerned. All weather interceptor pilots now had to be skilled technicians with an engineering bent of mind while still retaining superlative "hands-and-feet" skills, but this lesson was learned the hard way. In the beginning, new pilots, fresh from training on the Harvard single-engine propeller trainer, received only 30 to 40 hours' jet training on the Canadair-produced T-33 Silver Star before converting to CF-100s. A mere 50 hours were spent on the CF-100 before the pilot was sent "on squadron" and proclaimed operational. There were not even CF-100 ground simulators at that time to help the pilot hone his skills under expert supervision. Considering the vast array of technical skills involved in managing an aircraft of the sophistication of the CF-100, not to mention the demands of the kinds of missions the aircraft was designed for, it is no surprise that the initial loss rate was high. Today, high-performance fighter training takes about five times as much flight training time on much more "user-friendly" aircraft. This is in addition to highly realistic training in sophisticated ground simulators. Many still say it is not enough. It is *never* enough. As Chuck Yeager has stressed, experience is just about the only thing that separates the dangerous from the magnificent.

The first three operational CF-100 squadrons were formed in 1953. Considering the hurdles in turning around the experimental aircraft's problems, and the others related to tooling up for an improved version (with parts that were over 90 percent different, according to figures in *The Avro Canada C-102 Jetliner*), this was a remarkable accomplishment. One of the major drawbacks of this type was in its radar/fire control system, which required an approach to the target from behind, an area that was generally well-defended by Soviet bombers. Of course, this had nothing to do with Avro but rather with Hughes Aircraft and their radar/fire-control system. Hughes' problems in this area also contributed to the F-102 being equipped with much the same system used on the CF-100 rather than the, apparently technically challenging, Hughes MX-1179 system that had been intended for it. For the CF-100 Mk. 3 version, limitations in radar, serviceability, cockpit arrangement and equipment ensured it was replaced quickly once the almost all-new Mk. 4 became available.

As such it was a valuable aircraft in that it allowed Avro and the RCAF to learn, from operations, the lessons necessary before the impressive Mk. 4 became available. For Avro it allowed them the time and experience to secure adequate components largely from Canadian contractors and iron out the service-proven shortcomings. For the RCAF it allowed them time to develop a core of pilots and instructors, as well as a practical training syllabus (including physics 101!) for those who followed. By early 1955, the Mk. 3 was relegated to training while the Mk. 4 took over interceptor duties. While the problems of the Mk. 2 meant it only served as a trainer, the Mk. 3 being an operational trainer with weapons and radar meant that some of the training deficiency would be made up with better flying trainer samples, and more of them.

NORAD and NATO Cold Warrior: The CF-100 Mk. 4

The Mk. 4 was almost an entirely different aircraft from the Mk. 1 and Mk. 2, thanks to the talents of Floyd, Lindley and the crew at Avro. The addition of wingtip pods holding fifty-eight 2.75 inch folding-fin rockets (to complement the eight .50-calibre machine guns in the belly), and the introduction of the Hughes MG 2 radar/fire control system made the massively improved airframe a force to be feared. This radar allowed interception from a variety of angles ranging from the side to nearly head-on. It allowed

A CF-100 Mk. 4b of 445 Squadron RCAF on the way to Marville, France. It wears the NATO standard camouflage paint scheme. (Public Archives of Canada)

interceptions that limited the attacker's exposure to (rear gunner) defensive fire, while allowing angles of weapons release that presented the largest target to the area of dispersion of the potent rocket packs.

About this time Avro had sent a CF-100 Mk. 4 to the US for weapons systems trials with the USAF and Hughes specialists. The American response to the RCAF and Avro was that the Mk. 4 had the most potent and tactically useful weapons system then in service (it really was a very powerful weapons platform), but what the Americans were most impressed with was the reliability and serviceability of the Orenda engines. Considering they obviously felt the CF-100's radar and weapons were the best in the world, this is a very high accolade for the Orenda engine. Meanwhile, by this point, A.V. Roe Canada Ltd., a very young company, was the only one in North America producing both engines *and* airframes. Further, these A.V. Roe Canada projects were the first examples of either that the company had placed in service. For every nation except Germany, Britain and the United States, in that order, this was the first jet-powered radar-equipped all-weather interceptor, period.

During early testing of the Mk. 4, Zurakowski, (by then employed with A.V. Roe Canada after serving in the Polish Air Force, fighting in the Battle of Britain in Spitfires and working on the development of jet fighters at Gloster Aircraft in the UK), took a Mk. 4 prototype supersonic. He felt the aircraft had the kind of power to easily exceed its limiting Mach, even in level flight, if a pilot became distracted. Thus, for safety reasons, he felt obligated to find out what would happen to the aircraft if it exceeded its "placard speed." He nosed the Mk. 4 over at high altitude and soon broke the sound barrier, thus making the CF-100 the first straight-wing aircraft to do so. He recovered the aircraft and returned to Malton. The shock wave and resultant movement in the center of lift produced a strong nose-tuck but, unlike Frost's DH.108, the aircraft was recoverable and didn't come apart. Zura's diminutive frame obviously held a disproportionate amount of guts! It is also evident that Bob Lindley and his team had, through monumental (and economical) effort, overcome the structural limitations that had led the extremely erudite Stuart Davies to recommend a rather extensive shake-up in the engineering side of Avro management. This proof of the aircraft's durability and controllability was not appreciated by A.V. Roe management since they had tried to sell a swept-wing redesign of the airframe based on Frost's ini-

RCAF technicians working on the CF-100's MG-2 radar/fire-control system. (RCAF)

tial suggestions—which did *not* indicate level-flight supersonic performance even with more thrust and the swept-wing!

In fact, during my training in the Canadian Forces, I was told that a CF-100 was put on the NAE's structural test rig to see what the fatigue life of the airframe was in normal operations. I was told they simulated about 30,000 flying hours without problems and took it off the rig not because the aircraft finally fatigued, but because they needed to get on with testing other aircraft! The F-18 Hornet, for example, is limited to between 4,000 and 6,000 hours before it is finished.

During the 1955 Farnborough Air Show in Britain, Zura presented the CF-100 Mk. 4, the first foreign designed and built aircraft invited to appear there. His dazzling display, including tight turns within the confines of the airfield, stood out in sharp contrast to normal jet-fighter routines that consisted of high-speed passes, rolls and zoom climbs. (As is said today, it wasn't a typical "smoke-and-noise" display.) He beat up the airfield in tight turns at low level and especially dazzled the crowd with a "falling leaf" manoeuvre he had devised. He literally stole the show and the headlines proved it! Since a 1951 invitation to display the XC-100 at Farnborough had been can-

celled due to the structural problems, one can see that Europeans waited an extra three years to see the jet, yet were impressed nonetheless.

By the end of 1954, the Mk. 4 was being delivered to the RCAF, in quantity, with their up-rated Orenda engines. The CF-100 gained many names other than the official "Canuck" moniker. Often they were derogatory such as "Lead-Sled," CF-Zilch," and the most popular "Clunk." The feelings of the pilots varied from adoration to disdain, with the detractor's feelings usually being predicated on one of two factors; whether the pilot had come from the day-fighting Sabres or if he had experienced the Mk. 3. Pilot after pilot who flew Mk. 4s or 5s in the European theatre will confidently assert that, during the 1950s, no allied fighter, in daytime or night, bad weather or good could touch the CF-100, save the magical Orenda-powered Canadian Sabre, even in a dogfight. A couple of these Cold-Warriors, such as W/C "Irish" Ireland, have gone as far as to say that the CF-100 could even tangle with the Hawker Hunter and emerge victorious. Heady performance considering the Hunter replaced the Canadair Orenda Sabre in RAF service!

By August 1957, Canada had re-equipped four Canadian NATO squadrons in Europe with CF-100 Mk. 4 aircraft in response to an urgent NATO appeal to fill a major gap in NATO's all-weather and night defensive capabilities. It is accepted as fact that the CF-100, over ten years after its original design was laid out and during an era of explosive advances in aerodynamics and propulsion, was the *only* high-performance aircraft reliably defending Western Europe on many bad-weather days and nights and at long range.

As late as 1958, the CF-100 was chosen to compete for a contract to re-equip the Belgian Air Force. Zurakowski mentioned to this author in 1996 that the Belgians approached him personally (at Farnborough) for his appraisal of the CF-100 and mentioned a dissatisfaction with British and American aircraft and after-sales support. The CF-100 won out against British and American designs due to aggregate superiority and re-equipped the Belgian Air Force in 1958. This was apparently *much* to the chagrin of American manufacturers since the US government under the Mutual Assistance Plan was subsidising the purchase of Belgium's aircraft.

The USAF's most serious all-weather and night interceptor in Europe during the 1950s was the Northrop F-89 Scorpion, while the RAF was using a de Havilland Vampire

The Northrop F-89 Scorpion, the next best thing to the Clunk in the night and bad weather interceptor role. (USAF Museum)

A Lockheed F-94 Starfire, a radar-equipped version of the F-80 Shooting-Star. (USAF Museum)

A Republic F-84C Thunderstreak. (USAF Museum)

The Meteor night fighter, built by Armstrong-Whitworth.
(Hawker Siddeley)

variant and World War II-era Gloster Meteors. All of these designs were poor cousins compared to the CF-100 Mk. 4 or 5. Republic F-84 Thunderjets, Thunderstreaks and Lockheed F-94 Starfires were just targets to the RCAF "Clunk drivers."

A former RCAF and still (as of 1997) Air Canada 747 pilot, Jack Hubbard told the author the following story. He was part of the initial operational readiness check of the CF-100 when it replaced a USAF F-84 Thunderstreak squadron on the field in Germany. His squadron was ordered to scramble and report in to the USAF radar weapons controllers upon reaching 40,000 feet. All was well and upon reaching 40,000 feet, some nine minutes after the order to scramble, the pilots awaited further intercept instructions. They doodled along at this altitude for a time before radioing in to the USAF controllers requesting further instructions. Apparently, the controllers had left their post to have a coffee since it was expected the CF-100s would take much longer to take off and reach altitude based upon experience with their USAF predecessors. After a while, the java-sipping USAF controllers sauntered back to their posts and instructed the CF-100 pilots to return to base and scrub the mission since the ground radar was obviously broken. The Canadians asked what

the trouble was. The controllers responded that their radar indicated the formation to be at 40,000 feet and that since this was clearly impossible they should RTB to give them a chance to fix their equipment! The flight commander's reply (expletives no doubt deleted!) was something to the effect that "We are and for several minutes have been at 40,000 feet and I request you provide vectors and quit wasting our GAS!!!" The grins of the so-called Clunk drivers must have stretched their oxygen masks to the point of rendering them unfit for future operations! This is an interesting anecdote considering the F-84 Thunderstreak was a *day-fighter.* The nine minutes from scramble to 40,000 foot altitude is also right on the original CF-100 specification, obviously one that not even a single-engine, single-seat, USAF day-fighter could accomplish.

Another telling anecdote was provided by a CF-100 Mk. 5 pilot who was instructed to take off and climb to 30,000 feet with his element leader to a position near Toronto, Ontario. Apparently the leader was delayed in his take-off by some minor glitch so his wing-man scrambled first. Upon arriving at 30,000 feet over Lake Ontario and becoming bored waiting for his leader, he decided to orbit and climb—at the same time— for lack of anything else to do. Finally, his leader was able to take off and radioed en route asking for the grid position of his wing man. The "wingy" duly gave his position and mentioned orbiting by this time at 40,000 feet.

Lead replied "Roger, will meet you there." During lead's transit the wingman maintained his climb in the orbit.

Finally lead arrived and said, to the effect; "Number two, we are in position at 40,000 feet and don't have you on radar, state position."

Number two replied, "Lead we are at your co-ordinates climbing through 60,000 feet!" The leader's reply is unprintable.

This anecdote is especially significant considering the fact that the famed Lockheed "Skunk-Works", U-2 high-altitude reconnaissance aircraft was designed to operate with impunity at 70,000 feet, an altitude that was unattainable by the Soviet Union's best early-1960s interceptors. Even the mighty F-15 Eagle starts running out of engine and wing at 60,000 feet, even when it is relatively clean and light. The big engine nacelle volumes might have limited the CF-100's top speed, but the large additional upper surface area, shaped as it was, and the decent aspect-ratio wing resulted in a shape that produced a great deal of lift.

Although the CF-100 exceeded its specified speed requirement of 490 knots by more than 100 knots, by 1959 it was being left in the dust by new designs such as the B-52 Stratofortress and Soviet "Blinder" bomber and the commercial Boeing 707. Due to the cancellation of the Arrow program the CF-100 was forced to over-stay its welcome until finally replaced in 1961 by secondhand F-101 Voodoos retired from Air National Guard service. These beat-up birds were quite the sight with faded areas under the RCAF markings clearly betraying their earlier American service. One can only imagine how demoralizing this was to RCAF aircrews who had been proudly salivating over the astronomically superior Avro Arrow of their own nation's origin. As we shall see, even the Mk. 1 Arrow would have been very serious competition for the McDonnell Douglas F-15C in the interceptor roles for which they were designed. Today, however, some Canadian historians persist in rating the F-101B Voodoo as "excellent," an interesting assessment considering the serviceability problems, relatively low performance, and the fact that the aircraft never fired its limited weapons in anger to prove if it could perform its mission at all.

The CF-100 would soldier on until 1983, when it was retired from service due to lack of spare parts. At this time the aircraft was a powerful Electronic Counter Measures (ECM) aircraft with 414 Black Knight Squadron. This role has subsequently been filled largely by the even older T-33 Silver Star, an aircraft with considerably lower capability in any respect than the jet it replaced. The last flight of the CF-100 was made by a 414 Squadron aircraft (painted to represent the first XC-100 prototype) when this aircraft was flown to the National Aviation Museum (NAM) at Rockcliffe in Ottawa to join the collection. This aircraft is now on loan to the Canadian Warplane Heritage Museum in Mount Hope, Ontario as a static display aircraft. A curator at the NAM, Andre DuCharme, declares they took out the fuel tanks to ensure the CWHM didn't try to fly it! What a shame. Canada deserves to see its one and only home-designed fighter (to enter service) in flight. Orenda engines, once the power behind the best day and night fighters in NORAD and NATO, are still in operation in industrial applications world-wide.

The CF-100 of the Canadian National Aviation Museum on loan to the Canadian Warplane Heritage Museum. (R.L. Whitcomb)

Arrow RL 203 in an afterburner climb, from the painting "Thunder Before the Storm."　　(image by R.L. Whitcomb, 1996)

BOTH AVRO AND THE RCAF were keenly aware from the rapid progress of aircraft and weapons design in the 1940s and 1950s that the CF-100 would need to be replaced in about ten years. Considering that the normal development time of an aircraft of this type was about seven or eight years, they knew they needed to start working on a replacement even while the CF-100 was just entering service.

In late 1951 the RCAF formed an "All-Weather Requirements Team" to begin looking at a supersonic replacement for the CF-100. It should be pointed out that the sound barrier had only been broken by Chuck Yeager in a rocket-powered Bell X-1 as recently as 1947. This was done after the British had cancelled (in January 1946) a very similar design conceived in 1943, the Miles M.52, and had passed all their design information to the US (Bell Aircraft and NACA, the National Advisory Committee on Aeronautics, specifically) free of charge. It is odd that this design was cancelled in part because of genius inventor Sir Barnes Wallis' belief that breaking the sound barrier with a human-occupied aircraft was too dangerous. Oddly enough, this M.52 cancellation came eight months *before* Geoffrey de Havilland, Jr. was killed in a (possibly) supersonic dive in the DH.108 Swallow. This death really put the brakes on British supersonic research and many promising programs were cancelled by those holding the purse-strings. Obviously supersonic research continued, however, while the Americans grabbed the headlines and sold the hardware.

Arrow RL 203 from the painting and limited edition series "Northern Thunder." (image by R.L. Whitcomb 2002)

CHAPTER FOUR

The Avro CF-105 Arrow Weapons System

Per Ardua Ad Arrow

The impression that supersonic aircraft are just around the corner is quite erroneous.
—Sir Ben Lockspeiser, British Director General of Scientific Research for the British Ministry of Aircraft Production, 18 July 1946.

A wind tunnel model of the Miles M.52 supersonic research aircraft. The project was begun in 1943, and ended in 1946. (via Derek Wood's *Project Cancelled*)

Sir Frank Whittle, the inventor of the turbojet, quit his own company, Power Jets, over the M.52 fiasco since a derivative of his W.2B/700 engine, using afterburning and bypass "ram-burning" was finally proving successful and capable of giving the M.52 a highly-supersonic performance. Unfortunately the power-brokers of the era became convinced that only swept wing aircraft could go supersonic, and this influenced the M.52 cancellation, despite the fact it had a good supersonic wing design.

The M.52 appears to satisfy area-rule considerations slightly better than the Bell X-1 and could very possibly have given the first supersonic honours to Britain. The turbojet-powered M.52 also envisioned use of an engine bypass duct into which ramjet combustors were to be installed. The later Republic F-103, which made it to the mock-up stage after torturous development before being cancelled in 1957, also employed this concept and was, to the author's knowledge, the second design to do so. Bill Gunston's *Faster Than Sound* reveals wind-tunnel and engine performance figures from actual tests that demonstrate that the M.52 would have been supersonic—and by a comfortable margin.

Jim Floyd had taken over from Atkin as Avro's chief engineer in January of 1952 and had been spending a fair amount of time with Chamberlin in Avro's projects office studying supersonic configurations and design ideas to be considered for a CF-100 follow-up aircraft. They met the RCAF team in February to discuss their respective projects.

The RCAF operational requirements team issued their report in March and, while not producing an aircraft specification, agreed that Avro could assist them by studying the state of the art and submitting what they thought would be a suitable design. By June, Avro dutifully produced two designs. Both single-seat proposals relied on the delta-wing planform with one being twin-engined and the other using a single power plant. Both were to use the afterburning turbojet being designed by Orenda, the TR-9 Wakunda. The larger twin-engined version featured internal weapons storage of the Canadian Velvet Glove, radar-homing, air-to-air missile while the single-engined version was to be equipped with internal Falcon missiles, which were shorter than Velvet Glove. Dubbed the C-104/1 (single-engine) and C-104/2 (twin-engine), the single-engine version is more reminiscent of the much later F-106 than the F-106 is to the aircraft it was supposedly developed from, the F-102! The C-104/2 was developed into the Arrow. According to Jim Floyd:

> In June [1952] we submitted two possible designs, both with delta wings. The C104/1 was a single-seat, single-engine, low wing, tailless delta weighing 28,200 lb., with a wing area of 617 sq. ft., and powered by one TR9 engine (under study by Orenda). The C104/2 was a larger twin-engined, high-wing, tailless delta with a wing area of 1,189 sq. ft., powered by two TR9 engines. The advantages and disadvantages of the two designs were fully outlined in the brochure. The main advantage of the larger C104/2 was the very large armament bay, designed to stow internally a wide variety of weapons, resulting in the potential for using the aircraft in many roles, such as long-range interceptor, advanced trainer, bomber or photo-reconnaissance aircraft.

In other words, Floyd and Avro Canada were intentionally designing a multi-role aircraft, something the US would latch on to with alacrity many years later. The multi-role capabilities and thus export potential of the Arrow weapons system were completely lost on the Diefenbaker government (or so their recorded remarks

DELTA INTERCEPTORS · 1949 TO 1956 ·

Convair XF–92, –flying in 1949– strictly subsonic, basis of the Convair "1954 Interceptor" submission, the F–102.

Avro Canada C–104/1 design proposal to the RCAF June 1952

Convair YF–102A, On paper in 1952, first flew late 1954, incapable of level supersonic flight due to area rule problems

Fairey FD.2, on paper in 1952, first flight October 1954, world speed record March 10th, 1956 of 1,132 mph (demonstrated over 1,320 mph)

Dassault Mirage III prototype, on paper circa 1954, first flight November 17th, 1956

Convair YF–106A, on paper in 1954, first flight December 1956. Derived from the XF–92 and F–102, world speed record December 1959 of 1,526 mph

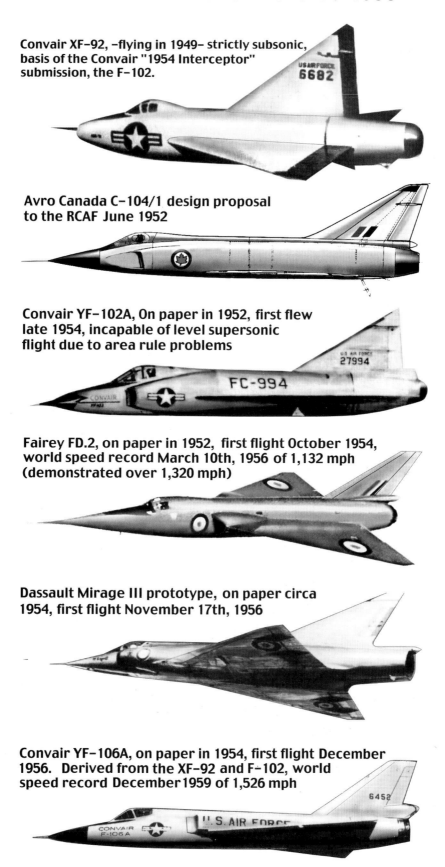

would suggest), and seemingly, on the Liberals they replaced. In other nations the concept of multi-role capability was taken as being something of a political red herring since none of the supposed multi-role aircraft were very good at anything! The British certainly came to appreciate the multi-role capabilities of the Arrow, however, as we shall see. But then they had been one of the few nations to benefit from a really excellent, multi-role aircraft in the past, the superb de Havilland Mosquito.

Considering the history of supersonic aircraft designs up to this time (1952), both early Avro proposals were exceptionally advanced concepts. With respect to the single-engined, single-seat C-104/1, its design was completely validated by the Fairey Delta Two (FD.2), Mirage III to 2000 designs, and eventually by the F-106 Delta Dart, which would finally become an excellent aircraft after simply a development nightmare. To see how far ahead Avro was at the time it is worthwhile to take a quick look at the progress of high speed delta-wing designs of this period.

Faster Than the Sun: The Fairey Delta Two

The title "Faster than the Sun" is from the remarkable book of the same name by Fairey test pilot Peter Twiss and refers to the FD.2's ability to outrun the rotation speed of the earth!

The 1947 British specification E.10/47 called for a piloted delta-wing aircraft to conduct "important research work with revolutionary possibilities in the design and operation of fighter aircraft." Boulton Paul produced the P.111 tailless delta and flew it while Fairey produced the FD.1

(Fairey Delta One), a small, cropped-delta, mid-wing design using a single Rolls-Royce Derwent centrifugal flow turbojet. It first flew at RAF Boscombe Down on 12 March 1951. Both used largely Lippisch inspired delta wings of rather thick design with blunt leading edges.

The Fairey FD.1 also had another trick up its sleeve. No doubt inspired by the late World War II German vertical-ramp-launched Bachem Natter, the FD.1 design included mountings for rocket boosters in the tail for just such a launching method. Test launches of models were done in the Australian Woomera range. Performance of both the piloted Derwent version and the rocket-launched models provided data which was rolled into a subsequent development, the fabulous Fairey FD.2. No doubt the success of the rocket launched test vehicles influenced Avro Canada to take a similar approach to proving some of the CF-105's design features. Presaging subsequent developments in the UK, at this time Avro also submitted hybrid rocket/turbojet fighter designs.

British Director of Scientific Research (Air), Sir Henry Gardner, suggested to Fairey that they design a transonic research successor to the FD.1 in February 1949. According to Derek Wood's excellent *Project Cancelled*, in October 1951 Fairey got a real design boost when Robert Lickley, formerly of Hawker's, joined Fairey as chief engineer. (After reviewing the present work, Jim Floyd produced documents from 1956 showing his respect and friendship with Mr. Lickley, and his appreciation for what the Fairey Delta Two meant for the Arrow program, then

The Fairey FD.2 (via Derek Wood)

under relentless attack by several government agencies and agents.)

Due to production priorities imposed by the British government (as in Canada and the USA) due to the Korean War, the FD.2 design progressed slowly. It was only in September of 1952 that production drawings were issued to the shops. This implies that the design was somewhat ahead of the Avro Canada delta project but not by much. When one looks at the development that led to the F-106 it becomes clear that both Fairey and Avro Canada were well ahead of the Americans.

While the FD.2 was supposedly designed for transonic research, (since the British government had become convinced it was too risky to try supersonic flight), Fairey built in far more performance potential. The Delta Two was an excellent and far-sighted design. It was a very sleek thin-wing pure delta design using a single afterburning Rolls-Royce Avon turbojet. To compensate for the high landing angles inherent with delta designs, a "droop snoot" was designed into the aircraft. This nose treatment was patented and later applied to the awesome Concorde. The wing had (until the Arrow) a very thin thickness-chord ratio of only 4 percent. It also had very generous control surfaces so as to assure good manoeuverability. Wood implies in his work that the Mirage III was a copy of the FD.2 and there is strong evidence to support his theory. One example is that a good deal of early flight testing of the FD.2 was conducted in France with full French and Dassault support. When the FD.2 displayed its pedigree to the French, the Dassualt 550 design was modified to incorporate the delta wing. In plan view, the Mirage III is virtually identical to the FD.2, even in size.

The FD.2 first flew in October 1954, which rules out its having been an influence on the Arrow's aerodynamic design. Flight testing was slow-paced with the first seventeen flights being subsonic, with the last one resulting in a belly landing and eight months of repairs. This mishap was due to the fuel collector tank having been collapsed by an internal build-up of air pressure during flight. Twiss was reluctant to turn back to base on this occasion because he *knew* the tanks were full (since he had watched them being filled) and at first wouldn't believe the gauge telling him he was out of fuel. He became more convinced when the engine quit. In *Faster Than the Sun* Twiss comments, with typical British understatement, that the FD.2 made a "rather fast glider at that!"

In the month of its return to flight status in August 1955, the Avon-powered FD.2, with Twiss at the helm, went supersonic without afterburner augmentation. This was over a year after the French performed this feat for the first time in the SFECMAS Gerfault, an experimental delta-winged jet that "supercruised" on 3 August 1954. By this time the Convair YF-102A, designed from the XF-92A delta-fighter concept vehicle, was flying and, despite having much more power than the FD.2 and Gerfault, was still barely supersonic, even with full afterburner! In the end even the YF-102A redesign of the subsonic-only YF-102 would have to be redesigned as the F-106, which looked much more like the FD.2 and Avro C-104/1 than it did any member of its own family.

Once the FD.2 had demonstrated the ability to "supercruise" and based on performance projections using afterburning, it became quite clear to Twiss and Fairey that the FD.2 could make a serious attempt at the World Absolute Speed Record for piloted aircraft. Reaction among the politicians and bean-counters was decidedly frigid despite Britain's having been left in the dust in supersonics by the US. Even Roll-Royce, according to Wood, was against the idea, warning that the Avon might disintegrate. Fairey eventually managed to get permission but had to pay for the record attempt out of pocket.

As Derek Wood relates in *Project Cancelled:*

> On 10 March 1956, the FD.2, with Peter Twiss at the controls, set the World's first four figure speed record, achieving a mean speed of 1132 mph at 38,000 ft over a 9.65 mile course. The record exceeded by more than 300 mph (37 percent) the previous record set up in August 1955 by an American F-100 Super Sabre. Never before had the record been raised by such a margin. The effects of this extraordinary performance sent a shock wave round the aviation fraternity in many countries. In the United States there was almost disbelief, followed by a long hard look at the technical merits of the airframe. In France, it meant a change in a military programme which was to lead ultimately to the highly successful range of Mirage aircraft."

Avro Canada, bearing in mind the accusations of the Canadian National Aeronautical Establishment (NAE) and others in Canada that the CF-105 design would not even be supersonic, were probably dancing on the rooftops. The Fairey FD.2 was broadly similar aerodynamically and especially in the supersonic drag department, to the Avro delta designs. The differences, however, were that the Avro designs were combat capable aircraft having provision for the internal weapons and radar/fire control systems with which to make them effective. The Arrow would also have a much higher thrust-to-weight ratio and range. Jim Floyd provided a letter he had sent to Dobson after his late 1955 trip to the UK. Apparently he came to the same conclusions regarding what the Fairey Delta Two's success meant for the Arrow program. This trip resulted in the RAF trying to acquire Arrows and in the Hawker Siddeley Group withdrawing its Thin Wing Javelin in favour of an Arrow submission to Operational Requirement 329, otherwise known as the F.155T all weather interceptor program.

The RCAF Interceptor Specification

In a concerted effort to ensure that the CF-100 replacement would be in service as long as possible, the final RCAF operational requirement (OR 1-1/63, "Supersonic All-Weather Interceptor Aircraft") was demanding in the extreme. It set out an aircraft requirement to follow up the earlier AIR 7-3, "Design Studies of a Prototype Supersonic All-Weather Aircraft." To the author's knowledge, not one interceptor design in service then or since has met all of the requirements set forth in these documents—although the F-22 Raptor will meet them, aside from the two-man crew stipulation. The RCAF's new interceptor had to have a Mach 1.5 manoeuver capability of 2 G (60 degrees of bank) at 50,000 feet altitude without losing energy (speed or altitude), and be ready for squadron delivery in October 1959. Two engines of very high thrust were specified to meet this requirement and provide safety over long distances. A crew of two was specified to share the chores of long flight times and exceedingly sophisticated on-board systems including the radar, fire control and weapons, which were also soon to be specified. (That selection took the RCAF's Operational Requirements branch nearly three years and did the program serious harm.)

This aircraft was designed to be a guided-missile platform at a time when the top fighters in the world were only armed with guns and unguided rockets, not far removed from World War II designs. Indeed guided missiles were still in the development phase and the Canadian Velvet Glove was one of the most advanced designs going. The combat radius for the aircraft was to be 300 nm on a low-speed intercept profile, and 200 nm for the supersonic intercept, both missions including supersonic combat of

significant duration. Internal weapons were prescribed for low drag, and required a very large bay for the long guided missiles then in design. The October 1959 date of entry into service was projected using the MX-1179/Falcon (a.k.a. MA-1 fire-control and weapons system) being designed for the USAF "1954 Interceptor" program. When something altogether more advanced than the stumbling MX-1179 and Falcon missile programs were specified for the Arrow, the entry into service date was pushed back to approximately 1960.

While these specifications were unheard of, they were arrived at using simple logic. The USAF had initiated development in 1949 of their 1954 Interceptor. The RCAF apparently took those requirements, inflated them by about 15 percent, added one engine and one crew member and dropped it on Avro's desk. When the RCAF later inflated their expectations in fire-control and missiles over the massive, crash American programs, they probably threw one too many straws onto an already straining camel. In effect, the RCAF was asking for a longer-range and higher-altitude version of the USAF 1954 Interceptor. The USAF never received, not even to this date, an aircraft fully meeting their own 1954 Interceptor specifications, and the resulting aircraft would not enter service until 1960 as the Delta Dart. The RCAF very nearly received the Arrow Mk. 2 in 1959-60, an aircraft that *exceeded* even the RCAF's higher demands. Other than the Sparrow missile, Avro had exceeded all performance objectives by a fair margin and even the ASTRA 1 system, Sparrow not included, was shaping up by the summer of 1958. I believe that the facts presented in this book prove that the Arrow Mk. 2, upgraded electronically, would still be the best of the high-performance interceptors in the world.

Floyd ruefully characterized this RCAF requirement as being a "beyond the state of the art project," with the RCAF team wanting "the moon!" He was confident, however, that the team Avro had assembled, with experience gained from the CF-100, Jetliner, and engine programs, was up to the task. One can only wonder about Floyd's personal feelings at getting involved with another government contract considering the checkered politics of the Jetliner and the harsh whipping they had received over the CF-100. Meanwhile Floyd's Jetliner Number One was still soaring through the heavens with the greatest of ease.

Avro wanted to keep the unknowns to a minimum in the design of the Arrow and recommended installation of the Hughes MX-1179 radar and fire-control system with Falcon missiles, both of which Avro knew to be high-priority projects with the USAF and therefore not likely to face cancellation. Both of these systems were under development for the USAF 1954 Interceptor project. Considering the high risk associated with using so many systems under development, this was a very wise choice. The RCAF disagreed, apparently mostly on the advice of AVM Jack Easton, chief of operational requirements, and specified a system that was far superior to the one that was only a glint in the eye of the largest military-industrial complex in the world. This system would evolve into the ASTRA radar/fire-control system and Sparrow 2D fully-active, radar-homing "fire-and-forget" missile. The latter especially proved to have very serious strategic implications for the RCAF when more of the military and civil service became fed up with the growing *projected* costs of the Arrow program, brought about largely due to expense projections relating to development and production of ASTRA/Sparrow—*not* the Arrow airframe or Iroquois engine.

At least, that is the view usually portrayed of ASTRA. There is evidence available to suggest that ASTRA was more successful than most people assume. Documents from RCA, the prime contractor, leave no doubt that ASTRA was *far* ahead of the competing US programs in both concept and technology. It can be argued that the integration of ASTRA set the standard which the US didn't even approach until the system (Hughes AWG-9) in the F-14 Tomcat. The earlier and almost ASTRA contemporary Westinghouse APQ-72 system used in the F-4 Phantom could perhaps be considered a low- tech system designed to introduce *some* of the sophistication and user-friendliness of ASTRA. (More on this later.) In *Storms of Controversy* Campagna asserts that early 1958 evaluations of the Arrow with ASTRA showed the total weapons system to be very promising. Campagna also points out that this Canadian Armament Research and Development Establishment (CARDE) evaluation wasn't released to *anyone* until 1960, far too late to help Avro, the Arrow program and the RCAF. Gerald Bull, who later developed superior artillery for South Africa and Israel, and the "supergun" for Iraq, worked at CARDE at this time and had been behind the Velvet Glove guided missile. Some readers will have heard of the secret American project *HARP,* (for High Altitude Research Project), which was actually Bull's development for launching satellites, via heavy guns, into orbit.

As with the CF-100, an RCAF team, this time led by Wing Commander (W/C) Ray Footit, searched the manufacturers

of the West to see if an aircraft capable of meeting this specification was on the boards anywhere. It is no surprise they returned empty handed with no aircraft investigated even coming close. The F-102 specification and aircraft were also investigated and rejected as having too short a range, too high a pilot workload, too small a payload, and one too few engines. Even the F-106 never came close. Avro was advised to continue refining their design. In July 1953 a ministerial directive from the Department of Defence Production was received by Avro authorising preliminary design of the C-105. The Arrow program was launched.

Another testament to the difficulties encountered in high-thrust turbojet design at the time is evidenced by the Rolls-Royce RB.106, the first engine specified for the Arrow. By early 1954 Rolls-Royce had abandoned this engine. The Curtiss-Wright J-67 was substituted and made necessary a redesign of the fuselage since the engines were closely integrated with the fuselage design. By 1955 this engine was likewise abandoned, this time by the USAF and again the aircraft engine bays had to be redesigned. The J-67 troubles also didn't help the Republic XF-103. Some feel the J-67 was cancelled for geo-political reasons (since it was a British, not an American, design) as much as any engineering difficulties.

The PS-13 Iroquois engine had originally been conceived by Orenda with an eye to the international military turbojet market and not for the Arrow program *per se*. When it was begun, coincidentally at the same time as the Arrow program was authorized by the government, it was felt to be a next-generation engine to succeed the engines originally proposed for so many aircraft, including those that the first Arrow drawings were built around. It was also the engine upon which the final Arrow redesign was based since they obviously couldn't count on any other manufacturer. Development was accelerated on the Iroquois when the J-67 evaporated, giving both the RCAF and Avro another taste of the effects on their businesses of dependency on a competing power. Avro, Orenda, the Hawker Siddeley Group, and the government of Canada all committed themselves to developing the highest-thrust, lightest, simplest and smallest afterburning turbojet the world had yet seen for their new interceptor, only a few years earlier than originally planned. The RCAF was in full agreement with this decision and pushed for it. Howe and certainly General Guy Simonds, Chief of the General Staff, were by now starting to hold their noses.

Avro was forced by these events to bite off an enormous mouthful. They even got the unwanted burden of project management for ASTRA and Sparrow, products they had little experience with, and systems they opposed. The solid-state ASTRA development set that appeared, highly promising in June of 1958 must be considered something of a miracle considering the technology required. The service version of the Iroquois was still probably about eight months away from production by Black Friday, quite a feat but just a little too late.

Avro was not only designing an aircraft to carry non-existent weapons depending on a non-existent radar with non-existent engines producing non-existent thrust ratings, but an aircraft to operate at record high-speeds and altitudes at long ranges. No wonder Floyd considered it "beyond the state of the art." To compound the headaches, the RCAF considered the development urgent due to an assessment of the threats likely to present themselves over the decade it was to serve, 1960-1970. For this reason Avro decided, in 1955, to adopt the "production from scratch" or "Cook-Craigie" method of production. This production method was named for its originators, Generals Laurence C. Craigie and Orval R. Cook. During the late 1940s, these two American officers had developed a concept of an aircraft development program in which the usual prototype stage would be skipped. Instead of waiting to start full-scale production until after the prototypes had passed flight testing and the bugs had been ironed out, the Cook-Craigie plan called for the delivery of pre-production aircraft direct to the flight testing phase before squadron adoption.

Confidential Avro documents from December 1953 show that Floyd was initially opposed to this high risk method, preferring to produce a prototype or two on experimental tooling to wring out and redesign from. Harvey Smith, Avro's works manager, was for the former method however, having used it in his previous job at Kaiser Motors in the USA. The USAF had also specified that the F-102 Delta Dagger be produced by this method to hopefully get it into service by 1954. Of course in the case of the Delta Dagger, this plan was a complete disaster. When forced to utilise the Cook-Craigie plan, Floyd ensured that Avro made maximum use of test rigs and solid pre-design techniques. He ensured that the Arrow was also the first computer-aided aircraft design. Avro proved the Cook-Craigie plan could work " as advertised." Today the United States has reverted to Floyd's (and Britain's) preferred method of building

prototypes, then pre-production aircraft, then the production version for the Advanced Tactical Fighter (ATF) and the Joint Strike Fighter (JSF).

Design Considerations of the Arrow

This section is largely based on information from Floyd's 1958 "Commonwealth Lecture" on the Arrow project to the annual conference of Britain's Royal Aeronautical Society (RAeS). The 1958 trip very nearly resulted in a repeat performance of Floyd's 1955 visit, which had resulted in an attempt by RAF and other British leaders to purchase 200 Arrows in 1956. (This is explored in Chapter Eleven.)

The reader may find the next section interesting as a comparison, in terms of technical benchmarks, of the Arrow design to other aircraft. The aerodynamic theory is also explored. Every effort has been made to express the information in terms that the reader will understand and enjoy.

WING DESIGN: THE KEY TO SUCCESS

At the time Avro designed the Arrow there was a somewhat acrimonious debate going on in the US over the relative merits of the delta wing versus the straight (trapezoidal) wing for supersonic aircraft. Some of the debate concerned the tendency of airflow over a delta (or swept) wing to turn outwards towards the wingtip. Some of the argument was also probably due to the flagrant refusal of the XF-92A and the YF-102 (first example) to break the sound barrier. With a large delta wing, the effect was even more pronounced, potentially leading to the airflow close to the surface reversing direction at the tips. This is obviously not conducive to lift production or low drag. The stealthy World War II German Horten IX (aka Gotha 229) jet-powered, tailless flying wing, when tested in the wind tunnel, was actually found to have reverse flow at the tips.

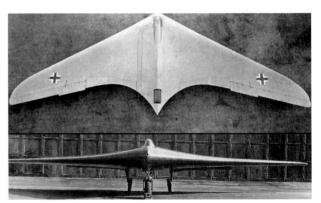

Two views of the Horten HD IX version one. This delta flying wing was modified to include two BMW.003 jet engines.

The Me.163 Komet, the first tailless rocket interceptor. It was a dangerous ride.

Unfortunately the delta seemed to come out of this argument poorly, as evidenced by ancient training materials, still in use in the Canadian Forces, concluding the delta is not the best wing design. Evidence that this condemnation was premature comes from the North American X-15 rocket plane program. Initially the X-15 was designed with a trapezoidal wing and separate tail. However once it flew and more information on the delta's characteristics (no doubt a considerable amount of this coming from Avro's wind tunnel work at NACA, the National Advisory Committee on Aeronautics) they tried to sell the USAF on a delta-winged X-15A-2 successor. This information and other interesting revelations about hypersonic flight are contained in Bill Sweetman's book on the Aurora spyplane. In reality, most modern fighters such as the F-15, SU-27 etc., all use cropped-deltas while adding a separate tail. The emerging generation of European fighters use a canard-delta arrangement, something Avro was looking at in 1957 for the Arrow.

The main originator of the swept wing and delta designs was Nazi Germany, even though Jack Northrop had produced flying-wing designs in the 1930s. The lead must go to Germany however since they appear to be the ones who first understood the benefits of the swept wing in combination with a thin profile (Thickness/Chord or T/C ratio). The Me-262 was the first combat aircraft to use swept wings and a Messerschmitt wing formed the basis of the wing used on the F-86 Sabre, which itself was a redesign of the FJ-1 Fury, a straight-winged US Navy jet of 1946.

The benefit of the swept wing design is twofold. First it allows a wing of a given T/C ratio to present a thinner profile to the direction of airflow once it is swept back. This is the secret of the swept wing; as you sweep the wing, the T/C ratio becomes smaller and the wing "appears" thinner to the airflow. Air molecules have less time to change

direction and conform to a curved surface as you increase speed into the supersonic range. This can cause the air to separate from the wing and cause a great deal of drag and loss of lift. As air speeds up to flow around a curve and reaches Mach 1, it produces a shock wave that adds an enormous amount of drag and radically changes the point on the wing where maximum lift occurs. It can also cause extreme structural loads, vibration and flutter. Unless the wing is curved very gradually and is very thin, this shock wave will have the tendency to move back and forth on the surface of the wing, often very quickly, with loss of control and structural failure the possible results. This is what happened to .John Frost's gorgeous DH-108 Swallow. A wing with a small thickness/chord ratio with gentle curves will minimize this effect, and at the speed of sound, the shock wave will move directly to the trailing edge of the wing making the wing behave normally again.

The Armstrong-Whitworth AW.52. (Hawker Siddeley)

Even before Frost turned the Vampire into the Swallow, Armstrong-Whitworth Aircraft, a founding member of the Hawker Siddeley Group, developed the AW.52 tailless research aircraft. This elegant design first flew as a glider in 1945, and by 1948 it was flying with jet engines, first two Rolls-Royce Derwents, then later with two powerful

The Avro 707B, second in the series of five Avro 707 research aircraft. It was the testbed for the Avro Vulcan bomber. The dorsal inlets would move to the wing leading edge.
(Hawker Siddeley)

The second prototype Vulcan bomber produced under the guidance of Stuart Davies. The Vulcan had the original pure-delta wing modified to alleviate pitch-up and stability problems, and this knowledge helped the Arrow design. The Vulcan would prove capable of an un-refuelled range of about 4,600 miles and remained in service for 26 years; until the end of 1982. (Avro UK)

Nenes by the same manufacturer. It would appear to have been over-powered. On 30 May 1949 the first use of a Martin-Baker ejection seat occurred from one of these experimental aircraft when a dangerous flutter developed in one wing-tip. After ejection the aircraft stabilized itself and glided into a field with barely any damage being done.

On 4 September 1949 Avro UK flew their first pure-delta jet, the Avro 707, as a test-bed for the Vulcan bomber. On the third version of this aircraft, which was considerably sleeker and had the engine intakes moved to the wing root, a sawtooth and notch were tried on the wing to confirm Avro Canada's arrangement for the CF-105 Arrow. (This information is taken from a letter between Floyd and Dobson from the period, however, no photos of this version have been found, perhaps for security reasons.)

The best supersonic wing, from a purely theoretical aerodynamic standpoint, is a straight wing of zero thickness, in other words, a flat plate one point thick. This is, in the material world, impossible, so the design is always a compromise between aerodynamics and structural concerns (this combination is termed "aeroelasticity"). The straight wing is limited structurally compared to the delta because, to achieve the required thin profile, only a short span can be supported by a spar of equal thinness and comparable strength. A good example of this is the F-104

Starfighter, an aircraft with very high wing loading and thus poor low speed handling, an exceptionally high stall speed, and poor high-altitude manoeuverability. (On the deck it was invincible.) An RCAF F-104 Starfighter pilot once related to the author that an engine-out emergency landing profile, consisting of a 360-degree spiral starting at altitude and ending on the runway, had to be entered at 18,000 feet on the Starfighter, at a speed of 240 knots!

The long root length of the delta wing also has several advantages in the real world. It can present a very thin T/C ratio while still being thick enough to carry a large quantity of fuel and stow the landing gear. It can thus be built large enough for a large aircraft while still preserving low supersonic (wave) drag, and provide a high amount of lift since it will have much more area than a straight wing, and it can also be strong since it can carry many stress bearing spars down its length. Its inherent arrow shape keeps it out of the supersonic shock (bow) wave produced by the nose of the aircraft until relatively higher speeds are reached.

DELTA-TAILLESS:

A further advantage of a delta wing is that the control surfaces, being at the rear of the aircraft, can be used to roll or pitch the aircraft, thereby dispensing with the need for another set of control surfaces such as the horizontal tail on conventional designs. A tail would add weight and

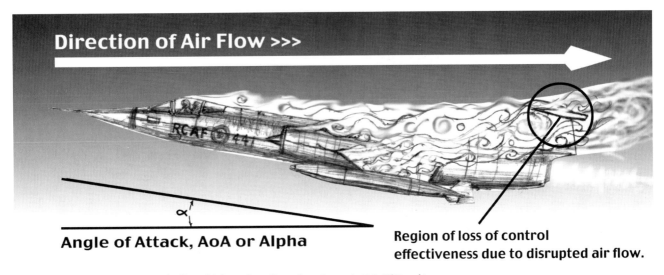

Tail "blanking" of high mounted tails at high angles of attack.   (image by R.L. Whitcomb)

markedly increase the supersonic and interference drag of the design. Tails also add headaches in design caused by airflow interactions with the mainplane and, potentially, with engine exhaust. A case in point is the control problems encountered with virtually all T-tail designs such as the F-104 Starfighter, F-101 Voodoo, and the Gloster Javelin. At high angles of attack (alpha) the turbulence coming off the wing and fuselage tends to "blank" the tail and causes decreased, or eliminated, control effectiveness in pitch and perhaps yaw as well. A flat spin caused by this phenomenon almost killed Chuck Yeager during the reaction-control assisted NF-104 high-altitude investigation program and was immortalized in the movie "The Right Stuff." Jan Zurakowski left Glosters in Britain for Canada largely due to a refusal of the Gloster designers to take his concerns about this, as he demonstrated it in the Javelin during flight test, seriously. It was probably as much a test of the Avro designers and management as it was the aircraft that induced Zura to take the CF-100 supersonic early in his employment. He has stated that he was quite impressed with the honesty and diligence of the Avro team.

Avro found that the best way to minimize trim drag (drag induced by any control surface deflection required for straight and level flight) and keep the center of lift where they wanted it, at the extremes of speed and altitude, was to introduce a "negative camber" profile to the wing. In other words, the wing was curved on the bottom, opposite to what would be considered a normal airfoil shape! This helped control the center of lift movement between very low and very high speed and was one of Chamberlin's tricks to make the delta behave at low and high speeds. The flat upper surface still represented the closest thing to a perfect supersonic airfoil, a flat plate, as it was perfectly straight from just behind the leading edge right to the trailing edge. This also provided the design with the happy feature of allowing the shock-wave to travel from the leading edge directly to the trailing edge once supersonic speed was reached thereby reducing transonic drag, center-of-lift fluctuations and control-surface flutter. It also made the entire wing a laminar-flow surface at low alpha. As a result, the Arrow was one of the first aircraft to smoothly break the sound barrier as if it wasn't really there.

THICKNESS/CHORD RATIO:

The ratio of the length down the fuselage (chord) of a wing to its thickness is a major factor in the drag of a wing. A low T/C ratio wing is a thinner one. Form drag (discussed in more detail later) is especially pronounced at supersonic speeds and is exaggerated by separate protrusions of items in the slipstream. A wing with a low T/C ratio will have serious advantages over a thicker one in form drag at supersonic speeds. The challenge is making it produce enough lift at low speed. The delta planform proved superior, in the eyes of Avro's designers, to the swept-wing or double-delta aircraft (with separate delta-ish tailplanes such as the F-4 Phantom, MiG-21 and to large degree most fighters in front line service today).

The Arrow wing had an average T/C ratio of 3.6 percent and a flat upper surface. By comparison, the F-4 Phantom has a 6 percent T/C ratio at the root while that of the F-15 Eagle is in the order of 5 percent. As discussed, thicker wings at supersonic speeds suffer from exponentially high-

er "wave drag" (drag induced by the shock wave). They also had penalties in center of lift movement and early laminar flow separation. The latter adds significantly to supersonic drag. The Arrow had a lower T/C ratio than almost any combat aircraft that has entered service (other than the F-104 Starfighter which beat the root T/C ratio of the Arrow by a mere .14 percent) while avoiding the sharp leading-edge which is not good for subsonic flight. All of the aforementioned aircraft have at least three *additional* drag-inducing tail airfoils as compared to the CF-105.

DELTA-WING LEADING-EDGE VORTEX:

Somewhat overlooked in many early commentaries on aircraft design are the delta's *excellent* lift characteristics. While it is a first-class supersonic layout since it tends to stay out of the bow wave, it also has exceptional low-speed handling characteristics. Indeed, from low speed to hypersonic flight, the delta is an excellent shape. The characteristic which really aids low-speed handling and thus manoeuverability is the fact that the delta creates an unusual leading-edge vortex of air that tends to keep the air attached to the wing at extreme angles of attack (60 degrees or more in some cases, while straight wings normally stall between 15 and 20 degrees). Again, since very high-altitude flight is actually like slow flying, this vortex phenomenon gives the delta a high-altitude advantage over a trapezoidal or swept wing—it can make more lift if the thrust is there to overcome the additional drag that high amounts of lift always create. This gives a delta-winged aircraft the ability to maintain higher alpha before the stall, and thus to manoeuver better at low speeds and in low air densities while maintaining control. Knowledgeable fighter pilots are incredulous at the mention that the Arrow *demonstrated* a stall speed of only 117 knots at *full* combat weight! Jack Woodman, the RCAF test pilot assigned to verify the Arrow's performance, is actually on the record as saying you really *couldn't* stall the Arrow. The speed they chose as the stall speed is where the sink rate became unacceptable for landing purposes. This is solidly F-18 Hornet territory with the F-18 achieving its low-speed characteristics by (drag inducing) massive flap and leading-edge slat deflections plus a large deflection of the tail plane. Meanwhile, the F-18 is known for being an excellent low-speed dogfighter. Considering the extra drag of all the Hornet's high-lift devices, it would be interesting to compare the low altitude acceleration curves of service Hornets against those of even the Arrow Mk. 1. It may have been a much different dogfight scenario than most would assume considering the Arrow's thrust and wing loading.

The vortex only forms when the angle of attack is increased, in other words the aircraft is pitched up. The sudden vortex formation was found to add so much lift that deltas were known to pitch-up during turning or pull-up manoeuvres and tended to make the aircraft tighten in a turn without additional control stick movement. This phenomenon was a real problem with the XF-92A as evidenced by the propaganda that the program was a "success" because it revealed that this vortex needed further study! This vortex, once formed, added massive lift unlike any conventional wing. This could cause anything from difficulties in accurately tracking a target to structural failure if not compensated for in time. This massive increase in lift, produced once the vortex formed, is the reason XF-92A test pilots Yeager and Lieutenant Colonel (LCol) Frank Everest are on record as stating that the turning ability of a delta-wing aircraft is unsurpassed. They also presaged Woodman's comments on the Arrow's delta when they said the delta, as installed on the XF-92A, just didn't want to stall and maintains lift and controllability at extremely high alpha. A later F-106 pilot said that if you pulled on the stick at high-speed it was a battle to maintain the turn and keep your head out of the instrument panel! (So much for those who say the Arrow would have been unmanoeuverable!) This turn-tightening problem was one that Avro had very wisely spent a great deal of time in understanding and designing solutions.

LEADING-EDGE SAWTOOTH AND NOTCH:

Avro sought to minimize the pitch-up problem and flow reversal at the tips associated with highly swept wings by introducing a notch and sawtooth at mid-span on the wing.

Avro's understanding of the vortex effects as presented to the Royal Aeronautical Society during Jim Floyd's October 1958 Commonwealth Lecture to the society. (Journal of the RaeS)

FIGURE 3 (*left*). Vortex pattern of plain wing.

FIGURE 4 (*right*). Vortex pattern of wing with notch and extended leading edge.

This view shows both the leading edge sawtooth and the leading edge slat designed into the Phantom after the mock up stage. The horizontal stabilators were also given anhedral to provide more equivalent vertical surface area to improve directional stability and the wing outer sections were given more dihedral. A considerable number of changes were made after the mock-up.

First, however, they tried it with only a notch. Their wind-tunnel tests showed that the effect was inconsistent (unrepeatable) from test to test and it was therefore not seen as a reliable solution. They then added the leading edge extension or "sawtooth" as is used on the F-4 Phantom, F-8 Crusader, and as incorporated on the new "Super Hornet" (just as the YF-17 Hornet prototype had), Saab JAS-39 Gripen and most other current designs. (For those aircraft such as the Eurofighter, F-22 Raptor and Dassault Rafale, there is a sawtooth when the leading-edge slats are deflected.) With the Arrow, this combination sawtooth/notch produced a small but powerful secondary vortex (at the point of the notch) that traveled backward almost parallel to the airflow, forming an aerodynamic "fence." It allows a much larger delta wing to be produced without suffering from flow reversal at the tips and thus tends to keep drag in check at high alpha, while enabling the wing to make lift. On the Arrow this vortex also crossed the point where the elevator met the ailerons giving improved control effectiveness to both control surfaces. At high altitudes this feature also reduced trim drag since it made the elevators more effective, and therefore less requiring of deflection.

Any wing with a sharp or pointed leading edge will stall sooner than one with a gently rounded one. For low speed manoeuverability this demands a compromise from the supersonic "flat plate" ideal. To give the Arrow better low speed characteristics, as well as a higher potential angle of attack or alpha capability, a drooped leading edge was incorporated in the design while the inboard sections were fairly rounded anyway. The leading edge (sawtooth) extension on the outboard wing sections provided an excellent area to incorporate droop.

To alleviate poor critical alpha characteristics on the early F-4 Phantoms, despite the incorporation of a leading-edge "sawtooth," a leading-edge slat was introduced to droop the leading edge under certain conditions and this markedly improved its dogfight performance. The Arrow would not have needed a slat on the leading edge to compete, since it had 66 percent lower wing loading to start with plus aerodynamic lift enhancing devices. One of these, included for low-speed handling, was the drooped leading edge which, in combination with the low wing loading, rendered slats unnecessary. It's apparent that the Arrow wing had excellent low-speed and high-alpha characteristics while producing very low drag at supersonic speeds due to the wing's extremely thin design and the aircraft's lack of separate all-flying horizontal stabilizers. Again, Avro seemed to put their computer technology to good use and had made advances in thinking in three-dimensional fluid dynamics rather than the old, additive "blade element" theory, something everyone, including NACA, had trouble grasping. The NAE, DRB and arguably the RCAF never figured out Avro's aerodynamics.

The McDonnell Douglas F-15 Eagle would use a similar wing design to that of the Arrow but would delete the notch/sawtooth since its shorter span and lower sweep angle didn't have the tip flow-reversal problems to such an extent. It still has higher wing loading which comparatively limits its altitude and manoeuverability, and this is borne out by the performance curves published in this work. Another feature the Arrow and F-15 share is how the engine location and fairing with the body result in extra low speed lift due to the engine exhaust inducing airflow over the fuselage. In essence the Arrow used a "pumped" wing and this meant that the elevators were located in an excellent place to also benefit from that extra induced flow, especially at low speed.

ARTIFICIAL WASHOUT:

An additional benefit derived from concentrating the droop on the outboard wing sections of the Arrow was that it built in "washout." Washout means that the wing either physically or aerodynamically incorporates twist, with the tips having a lower angle of incidence than the root. This ensures that the wing will stall last towards the tips thus maintaining aileron (roll) control in a stall or spin situation, which is vital. The early deltas stalled first at the tip due to span-wise flow causing a breakaway at the tips.

Leading-edge droop can be seen at the right wingtip on this F-15C. So too can the sawtooth on the horizontal stabilizer, both features being incorporated for the same reasons as on the Arrow.
(image by R.L. Whitcomb)

This stalled section was, on a delta or highly swept-wing, behind the center of gravity of the aircraft so that when that region stalled, the aircraft would pitch up since only the portion of the wing in front of the center of gravity would be making lift. Avro found means to control this span-wise flow and managed to add washout (twist) to the wing aerodynamically rather than physically, another drag reducing feature. This was also done, in part, by designing the wing to have a lower T/C ratio at the root than at the tip, an unusual feature well suited to the delta wing. (Republic Aviation had experimented successfully with this concept on their bizarre-looking Thunderceptor derivative of the F-84F Thunderstreak.)

Virtually all wings incorporate washout, most by using physical twist due to simpler design and manufacture. For an illustration, one should look at side-view photos of the Arrow wing compared to that of the F-18 Hornet. The Arrow wing had *all* aerodynamic twist, none being added with actual physical twist, whereas the Hornet has significant physical twist. The Avro Jetliner also had all aerodynamic twist, but achieved it through incorporation of a modified leading-edge profile.

On the Arrow, the addition of leading-edge droop was found to increase the buffet boundary (buffet is encountered just before the stall) by over 60 percent. This shows a very significant improvement in the high-alpha and, thus, manoeuvring capabilities of the Arrow. Testing of the Arrow wing demonstrated that the leading-edge droop, designed for low-speed handling, added insignificant amounts of supersonic drag up to about Mach 2.5. This would, at first glance, appear to be a lower-drag solution than either the F-18 Hornet or F-16 Falcon wings, both with considerable physical washout or twist, and hard-angle leading-edge drooping slats. Again the delta's lift advantages seem to guarantee an excellent low-speed "dogfight" performance with very low drag and high lift. In reality it appears to be one of the best thought-out wing designs up to this day, especially when the aerodynamic flourishes are considered.

DRAG REDUCTION: IN SEARCH OF SPEED, RANGE AND HEIGHT FORM OR PROFILE DRAG:

This term refers to more than just the aerodynamic drag produced by the frontal area of items encountering the slipstream, i.e.; the drag produced by the necessity of air "bending" around a shape it runs into. Again, for a clean aircraft, wing thickness and size are major factors when considering form drag. For a little background, it is interesting to look at the Spitfire design of 1936. This aircraft, designed by the truly inspired Reginald Mitchell, had, for its time, a very thin wing. The long fore/aft length of the wing combined with its relative thinness to produce an exceptionally low T/C ratio on the Spitfire which was its secret for attaining high speed. The extra area gained by its resulting, large square footage also gave it low wing loading which made it very manoeuvrable. The svelte overall form of the 1936 Spitfire gave it one of the highest "critical mach" numbers of any aircraft designed before or during the war.

Arrow flutter model in the wind-tunnel. (Journal of the RaeS)

A 411 Squadron (RCAF) Spitfire Mk. 11a in the hands of Buck McNair. (From the painting "Grizzlies Cut Their Teeth" by R.L. Whitcomb)

Unlike the Spitfire, the P-51 Mustang was designed after the phenomenon of "compressibility," (which determines critical mach) was discovered. Compressibility is the phenomenon of air speeding up as it travels over a curved surface and approaches supersonic speed. At supersonic speed the ability of air molecules to get out of the way fast enough disappears (the air's willingness to be compressed) and it reaches a point where it produces a shock-wave, or hard "pile up" of air at the point where it has been forced to exceed the speed of sound. The effects of the shock wave formation on a curved wing have already been discussed as they related to the DH.108 Swallow. The Mustang used a special "laminar-flow" airfoil to counteract this effect which gave it its high top speed and low drag (which, once the Allison engine was replaced by the Rolls-Royce Merlin, combined to give it its long range). As discussed previously, the Spitfire had a critical mach of .91 vs. the Mustang's .85.

Thus, for low drag an aircraft should be as "clean" as possible, i.e.; it should have an absolute minimum of extra bulges and contours applied to the basic aerodynamic shape. The aerodynamic shape itself should occupy as little volume as possible, and the volume it does occupy must expand from the nose smoothly, with the overall volume progression being tailored for the speed range of the aircraft—a subsonic aircraft should have a relatively large, rounded nose and airfoil, while a supersonic one must be rather pointed and keep the volume progression from nose to tail very gentle.

PARASITE DRAG:

Parasite drag refers to the drag of any items not contributing to lift. The fuselage on *most* aircraft is usually a large contributor to this form of drag.

Any protuberances, bumps and curves on an aircraft will produce drag. At supersonic speeds this penalty is compounded because these features will add their own shock effects. In this respect the Arrow is still light years ahead of any combat aircraft in service. It had adequate internal fuel capacity to provide its long-range needs without resorting to external tanks. It was designed to carry its weaponry internally as well. It had a delta-wing which required no extra tail surfaces. It had only one fin. It satisfied its area rule requirements well without resorting to subsonic drag increasing noticeable pinches and bulges. One area that has been largely ignored is the fact that the Arrow used a revolutionary, and still largely un-copied, cam/knuckle control-surface actuation system that was housed entirely in the wing. Thus, there were practically no protruding fairings for the hinges and actuator arms. (Towards the tips there were, on the underside of the wing, small curved protrusions over the knuckles that, due to their not having any right angles and being as shallow as they were, added very little drag.) Avro's brilliant hinge design also ensured that there were no gaps on the "active" side of the control surfaces by incorporating a double piano-hinge assembly that assured low drag no matter which way the control-surfaces were deflected. The F-15 Eagle and F-18 and others have large 90 degree fairings over the actuator-hinge mechanisms which add considerable supersonic drag. Ninety degree angles on an airframe impose significant drag penalties at supersonic speed due to the formation of hard shock waves which impact the surrounding structure thereby aggravating the "interference drag" problem. Right-angles on an airframe are also the ideal shape to reflect radar and thus betray the airframe to surveillance radars and radar-guided missiles.

By any standard, the Arrow was an exceptionally clean machine. Even the phenomenal Lockheed SR-71 with two engine shapes in addition to the fuselage, two tails, and two (or three) underside stabilizing fins cannot compare to the Arrow in terms of aerodynamic cleanness. The SR-71 also has, for heat absorption purposes, corrugated wing skins. Indeed the combined curvature of the wings, meeting a similar curve of the engine nacelles, right at the point where the engine intake spilled extra air outboard, caused such a pressure disturbance that it severely limited the economical cruise speed of the SR-71 for quite some time! All this air colliding at one point was simply like a wall the aircraft could not break through until a great deal of effort was expended in modifications. Furthermore, the only recently admitted stealth characteristics incorporated into the A-12/SR-71 were obliterated when it was discovered that the aircraft was directionally unstable and had to have 90-degree-angle ventral fins applied. To get an idea of the speed capabilities of the Arrow shape alone, one should consider that the Mach 3.2+ SR-71 was almost twice as heavy as the Arrow and had about the same power as the Iroquois-Arrow would have had. It also had much greater frontal area and interference drag due to all the bulges, twists, engines and fins sticking out. It had only slightly more wing area and thus higher induced drag at altitude. In fairness however, it would have had less trim drag and the reasons for this will be discussed later.

INDUCED DRAG:

Induced drag is simply that portion of an aircraft's drag total at a given altitude and speed caused by the production of lift. Drag due to lift. Old school theory taught that a very high aspect ratio (large span to chord ratio) on a straight-wing provided the lowest drag for a given amount of lift. This is where the "acrimonious" American debate got heated, still gets heated, and where Parkin and fellows in the Canadian government research facilities really dug in their heels. The delta-wing boosters were arguing that the delta was naturally better for induced drag at subsonic speeds *and* supersonic speeds. The trapezoidal fans felt the opposite. The author thinks that the latter didn't understand the leading edge vortex phenomenon and merely assumed it made more drag. The reason the delta made more drag seems to be because it could operate at angles of attack beyond where the trapezoidal wing would stall, and made even more lift in the process! Avro seemed to achieve a breakthrough in induced drag and controllability on the Arrow wing—and Dr. Courtland Perkins, Chief Scientist for the United States Air Force was hungry for those figures by 1957.

(Today, Paul Salvian, a former assistant to the structural engineer for the de Havilland Canada Dash 8, constructs simple, catapult-launched scale flying-models (gliders) of many aircraft which he markets as "Paul's Jet Aircraft for Kids." He was stunned, after modifying his Arrow model, wing included, to genuine scale with information provided by this author, to discover the Arrow models soar farther, and are more stable, than *any* of his other models. This includes scale models of high aspect-ratio, unswept, high-performance *gliders*. On relating this information to various people, the only one not surprised was Jim Floyd!)

The point is that while a glider style wing has less induced drag than one with a lower aspect ratio, there are so many other considerations in the total package that a blanket statement as to any wing's suitability is impossible unless all considerations are known. Deltas make lift like no other wing once pitched up, and high-aspect ratio wings are unsuitable for supersonic flight. Avro decided to use the delta wing based on their research, while others were watching the unhappy results of the Convair XF-92 and were avoiding that wing type like the plague, with NACA's blessings. The fact that the entire upper surface of the Arrow produced lift also provided lift and drag bonuses.

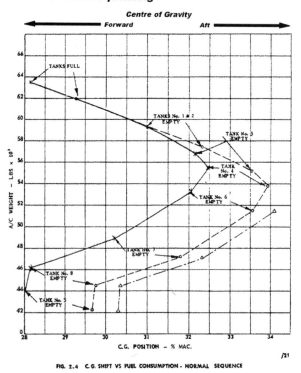

CF-105 Fuel Sequencing

Centre of Gravity

Forward — Aft

FIG. 2.4 C.G. SHIFT VS FUEL CONSUMPTION - NORMAL SEQUENCE

TRIM DRAG:

Drag produced by any control surface deflection required for straight and level fight is termed "trim drag." Trim drag is a major component of drag in high-performance aircraft at the extremes of their speed and altitude range and is improperly ignored in most written presentations of aircraft designs.

It was known that, as speed and altitude varied over the very wide speed range intended for the CF-105, the alpha and thus the point on the body of the aircraft where the lift was centered (center of pressure or center of lift) would change. It would also change with speed. Both cases are counteracted in almost every aircraft by deflection of the elevators to keep the aircraft straight and level across its speed and altitude "performance envelope." For example, at low speed the aircraft would fly somewhat nose up (at a high alpha), and to keep it there, the elevators would have to be deflected upwards. At high subsonic speeds and low-to-medium altitude, the elevators would actually be deflected slightly downwards on a properly designed delta-tailless aircraft since at subsonic speeds the center of lift is located farther forward than it is in supersonic flight, tending to cause the aircraft to pitch up. At high altitude and high speed, low air density actually results in aerodynamic conditions similar to those of low-speed flight. At an aircraft's "absolute ceiling," in any aircraft, the eleva-

tors are either deflected upwards, completely eliminating any capacity for a further climb, or the angle of attack of the aircraft and the resultant drag exceed the amount of thrust available to maintain speed, and thus altitude.

Supersonic speed also causes the center of lift to move rearward resulting in a nose-down pitch force. Thus in the thin air of extreme altitude and at supersonic velocities, the elevators would again be deflected upwards. (Pondering these phenomena says something unkind about the F-111 Raven, F-14 Tomcat and Tornado's "swing-wing." Unfortunately, at supersonic speed, the swing-wing's sweep moves the center of lift back, which aggravates the natural rearward shift that occurs at supersonic speed. The sweep does, however, help move the center of gravity of the variable-geometry aircraft in a favourable direction, yet the wing-glove retractable vanes of the F-14 Tomcat, since de-activated in efforts to reduce weight and complexity, and the large sawtooth on the MiG-23 which vanishes at the forward swept position, show that it isn't enough to counteract the negative effects.)

For the Arrow, Avro incorporated the negative camber of the wing to reduce this effect. They optimised that camber at .75 percent negative, which gave a good compromise across the performance envelope. Avro also ensured that they programed the fuel consumption to move the center of gravity as far rearward as possible by the mid-point of the flight, which would coincide with the highest speed and altitude portion of the mission.

Manoeuverability Factors: Wing Loading, Power Loading, Control Effectiveness, Critical Alpha and Load Limit

WING LOADING:

The Arrow design had a wing area of 1225 square feet. Compared to contemporary and modern fighters, this resulted in a very low wing loading when the weight of the aircraft is compared to the area available to "carry" it. The simple secret to the phenomenal manoeuverability of the Mitsubishi "Zero" fighter of World War II was its low wing loading. No high-performance fighter of the war could match it in a turning fight, not even the Hurricane or Spitfire. When it came to altitude performance, the Zeros ran out of engine long before they ran out of wing. Those who battled the Zero successfully relied on superior power, speed, and climb rate to defeat them. In simple terms this is known as "fighting the engine" rather than "fighting the airframe." Against any aircraft up to the F-15A, the Arrow would have been able to fight both the airframe and the engine.

At high altitudes, low wing loading is absolutely critical to the manoeuverability and speed of an aircraft. At these heights the air is so thin that a large wing is necessary to provide enough lift to support the weight of the aircraft. A smaller wing would invoke such severe trim and/or induced drag penalties as to exceed the amount of available power and make the aircraft stall. The U-2 spyplane used very high aspect ratio wings, glider-style, to minimize wing loading and induced drag and thus develop enough lift to achieve its very high altitudes. (U-2 equivalent altitudes were not reached by the Soviets with any serious payload until the late 1980s with their Mystic aircraft. This fact says a lot about the aerodynamic, structural and materials design of the Arrow, not to mention her power plants). The Arrow has the lowest wing loading of any interceptor the author knows to have entered service. This is pointed out in the statistical charts later on.

POWER LOADING:

This is the ratio of weight to the amount of thrust available to carry it, its inverse is equally valid and is called "thrust to weight ratio." The Arrow had a very high thrust to weight ratio (or very *low* power loading) and was about the best in the world in this respect until the F-15A Eagle which entered design in 1969. Tables in this work compare the power loading of the various Arrow versions to various aircraft.

CRITICAL ALPHA:

The ability of an aircraft to achieve high alpha without causing flow separation (and then the stall) is a major factor in potential manoeuverability. Think of hanging your hand out the window of a speeding car. As you raise the front of your hand against the airflow, the weight on your arm diminishes. The angle of your hand to the angle of airflow (horizontal) is the angle of attack or alpha. As you increase this angle, the weight on your arm is reduced to perhaps the point where your arm is actually lifted off the doorframe. If you continue to increase the angle, you will notice that your arm suddenly plops down again on the doorframe. You just discovered the "critical alpha" of your hand-airfoil. Or to put it in less "aero-speak" terms, you have found the angle of attack where your hand stalls.

A delta wing has an innate high alpha capability because it naturally produces the vortex already described, which, if it can be controlled and kept from reversing at the tips, produces a great deal of lift. This, in crude terms, is caused because a swirling vortex (spiral of highly energized air), separates from the lifting surface (wing) much later than normal airflow would. Avro incorporated the notch/sawtooth to do just that: take advantage of natural phenomena to develop a vortex where they wanted and then use it to improve the high alpha characteristics of the wing. They further introduced leading-edge droop to add even more high-alpha capability, especially for low speed handling. The leading-edge notch and sawtooth on the CF-105 did exactly the same thing as the long LEX (leading edge extension) does on the F-18, F-16, the Soviet's MiG-29 and Su-27. On these designs the LEX creates the same type of vortex and it is used to produce both an aerodynamic fence, (to keep the airflow over the wings moving in the direction of travel so the wings make more lift) and to create a core of high energy air to prevent airflow separation and loss of lift. The F-16 is advertised far and wide

A Tomcat showing the ability of the swing-wing to emulate the delta and produce the leading edge vortex. The F-14A had higher wing-loading than the Arrow and while weighing nearly as much empty, had roughly half the dry thrust of the Arrow 2. (Frank Ertyl via M.A.T.S.)

(especially during USAF air show presentations) as *the* aircraft that is capable of extraordinarily high alpha before the stall. The F-16, by the way, is limited to about 26 degrees of alpha before encountering control problems. The F-18 is even better in this regard but the exact figure is, to the author's knowledge, classified. Let's just say that it is confined to about 28 degrees during air shows to allow the aircraft to recover without crashing should one engine fail at such a low altitude.

More than one Avro engineer has stated to the author that the Arrow was wind-tunnel tested to 45 degrees of alpha before separation (and stall) at low speeds. This figure has also been published in works on the Arrow. Other sources claim the delta-wing makes lift up to 60 degrees of alpha, which is about 40 degrees more than a normal, straight wing can produce before stalling. Zurakowski related that the aircraft was test flown at up to 25 degrees without problems. Considering the F-16's reputation and 26-degree limitation, one must applaud Avro's success. Landing attitudes were restricted to 15 degrees of alpha for runway visibility reasons, and because the landing gear geometry limited its landing alpha to about this angle. This latter limitation was applied to prevent the exhaust nozzles from striking the runway. As such it landed "hot" (fast)—but not as hot as an F-104 and some other jets to have entered service. The pilot would also have had excellent controllability and thus safety on approach. Since it landed so much above the stall (it stalled at less than 117 knots when low on fuel while it landed at about 160) the pilot would have been able to keep the nose high for a good portion of the landing run and thus reduce the landing roll through aerodynamic braking. (Aerodynamic braking was glamorized very effectively in the movie "Space Cowboys.") The author has occupied the back seat of a CF-5 while the nose wheel was off the runway and the drag chute was deployed. Flight testing of the Arrow didn't get that far before cancellation.

CONTROL EFFECTIVENESS:

To turn all this lift and alpha capability into useful manoeuvres requires effective control surfaces that can produce a high rate of change in alpha. One look at the Arrow wing will show the elevators and ailerons to be simply enormous relative to the size of the wing. In the case of the elevators, this was done due to a relatively short "moment arm" (distance between the center of gravity and the control surface) to assure good responsiveness at low speeds. That being said, most modern aircraft with the

engines located at the extreme rear of the aircraft have short moment arms as well. Again one should note that the vortex created by the leading-edge notch/sawtooth passed over the joint between them imparting added effectiveness to both. The Arrow also had the first computerized (fly-by-wire) flight control system. Problems with the pitch-up and turn-tightening characteristics of Convair's deltas, coupled with the fact that they didn't seem to want to stall, should end all serious debate about control effectiveness as far as the delta's ability to make lift and turn. Avro actually had to modify the flight control system to limit the control effectiveness for flight at high speeds and low and medium altitudes. This characteristic did not hurt low-speed lift since then lift would be generated by a high angle of attack and leading-edge vortex control. Control effectiveness was assisted by the fuel consumption sequencing pattern which made sure adequate control authority existed at the extremes of operation. This reduced trim drag greatly as a fringe benefit.

By cancellation date the design and programming of this system had not progressed to the point where the ailerons were used as elevators and vice versa (cross-programming). However, it was just a matter of test flying the aircraft and developing the parameters under actual flight conditions, then programming them into the flight control computer to give it this capability. The Arrow Mk. 3 preliminary proposal demonstrates that Avro had done some computer modelling in that direction, programming in 4 degrees aileron up deflection above 40,000 feet as a desirable feature for the Mach 3+ Arrow 3. The F-18 Hornet uses such a system to great effect, but it took a great deal of flight testing to develop and refine it. Indeed the Hornet, about 30 years after its initial design, is still being tested and honed in this department. As it was, Zurakowski described the Arrow as having an excessively fast roll rate and the flight control system was modified to reduce this on the prototypes. Zurakowski and Woodman also described the aircraft as being very sensitive to pitch inputs, something that bodes very well for manoeuverability since this means that it had high control effectiveness and thus could change alpha very quickly. Indeed, Woodman complained after his first flight that a mere 1/5 inch of control stick movement would subject the aircraft to .5 G acceleration when the controls were calibrated for "linear" sensitivity. In other words, only two inches of movement were required to effect a significant 5-G turn. The system was then modified to include a "gradient" whereby the stick was made less effective near the center position while preserving total pitch authority at the extremes of its movement area. On Woodman's second flight in the Arrow he found the stick gradient to be "excellent." Since Woodman found the less sensitive "toned down" filtering on his second flight more to his liking, one can see that the Arrow had awesome natural control sensitivity.

Again, Avro designed the fly-by-wire system to minimize sensitivity at combined high-speed and at low-to-medium altitudes to protect the pilot and aircraft since it had so much lift and control authority built into it that to do otherwise could endanger the aircraft and crew. While Avro knew the Arrow had plenty of control authority and lift-generation potential at low speed, an Arrow configuration was proposed using a canard to reduce trim drag for an even higher-speed, higher-altitude Arrow version.

The Arrow Mk. 1, taking off at a weight about 5,000 pounds heavier than that of a combat-loaded Mk. 2, lifted off at 170 knots. F-15 Eagles take off at about 210 knots. It is easy to see which would be the best dogfighter.

LOAD LIMIT:

Maximum G is the structural limit of the airframe and thus is also a limit on alpha and manoeuverability. A fast alpha increase loads the wings with a great deal of force. Think of the weak-kneed feeling experienced when an elevator lifts off abruptly. This is perhaps an acceleration of 1.2 G. The Arrow was designed to be flown in normal operations at up to 7.33 G *at combat weight and supersonic velocity*. At this level of G force, your head, as an example, normally weighing perhaps 15 pounds, will weigh 110! (Not difficult to see why it is hard for a combat pilot to withstand high G while swivelling his or her neck to look for the enemy!) The Mk. 1 Arrow prototypes weighed 49,000 lbs empty. At 7.33 G, the wings would have to bear a load equivalent to over 400,000 lbs! The CF-18 Hornet is currently limited to 7.5 G maximum, *clean and light*, and is restricted to less when it is at any useful combat weight. The performance curves shown later also show that the powerful F-15C, even in the comparatively light air-to-air combat configuration, with no tanks, is limited to only 5.5 G.

SUPERSONIC AERODYNAMIC CONSIDERATIONS
SEARS-HAACK BODIES AND WHITCOMB'S AREA RULE:

Sears and Haack were Scandanavian aerodynamicists who investigated simple shapes to see how shape should change with intended speed range. As already mentioned, a curved surface causes air to speed up, and when the speed of the air reaches supersonic speed (Mach) a shock wave is formed. Every time a shock wave is produced, aerodynamic drag jumps. This is the reason it was so difficult for early

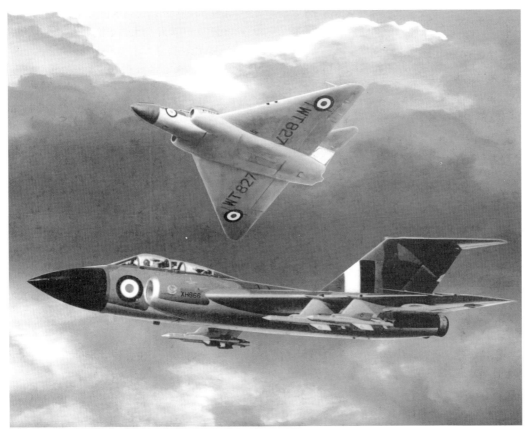

Gloster Javelins. The aircraft was far too bulbous, occupying far too much volume at the maximum point down its length relative to overall aircraft length (fineness ratio) to be a viable transonic or supersonic aircraft. The horizontal stabilizers were easily "blanked" and the plain delta-wing had problems with pitch-up. Avro Canada learned from Gloster's mistakes. The Javelin served until 1968—this longevity due purely to a lack of an acceptable replacement.
(via Aviation Bookshop with retouching and compositing by R.L. Whitcomb)

This CF-5 shows the pinched waist at the point of maximum wing volume.   (image by R.L. Whitcomb)

jets to break the sound barrier: while many had reasonably low subsonic drag, (even while neglecting the "flat plate" theory), the formation of the shock wave as the aircraft approached supersonic speed caused more drag than the relatively low-powered engines of the day could overcome. Small bumps, routinely incorporated for things such as control surface hinges, gun blisters, exhaust cowlings and the like added so much drag at supersonic speed that many early designers felt it would be impossible to break the sound barrier in a practical piloted aircraft. Meanwhile, these same minor protuberances had caused little difference in the subsonic regime. The reader will recall that the perfect supersonic lift-producing shape is a flat plate with no curves. Again, this is impossible since a "point" has zero size and is impossible to physically produce. For a low-drag aerodynamic "shape" one must construct a vehicle with the smallest volume possible to get as close to nothing as one can. In subsonic flight, the front of the aircraft was found to have the lowest drag when it was quite rounded. In terms of Sears-Haack thinking, this would represent a total aircraft volume shaped like a teardrop with the blunt end going into the wind. This was far from the reality with supersonic aircraft however. The conclusion was that the ideal supersonic "real-world" shape was a round form that was symmetrical from front to back and ending in two points, similar to a barley seed. Hypersonic shape needs seem to reverse the subsonic teardrop.

To understand this concept one must consider the aircraft as a whole. To the fuselage shape with a cockpit sticking out, intakes providing their own bulges, the wings providing two very large protrusions of their own, are added any tail surfaces, fuel tanks, weapons pylons, control-surface hinge fairings and other volumes. When you think of these protrusions cumulatively over the length of the aircraft, one can see how air would have to contort, twist and turn to get around this form. To quote Floyd, "anytime you bend air, you have to pay for it." The fee is increased drag. The payment is either lower speed or higher thrust. This is form drag in a nutshell. At supersonic speeds it is a very important consideration because the effect of each protrusion, especially objects which stick out at 90-degree angles, is much higher than at subsonic velocities.

NACA Langley's Dr. Richard Whitcomb (no known relation) actually regarded an aircraft as a total volume flying through the air rather than as individual areas to be considered separately then added together when predicting a supersonic body's performance (the latter corresponding to "blade element" theory). His thinking mirrored a more three-dimensional fluid-dynamics approach which was right down Avro's computer-packed alley. He found essentially that the cumulative volume of an aircraft, considered as a whole from front to back, should correspond to the Sears-Haack supersonic barley-seed ideal. If the cumulative total of each of the items of the aircraft form could be adjusted in volume to represent a Sears-Haack volume-shape for the intended speed range, Whitcomb theorized that transonic and supersonic drag could be greatly reduced. The way to think of this is to take a plasticine model of an aircraft and carefully roll the wings and everything else into one round shape with the wings etc. increasing the bulge only in the section that runs down the length where they occurred originally.

Whitcomb took the research from theory to practical application by proving that a supersonic aircraft should be long and pointed at the front and, where large volume increases were encountered, (such as where the wings were located), the fuselage should be "pinched" to occupy proportionally less volume. This was termed the "area rule" and is now commonly and incorrectly referred to as the "coke-bottle" fuselage.

An excellent aircraft in which this theory is applied is the Northrop T-38 Talon/CF-5 Freedom Fighter which has the fuselage very noticeably pinched where the wings join the fuselage. It was largely ignorance of area rule that limited the potential speeds of, as examples, the F-80 Shooting Star and the CF-100 Canuck. Even the SR-71 Blackbird ran into a wall (of air) due to this effect. Needless to say, if the airframe can be devised with relatively straight profiles and still conform to this ideal, performance will be even better. Enter the CF-105.

Whitcomb didn't release his findings until December 1953, and the USAF endeavored to keep them secret, according to *Faster Than Sound*. This was too late to influence the design of the YF-102 first prototype. Whitcomb's 1953 area rule papers, for only the transonic region, were supplemented in 1956 by a further paper on area ruling for supersonic speeds. A D. Kuchemann, working at the Royal Aircraft Establishment (RAE) at Farnborough, England, also produced data demonstrating the need to area rule aircraft. Kuchemann however, worked with physical models by carefully observing the streamlines (probably with smoke injected) across a wing and fuselage, which produced the same effect.

604-105-2

CF-105 SUPERSONIC ALL-WEATHER FIGHTER

SECRET

The cover page of Avro's 1955 CF-105 development proposal to the government of Canada shows the Arrow design as it was before area-ruling, leading-edge droop, and other refinements. (via Jim Floyd)

The Arrow was modified very early in the design process to better conform to the area rule. Without question this was done because of the extreme difficulties that the YF-102 encountered. On the YF-102A redesign, the nose was lengthened, the fuselage was reduced in volume as much as possible where the wings began, the area around the engine nacelles was reduced and modified, and two tail blisters were cobbled on. It was a much different aircraft. To check the effects of area rule on the Arrow, wind-tunnel and

rocket-launched tests were carried out on models using variations between "no-area rule" and "super-area rule." The modifications showed a significant reduction in transonic and supersonic drag. To further validate their design, one of the Douglas Nike-missile-launched test models incorporated a structurally impractical super-area-rule shape, and its drag was compared to the less-modified design. Happily for the Avro team the tests did not show any worthwhile improvement, probably since the bends in

Schlieren camera photo of an Arrow wind-tunnel model at around Mach 2. The lines show shock wave formation. The Arrow was an extremely clean design, yet note all the shock disturbances. An aircraft with more flying surfaces, external weapons, tanks, hinge-fairings and any other protrusions would have a great many more shock effects (and drag) to contend with. (via Peter Zuuring)

the airframe created *more* drag than the better Sears-Haack conformance saved. With only very minor changes, the Arrow was found to be "right the first time."

Again, shock wave formation is a major factor in supersonic drag. At exactly Mach 1, the shock wave is basically perpendicular to the aircraft; it's like a wall in more ways than one. In this case it is called a "normal" shock. As speed increases past Mach 1, the shock wave begins to bend backwards at an angle from the leading edges of the craft and is then termed an oblique shock due to the angularity. If the main (bow) shock wave impacts the wing tips, unhappy things occur, including vibration and flutter which can be potentially destructive. This is one of the limitations of a straight-wing supersonic design since, to provide more lift, the span of the wing has to increase. This wide span can soon encounter the bow wave; this is another reason why the wings on the F-104 were so short, and why hypersonic and space plane designs such as the space shuttle and the Aurora (if it exists—some say it's called Astra) hypersonic spyplane use a delta planform.

In Bill Sweetman's book on the Top Secret Aurora hypersonic spyplane a very interesting illustration is reproduced from a 1983 USAF document on hypersonic flight. This diagram shows several possible hypersonic aircraft designs starting with a Mach 3 to 5 "proof-of-concept" aircraft. This

A US Navy F/S-18 Hornet piercing the sound barrier. A solid wave is moving over and under the aircraft to the trailing edges. The activity around the protrusion on the top of the wing gives an idea of the extra drag any bumps cause. Behind this wave the water vapour is visible: the expansion behind the leading shock wave cools the air, condensing the water vapour into droplets, with the opposite effect behind the terminal shock making it invisible again. This can normally be seen only at low altitude and in hot, humid weather. (US Navy, taken by John Gay)

The F-4 Phantom II mock up before many radical changes. (McDonnell)

shows the Arrow planform, including intakes, *exactly*. The Arrow wing was sufficiently swept to allow a top speed of at least Mach 3.5 before this phenomenon would present a problem. To get even more speed they simply had to extend the nose (as they did on the Mk. 4 and PS-2 design).

SUPERSONIC INTAKE DESIGN:
MAKING POWER OUT OF THIN AIR

Intake design is critical to the success of a supersonic aircraft. It must be designed to provide enough air over the entire speed range of the aircraft. It must not cause turbulence before the air enters the engine compressor section. Pressure recovery is the yardstick by which an intake's efficiency is measured, with 100 percent being considered perfect by most designers since any duct incurs some losses over length. Pressure recovery tends to vary over speed since at low speeds there is little "ram" effect to help push the air into the intakes. At high speeds there is a tendency for more air to hit the intake opening than the engine can swallow. This results in intake "spillage," which in effect is like having the air pile up in front of the intake and then spill around the sides. This can cause enormous drag and affect the air inside the intake as well as the aerodynamics of the aircraft body due to pressure disturbances and turbulence. It is like plowing air as a snowplow does snow.

Oddly enough, the Iroquois engine and Arrow intake system were designed to allow a shock wave to form at the engine's first compressor stage. The first stage of the Iroquois engine was designed to give the air an extra "smack" to speed it up to transonic speed. It was in effect

designed to get *over* 100 percent pressure recovery by benefitting from the compression of the shock wave. The A-12/YF-12A/SR-71 made use of the same idea by designing the inlet "spike" to move *aft* {highly unusual} as speed increased, to place the shock wave at the engine nacelle opening. This seemingly strange concept also required huge intake spill doors just aft of the spike on the SR-71.

Shock waves generally must not enter an intake since this can cause extreme turbulence and pressure distortions. The Arrow's intake at Mach 1.8 (the Hornet's maximum speed) was 96 percent. At Mach 2 this dropped to 86 percent. Statisically speaking, this is still an excellent performance today. The Hornet also swallows the shock at Mach 1.8 causing intake "buzz" (from the shock wave jumping in and out of the throat very rapidly). By any standard the Arrow Mk. 1 and 2 intake was an excellent design.

The CF-105 Mk. 1 and 2 designs used a "fixed geometry" intake which means the opening was fixed at one size and could not be varied in flight. Most of the aircraft up to the time of the Arrow used a similar system. Later aircraft such as the F-14, F-15 and others use a variable intake. The ramps and other devices reduce the size of the intake to control intake spillage and the formation of shock waves at supersonic speed. The F-18 and F-16 both still use fixed geometry intakes. It's worth pointing out that most fixed intakes are limited to Mach 2 or under. (The author was shocked to learn that the F-22 Raptor uses a fixed intake.)

The Arrow's long intake bleed-ramp was designed to produce a shock wave at supersonic speeds well ahead of the intake opening and thus keep it from touching the intake lip at speeds up to Mach 2.3. In reality this may have occurred later due to some compressibility of the airflow behind the bow wave and the ramp's own secondary shock wave, suggesting potentially higher speeds than Avro projected. This opinion seems justified since the F-4 (which appears to have copied the Arrow intake) and especially the F-106 had comparatively short intake ramps yet achieved speeds of Mach 2.2 and 2.31 respectively in clean and light specially prepared record attempt aircraft.

On the Arrow Mk. 2, concerns about shock wave impingement at the intake lip and *perhaps* airframe heat absorption/dissipation were felt to be the limiting factors as far as aircraft speed was concerned, rather than thrust. The long intake tunnel also boded well for high alpha operations. In aircraft such as the MiG-29 and Su-27 with their short intakes, turbulence at the inlet has little distance in which to smooth out and this condition can result in airflow distortion at the engine compressor face. It is thought that at least one of the public air show crashes of the MiG-29 was due to intake pressure recovery problems brought about by uncontrolled yaw after an engine failure. As a testament to excellent design, the Su-27, meanwhile, does the "Cobra Manoeuvre," which involves momentary alpha of around 90 degrees. The Arrow intake was wind-tunnel tested at AOA's up to 9.5 degrees and yaw angles of 6 degrees and was found invulnerable to flow distortions. Admittedly, this was not a wide range of study by today's standards. Apparently the intakes proved invulnerable in tests limited at 25 degrees alpha in actual test flying, very competitive with today's fighters.

The intake ramp on the Hornet, Arrow and all supersonic aircraft is set a couple of inches away from the fuselage. This is to ensure that the intake doesn't ingest the low-energy and turbulent boundary layer formed against the fuselage. These intakes also have a strip of perforated "bleed" holes on the ramp just in front of the opening, which are connected to a "cascade" inside the ramp that ejects boundary layer air rearward under the aircraft. On the Arrow, the opening of the cascade is located under the fuselage. As the aircraft gained momentum, suction at the bleed holes would increase with speed. This accomplished two goals. First it sucked away the turbulent, low-energy air coming off the bleed ramp preventing it from entering the inlet. Secondly, as speed increased, so would the suction at the perforated strip thus decreasing intake spillage requirements at the right time. The bleed system naturally tended to adjust itself, thereby delaying the point where

> UNCLASSIFIED
>
> JOINT REPORT ON AN RCAF-DRB-NAE VISIT
> TO N.A.C.A. LANGLEY LABORATORIES TO DISCUSS AERODYNAMIC
> PROBLEMS OF AVRO CF-105 AIRCRAFT - 19 NOVEMBER 1954
>
> SUMMARY
>
> N.A.C.A. comments on CF-105 design problems are summarized as follows:
>
> (a) The Company's estimate of zero lift drag at subsonic and supersonic speeds should be increased by 50 percent or more.
>
> (b) Substantial reductions in drag throughout the supersonic speed range should be possible by proper application of the area rule.
>
> (c) Present intake lip design is likely to result in prohibitive drag penalties at supersonic speeds.
>
> (d) The high drag due to lift associated with low aspect ratio delta wings makes them poor planforms for high endurance and long range.
>
> (e) The high drag due to lift is not improved by the negative camber proposed by the firm. Correctly designed positive camber should be used to reduce substantially both drag due to lift and trim drag.
>
> (f) A wind tunnel programme would be required to develop the means proposed by A.V. Roe to ensure intake stability.
>
> (g) The CF-105 wing planform is of the type which gives serious pitch-up tendencies. Cures developed in wind tunnels do not always work out in flight.
>
> (h) The directional stability characteristics of the CF-105 are poorer than had been experienced in the United States. A wind tunnel programme should be pursued.
>
> (i) All steps should be taken to ensure aerodynamic stability before resorting to electronic means.
>
> (j) It is possible that the use of elevons rather than separate elevators and ailerons would result in lower trim drag and higher reversal speed.

Joint report denigrating the Arrow design. Testimony suggests the origin of these criticisms was Julius Lukasiewicz of the NAE. (via Peter Zuuring)

drag would be increased from spillage. The British NAE mentioned that the Arrow's bleed/bypass system would dramatically increase the speed potential of the aircraft over conventional designs before spillage became a problem. They found Avro's work on the intake "especially laudable."

Avro was accused, again by the Canadian NAE (seemingly with some support from NACA) of having an excessive ramp angle in front of the intake. This angle was 12 degrees. Meanwhile, the F-4H1 Phantom prototype had an angle of five degrees. This was found in flight test to be insufficient and was increased first to 10 degrees, and finally to 15. Again Avro suffered for having done it right the first time.

The assessment of the Arrow's aerodynamics by the Canadian government research facilities and scientists took a very narrow view. Dr. John H. Parkin and Julius Lukasiewicz, two of the leading lights of the National Aeronautical Establishment, and many others couldn't comprehend the aircraft's unique requirements, and the features of the delta-wing. They certainly couldn't grasp Avro's new lifting body theory and many of the design features. To substantiate their feelings, the Defence Research Board (DRB), NAE, and RCAF descended on NACA's Langley high speed aerodynamics facility to discuss "Aerodynamic Problems of Avro CF-105 Aircraft." The general conclusions are shown in a page from the joint report.

As with all projects Jim Floyd had been involved with, the Arrow was designed to incorporate plenty of room for growth. The Arrow was designed to a Mach 1.5 specification but the team knew that with advances in propulsion and an ever-evolving Soviet threat, they would be wise to provide room in the aerodynamic design for increases in speed. In fact they really outdid themselves, and in many regards the Canadian experts in the DRB, and NAE and RCAF couldn't comprehend much of what Avro was doing. This was *most* unfortunate for Avro. From the NACA participation, we can see that by the end of 1954, even these experts were having difficulty keeping up with Chamberlin, Lindley, Pesando and Floyd. This despite Avro's thick performance reports that thoroughly describe design and development and the reasoning behind their decisions, including references to what was going on elsewhere then and historically.

Unfortunately this NACA visit did not include Avro's designers and engineers. One would assume they were somewhat taken aback when confronted by such expert opinion condemning the Arrow as a ridiculous, and probably dangerous, design. No doubt they made strong representations to be allowed to defend their design and another conference was arranged at NACA Langley. Present at this 20-21 December 1954 meeting were: Ira H. Abbott, M.B. Ames Jr., John W. Crowley, Hugh L. Dryden, and E.O. Pearson of NACA headquarters. Ames and Dryden are legends today, each with a research facility named in their honour. Richard Whitcomb, inventor of the area rule and supercritical wing was present as the Langley transonic expert. Thomas A. Toll was also there for Langley Aeronautical Laboratory, with all the Langley staff reporting to Robert Gilruth. Gilruth was not present at the meetings but figures in our story later. Charles W. Frick was present from the NACA Ames Aeronautical Laboratory. From NACA's Lewis Flight Propulsion Laboratory was D.D. Wyatt. From the Canadian NAE were R.J. Templin and D.C. McPhail. The DRB was represented by A.W.R. Gilchrist and J.J. Green, while the RCAF sent AVM J.L. Plant, G/C H.R. Footit and S/L A.W. Armstrong. From Avro there were Fred Smye, Jim Floyd, Jim Chamberlin, Bob Lindley, J.S. Dobranski, John Morris, F.A. Woodward, and J.H. Lucas.

The meeting was chaired by Hugh Dryden, and according to Floyd the first marathon day resulted in a sleepless night whereupon he decided to put to paper what he felt had been discussed, and more importantly *agreed upon* the day before, for discussion on day two. The subsequent paper, penned by NACA chairman Ira Abbott, was far more favourable to the Arrow but still included a few flags, though no outright disagreement. Harry Keast would write, late in life, that NACA themselves actually felt Avro was being conservative, suggesting the hedges in the final document were a concession to the anti-Arrow faction. In reality all of the original objections to certain design elements would prove that Avro was far in advance of current thinking, and that few were operating at such an advanced level in some of Avro's specialties.

The flight which really put to rest any questions about the Arrow's drag and performance was Potocki's Mach 1.96 run of 11 November 1958. On this flight the underpowered Mk. 1 Arrow exceeded Avro's original top level speed projections for the Mk. 2, proving all the critics wrong. Dr. John H. Parkin (director of the NAE) and Julius Lukasiewicz (the NAE's aerodynamics expert) however would remain hostile to the Avro design, with the latter actually going on television in the 1990s after the first showings of the CBC miniseries "The Arrow," to remove all doubt.

The Arrow intake system incorporated several other advanced methods to prevent spillage and also assist thrust. A set of bleed/bypass gills was placed inside the intake duct just ahead of the engine itself. These gills would automatically open when pressure reached a certain level in the intake and divert this air around the engine and up to about Mach .5 the gills would dump a percentage of it overboard via another set of gills ringing the engine nacelle skins. This is actually very similar in intent to the SR-71's later bleed/bypass door system. This system not only took care of spillage, it also helped cool the engine and since it acted as a heat exchanger in the direction of flight, it also added thrust. This was a brilliant design and the best modern jets use a system that is virtually identical.

PROVING THE DESIGN ON THE GROUND

Avro had made use of the new and largest *digital* transistorized computer in the world, the IBM 704, as well as their own enormous analogue systems, to solve the thousands upon thousands of mathematical problems. Thirty

Avro's analogue computer room, only a portion of the computing power of the company in the mid 1950s. Avro also had an electronics design division and were making full use of digital and transistorized technology. (via Jim Floyd)

Avro's digital computing room with the IBM 704 mainframe. Documents from Avro suggest that some US manufacturers really didn't value computers very much in those days, as suggested by a comment from Douglas Aircraft that they had an overabundance of computing power in 1959! (via Jim Floyd)

engineers and mathematicians were employed to feed just the IBM 704 computers a steady diet of formulae to test the designer's theories and predict all the variables. To the author's knowledge, the Arrow was the first computer-aided aircraft design. Even the A-12/SR-71 was a "slide rule" aircraft, as former Lockheed Skunk Works head Ben Rich relates in his appropriately titled book *Skunk Works*.

Full-size test rigs were constructed to simulate everything from fuel systems in all flight attitudes to aircraft-wide electrical, air conditioning, hydraulic and other

system simulators. This seemed to stem from an idea hatched by some technicians who had the pleasure of testing and troubleshooting the electrics of the CF-100. From *Jet Age*:

> There was a time nearly 4 years ago (1951), that Herb Stangel and a few of the boys decided there must be a better way to check the CF-100's complex electrical system with its maze of junction boxes, relays, switches and motors than crawling around in the belly of the aircraft. They found one—a test bed which contains every bit of equipment found anywhere in a CF-100, including the device for firing rockets. To test any item, they merely put it into the test bed where applicable. It was such a good idea that it's doubtful Avro ever will make another aircraft without first building a test bed.

Actual aircraft components were thus incorporated in these simulators and test rigs to the largest extent possible.

The metal test airframe was attached to a complex assembly with up to thirty hydraulic systems being used to load some 1,100 different points on the aircraft structure to determine the ultimate strength (breakage point) and fatigue characteristics of the structure. Some 3,000 strain gauge stations and 300 deflection gauges were located around the static test airframe. Computer-controlled heating lamps were used to simulate temperatures that would be encountered at supersonic speeds and explore their effect on the airframe.

Avro constructed a computer-controlled, flight-control-system test rig. This system was initially used to develop the hydraulic system and components for the aircraft. Once complete, the fly-by-wire flight control system was developed on top of the mechanical system. Once *this* had been completed, the entire system was developed into a flight simulator to familiarize the pilots with how the Arrow was expected to perform in flight. This system was capable of synthesizing the fire-control and radar inputs with the flight characteristics of the aircraft giving realistic cockpit instrument readouts and control feedback to the pilot. Once actual performance data was achieved in test flights, the simulator computers were updated with the improved data. Obviously this is a very efficient and cost-effective method of development.

A full-size air-conditioning and pressurization test rig was constructed. This system was vital to the aircraft since at the high altitudes where the Arrow was designed to fight, the air is very thin. Along with the cabin area, air-conditioning capacity was required to cool the radar and other computer systems which incorporated transistors and even very early integrated circuits but still retained some of the miniature vacuum tube technology. Avro produced a system of insulating panels that were movable from test rig to test rig, allowing the components to be tested over the entire operational range of the aircraft, from -65 to 250 degrees Fahrenheit. This is a huge temperature range and presented many challenges for the design team.

One of the launches of the Arrow test models at NACA's Wallops Island facility. (courtsty Jim Floyd)

A one-sixth scale model was constructed to prove the intake design. It included the nose, canopy, intakes and bleed systems to explore the pressure and flow patterns in the intake. They tested a full thirty-seven inlet designs with 1,283 points in the intake where data was collected. A Schlieren camera, which makes shock waves visible, was also employed. A full-size intake test included pressurizing the duct to the pressures and temperatures expected at high speed and altitude, whereupon 50-calibre rounds were blasted through it to see if it would cause explosive decompression. Explosive decompression would mean that the intake would rip open or explode like shattering glass in the case of battle damage. It remained intact during the test.

Wind-tunnel tests were conducted on a wide range of design variations in Canada and at high-speed facilities in the USA. About 4,000 hours of wind-tunnel testing was compiled in runs of about one hour each. These were conducted at the NAE in Ottawa (with the NAE manufacturing some of the models), at the Cornell Laboratories in Buffalo and at the NACA tunnels in Langley Field and Cleveland, Ohio, and finally at the Massachusetts Institute of Technology (MIT). These last two facilities were the most advanced in the world. These tests proved invaluable in assisting the design, in proving concepts, and in establishing the stability factors of the aircraft. Of course all data was given to the Americans free of charge. Meanwhile, in works describing the development of the F-4 Phantom, it has been said that the changes to the intake and wing (to concepts identical to the Arrow) were done due to wind tunnel data that "became available" in 1955.

To verify theoretical flight and drag calculations and wind-tunnel assessments, eleven heavily-instrumented free flight test models were launched on Nike missiles to investigate supersonic characteristics. These tests were done in Canada at the CARDE missile range near Point Petrie (near Belleville) in Ontario, over Lake Ontario, and at NACA's Wallops Island facility in Virginia over the Atlantic ocean. Models that would evolve into the Convair F-102 and B-58 Hustler were tested in an identical manner at Wallops Island.

The first two launches were of rather crude Arrow scale models to make sure the model would separate from the missile's booster section properly. This separation depended on the missile having higher drag than the model under test so that when the booster flamed-out, the missile section would decelerate faster than the model and the two would part company. The models had

One of the rocket-launched Arrow models on structural test. It was vital that the models flex and exhibit the same physical characteristics as the full-size aircraft. This allowed them to both validate drag projections and also to quantify the effectiveness of controls. (Avro Canada)

sixteen radio channels on which to relay data to the ground installations for various flight parameters. They were also filmed on kine-theodolite cameras, taking hundreds of frames per second to enable the engineers to plot the performance of the flight. Two of the later models were equipped with controls and instrumentation to explore directional (yaw) stability and two more were similarly equipped to explore longitudinal (pitch) characteristics. It was calculated that the relatively low altitude and thus thicker air of the launches would adequately represent the characteristics of the full-size aircraft at high altitude.

The test launches done in Canada were not altogether successful, partly because the RCAF had moved a key tracking radar to Cold Lake, Alberta. The western copies of the German kine-theodolite cameras were also unreliable. The only really reliable information came from Avro's own highly instrumented ground telemetry installation installed in a truck. This same truck would be used to gather data from the actual flying Arrows through the heavily instrumented weapons pack via a radio data-link to the ground. The models' radio test (telemetry) equipment was so effective and robust that one of the models,

at the end of its flight, skipped off the surface of Lake Ontario and continued to provide data to the astonished monitoring technicians! Two launches, of a "super-area rule" Arrow and another fully instrumented version were fired from the NACA range at Wallops Island, Virginia. The information from these launches was first class since the radar and cameras were functioning properly.

All of the Avro involvement with NACA, at Langley especially, gained Avro the respect of some scientists that are today icons of the air and space ages: Dr. Richard Whitcomb and Dr. Hugh Dryden. Whitcomb worked under Dr. Robert Gilruth who ran the Langley facility while Dryden had run the NACA Flight Research Center at Edwards Air Force Base in California which was later renamed for him. Dryden chaired the two day conference between Avro, the DRB, NAE, RCAF and other critics who had made representations that the Arrow would not be supersonic, would break up in flight, etc. Gilruth would later employ Jim Chamberlin and over twenty-five other former Avro-ites for the space race, Chamberlin as the engineering manager of NASA's Mercury and Gemini programs.

STRUCTURAL DESIGN

The actual structure of the CF-105 was reasonably conventional in being a mostly aluminum/magnesium (Dural) stressed-skin design. Titanium and special steels were also applied for skinning in some areas, especially around the engines as well as for fastening and other high strength and small size components that demanded it. The methods of fabrication were very advanced, as were the specialized light-alloys (magnesium and aluminum based alloys) that were developed for what one British engineering scholar felt would become *"the ultimate light-alloy airplane."* Avro certainly had more than a few revolutionary ideas, and leadership in computerized design and production techniques would prove a huge advantage that Avro exploited to the hilt. Gunston asserts in *Faster Than Sound* that a later aircraft was the first to have major components machined by computerized production equipment. Again, Avro was first. Many have related that Avro was well advanced in using computer-aided design. The computers, once fed the final design (produced with the assistance of computers), also produced punch-tape code for the heavy machining equipment (such as their huge wing-skin mill) which would configure the machine and produce the part using CNC (Computer Numeric Control) techniques. This will be a surprise to many, but then, when it came to the Arrow,

The Arrow structural test airframe in the test rig. An enormous amount of stress and fatigue testing was done here. (Avro Canada)

few did realize how advanced everything about it was, because it was first in so many areas.

The high delta-wing design was chosen for a number of reasons. This design allowed the easiest access for engine changing and maintenance. An engine change could be done in the Arrow in about half an hour—a phenomenal feat, then or now. High-wing designs also have exceptional roll stability in gusts and crosswinds. Indeed, for a fighter, a high-wing design can have *too* much roll stability, making it slow to roll when the pilot wants it to. The Arrow had four degrees anhedral that not only made the landing gear shorter, but also made the roll rate faster. Again, Zurakowski stated to the author that the Arrow had *too* high a roll rate and that the flight control computer parameters were modified to reduce it. While the Arrow roll rate of 360 degrees per second was very good, the Northrop designed CF-5 Freedom Fighter had double this rate and required a mechanical stick-limiter to prevent an overly excited pilot in training from putting his helmet through the side of the canopy! (While the F-5 had an astonishing roll rate, its more important pitch rate was poor.)

Having the wing mounted high also had advantages in terms of aerodynamics, strength and weight. The four stress-bearing spars were in effect bolted together down the spine forming one lifting surface and one structural member. This was ideal since the skin and spars formed one strong stress-bearing assembly to which the fuselage was bolted, rather than bolting two wings to a fuselage as on many other designs. This is an important consideration in design since having as much area as possible producing lift reduces parasite drag and makes for a more efficient design overall. There would be no chances taken in the design of this wing after the problems with the CF-100!

To this solid wing/spine assemblage was attached the vertical fin. The main stress bearing spar of the fin was extended some distance and dropped down inside the airframe to provide strength against side moments. The fin would be subject to considerable sideways stresses from turbulence, rudder inputs and any sideslip encountered.

Commentators speak of the blending of the fuselage and wing on aircraft such as the F-16, SR-71, MiG 29 *et al* as being beneficial in helping the fuselage produce lift. On the Arrow no such blending was required since the top of the fuselage, wing *and* intake were one continuous, flat, surface. In effect, the *entire top of the aircraft was the wing*, making the Arrow, in very real terms, a "lifting body." This point is a major one and is a considerable advantage when compared to even the SR-71. The F-15 and F-22 and current Soviet fighters share this philosophy to a large extent.

MATERIALS

Avro was leading the West in the use of the exotic metal, titanium, although in the 1950s it was both extremely scarce and presented many difficulties in its manufacture and use. Besides Orenda's use of titanium in the Iroquois engine, it was used on the CF-105 for engine hot-end shrouding (like the much later F-15 Eagle), and for structural joints and fastening applications to both save weight, and satisfy small size requirements dictated by the very thin wing. Titanium was considered for larger structural members but was rejected in favour of high-strength aluminum alloys because Avro found that, at the temperatures expected at a sustained Mach 2, new zinc and aluminum alloys, some of them developed exclusively for the Arrow by A.V. Roe Canada's subsidiary (Canadian Steel Improvements Ltd., a Canadian mirror of Hawker Siddeley's High Duty Alloys company in Britain), were up to the task and were stronger by weight. While they tried to maximize the usage of light alloys in the Arrow design, titanium and exotic composites were kept in mind for future developments, as we shall see.

The majority of the structure of the Arrow was machined from a fairly typical aerospace quality aluminum-magnesium alloy, 7075S-T6. The wing was covered in a special aluminum/magnesium alloy, 75ST. These covering panels were not made from normal sheet-metal of uniform thickness but were machined from solid billet. Regular "sheet" stock was normally rolled at the mill and would have resulted in a rather wavy surface and had other limitations. Arrow skins were machined on their own CNC equipment to the exact thickness required for the local strength anticipated, often including integral stiffeners (machined out of the billet with the skin in one piece) to save weight, expense, and avoid other problems. Enter Avro's "Men From Mars," who suited up to machine the one-piece fuselage formers from the challenging 75ST alloy for the Jetliner. The engineers felt that the heat-treated alloy would have residual stresses that would be relieved during machining and thus allow the material to distort. Once attached to the wing, these distortions would then transfer unwanted stresses to the structure itself. To prevent problems the panels were machined, then stretched by two percent, solution-treated and artificially "aged." Even then the final machined skin was stress-relieved as a final step. The end result was a perfectly shaped distortion-free panel of the exact local strength required that was corrosion-resistant and would not distort with time.

Some components were made from an (at the time) new aluminum alloy, No.7079, which could be machined without having internal latent stresses build up, to a part size of about 6 inches in thickness even with heat treating.

Other external surfaces were produced from a special magnesium/zinc alloy for areas demanding the ultimate in strength-to-weight ratio performance and heat absorption characteristics. The alloy designation is ZE41H24 and was used because it did not lose its strength or dimensional conformity at temperatures of over 250 degrees Fahrenheit which would be produced at over Mach 2. (Mach 2 speed results in aerodynamic skin friction temperatures—kinetic heating—of about 200 degrees Fahrenheit.) Avro developed special hot-forming techniques for this alloy. Up to this point aluminum alloys were known to lose their strength at about 200 degrees, which limits an airframe to Mach 2. Avro had the engineers working on titanium, which is actually weaker by weight than this zinc alloy, for even faster Arrow versions, well in advance of the A-12/YF-12A/SR-71. Even so, since the higher heat areas used a material that was capable of 250 degrees, it is clear that the Arrow Mk. 1 or 2 would have been capable of sustained speeds well above Mach 2 and short term dash speeds considerably above this provided the thrust was there. Another Arrow myth shattered.

Avro was also using composites. Examining a piece of composite from the Mk. 1 shows a fibreglass honeycomb material using phenolic resins and incorporating a metallic puddle-welding technique! Indeed a honeycomb, glass-fibre microballoon filled insulation material proposed in mid-1958 for the Mk. 3 Arrow bears more than a passing similarity to the most highly classified item on the (circa) 1964 Gemini space capsules, the heat shield itself! But then Chamberlin and Lindley, gentlemen very involved in the Arrow design, were also very involved in the Gemini spacecraft.

The fuselage was designed around the engines, intake, weapons bay and cockpit requirements. Its length was largely dictated by the requirement to have an internal weapons bay larger than that of a B-29 bomber. The location of the engines at the rear of the aircraft avoided any problems with supersonic exhaust "plumes" and their shock waves which can have dramatic drag, control and structural consequences if they impact the airframe. At high Mach numbers the exhaust plume also effects the area rule principle. Happily for Avro, the then little understood exhaust plume effect tended to fill in the Sears-Haack volume behind

Top is the YF-102 (subsonic) original with the original canopy. Bottom is the YF-102A after extensive modification.

the airframe and was largely responsible for the Arrow, in flight test, recording about 20 percent lower supersonic drag numbers than even Avro had projected. Engines at the extreme rear of the aircraft were a new idea at the time. Most designers up to that point had placed their engines (and almost everything else) as close to the center of gravity and center of lift as possible. This contributed to their poor "Sears-Haack" conformance and also made them heavier since they required long jet pipes. Those jet pipes were also always prone to overheating. Some British designers resisted this kind of design, considering integrated engine/fuselage designs to be "a hot can of worms." This last from Wood's *Project Cancelled* in reference to some designers' views of the later TSR.2 engine placement.

CANOPY DESIGN

The canopy was pointed at the front similar to the revised YF-102A and later A-12/YF-12/SR-71 design. The hypersonic X-15 rocket-plane also shared this arrangement. The frontal "V" shape is not the ideal from the point of view of forward visibility but at the speeds the Arrow was projected

to achieve it was seen as the only design because it had the lowest drag. It would also not build up heat nor have to endure the same kind of aerodynamic loads as a flat-front screen would. The quartz glass used was very thick in order to provide the "hot-soak" heat absorption properties required and was installed similarly to the NAA X-15 in a stress-free "floating" arrangement. It was also specially made to ensure there were as few impurities, built-in stresses or tiny air bubbles present as possible. One engineer related how an almost invisible bubble in some glass under heat test would grow (along with his eyes!) to an unbelievable size then almost disappear again once the glass had cooled. The canopy skin alone was expected to reach temperatures of up to 300 degrees Fahrenheit!

Avro was criticized by the RCAF at the time for using this pointed-front canopy design and is so criticized to this day. An *Airpower* magazine special on the SR-71 reports on similar machinations that occurred in the SR-71 development. At the time Lockheed was considering putting a flat panel in front, similar to that of the F-104, to reduce the distortion of view that some felt was preventing successful air-to-air refuelling. They found other means to correct the problem, much to the relief of the nervous test pilot. Avro's solution to a distortion problem had been to put a vertical black screen between the two front panes of glass. Lockheed's solution is unknown. The RCAF wrote Avro more than one blunt letter demanding an F-104-style canopy. An experienced fighter pilot mentioned that the Arrow would be a "sitting-duck" with such poor visibility from the cockpit. While the Arrow could have given a good account of itself in a dogfight, with superior altitude and speed, only a foolish pilot would engage in one in the first place, as opposed to remaining aloof and "dropping missiles." Avro's wisdom in this regard, exemplified by their refusal to comply with an RCAF demand for an F-104 type canopy, until all the unknowns were fully understood, and/or materials technology provided a solution, was one reason why they gained a reputation for inflexibility and arrogance. Clearly, the Arrow was designed for longer hot-soak periods at high supersonic speed than any combat design to this day. It seems Avro wasn't going to let RCAF staff officers risk RCAF pilots! Some latter-day critics seem to feel perceived poor visibility through the canopy was a sufficient reason for cancellation of the program. One might imagine it would be more pragmatic to just change the canopy. Avro was willing to look at that option, but only once the actual heating and other stresses on the canopy design were known from service flying. They did not want to risk the integrity of the design and were conservative.

The canopy shells were machined from ZH62, an alloy which remained quite strong at temperatures of over 300 degrees Fahrenheit and could be heated and cooled over and over without losing its dimensional or strength properties. At high altitude, the cockpit would be highly pressurized compared to the outside air and the outer surface would be very hot from skin friction at high speed. The material was cast into shape and then machined to its complex, compound curve shape and was weldable. Today the machining of this complex shape would be exceedingly expensive due to the current method of programming a computer-controlled milling machine to do the job. A Canadian machine shop won the contract to produce the canopy shells and devised a very ingenious method to machine the part from its rough casting. A milling machine was adapted to have a hydraulically controlled, three-axis moveable cutter. Hydraulic actuators were connected to a hand-held follower with levers and arms moving the hydraulic valves, making the mill cutter follow the movements of the operator's hand. This "tracer" arm was hand-moved over a wooden canopy shape following the multiple curves, with the mill cutter following along and milling the casting to the shape and size of the wooden pattern. Final finishing was done by hand. If the final canopy framing piece was found after forming to have porosity, the fact that it could be welded would save the part from the scrap heap. It was a most ingenious and effective way to produce a complex form in an economical and reliable fashion.

This Canadian company was founded by a skilled European tool-maker who spent hundreds of thousands of dollars setting up this business, with his first contract being from Avro. Avro provided technology and technical assistance to most of the companies with which they worked, simply because they had to in order to get the quality, *in Canada,* that cutting-edge aerospace production required. Avro had a vested interest in raising the standard of industry in Canada.

CREW ESCAPE SYSTEM

The crew escape system was also state-of-the-art. Martin Baker, the British pioneer of the rocket-assisted ejection seat, allowed Avro to use his newest seat design, the Martin Baker C-5, in the Arrow before any other aircraft did. Dummy firings were conducted from the metal Arrow mock-up and at the RAE in Britain. The seat was also successfully tested on a rocket sled in the USA. It was proposed to simulate an ejection in a rocket-sled configured as an Arrow cockpit but this had not been done by the cancellation date. Meanwhile, Convair was blasting live bears out of rocket-sleds to test their seats. One would think a dummy, loaded with accelerometers, would be suitable and considerably more humane!

The canopy clam-shells on the Arrow were designed to remain attached to the aircraft during ejections, with the halves being snapped open and locked while the seats roared up the ramps. Since the clam-shells and front canopy thus blocked the airflow, one can see that the occupants would be in a relatively turbulence-free zone while abandoning ship. Aircraft that jettisoned the entire canopy sometimes caused failed ejections or injured the occupants due to wind-blast. This is why the face-blind ejection handle, common at the time and located above the occupant's head was abandoned later—because the turbulence often prevented the occupant from even getting his hands on this type of handle. Both were well shielded in the Arrow in such a case.

Avro found that the manual ejection system, where the pilot orders the navigator to eject and then follows once the navigator has departed, took about eight seconds from the bailout command to the time both were clear of the aircraft. Avro was looking at an automated system where the pilot could eject both occupants automatically. They calculated that they could reduce the total ejection time for both crewmen to about 2.5 seconds from the bail-out command by this method. This is an excellent performance today as it takes about 1.2 or more seconds even now to get a single man out of an aircraft once the lever is pulled.

INTERNAL WEAPONS CARRIAGE

Internal weapons were specified for the Arrow since Avro calculated that they could not stay under the drag coefficient of .020, at combat height and speed, while using external weapons. The weapons pack could be changed while the aircraft was running and being "hot-fuelled" on the ground between missions—in a matter of minutes. Turnaround time was to be 10 minutes including re-arming and replenishment. This is very good. Weapons loading on a conventional and drag-intensive current design is considerably more involved. The interchangeable weapons pack also allowed the role of the aircraft to be changed at will. Mission-specific systems were designed to be housed in the weapons pack itself to instantly reconfigure the aircraft's onboard systems for whatever role its payload demanded.

Artist's concept of the Mk. 2 Arrow with the MA-1 system. This shows the armament arrangement, with both heat-seeking and radar-guided Falcon missiles, with the rear ones in the process of extension. In reality the missiles would extend, fire and retract one-by-one and the tank would be gone by that stage. Avro was projecting the 21st Arrow to be the first to meet their expectations for the engine and other systems.   (image by R.L. Whitcomb)

Some have felt that the opening of the weapons bay doors in supersonic flight would have caused the Arrow to break up in flight. They vastly underestimated the credentials of those who designed the Arrow. The F-101 Voodoo, F-102 Delta-Dagger and F-106 Delta-Dart all used similar but less sophisticated systems at supersonic speeds and still returned safely to base. The upcoming F-22 Raptor of course uses a similar system yet once again the doors remain open during weapons deployment!

The Arrow used an ingenious system for the initial Sparrow missiles, whereby the doors were segmented, meaning that as the missiles extended only the portion of the door assembly that the missile was moving through would open, then they would close as the weapon cleared that area. The entire door assembly was closed once the missiles were completely extended with tiny flaps remaining open to conform to the protruding missile struts. This was designed in because the Sparrow 2D's own semi-active homing seeker would have to lock onto the target before firing, and this could take some time. Avro also explored a semi-recessed, or "conformal" carriage method for the Sparrows.

Once ASTRA/Sparrow were cancelled and replaced by the MA-1 system with Falcon missiles, the system allowed for missile extension, firing, retraction and door closure—all in less than a second. The missiles, with their seekers already updated with targeting information from the radar and/or infra-red sensors, would extend, fire singly and retract. The Arrow fly-by-wire system was designed to automatically trim the aircraft during weapons extension with the aircraft remaining rock-steady during target tracking and lock-on.

On a more strategic and political note, this internal weapons design must have simply terrified the Soviets. They would have had no way of knowing whether an Arrow was configured for interception duties, photo-reconnaissance or even tactical nuclear bombing since its payload was internal. (Campagna, in *Storms of Controversy* relates meeting a former East German officer who related that, during the Arrow program, the East Germans got

The F-22 Raptor shows off its smooth underside and internal weapons. Hinge fairings are also similar to those visible on the Arrow. Sidewinder bays are open.
(courtesy Lockheed Martin)

weekly briefings on the progress of the design. Meanwhile the author wonders if the Sputnik launch was intentionally done on the day of the Arrow unveiling to steal its thunder and reinforce the belief that the missile age had dawned, and that interceptors were thus obsolete.) The F-106 had an internal weapons volume not that much smaller than the Arrow. It was the largest competitive design but since it was divided into two sections, it meant the Arrow's weapons bay would have had the greatest "concealed weapon" paranoia factor associated with it in the Soviets' eyes. The bay's large volume, and especially its un-interrupted length, meant that boosted "stand-off" weapons of larger size, range and payload could be carried. The possible repercussions of this seemingly minor fact should not be underestimated. At arms negotiations, weapons systems with this "you never know what it's packing" capability have always been major bargaining chips and bones of contention. Imagining what an aircraft *could* carry sometimes seems to have created more fear than many weapons that actually *were* carried.

Photo showing the size of the Arrow main landing gear leg.   (Avro Canada)

LANDING GEAR

The Arrow used a wing-stowed and rather long landing gear system that retracted inwards. Its wide stance was a strong point since it improved landing characteristics and runway stability. According to several sources, in World War II the Germans probably lost more Bf-109s due to landing and take-off accidents caused by its very narrow landing gear than through actual combat. The extremely thin wing of the Arrow caused gear-design headaches since the size of the legs and tire width were limited by the stowage thickness available. Tandem wheel assemblies were devised using very narrow, effectively solid tires to take the weight of the aircraft. The legs also twisted and shortened during retraction to fit inside the wing space available to them. Even so, there was about 14 inches of depth available in the Arrow wing.

Zurakowski related that Dowty proudly presented their design to Avro as the "most complex landing gear ever designed." Jan mentioned thinking that he would have preferred them to have designed the most simple gear ever but kept his mouth shut since the proof would be in the flight-test. Of course the proof, if negative, would risk *his* life not those of the designers!

The legs themselves were of a super-high tensile strength (280,000 psi strength), forged steel alloy to bear the stresses of a fully loaded aircraft. The legs were machined to slightly larger than finished size, then forged and heat treated to increase the strength. They were then machined down a few thousandths of an inch to final size to remove a thin brittle layer caused by the heat treatment. Some critics point to the landing gear as being the Achille's heel of the design since it was the cause of one landing accident. This accident was caused by the failure of the gear to twist the bogies to align with the aircraft centerline during extension. An internal chain linkage was used to accomplish this and a guide problem resulted in the chain hanging up. The design was modified and a similar incident never occurred again.

The gear was clearly up to its task structurally since the prototype aircraft, again with the heavy engines and nose ballast to balance those engines, plus the heavily instrumented weapons pack, were actually operating beyond the designed combat weight of the Mk. 2! The Mk. 1 test aircraft operated at a take-off weight of about 67,000 pounds while the normal gross weight of a loaded Mk. 2 was projected to be 62,431 pounds. Most importantly, the real stress on a landing gear occurs at landing. With the weight of the J-75s and their ballast, plus a heavy weapons pack, the test Mk. 1s were landing at weights far beyond what they were designed for. Even so, Avro's stress department considered that the landing gear design would have to be changed if the aircraft was ever to operate at take-off weights in excess of 80,000 pounds.

During taxi trials it was found that the brake systems were not up to the job during emergency braking tests. They were originally also designed for a slightly lighter aircraft, but, as in most all aircraft design evolutions, the weight had increased somewhat with time. (While critics again pillory Avro for weight escalations, the secret June 1955 development proposal for the Arrow states a take-off weight of *around* 60,000 pounds, little different than it was at the end.) The increase in braking force required (due to the Physics 101 formula *Force Equals One-Half Mass Times Velocity Squared*) forced some changes due to the extra weight the brakes had to decelerate. These early brakes overheated to the point where they caused some blown tires and magnesium wheel fires before they were replaced with a braking system of higher capacity. Considering the small size of the wheels and thus the area available for brake enlargement, the required increase in braking ability must have been fairly minor. Woodman related that on one of his test flights the drag-chute failed to deploy and as such he only required moderate braking, intermittently applied, to bring the Arrow to taxi speed well within the runway available. He said later that with a streaming drag-chute, the Arrow would stop within 6,000 to 6,500 feet of runway with little or *no* braking. Again, this was on a Mk. 1, which landed about 3.5 tons heavier than a Mk. 2 would have.

FLIGHT CONTROL SYSTEM:
THE WORLD'S FIRST FLY-BY-WIRE AIRCRAFT

The most advanced contemporary designs and even many current combat aircraft (like the F-15C) use a fully-powered flight control system. In other words, a mechanical/hydraulic linkage translates the pilot's control input from the stick directly into a corresponding movement of the control surfaces. Cams, levers and proportioning valves might add modifications due to performance requirements at different speeds, weights, configurations and altitudes with a powered system yet the stick still moves a valve directly that sends hydraulic fluid to a control actuator with any proportioning effect of flight control servos and artificial pilot "feel" (feedback) being a secondary "add-on."

Avro decided to develop a revolutionary control system for the Arrow. The wide speed and altitude ranges of the aircraft were major influences in this decision. So was the fact that the aircraft was the first with negative stability, in some performance regimes, intentionally built in. High angles of attack required in thin air would "blank" some of the tail fin and thus reduce its effectiveness. This is the reason why the F-15 and other aircraft have twin tails. These twin tails have the problem of producing pressure disturbances in the air which hit the adjacent tail and produce even more drag and other aerodynamic effects than just the frontal area increase would suggest.

Avro designed the Arrow with a large single fin knowing that in some potential flight conditions, especially above 40,000 feet, the aircraft could become directionally unstable. A 50 percent larger fin area was explored as were underside ventral fins to improve directional stability. Ventral fins were used on the F-104, SR-71, Convair/General Dynamics F-111, F-14, F-16 and other later designs for this reason. Avro considered the drag and performance penalties too high. Their solution was to develop a sophisticated computer-controlled flight control system. Today this is called "fly-by-wire." This system provides a wide range of advantages over the boosted concept. As speed increases in any aircraft, (at a given altitude) the amount of control input required to affect a change is reduced. A fly-by-wire system can automatically counteract this effect with the benefit that the pilot will not have the tendency to pull too hard under high-speed conditions and overstress the airframe, which could cause the aircraft to break up in flight. Similar computer parameters could prevent the pilot from again pulling too hard at slow speed and stalling the aircraft close to the ground. It also monitored the amount of skid and automatically corrected it without requiring the pilot to make constant, and perhaps humanly impossible tiny and fast corrections with the rudder. These automatic rudder inputs were accomplished without causing the pedals to move. The NAE found this unacceptable, feeling that Avro should have been able to design it without any artificial control gradients that varied with speed. With an aircraft of the speed range and performance of the Arrow, this writer is confident in saying it just can't be done effectively.

Skid (yaw) above 40,000 feet was the only dynamically unstable flight control regime of the Arrow. Dynamic instability means that if a deviation in aircraft attitude is caused by a gust or any other force, that the deviation will continue and accelerate, and uncorrected, would result in loss of control and potential aircraft break-up. (Clearly then, the XF-92A was dynamically unstable in pitch once the nose was pitched up as evidenced by the turn-tightening problem.) In the CF-105 any yaw control system malfunction detected by the system would result in it automatically switching over to the emergency system with a cockpit indication to the pilot. It is interesting to ponder the F-16 at this point. It was longitudinally unstable which means that the horizontal stabilizers actually produce lift in normal flight on this aircraft. This is highly irregular. A flight control system malfunction could cause this aircraft to pitch up and tighten its pitch rate to the point of aircraft destruction and/or the death of the pilot. This was supposedly designed in to allow a fast manoeuvre capability for the aircraft. Considering the pitch authority of the Arrow and other competent designs one must wonder if it was necessary or simply done to reduce the induced and form drag of the F-16 by making the tail provide lift thereby allowing a smaller wing.

On the longitudinal (pitch) axis, the Arrow was designed, in the words of Floyd "on the margin" of instability to ensure quick pitch control response, so necessary for good manoeuverability. At some speeds, altitudes and weights, especially above 40,000 feet, the aircraft was slightly longitudinally "relaxed" or statically unstable, which is minor compared to being dynamically unstable. In the case of a damping system failure, an oscillation induced in this case would continue, but would not aggravate itself unless the pilot mistimed his corrections. Artificial stability augmentation was added about all three axes with special attention to redundancy on the yaw axis, due to the dynamic instability in certain flight performance states.

In *Faster Than Sound,* Gunston states (page 209):

> It follows that today's aircraft designer can, from the very start of a design, plan an aircraft in such a way that it totally relies on a lightning-fast and completely reliable control system in order to fly, to manoeuvre, to avoid structural failure. This is still a fairly new capability; until about 1970 it was impossible.

An interesting passage considering he also points out, on the same page, that the first aircraft to test Active Control Technology (ACT, which allows instability to be designed in) was an Avro Lancaster in 1948-1950! Anyone who has seen video of the Arrow on final approach, with the elevators flickering every bit as fast as they do on an F-18 or F-16, will know the Arrow had "active controls."

For those who would argue based on digital "at the speed of light" response, Floyd mentioned in 2001 that the electronic portion of the Arrow's flight control computer was *digital and transistorized.*

The flight control system on the Arrow had three modes, much like the CF-18 Hornet of about twenty years later. In the automatic mode, a movement of the control stick was translated into a corresponding level of electrical output by the "stick-force transducer". This signal was measured by the command servo which, through the flight control computer, analyzed speed, altitude and other flight factors to decide exactly what the pilot wanted the aircraft to do and how best to do it. The command servo (not the stick) would then move the valves that controlled the hydraulic actuator system to produce the calculated movement of the control surfaces and the stick would follow. This happened so quickly that the system was "transparent," i.e.; it felt completely normal. Some authoritative sources have claimed the Arrow did not have a "true" fly-by-wire system. They are ill-informed. To give the pilot some feed-back as to the magnitude of change being affected on the control surfaces, and thus the corresponding stresses to which he was subjecting the aircraft, an artificial feedback system was included which translated into resistance pressures on the stick. In simple terms, this allowed the pilot to feel what the aircraft was doing in flight.

As an illustration of how far-sighted this design was, one only has to look at the second fly-by-wire combat aircraft, the F-16 Falcon, for a comparison. This design, created almost twenty years later, initially had a side stick to control the fly-by-wire system which did not move. (This was not Convair/General Dynamics' first unusual control system either. The F-106 had an odd, two-handed, narrow-forked yoke on top of their stick.) There was no stick movement to give the pilot an idea of how much of a change to the flying condition he was asking for, and no feedback to tell him how his inputs were affecting the aircraft. Early testing revealed that most pilots would find the aircraft unflyable and that, even once trained on this system, a panic situation that one could expect under combat conditions could lead to inputs of such magnitude as to cause the aircraft to break up in flight! The Arrow never experienced an emergency caused by its flight control system but its second landing accident was (perhaps wrongly) attributed to it. An early YF-16 Falcon pre-production aircraft had a pilot-induced-oscillation (PIO) crash during testing, caused by the flight control system

(and the pilot's overcompensation) which was dramatically captured on film. The Airbus fly-by-wire prototype crashed at an air show for similar reasons. The YF-22 Raptor prototype also crashed due to flight control problems resulting in pilot-induced-oscillation. Even an F-14 test aircraft (with no fly-by-wire) crashed due to PIO with one of the crew members almost parachuting into the flames of the wreck!

The Arrow engineers clearly had "all their ducks in a row" when one looks at the record. The Arrow prototypes even had a simple rheostat dial installed in the cockpit allowing the pilot to "dial up" whatever amount of stick effectiveness he desired. It must have been a blast to play with on those boring flights when the ground telemetry engineers were demanding: "OK, now one degree left yaw at 20 knots increased airspeed." On the other hand, could any flight in an Arrow be boring?

On an early test flight, Zurakowski had Arrow RL-201 suddenly dip a wing opposite to his control input on take-off. He instantly flicked off the automatic flight control system, (the switch being located by the thumb on the joystick), corrected the roll and carried on with the test flight. This demonstrated, besides Zura's grace under pressure, the inherent safety of the flight control system. Upon landing and subsequent investigation, it was found that some control micro switches were wired backwards. In Peter Zuuring's *Arrow Scrapbook* Avro is criticized for having the aircraft's wiring all of one colour. Meanwhile assembly photos of the upcoming F-22 Raptor show that nothing has changed, this because virtually all aircraft connections are Cannon plugs or Veam connectors which cannot be joined incorrectly. (This happened on the Arrow due to it being an early development aircraft.)

All flight control surfaces were actuated by dual-sided hydraulic rams having two separate and independent hydraulic systems (one from each engine) to power them. This is better than single redundancy. In effect they were like having four rams in two with two hydraulic systems to run them. Any portion of the control system could go down and at least one other way to get the job done would be available. In an extreme case, one engine could fail along with both opposing sides of a pitch or roll actuator. Even then, degraded controllability would be available from the other wing. The Arrow had the world's first flying 4,000 psi hydraulic system to minimize the size of the actuators for the thin wing and fin. The second was developed for the Rockwell B-1 bomber.

In manual and automatic modes the stick force transducer generated a voltage that was amplified and processed by the command servo. In the emergency mode, the command-servo reconfigured directly connecting to the hydraulic control valves so that a given deflection of the stick would result in a linear amount of control surface deflection. In other words half stick movement would result in half control deflection as in most powered and boosted systems. These three modes provided triple-redundancy for the flight control system itself on top of the double-redundant hydraulic systems. (Actually, since Avro's damping system was built semi-autonomously and had its own back-ups, the total system had better than triple-redundancy in many respects.) The NAE also questioned Avro's far-sighted control system design, again predicting it would break up in flight. One can imagine at least one YF-16, Airbus and YF-22 pilot would have been very happy to have had the same system in their aircraft!

So far our appraisal of the Arrow's fly-by-wire system has only looked at pilot control and stability concerns. A further advantage of this system was its ability to integrate other mission factors. One of the biggest revolutions in systems design incorporated into the Arrow was the integration of the fly-by-wire system with the fire-control system and radar. The term "fire-control system" refers to the systems involved in radar tracking, electronic countermeasures (ECM), and weapons (fire) release aspects of a combat mission. The Astra/Arrow was to integrate the ground and onboard radar systems, radar and inertial navigation systems, actual flight conditions of the aircraft and weapons release preferences into a synthetic, dynamic package, all of which combined under the pilot and backseater's control to provide the ultimate in combat system effectiveness. Avro and their subcontractors had gone a long way in this area before ASTRA was cancelled, yet the separate "black boxes" (computers) were adaptable, with some extra effort, to other radar/fire-control systems.

Unlike previous designs, and unlike almost all subsequent designs, the Arrow was designed to be controllable from the ground via data up-link. It was felt that, with the long ranges and fantastic closing rates involved in a supersonic interception, that human flightpath management and weapons release might be inefficient or impossible. For this reason the Arrow was designed to be controllable from the ground for the mid-course and attack phases of its mission with the backseater able to modify the profile, radar and ECM and other modes at will. Some say that a ground controller could land the Arrow through verbal cooperation with Precision Approach Radar (PAR), with the PAR operator talking to the remote pilot in the same way he would a "real" pilot in zero visibility. One would assume the pilot would still have to select gear-down and handle the braking and shut-down chores.

Ground radar tracking, the radar returns of the Arrow aircraft itself, its speed, altitude, weapons release parameters, closure rate and other information could be relayed literally at light speed in both directions and integrated to produce the optimum manoeuvre and weapons-release flight profile for the aircraft. This would be up-linked in real time to the aircraft flight control computer and result in both a flightpath change and control-stick movement being affected automatically in the aircraft itself. The pilot could override any of these corrections by applying a given amount of stick pressure. This was a huge leap in combat aircraft system design and is still exceptional forty years later! This was not a pie-in-the-sky, future add-on for the Arrow at the time of its flight testing. The computer "black box" (actually it was orange) to handle these chores was produced by Minneapolis-Honeywell and was installed in all the flying Arrows directly aft of the air-conditioning outlet on the spine. Incidentally, Minneapolis-Honeywell also provided the fly-by-wire control system for the second fly-by-wire aircraft, the experimental hypersonic X-15, which flew for the first time seven months after the Arrow was cancelled! Unfortunately an early X-15 also broke in half on landing due to being under-stressed despite being of mostly titanium structure. Another broke up in flight when the flight control system malfunctioned. Minneapolis-Honeywell also provided the fly-by-wire systems for the Mercury capsule and the Gemini spacecraft.

The second X-15 after a hard landing in the hands of Scott Crossfield. (NASA Dryden)

Before we look at the actual construction milestones achieved with the Arrow, once the exhaustive and computer-aided design testing was finished, it is worthwhile to look at the only competing delta-winged interceptor project: the Convair XF-92/YF-102/F-102A/F-106A program. It is a telling pity that the true facts, actual performances and real costs of this development were not known to the Canadians. They undoubtedly would have served to vindicate the Arrow program.

The USAF 1954 Interceptor Project: Trials and Errors

Much of the information in this section is based on Joe Baugher's wonderfully researched articles which are available online (see the bibliography).

In 1949 the USAF decided they needed a supersonic high-altitude fighter to counteract the intercontinental bombers that were revealed during the 1947 Tushino air show in Moscow, where the TU-4 Bull bomber (copy of the B-29 Superfortress), two jet-bombers and one jet-fighter shocked the Western military attachés who were invited to watch. This supersonic interceptor, termed the "1954 Interceptor," was to be in service by 1954. The contract attracted nine bidders. Performance expectations were similar to those later used by the RCAF for the Arrow with some notable exceptions. Intercept speeds of Mach 1.5 at altitudes up to 70,000 feet were called for, but the aircraft was only to be short to medium range. What the USAF felt was medium-range, however, was short-range according to the RCAF's requirements, which involved more fuel burned in longer-duration combat. The USAF later considered its F-101B Voodoos to be long range whereas the RCAF considered this plane to be medium range. Guided missiles, which were deployed by the Germans in World War II, were specified as the armament. The politicians accepted a single-seat, single-engine design from Convair derived from the XF-92A delta-wing X-plane. While the USAF 1954 Interceptor and RCAF OR 1-1/63 specification would share ultimate speed and altitude performance expectations, the RCAF requirement was more demanding in terms of range, crew, powerplants and onboard systems. USAF combat ceilings were also based on a 1.2G manoeuvre benchmark (i.e.; it had to sustain a 1.2G turn without bleeding energy—without losing speed or altitude) while the RCAF combat ceiling for their interceptor required a *much* more stringent 2G manoeuvre capability at the same altitude.

One submission was from Republic with their F-103 proposal. This design proposed an extremely advanced aircraft capable of achieving a Mach 4 performance at altitudes of up to 80,000 feet. This was clearly a quantum leap in the state of the art for 1949 and the F-103 was cancelled in 1957 (with only a mock-up having been built), presumably because of development difficulties.

Of the nine submitted, the two designs which were selected were, as evaluated by the USAF, the two *worst* in terms of overall technical and military merit. According to Baugher's research, the Convair design that eventually equipped the USAF as their front-line interceptor was the *worst* design in their eyes. This aircraft proposal was based upon an enlarged XF-92A from Convair, with the nose "pitot" intake giving way to a radar/fire-control system and the intakes moving to the sides. Both this and the F-103 submissions were to be partially or wholly powered by the Bristol Olympus derivative Curtiss-Wright J-67, which added an afterburner to the British engine. The F-103, however, was to employ a "variable-cycle" propulsion system, with the J-67 turbojet being by-passed at high supersonic speed, and the air fed to ramjet combustors ringing the turbojet's circumference. These were intended to more than double the high-speed thrust of the primary turbojet. This concept was similar to the 1945-46 Miles M-52 design that was produced to assault the sound barrier. The F-103 design meanwhile only had side windows and forced the pilot to view the frontal aspect through a narrow field of view with a periscope, similar to the system proposed by Avro UK in 1954 for their SR-71-similar Avro 730 design.

The Convair entry in the MX-1554 1954 Interceptor project was closely related to the experimental XF-92A which Convair had built in 1948 as a test bed to provide data for their proposed F-92 Mach 1.5 fighter. The XF-92 was designed to reach level flight speeds of Mach 1.2-1.5 yet it flagrantly refused to even break the sound barrier. So would the YF-102 except in a steep dive, where it achieved Mach 1.06. Apparently, they felt that the same basic design with more thrust would achieve the design goals.

The chubby XF-92A. The vertical stabilizer was too far forward, among other things. (USAF)

The wing design of the XF-92A had been conducted in consultation with Alexander Lippisch who had done pioneering work in Germany on tailless and delta-winged aircraft before and during the war. Dr. Lippisch was not unknown to Avro. As related in Bill Zuk's book on the Avrocar, John Frost, while working on his flying saucer theories, consulted with Lippisch in the mid 1950s. The most memorable Lippisch-inspired design was the Me-163 point-defence rocket interceptor.

Convair had become convinced that the delta configuration provided a viable solution to the problems of supersonic flight. The XF-92A had been the first powered, delta-wing aircraft to fly in the Allied nations, with the second belonging to the Hawker Siddeley Group in the form of the Avro (UK) 707 delta-research aircraft of about a year later. The F-92 project had itself been cancelled before any prototype could be built, largely because the XF-92A showed real problems with Lippisch's thick, blunt leading edge delta, and because the aircraft speed fell well short of the specification. The XF-92A was strangely promoted as a success at the time, in that it showed the delta wing, once pitched up, pro-

The Horten Ho IX. This stealthy tailless jet fighter-bomber design flew before the end of the war, promising good performance.

duced a considerable amount of additional lift. Unfortunately this aircraft also displayed a dangerous turn-tightening tendency once the nose pulled up. The cause of this, besides the leading-edge vortex, was the fact that, due to span-wise flow, the air separated *first* at the tip, which was located behind the aircraft's center of gravity, which moved the center of lift dramatically forward. In effect it was like someone jumping off a balanced see-saw causing the aircraft to pitch up and depart from controlled flight.

On 11 September 1951, Convair received a contract for its delta-wing design which was assigned the designation YF-102. Work on the competing Republic design was also authorized, and that aircraft was assigned the designation XF-103. The reason the Republic submission received the "X" for experimental while the Convair entry got the "Y" for pre-production was because the F-103 design was deemed so advanced that it was expected to take longer to

develop and thus miss the 1954 service date. Why Convair got the Y is anybody's guess considering that the XF-92A was a failure, and that Convair's Consolidated and Vultee parents had never, despite their best efforts, produced a successful fighter.

In order to expedite the development of its 1954 Interceptor program, the Air Force adopted the Cook-Craigie development method. As mentioned in the Arrow design section, the Cook-Craigie method is inherently risky and is in essence a "crash" style of development. It can result in costly and time-consuming fixes not only to the development aircraft but also to expensive hard-tooling if unexpected problems turn up. Considering however that the USAF had contracted Convair to have an operational Mach 1.5 cruising delta interceptor, using guided missiles, on the tarmac in 1954, the program needed to be a crash one.

The YF-102 was to go from paper, to hard-tooled pre-production aircraft, and if all went well, mass production and only drop the "Y" designation in the process. That Convair had learned the lessons necessary to take this bold step from the XF-92 was anything but obvious. The XF-92 and the YF-102 were substantially different designs. One significant difference being that the intake design, so crucial for supersonic flight, was entirely different between the two aircraft. But even the redesigned F-102 intake would prove inadequate and have to be redesigned and improved several times.

By December 1951, it was apparent that the Curtiss-Wright J-67 engine and the MA-1 fire-control system would not be ready in time. (Radar/fire-control development problems were also being faced at this time in providing a system for the CF-100) This forced the USAF to change its plans. At that time, the government allowed the USAF to reverse-engineer its air defence plan based on what they felt Convair would actually produce. An interim, lower-performance version of its 1954 Interceptor, was authorized to allow the USAF to get the basic interceptor into the air at an earlier (yet still later than 1954) date while a redesign was to produce an aircraft to meet the specifications. The interim version was to be designated F-102A, with the fully-developed, advanced version being designated F-102B. The F-102A's engine was to be the less-powerful Pratt & Whitney J-57 turbojet, but the F-102B was to retain the high-thrust J-67. At the same time, the J-67 engine was experiencing difficulties of its own, perhaps of a political nature, although Sir Stanley

Hooker of Bristol Aero-Engines stated in his autobiography, *Not Much of an Engineer*, that the Curtiss-Wright engineers were less than prodigal. This is because the Bristol engines were producing considerably more dry thrust (without afterburner) than the Curtiss-Wright "updated" versions, although the requirement for an afterburner meant that more unburned oxygen was required in the afterburner can, perhaps limiting the dry thrust of the Curtiss-Wright version. Avro would later be discouraged by the US from allowing Curtiss-Wright to license-produce the Iroquois, supposedly because the latter was poorly run. One must assume that some of Curtiss-Wright's problems were due to resistance on the part of the US to the production of foreign engines for US defence purposes.

With the cancellation of the J-67 engine, Convair and the USAF had to consider alternative power plants. They would finally settle on the Pratt & Whitney J-75. On 27 October 1953 the J-67 was abandoned, requiring a redesign of both the Arrow and the F-102B. By design or default this cancellation clearly didn't help the Arrow development—considering the Avro engineers felt the J-67 would be a viable engine as late as mid-1953 when the Arrow program was launched.

The F-102A would be equipped with an interim fire-control system, but the F-102B (which was later re-designated the F-106) was be equipped from the outset with the highly-sophisticated radar/fire-control system being developed by Hughes under project MX-1179 (which, in combination with the company's Falcon missiles, was known as the MA-1 system). This was to operate in a computerized ground control network. (This same fire-control system was proposed by Avro for the CF-105 but, three years after program-launch, the RCAF felt they should have a radar/fire-control system and weapons that were far more sophisticated than these ultra-high-tech American developments. According to many sources this was a fatal decision, and made the Arrow program vulnerable to American politics and American-owned companies, including Canadair which, at the time, was owned by Convair/General Dynamics.

By mid-1953, the MX-1179 fire-control system was slipping badly, and it took another year before an experimental installation could be installed aboard a T-29B for testing. Up to 1959 there was only one ground development station in operation for half of the MA-1 system's brain, the eagerly awaited SAGE network of computerized ground-control installations. (MA-1 was designed to work with SAGE, the Semi-Automatic Ground-Environment, which was a "close-control," Ground Controlled Intercept [GCI] system, something the Americans ridiculed after about 1979 when the F-15 Eagle arrived, employing the Arrow and F-4 Phantom's "autonomous," or independent, method of operation.) The SAGE network also included an inherent "licensing system," for lack of a better term, should nuclear weapons release authority ever have been sought for defence.

In reality Convair's 1954 Interceptor prototype, selected by the US government from eight superior designs (in the opinion of the USAF), barely even flew in the year in which it was originally to have entered service. When the YF-102 did fly on 21 December 1954, it too was found incapable of breaking the sound barrier and displayed only marginally improved speed performance compared to the XF-92, despite having an engine with a smaller diameter and much more power. It too "ran into the sound barrier" and could not pass. Meanwhile F-86 Sabres, both American and Canadian, were making booms with annoying regularity worldwide. The ten pre-production YF-102s, produced on expensive and laboriously produced hard-tooling were quickly halted on the production line for modification to both the aircraft and tooling.

To make the YF-102 supersonic, radical area-rule modifications were called for. The aircraft, according to a Discovery Channel "Planes of Fame" episode, required a 15-foot fuselage stretch (which must be exaggerated), pinching of the aircraft's waist, the addition of two blisters on the tail and a canopy redesign—among other things. Even the revised F-102 would prove to be a flop and resulted in an aircraft only capable of an honest Mach 1.2 after it was stretched, refined and area-ruled.

This was far from the 1954 Interceptor specification and called for another complete redesign culminating, after its own development problems, in the successful F-106. The F-102 Delta-Dagger proved in stunningly expensive style the risks of the Cook-Craigie method where pre-design ability was lacking. North American Aviation had, in the meantime, successfully used the Cook-Craigie plan to produce their F-107 fighter, which was not put into production. Shaw's *There Never Was an Arrow* points out that to merely change the F-102A into the F-106 (using the same wings and many other components) cost $150 million. Meanwhile the entire airframe, tooling and production of the first several all-original CF-105 airframes cost only about $111 million, or $118 million in US funds at the exchange rates of the era.

An F-106 Delta Dart unleashing the unguided Genie nuclear air-to-air missile. (USAF)

Much of the money that had originally been planned for the F-102B now had to be diverted into fixing the F-102A's problems and thereby provide the means to come up with a viable design for the F-102B. These problems were mainly related to structure and a misunderstanding of supersonic theory. Consequently, the F-102B fell even further behind schedule and began to lose some of its original high priority as a consequence. This was due in part to the McDonnell F-101 Voodoo arriving on the scene in 1954 and far exceeding the F-102's performance. Modifications began, to make it SAGE compatible and to turn it into an interceptor.

Seventeen F-102Bs were ordered in November 1955. The F-102B mock-up was ready for inspection in December 1955. On 18 April 1956, the USAF finalized the F-102B production contract of the previous November, earmarking all of the seventeen aircraft ordered exclusively for testing. One prototype was to be delivered in December 1956, with the others to follow in January 1957. This cautious method was far from the Cook-Craigie plan first envisioned for the 1954 Interceptor. On 17 June 1956, the designation of the F-102B was changed to F-106A. This re-designation was a recognition of the vast technical difficulties that had distorted the original F-102 program out of all recognition and the fact that the final aircraft was almost an entirely different design. It was also probably done to dispel some of the lingering aroma from the XF-92/F-102 debacle. At the same time, the USAF finalized the specifications for the 1954 Interceptor, specifications which the F-102 had so remarkably failed to approach. The specification required a maximum speed of Mach 2 at 35,000 ft with a 70,000 ft altitude capability. This performance would not be met in its entirety even by the F-106. The Arrow Mk. 1 came clos-

er while using de-rated (not developing design thrust) J-75 engines and thus being 44 percent underpowered compared to the Mk. 2 with Iroquois engines.

In late December 1956, the first F-106 flew, and also failed to meet its objectives. It was only capable of a maximum 57,000 feet and Mach 1.9 at a lower altitude. Acceleration was especially slow, taking four and a half minutes to accelerate from Mach 1 to Mach 1.7 and an additional two and a half minutes to reach Mach 1.8. Fuel control problems also caused engine "flame-out" problems and this would plague the F-106 at least until the 1961 "Dart Board" modification program was completed. Obviously, engine flame-outs are especially dangerous in a single-engine design.

By 1957 the F-101 Voodoo, originally designed as a long-range bomber-escort fighter, had been ordered into production as an interceptor, no doubt because even then the F-106 was still having serious development problems. The interim re-design of the F-101 escort fighter to carry the MA-1 interception system's brains, eyes and teeth had made this option even more appealing. SAGE and MA-1 operational experience could be gained on an aircraft that could do the same job, more and less in terms of range and speed, made it irresistible to the USAF. All interested and informed parties knew the F-101, no matter how heavily sold, could never rival Avro's Arrow. The F-101 was essentially a subsonic, or maximum Mach 1.2, combat speed aircraft at around 36,000 feet altitude and had a maximum speed of about Mach 1.6. This aircraft would be employed, second hand, by the RCAF soon after the Arrow cancellation. Even this aircraft, in RCAF hands, would sometimes beat the vaunted F-106 in Canada-US weapons competitions such as "William Tell." This must surely be a testament to the two-seat versus single-seat concept, especially where effective execution of the complex SAGE concept was concerned.

In September 1956, the USAF again reverse-engineered its requirements to suit Convair and specified that the F-106A be available by August 1958. They also specified that it be compatible with the Semi-Automatic Ground Environment (SAGE) system up to a radius of 430 miles with a combat speed of Mach 1.5 and an "intercept" ceiling of 70,000 feet. These numbers were *pure fancy* as a single-mission specification, although they were almost certainly fed to the Canadians, British, and perhaps even the Soviets! As pointed out in *Storms,* in 1958 RCAF staffers were pleading with the RCAF's Air Marshal Roy Slemon, second in command of NORAD, (the North American Air Defence Command) to try and get performance figures for the F-106 that could be compared directly with those of the Arrow. The letter asking for this pointed out that it "almost seemed as though the US was deliberately withholding this data." In 1968 the F-106A finally got long-range external tanks which extended its maximum *purely subsonic* combat radius to 375 miles! Avro's combat radii, even the slow speed ones, always included supersonic combat of at least five minutes' duration. Anyone familiar with fighter operations will have an appreciation of how much fuel that consumes. As for the F-106's 70,000 ft "intercept" altitude, it relied on the ability of the missile to climb for a significant distance to accomplish this task. The one specification the aircraft would meet was a top-speed of Mach 2 at 35,000 feet in level flight, though certainly not with external tanks.

At Avro, in an addendum to Performance Report 13 dated April 1958, an early Mk. 2 Arrow would be able to maintain about 68,000 feet for a time before having to head for thicker air. This was just after the first flight when the new drag data, from actual flight test, was not known. These "zoom ceilings" started from the various supersonic "power-limited" ceilings (at different Mach numbers) projected for the Mk. 2 from wind-tunnel testing and computer modelling. Since the Arrow was found to have about 20 percent lower drag than projected, and the Arrow Mk. 1 nearly reached the ceilings projected for the Mk. 2, one can see that the performance of the Mk. 2 would have been *far* superior to the F-106 in every respect. Indeed one performance curve the author has seen (from Performance Report 15 [PR 15]) shows the *developed* Arrow 2 as being

capable of pulling 6G at 50,000 ft. This isn't sustained G; however, the ability to make this much lift at 50,000 ft is exceptional. The F-106 was reported capable of 4G at 45,000 ft, while the F-22 Raptor is figured at 5G at 50,000 ft. Performance Report 15, released in late 1958 after the Arrow's *true* supersonic drag was quantified from flight test, also reveals the Arrow 2 would have reached 50,000 ft and Mach 2.0, 4.8 minutes after scramble order.

The F-106 intakes were also a complete re-design from the F-102, being a crude, variable-ramp type moved well aft to help address the area-rule and drag problems of the F-102. The shape of the fin and rudder were changed and a new undercarriage was fitted with steerable twin nose-wheels.

As on the F-102A and Arrow, the all-missile armament was housed internally in a ventral weapons bay. This armament consisted of a single Douglas MB-1 (Air-2A or -2B) Genie unguided rocket equipped with a nuclear warhead, plus two Hughes GAR-3 radar-homing and two GAR-4 infrared-homing (later re-designated AIM-4E and AIM-4G respectively) Falcon air-to-air missiles. The Falcons were equipped with conventional high-explosive warheads and could be launched either in salvo (all at once) or pairs but not singly. The unguided 2.75-inch, door-enclosed, folding-fin rockets of the F-102A were omitted. No gun was initially designed into the F-102, F-106 or CF-105, F-101 or F-4. The F-106 was only capable of firing *two* Falcon missiles at a time (rather than one at a time), plus the single Genie nuclear air-to-air rocket. This was due to the weapons bay doors being actuated by compressed air that was contained in an internal tank with limited capacity and no replenishment capability! In other words, the doors could be cycled a grand total of *three* times per sortie. The Arrow suffered from no such absurd operational limitation, the door actuators being powered as long as the engines were running and there was hydraulic fluid in the system.

The F-106 was initially equipped with a side-mounted control stick, but this was later moved back to the center and provided with a two-handed yoke grip for radar, weapons, navigation suite and aircraft control. This was an early effort to maximize the effectiveness of the single pilot in a demanding environment. This yoke system required having both hands doing different things on the control stick. This would make for some special challenges. First, the pilot's hand was not physically on the throttle, which is in itself an important part of the total flight-control system.

Second, the potential for hand movements involved in weapons and radar control being transmitted to the stick and thus resulting in course and tracking deviations is obvious. Both of these problems compounded the duties of the single crewmember who many experts already felt was stressed to the point of losing effectiveness in a normally degraded combat environment. The introduction, sixteen years later, of the Hands-On-Throttle-And-Stick (HOTAS) set up used in the F-16, F-18 and others improved the controllability and workload situation for the pilot but some still feel the pilot is overburdened.

The ejection system of the F-106 is another interesting topic. Originally, the F-106 had a seat similar to the F-102, this being an open, rocket-powered design similar to that used on aircraft of the day and since. Convair, with some justification, convinced the USAF that this design was inadequate for supersonic ejection and developed their own seat which was known as the "B" seat. This interesting design required the pilot to pull the "D" ring, which resulted in canopy jettison, shoulder harness and leg-garter retraction, then foot and seat pan elevation and leg guard deployment. Following this, rotational thrusters would fire, rotating the seat to a horizontal attitude at the top of the cockpit. Once there, gas-operated stabilization booms would extend, attachment bolts would explosively disconnect and the main ejection rocket motor would fire.

Of course, all of this would take time and any weak link in this pyrotechnic daisy-chain would prevent successful ejection. Time is of course very short when your aircraft is disintegrating in a fireball beneath you! Convair had devised an incredibly complicated system to optimize survival in a narrow region of the aircraft's performance envelope. Not surprisingly, there were failed ejections and pilot fatalities with this complex device. Pilots were singularly unimpressed. They demanded, and got, a reversion to a Weber seat similar to the Martin-Baker design employed on the Arrow.

In late 1961, US Secretary of Defense, Robert McNamara, proposed reopening the F-106 line for production of an additional 36 aircraft. By this time it seems the USAF was so frustrated with the aircraft's problems and delays and impressed by what they were hearing about US Navy F-4 Phantoms that the USAF Generals requested a competition between the two aircraft. This was "Project High Speed." Using the autonomous concept versus the GCI method of SAGE, the F-4's APQ-72 radar/fire-control system, also benefitting from a larger radar dish, demonstrated superior performance to the F-106's MA-1/SAGE system. As a testament to the delta wing's manoeuverability however, the F-106 proved to be the superior dogfighter. These results were diametrically opposed to expectations. As a result no new F-106s were produced and F-4Es were developed for the USAF Tactical Air Command, with a secondary interceptor function.

With the F-102/F-106 program, wing camber, cockpit arrangement, engines, intakes, radar, weapons systems, fuel systems, ejection systems, fuselages, fins, airbrakes, weapons bays and more were all modified or changed outright. Some sixty-three major changes were made to the radar/fire-control system, and sixty-seven changes were made to the F-106 airframe alone (not including changes to the F-102). The F-106's maximum speed was eventually raised to Mach 2.31 in, if competing US record-attempt aircraft are a guide, a stripped and specially tuned airframe.

A Note on Performance Specifications

It is worth noting that USAF service (not absolute) ceilings were based on the ability to sustain 1.2G at the stated altitude without losing speed or height. A 1.2G standard (or bomber) rate turn requires an angle of bank of 15 degrees no matter what the speed, height or weight of the aircraft. Similarly, a 2G steep or fighter rate turn requires an angle of 60 degrees of bank. Thus a particular G loading relating to a "combat profile" entails more than just the ability to pull a modest amount of G structurally, becoming a consideration of all the best attributes of the aircraft as a whole. Analysis of this "flight envelope" of an aircraft has forever spoken to the need for more power, less drag and more lift.

The RCAF meanwhile had established a combat specification for the Arrow even more demanding than the British convention. The British established a fighter's combat ceiling and combat altitude with the speed that could be maintained under a 1.5G turn. For OR 1-1/63 the Canadians upped this to 2G. All comparisons of US aircraft performance against the Arrow and British designs should bear in mind these more demanding British/Canadian requirements. As an illustration of this seemingly insignificant .8G turn difference between the US and Canadian rating systems, 1.2G requires an angle of bank of only 15 degrees while 2G requires a full 60 degrees of bank! Obviously, there is an *enormous* difference in the lift (and therefore thrust) required to maintain altitude between these "bomber-rate" and "fighter-rate" turns. The F-106 would realistically be roughly capable of about a Mach 1.5 combat speed at 1.2G and 50,000 ft. A far cry from the Arrow specification for a Mach 1.5 combat speed at 2G and 50,000 ft without losing energy. By the fall of 1958 Avro was projecting a Mach 1.8 combat speed at 2G and 60,000 ft, exceptional even today. (PR 15 and Floyd's testimony.)

Popularly published US figures tend to demonstrate the best singular performance numbers of a design and do not publicly tie the specifications together into a comprehensive, combat performance specification. This is a very important point for our purposes. While an aircraft may have a maximum speed of Mach 2 at 35,000 ft, its service ceiling, like on the F-16 of around 50,000 ft, may only be reached at a mere Mach 1.2 and the aircraft will have very little manoeuverability at all. Meanwhile the RCAF 7-3 Arrow specification called for the ability to sustain 2G at 50,000 ft and Mach 1.5. As for combat radius, the RCAF specification called for 200 nm on a high-speed mission and 300 nm on a low-speed mission that still included 5 minutes of air combat. Even before the F-106 was entering limited squadron service in 1959, the Arrow Mk. 1's flight test numbers had demonstrated the ability to achieve a combat radius of 575 nm on a low-speed mission with the Mk. 2 version. Again, the Avro low-speed missions included supersonic combat. The Arrow 2a, which Avro hoped to introduce on the line after the first 37 under contract, was set to achieve a 575 nm (661 statute miles) combat radius *supersonic*. Performance curves published later show that even the early Mk. 2s would have been able to sustain 2G at altitudes above those that the powerful Block 52 F-16Cs (a late production batch with much more powerful GE F-110 engines than those of the F-16A) could reach straight and level.

Arrow Production Milestones

Despite the necessity to change the Arrow design three times due to the proposed engines falling by the wayside one by one, Avro was able to turn out the first aircraft in a comparatively short time. This is impressive considering the monumental effort Avro expended in testing and research to "performance-specify" their design before construction. The British, when evaluating the Arrow project in December 1955, stated that Avro had spent about twice the money on project development compared to British projects—due to the extensive research and development program to prove the design before construction. This same British team compared the Arrow to the British "Thin-Wing Javelin" (TWJ) then in design as their supersonic all-weather interceptor, and concluded that the CF-105 was far superior, and would be cheaper to purchase "as is" from Canada than through licensed production in Britain or with substitution of British engines, weapons, or electronics. One should note that they were basing their appraisal on Avro's

Four of the men most responsible for the Arrow design (l to r): Bob Lindley, Chief Engineer; Jim Floyd, VP Engineering; Guest Hake, Arrow Project Designer and Jim Chamberlin, Chief of Technical Design (also Chief Aerodynamicist). Floyd's dark-reddish hair is already nearly snow-white from stress. As he said, the times at Avro Canada were like "controlled panic" for over a decade. The pressures of design, production and especially politics took their toll on everyone.   (Avro Canada)

drag numbers which the British further inflated for the sake of prudence. As we have seen, even Avro's lower drag estimates would prove to be considerably too high!

The first wind-tunnel tests were conducted only two months after the project go-ahead in July 1953. A wooden mock-up was completed by February 1956. Only a single year passed between project launch and the release of the first production drawings despite all the testing required to prove the design. The metal mock-up was produced largely to production type drawings and with mainly production materials and tooling. As such it helped with tooling development. Only 28 months were required from the first production drawing release to produce the hard-tooling, build a static test airframe, test the components in all the rigs already described, and actually construct the Mk. 1 prototype. On 4 October 1957 the first example of

Canada's new shining sword, Avro CF-105 Mk. 1, RL-201 was presented to the public. Minister of Defence George Pearkes, VC acknowledged, on that occasion, his agreement with the RCAF that interceptors and missiles would, in the future, prove complimentary. Sputnik also launched its tiny radio transmitter into space on that day, sparking the paranoia of the "missile age." The beautiful and ultra-sleek, even by today's standards, aircraft was an awe-inspiring sight. It was certainly an awe-inspiring performance in construction and engineering, especially considering the aircraft would exceed its performance specifications by 20 percent in the aerodynamic drag department and, even with de-rated J-75 engines, approach the specifications set for the Iroquois-engine version! It is worthwhile to consider the other aircraft designed to meet specifications even approaching those of the Arrow.

Arrow Mk. 2 vs. F-106A

Design and actual production of a hard-tooled Arrow interceptor had taken Floyd, Guest Hake (the Arrow program designer), Chamberlin, Lindley, Lindow, Pesando and so many others only forty months. By contrast, the Convair XF-92A aircraft was built in 1948 having already undergone design in consultation with Lippisch, of World War II German secret-weapons fame. Convair received a contract to produce an interceptor based on this design in September of 1951. It took a full fifty months just to produce the F-102 mock-up! The F-102, even after being stretched, would only prove capable of Mach 1.2, far below requirements! While this was going on a complete redesign was in progress to modify the F-102 to a new configuration which resulted in the F-106. The F-106 Delta Dart first flew on 26 December 1956. By this time, both the Fairey Delta Two and the Lockheed YF-104A had achieved Mach 2 in level flight. As for the F-102, its performance was clearly not up to specifications, causing the second example to be delayed until February 1957. Yet another intake redesign improved its performance. Troubles with engine reliability, the radar/fire-control system and cockpit layout caused further delays. All in all, the process from first flight of the technology demonstrator XF-92A aircraft to production of a prototype roughly equivalent to the 1954 Interceptor specification version took over *seven years* despite being a continuous priority development in all respects. It took Avro forty months to *get it right the first time!* Even so the F-106 is still considered by many to be the best interceptor the USAF has deployed. This appraisal, by USAF Air Defense Command pilots, includes the F-15 Eagle! They consider it a retrograde step in the interceptor performance regime. This praise of the F-106 could only happen in an Arrow-free environment.

The F-106's combat weight was 38,700 lb. while that of the Arrow Mk. 2 was about 62,431 lb. Respective afterburning thrust was 24,500 lbt (pounds thrust) for the developed J-75 as compared to 52,000 lbt on the Arrow Mk. 2, with two undeveloped Iroquois. This provided a combat-weight power-loading for the F-106 of 1.27 lb/lbt. The Arrow 2, using a still-limited Iroquois with a lower afterburner augmentation ratio would have had a combat weight power loading of 1.09 lbs/lbt—nearly 20 percent superior. This comparison is with an F-106 at half internal fuel. Without external tanks it was extremely limited in range.

The Arrow Mk. 2 had an internal fuel capacity 2.3 times that of an F-106 relying on two large capacity *external*

An instrumented weapons pack for the Arrow. These packs weighed considerably more than a missile pack would have. This test pack design was Kay Shaw's work. (Avro Canada)

tanks that didn't appear until the late 1960s! The Arrow also faced lower power demands per pound of airframe than the F-106 because the CF-105 had over twice the power available in an airframe with only about 25 percent greater frontal area. With a crew of two, a larger radar dish, greater weapons capacity, more excess thrust, yet 15 percent more relative internal fuel than the F-106 *with* two large external tanks, the Arrow was far and away a more effective interceptor platform. This certainly goes against Diefenbaker's statement that the Arrow was deficient in range. Indeed, it was ready to achieve a supersonic combat radius in the Mk. 2a version of at least 575 nm and do so with a combat speed of Mach 1.8 rather than Mach 1.5! This range performance is very nearly *three times* the RCAF specification. As Jan Zurakowski reiterated in a note in August 2001, when Diefenbaker explained his reasons for Arrow cancellation to the House of Commons, it was due to a perceived shortcoming in range. Zura also wrote that Diefenbaker reinforced this impression in public. Range is about the only thing that remained classified, to the extent that Avro couldn't legally challenge the statements in public.

CHAPTER FIVE

The ASTRA Radar/ Fire Control System

Just Slightly Ahead of Its Time

THE RCAF REQUIREMENT for the Arrow weapons system was essentially a long-range extension of the USAF "1954 Interceptor" specification, but with systems requirements above those of the American aircraft due to the RCAF's choice of the autonomous concept vs. the GCI (ground control intercept) network, which became SAGE. This was necessary to cover the large, hostile wilderness areas of Canada, which could not be achieved without enough ground radars, airfields and aircraft to allow a short or medium range aircraft to do the job. It was a wise and far-sighted decision. Nothing can cover Canada's land and sea territories like aircraft.

Avro assumed, from 1953 to 1956, that the RCAF would choose the Hughes MX-1179 airborne radar set, then under crash development in the US, and the Hughes Falcon/Genie missile systems, which together made up the MA-1 system. This too was a logical choice since the US was pouring Fort Knox into these systems and their SAGE ground environment. It was not, however, *deployed* as one reference book states. Even by 1959 there was only one SAGE development site in the US, and the F-106 would not enter service with MA-1 and SAGE until 1960. Initially contracted for 1951, the 1954 Interceptor system was indeed a long development program. The F-102 was also intended to deploy MA-1 and SAGE, but they were not ready. The F-102 was forced to use the same basic radar system as the late Avro CF-100s.

The RCAF decided as a result that the Arrow required an extremely advanced system in order to operate alone in a

AN/APQ - 72 STARBOARD SIDE

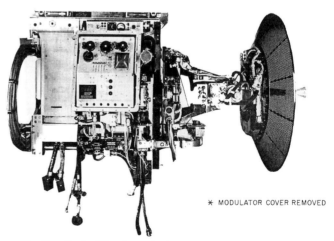

* MODULATOR COVER REMOVED

The Best Radar/Fire Control of the 1960s, the Westinghouse APQ-72 for the F-4 Phantom II   (Historical Electronics Museum)

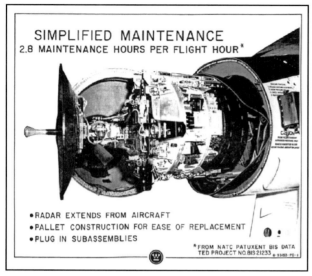

SIMPLIFIED MAINTENANCE
2.8 MAINTENANCE HOURS PER FLIGHT HOUR *

• RADAR EXTENDS FROM AIRCRAFT
• PALLET CONSTRUCTION FOR EASE OF REPLACEMENT
• PLUG IN SUBASSEMBLIES

*FROM NATC PATUXENT BIS DATA
TED PROJECT NO. BIS 21233

A page from a Westinghouse product package promoting the APQ-72's "new" features from around 1960. Advertised as being firsts, the rack mounting and extension system were actually first applied to ASTRA.   (Historical Electronics Museum)

heavily jammed environment. Chief of Operational Requirements, AVM Easton, headed an investigation of the systems in development and evaluated the Hughes MA-1 system and SAGE. The conclusion, with perhaps too much foresight, was that the MX-1179 radar would not be integrated enough with the aircraft flight control system for accurate automated weapons delivery, and would not have sufficient search and track range to make the most of the speed and range capabilities of the Arrow airframe. Easton also found the Falcon missile deficient in many respects. The Falcon was an unreliable missile right through the 1960s, and by the time it was fully developed, was obsolete compared to the Sparrow and Sidewinder alternatives. Early versions didn't even have proximity fusing, meaning the missile was supposed to bury itself in the target airframe before it would detonate. This doesn't happen often, since only the first part of a missile's flight is actually powered by the rocket, after which the motor quits and the weapon relies on inertia, and many modern missile "kills" result from the missile exploding close to the target, rather than driving into it. Another shortcoming the RCAF saw was the requirement with most radar-guided missiles to keep the target illuminated by the aircraft radar. This can make the intercepting aircraft vulnerable since it means the aircraft must generally keep closing the distance to the target bringing it progressively into the target's defensive weapon envelope.

For 1956 however, the ASTRA and the Sparrow 2D systems were very wishful thinking. ASTRA was to include full integration of the navigation functions, radar, data-link from the ground, electronic countermeasures and inputs of the navigator/weapons officer with the flight control system of the aircraft. Since the Arrow flight control system was built with "fly-by-wire" technology, this was at least possible. It seems that when Avro discovered that the RCAF wanted a fully digital and fully transistorized "all-can-do" intercept *and* bombing set, Avro balked. Avro seems to have mitigated, quite forcefully, for a two-phase program consisting of an interim ASTRA 1, and a fully digital and solid state ASTRA 2. They hoped the ASTRA 2 set would be ready for service by the time the Arrow's trials and development were completed and the service Arrow 2s were coming off the assembly line.

It is worth exploring the top radar system deployed during the 1960s before looking at ASTRA in detail. We will not get too far into the MA-1/SAGE system here since it is described elsewhere in this volume. MA-1/SAGE, as deployed in the F-106A at least, was also surpassed by the APQ-72 system of the F-4 Phantom II.

According to documents generously provided by the Historical Electronics Museum in Linthicum, Maryland (established and formerly sponsored by Westinghouse), the APQ-72 was begun on 30 August 1957—well after ASTRA was underway. It was supposedly a development of the APQ-50 system in use in some US Navy aircraft but this seems unlikely due to the much more advanced nature of the APQ-72. The APQ-50 used an electrically-actuated emitter/receiver (dish) of only 24 inches diameter, and was only a "search" and gun-laying radar. The APQ-72 by contrast had a hydraulically slewed dish of 32 inches diameter and included passive missile guidance and launch computation plus ground mapping, navigation, ECM (electronic countermeasures), a secondary passive search and tracking system using infra-red, home-on-jamming and other features. It was quite a leap in capability from the APQ-50.

ASTRA meanwhile had all of these abilities and more, and was the first radar in the West to use infra-red detection and tracking. ASTRA was to manage fully active homing missiles however, something that would not be deployed in the US until the 1990s. ASTRA also had more polarization options for the antennae, which improves detection, tracking and ground mapping resolution in rain and bad weather.

The first Westinghouse APQ-72 development set was delivered in December 1958, three months after ASTRA

The Astra mock-up radar, shown in a frame from Avro footage, being extended out the nose of the Arrow wooden mock-up. Its rack mounting system, suspended on shock mountings, was to isolate the system from vibration and shock, plus allow for easy access for servicing. It was the first to use such a system. (Aviation Videos)

was cancelled. It cost the US only one million dollars to develop this set according to estimates included with the documentation, while over twenty times this amount was spent on ASTRA. The first production APQ-72 was completed a year after the development set. The first ASTRA 1 (analogue) development set was delivered in June 1958 after over two years' development.

APQ-72 was fully analogue and used miniature vacuum tube technology. As such it was not a "look-down, shoot-down" system although it was regarded to be a major advance in this area. This also meant it had difficulty discerning ground features and moving targets below the aircraft horizon due to ground clutter. Real "look-down, shoot-down" systems didn't appear in service until later since they require very clean microwave generation and sophisticated filtering to remove ground clutter. The first step in this progress was development of a solid-state microwave source producing a clean digital signal. Further advances came about once the processors and filters became transistorized and digital and thus able to make use of the digital output of the new signal generator. The APQ-72 was pitted against the MA-1/SAGE system in the 1960 USAF *Project High Speed* competition between the F-106 Delta Dart and the F-4 Phantom II. As mentioned previously, the results were opposite to what was expected. The F-4 was found to have the superior radar while the F-106 was found to be a better dogfighter. Since APQ-72 used vacuum tubes, it required a great deal of

cooling. Fully three quarters of the APQ-72 system's power was used to cool the system leaving only one quarter for signal generation, reception and processing. ASTRA meanwhile reversed these two figures, leaving something like three times the output available for the real purposes of a radar/fire-control system.

The first digital "look-down, shoot-down" radar to fly, according to Westinghouse at least, was the "Coherent Pulse Radar" developed by Westinghouse on top of their basic APQ-72. This unit used transistors and included digital signal filters and a solid-state microwave source. As we show elsewhere however, APG-18 for the F-108 and later the YF-12A was also obviously an earlier, perhaps ASTRA contemporary "look-down, shoot-down" system. Westinghouse's Coherent Pulse system first flew in 1967, however it was not combat capable since it was designed to show the improvement over the old system and thus only a portion of the scan area was processed digitally, the majority of the scan area being handled by the "noisy" tube technology and analogue filtering. This Coherent Pulse system seems to have been developed into the set for the early F-16 Falcons, a set which lacked any radar missile capabilities. The ground mapping and other refinements certainly improved safety for the crews if nothing else. When the history of the Hughes ASG-18 and APQ-72 are considered against the Westinghouse announcement, it seems the digital aspects of Hughes' work were part of the American "Black" development list and no word of its core technology was to leak out. Again the implication is that many technologies evolved, secretly, somewhat earlier than conventional wisdom suggests.

The AWG-9 of the ill-fated USN F-111B and later F-14 Tomcat, was a better "look-down, shoot-down" radar, however it still used analogue filtering which made it something of a middle step in the evolution. The AWG-9 took over honours as the best radar in the West from the old APQ-72 system when it was deployed in the F-14A Tomcat. It had some digital processing and a solid-state microwave source yet it still required a fair amount of miniature vacuum tube and analogue hardware. It became the best radar of the 1970s and early 1980s until it went fully digital as the APG-71, but ran into competition from the F-15's APG-65, again by Hughes.

In contrast to the APQ-72 system of the Phantom, ASTRA used 75 percent of its power for processing and signal generation. Total power was about the same as the APQ-72 therefore it was about three times as efficient, and would have something like three times the effective range. ASTRA had a huge dish of 38 inches helping its range and accuracy. How did ASTRA 1, in 1958, achieve this efficiency? It was transistorized and thus required little cooling. In fact ASTRA appears to be the first transistorized radar of any capability for interceptors. After detailed study of the APQ-72, including how the switches are designed and arranged, it really seems as though the APQ-72 was nearly identical to ASTRA 1 in most visible respects. Westinghouse claimed the APQ-72 was the world's first integrated, retractable, chassis-mounted radar. In reality ASTRA 1 was. Indeed ASTRA, like the APQ-72 was rack-mounted on a vibration and shock isolating carriage that could be extended out the front of the aircraft for servicing. Even the ground connections were virtually identical for the test/cooling/power cart. APQ-72 appears to be only slightly less sophisticated than ASTRA 1 in all modes of operation and was advertised as the second system to include an infra-red detection and tracking function in the West. Again ASTRA was first although the MA-1 system would be modified, in some cases, to accept it. APQ-72 was far inferior however in two key respects: it was not fully transistorized, and it did not have a digital-ready signal source. By the time they crammed it into the expanded nose of the F-4B, it also had a slightly smaller dish.

ASTRA was announced by C.D. Howe as a "go" in June of 1956. Avro was mortified since they knew full well the technical hurdles they would have to overcome for this "all singing-all dancing" system. Despite their consistent objections they were tasked with project management. For some reason the USAF did not want Hughes to develop ASTRA. The RCAF approached Hughes to see if they would undertake the project. They were offered the Hughes MX-1179 and Hughes Falcon missiles (together making up the MA-1 system) or nothing. Hughes would be contracted to build the system for the F-108 Rapier, and there can be little doubt that work was started on this set before ASTRA was added to the Arrow project in mid 1956, since studies and development were already ongoing for the USAF Long Range Interceptor Experimental (LRIX). The RCAF would undoubtedly have wanted it, if this system's mid-1960s performance in the YF-12A is any indication.

Avro's trade discussions would certainly lead them to suspect a serious evolving digital system even while they were trying to get the MA-1 system operational. One might wonder if the fact that they would not build ASTRA, which was very ASG-18 similar, provoked the RCAF to demand a system with those attributes, which was what the ASTRA system was, and this led them to shop elsewhere.

ASTRA certainly cost Canada far more than the APQ-72 and perhaps even the ASG-18 system yet Canada received only the MA-1 system, a tube technology system tied to ground control and indeed, as deployed in NORAD, tied to USAF control. Nearly every book on the subject of the Arrow states that ASTRA technology was given freely to the US agencies around the date of ASTRA cancellation, September 1958. Without question, Avro worked cooperatively with the American designers whenever possible. All Arrow performance reports that the author has seen, including the annexes, appear to be written as though Avro assumed the appropriately cleared USAF sources would be copied as a matter of course. The inclusion of "mission 7" in these performance reports was tailored exactly for the USAF to compare with their LRIX specification.

Westinghouse would have been in the ideal position to capitalize, based on their primary subcontractor arrangement with RCA Camden, the ASTRA prime-contractor. It would be interesting to know who developed the digital microwave source at the heart of ASTRA and ASG-18 and probably AWG-9 for the F-111B and Tomcat. It is clear that Avro knew Hughes was at work on an advanced "pulse-Doppler" radar for the F-108 at least as early as 1957. Jim Floyd does not recall the name ASG-18 being applied at this time however, while it was his department's document that mentioned Hughes pulse-Doppler work at the time.

Officially, the USAF apparently felt Hughes was overburdened with the MA-1 system and were trying to ensure another manufacturer could compete with Hughes, thereby securing an alternate supply source. They suggested the RCAF contract RCA (Camden, New Jersey) to do the job and the RCAF complied. It seems odd that RCA became the primary supplier for ASTRA considering Westinghouse's much greater experience in developing intercept and ground mapping radars. It was for good reason they chose Westinghouse and Minneapolis Honeywell as secondary contractors. Minneapolis Honeywell were of course well qualified considering their later success with the fly-by-wire systems for the Arrow, North American X-15, the SR-71, NASA's Mercury and Gemini. Once developed, all ASTRA production was to be done in Canada. Much of the development was done there as well.

The navigator's "office" in the Arrow mock-up with the ASTRA suite. Switches, displays and modes were virtually identical to those used in the APQ-72, with the advantage going to ASTRA in flexibility and some key display areas. Electronic sophistication was another story altogether. (Avro Canada)

RCA Camden was however a good choice for the ASTRA development, in that they had produced the single greatest electronic advance of the century to that date—they invented the television. Turning an image into an electrical signal, transmitting it, receiving it and turning it back into an image are nearly all techniques employed in radar.

The ASTRA development, according to a 1957 RCA ASTRA progress report, was to follow two steps, designated ASTRA 1 and ASTRA 2. ASTRA 1, including the development set, was to be fully transistorized but used an analogue processor. Avro also added a third stage to the development, seeing as it was so challenging, and made the first sets manual, with automated features being added after the first 15 development flying sets. This would make the manual set virtually identical to the APQ-72 with the automatic set very close to the AWG-9 developed for the F-111B, and improved for the F-14 Tomcat. The ASTRA 2 system, once the parameters were set out in the analogue system, was to be fully transistorized and fully *digital*. ASTRA 2 was also, apparently, to be a pulse-Doppler set if schematics reproduced in *Arrow Scrapbook* are a guide. As such it would be at least equal to the ASG-18 and AWG-9 of the never-adopted US Navy F-111B and more probably approaching the sophistication of the digital version, the

APG-71 of the late 70s. If Air Vice Marshal Easton's representations are accurate, his specification was superior to anything even on the boards in the United States, and he surely would have known about Hughe's pulse-Doppler system if it was in development when the RCAF went shopping. Combined with the Arrow's fly-by-wire system such a radar/fire control system would not be equalled in intent and core technology until the F-18 Hornet, although ASTRA would likely have had longer range.

No wonder Avro was resisting this additional requirement for the Arrow and were predicting extreme expense for ASTRA! Would they have pulled it off? They appear to have done so, with the mostly analogue ASTRA Mk. 1 development set. Documents suggest that at least the 37 development Arrows would have been equipped with a semi-transistorized Mark 1 set. Once all the parameters were established in the analogue set, emulating them, and improving them digitally would be relatively simpler. The question remains if ASTRA 1 had the digital signal source or not, and if so whether it was perfected. The cooling and signal generation ratios suggest it was. The fully digital all-can-do ASTRA Mk. 2 set would surely have been expensive although they were well along by September 1958 when it was cancelled.

The analogue ASTRA-1 development set. Its transistorization (and klystron tube digital source?) still made it about 15 years ahead of its time as service samples go. The ASTRA-2 digital set was even more advanced. (via Peter Zuuring)

Avro's program management of ASTRA, reluctant or otherwise, made them privy to, and indeed responsible for, all the technology *and* how it was integrated in not only ASTRA but into the onboard systems of the fly-by-wire and data-link-flyable Arrow, and indeed with the parent company's Iroquois. All of this means that Avro was involved in the cutting edge in all the major aerospace sciences and were indeed contracted for aircraft, missiles, engines, electronics, fire-control systems, and so much more. No aviation corporation in the world, really, had this range of boasting rights. But then Avro had little choice considering the tasks they undertook on behalf of the government of Canada. As we have seen, some of the government research establishments were far less advanced in technologies like supersonic aerodynamics.

Some might ask if it is valid to claim this development was "Canadian" since much of it was done at RCA in the United States. This development, however, only took place as early as it did because Canadians paid for it. Derek Wood makes an excellent case in *Project Cancelled* to show that a considerable amount of American technological development was paid for by the British. In Nicholas Hill's article "Blue Streak— Its Brief Life as a Weapon," he agrees with Wood, as do many other researchers.

Arguably the US intelligence services had the information, or much of it, before cancellation of ASTRA anyway. Such cutting edge technology would be a normal target of the CIA's industrial espionage section. Meanwhile in Bill Zuk's *Avrocar* work, there is a lovely photo of Avro's John Frost with a very Cold Warrior looking General Trudeau, apparently head of the US Army foreign intelligence office. Anyone who has read LCol Philip J. Corso's *The Day After Roswell* will have gained some familiarity with this gentleman. According to Corso, he was a wise gentleman with a distrust of the CIA's methods and motives!

Once Hughes had turned down the ASTRA development, they suddenly started development of a "look-down, shoot-down" radar of their own which, coincidentally, shared a 38 inch dish and the ability to manage fully active homing missiles. This was for the LRIX contract, won by North American Aviation with the F-108 Rapier. It has been discussed how "Arrow similar" the F-108 was. During tests of this system in the YF-12A, this radar was found to have a detection range of up to 500 miles, and a missile launch at Mach 3 and 70,000 feet hit a target flying at very low altitude. This target was travelling head on to the launch aircraft, which definitely improved the radar's ability to track it and also suited the missile's easiest flight path, yet it was an astounding performance nevertheless. The later AWG-9, again by Hughes, really only has a reliable detection range of around 150 miles. This leaves a big question of course. Why the backward progress?

Four possible scenarios present themselves: AWG-9 has a much longer range than advertised, the ASG-18 figures were highly "massaged," or radar progress was actually reversed to allow the Soviets to (almost) keep up. The Soviets supposedly did not develop a "look-down, shoot-down" radar until the 1980s and all of their units up to this time were tube technology. A fourth option is a combination of the above, and this is the probable truth of the matter.

Obviously much of the above, as to reasons for events, is speculation, but one must admit APQ-72 came pretty cheap and fast, while the ASG-18 also bears dramatic similarities to ASTRA. It took Hughes, now the acknowledged leader, nearly a decade to field the MA-1 system and nearly as long to get the ASG-18 into the YF-12A.

When the Diefenbaker government later needed to build a Doppler-radar bombing capability for the F-104 Starfighter, they discovered Canada had the ability "in-house" due to previous experience in developing ASTRA. This is admitted in Cabinet documents. Despite how similar RCA-Westinghouse ASTRA 1 and the Westinghouse APQ-72 really were, Canada officially signed-off on ASTRA/Sparrow technology in 1958 and with that the right to blame the US for their success, or share in the profits!

An Iroquois engine in the Orenda facility. While it appears simply massive, it was comparatively small and light for the thrust output.
(Orenda Engines)

THE FIRST SUPERSONIC FIGHTERS (under the C-104 designations) Avro presented to the RCAF all-weather requirements team contemplated installation of Orenda TR-9 "Wakunda" powerplants providing around 12,000 pounds of dry thrust. The government and RCAF were not interested in funding this engine since British and American aero-engine manufacturers were developing several engines of this thrust class including the Rolls-Royce Avon (nearly 10 years after it was conceived) and the General Electric J-79. The Wakunda was a logical evolution of the Orenda incorporating more compressor rotors. It was a Winnett Boyd design suggesting it may not have been two-spool and if this is the case it would have been a questionable advance. Some at Orenda, the Canadian government and the RCAF wanted to leapfrog all developments on the boards at the time. The reasoning behind this risky decision was to hopefully extend the useful life span of the RCAF's next generation interceptor, and thus in the end save money.

Orenda and A.V. Roe Canada also wanted to up the ante and develop an engine with the highest thrust-to-weight and size ratios dreamed of at the time. Their reasoning was simple. Potential customers such as the US, Britain and France did not possess, and were unlikely to possess for some time, an engine of this power and efficiency. They knew all too well that to sell an engine abroad, it must be clearly and markedly superior. Considering the "Buy American Act" and the American track record in this regard, A.V. Roe's reasoning was sound.

Orenda's designers decided upon a bell-mouth opening of 42 inches, the same as what had been designed into the engine bays of the CF-105 design when the Rolls-Royce RB-106 was proposed. This powerplant was cancelled after some work on the Arrow design had been completed and resulted in Avro then turning to the Curtiss-Wright J-67 turbojet for propulsion. This engine, licensed from Bristol's non-afterburning Olympus design, would also be cancelled, affecting not only the Arrow design, but that of the competing F-102B/F-106, the XF-103 and other aircraft as well.

Orenda had not designed the Iroquois for the Arrow project however. It was begun under a private venture by A.V. Roe Canada Ltd. simply to produce the most high-technology, and high-thrust supersonic engine in the world. The size of 42 inches was probably meant to suit the engine for any aircraft the Olympus, Gyron, and J-75 could fit, and thus help fill the void left when the J-67 and RB-106 were

CHAPTER SIX

The Mighty Iroquois

The Sound of Freedom?

cancelled. Due to the failure of anyone else to produce an engine approaching the technology of the PS-13 Iroquois, Orenda had taken on a serious challenge. In retrospect, the Iroquois would very likely have realized all performance expectations, and probably would have become the top supersonic engine for at least the next ten years, and still one of the very best today. It arguably could have been the propulsive "defender of the free world" for at least a quarter century, largely undeveloped. As the specifications to follow will demonstrate, probably the best engine to actually enter service, then or since, in terms of thrust to frontal area, was the Bristol Olympus in its various forms. The Iroquois had been designed to exceed the Olympus in all measures from the beginning.

The early, undeveloped Iroquois, in 1956 during an early endurance test, was developing the highest dry, and afterburning thrust figures for turbojet engines, to the best of the author's knowledge, on the planet! It was doing so with about a third fewer parts and less weight than the other emerging high performance military turbojets. The Iroquois Mk. 2 specification also proclaimed about a 10 percent fuel efficiency advantage over these emerging designs dry, and was about 25 percent better wet. Considering the relatively low compressor ratio (chosen for high altitude high speed performance) this was quite an achievement. Simply put this engine was designed to be, and showed every promise of becoming the most powerful, lightest, simplest and most fuel efficient engine on the globe. The PS-13 also had a smaller compressor bell-housing inlet diameter than these generally later designs. This means lower installed size and thus less aerodynamic drag. Further to the size consideration, the Iroquois also had much of its machinery located *inside* the engine. What remained attached around the outside of its outer case was arranged and sized so that even this dimension was proportionally smaller than on most contemporary, and later designs. All of these advantages gave it quite an efficiency advantage and meant that an aircraft using it could carry less fuel, be smaller and lighter, and fly faster and higher. This would have made it irresistible to anyone wanting cutting edge performance for defence and also would allow an airframe, such as the B-52, to have its life and performance extended.

The Iroquois had more than its share of "firsts," though probably not one advance that is commonly attributed to it. It was the first two-bearing/two-spool design, using one combination (combining thrust and radial loads) bearing assembly for the compressor, and one for the turbine rather than the usual three bearing set-up using one set at each end of the compressor, and another at the turbine section. To do so the central casing had to be dispensed with, and to do this the central core of the engine was made to rotate on inner and outer tapered drum-shafts, one rotating inside the other. All the stator sections had to be suspended, between the rotating blade sections, from the outer case. It was thus an "overhung" design and was revolutionary in concept. Aspects of this concept were copied far and wide. Orenda probably got part of the idea, that of a drum type rotor rather than a thin shaft, from Hermann Oestrich's work on the French ATAR engines.

The Iroquois used an audacious (for the day) compressor design using only 10 sections consisting of 3 low-pressure (LP) and 7 high-pressure (HP) rotor discs. Most contemporary and later 2-shaft turbojet engines would use between 15 and 17 stages to do the same work. Two-spool engines using as few as 10 to13 sections would not appear in service until the F-18 Hornet and F-15 Eagle respectively. An engine of the same thrust but using one less compressor section is slated for service in 2010 with the F-22 Raptor. Less blades in the way of airflow in an engine increases the miniaturization potential, but more work is required of each remaining stage. For the Iroquois excellent compressor matching design capability was a stringent requirement for success since so much more work had to be done by fewer parts. Meanwhile single shaft designs, such as the ATAR turbojets in the Dassault fighters, were using 7 to 8 compressor sections yet were only producing slightly better than half the thrust from the same diameter and length.

To generate the mass airflow required in such a small package, the Iroquois designers developed a transonic first stage. In other words, across the length of these blades the airflow was expected to be at or above the speed of sound. This was a huge step. This develops supersonic "shock-waves" usually deemed destructive and unmanageable across a rotating, ambient air pressure-fed fan arrangement. (For illustration, one can see how all piston-engined aircraft tried to turn the propeller mostly within the speed of sound as measured at the blade tips. RPM above this could induce such twist and vibration as to threaten the engine and aircraft structure, not to mention the prop was not effective above this speed and tended to cavitate. Current turbofan engines, such as Sir Stanley Hooker's Rolls-Royce RB-211 used in many commercial jet passenger aircraft, turn the front fan so that the tips are at

The USAF was very interested in the Iroquois to power the B-52 and other aircraft. It would have provided a major performance boost and made less smoke.   (image by R.L. Whitcomb)

Mach 1.5. Avro had, many years ahead, jammed a transonic front fan in the first stage of a turbojet engine. This was radical thinking. Again, engine strength and thus materials, were critical factors. So was the need for Orenda to have their aerodynamics down cold! Harry Keast and Burt Avery were on the job; brilliance un-impeached by right of the category-leading Orenda engine used in the CF-100 and the best Sabres (Canadair-built CF-86s) flying in NATO, the RCAF and in other nations. They also had in the company the best digital computer technology with which to crunch the numbers.

All in all, Orenda had taken on some real challenges. They were, quite simply, determined to produce quantum leaps in engine aerodynamic, structural and material design, and to do so using largely undeveloped technologies, ones that Orenda considered would be viable in combination. The Iroquois was, in reality, taking advantage of the most visionary thinking in the field up to that date, yet was contributing a number of its own innovations.

As such, the Iroquois 2 specification (which probably only the Iroquois 3 would have met reliably) quoted a record shattering mass air flow of 350 lbs per second according to the period publication *Aircraft Engines of the World*. Since the Iroquois apparently exceeded even

the lofty dry thrust figure of this Mk. 2 spec (23,000 lbt) on early test, it must be assumed the engine would do this mass flow. This figure is still un-matched for an engine of a similar diameter to the author's knowledge. Of course mass flow is the yardstick, compared against diameter and weight, by which any engine is measured. For the PS-13 it is a figure about 35 percent better than the larger and heavier Pratt & Whitney J-75 which would power the F-106 Delta Dart, Republic's F-105 Thunderchief and the Lockheed "Skunk Works" U-2 Spyplane. A mass flow of 350 lbs per second is considerably better than that of the engine that powers the SR-71 Blackbird, the Pratt & Whitney J-58, an engine with 44 percent larger frontal area and 1,700 lbs more weight. The J-58 was also about five years later in coming and was a single shaft design.

As specified, the Iroquois would have given the CF-105 a range and performance advantage over any other designs. It could have given the A-12/YF-12/SR-71 a real performance boost, and would have been available sooner. Indeed documentary testimony from the USAF mentions their interest in having the PS-13 power the B-52 particularly, and other aircraft potentially. Republic later offered an Iroquois equipped F-105 Thunderchief as a defense pro-

Engine men (l to r): Charles Grinyer, W.R. McLachlan (V.P. Orenda Engines) and Rolls-Royce's Lord Hives. (Jet Age)

duction and development sharing option, with the USAF to receive some. Based on performance by inch of size, thrust to weight and fuel economy, the Iroquois should have powered many category leading aircraft thereafter! But then, the USAF was always interested in having the best equipment, as was the case with the Avro Jetliner, but was almost never allowed to procure it due to restrictions from political sources. The English Electric Canberra bomber (USAF Martin B-57) and the later Hawker Harrier (license built by McDonnell Douglas) are notable exceptions. The larger trend notwithstanding, a service Iroquois living up to its expectations would have been extremely hard for even the Americans to resist.

Even the XB-70 Valkeyrie would have benefitted from installation of the PS-13 since this engine was over 10 inches smaller in diameter and still lighter than the GE J-93's it flew with yet had roughly the same design thrust! It has also been pointed out (by former Pratt & Whitney America engineer Evan Mayerle) that the Iroquois would have been an ideal "core" engine for a high-output turbo-fan version for airliners. Orenda had a high compression ratio version of the Iroquois in design for use at lower altitudes and speeds. It is known that Convair looked at non-afterburning engines of the Iroquois thrust class as potential powerplants for the B-58 Hustler. It is also known that Convair/General Dynamics tried to acquire Iroquois technology after Black Friday and had looked hard at the engine earlier. Such engines would allow this (and other) aircraft to cruise supersonically while avoiding afterburner use, improving the aircraft's range and payload. The good fuel consumption figures the low-compression Iroquois 2 achieved boded very well for a very economical high-compression non-afterburning civil version. Orenda appeared

to have been studying turbofan variants also using the Iroquois basic core. Had this born fruit a turbofan engine of the size capable of powering today's largest jumbo-jets might have appeared several years early.

As it stands, Orenda was working on at least three versions of the Iroquois: the Iroquois 2 high-performance high-altitude engine, the Iroquois 3 even higher performance military turbojet, and a high compression high-fuel-efficiency commercial or lower altitude and speed military version. This is speculation, but the author believes that the Iroquois 2 turbine section would be mated to an enlarged compressor section including a fan section for a very high efficiency turbofan. This is because it appears that the turbine section was actually over capacity compared to the compressor on the Iroquois 2. It seemed to overdrive the compressor resulting in requirements for rotor brakes and compressor spill ducts to vent the compressor when it reached too high a compression and temperature state. Using this turbine section to drive an additional fan stage at the front of a turbofan version of the Iroquois seems to make too much sense for Orenda to have dismissed it. Turbofan version or not, the efficiencies promised by a high compression version of the Iroquois 2 or 3 engines promised to make them commercial and lower speed and altitude military engines *par excellence.*

Apart from the transonic first compressor stage, the Iroquois had another interesting feature. It was designed to bleed compressor air from around the LP compressor, through the ancillary machinery enclosure, to the hot section and afterburner shroud. This would help cool the engine and allow an increase in mass flow. To do so Orenda enclosed the machinery section in a sealed shroud that forced the air to eject rearward between the inner and outer walls of the engine's variable nozzle. In reality this made it a by-pass turbojet, a concept the author has not found on any previous engine. The J-58 for the A-12/YF-12A/SR-71 however would later employ this concept using tubes arranged around the outside of the engine but forcing the air back into the afterburning section. It was a great concept and would be developed further on the engines for the F-15, F-16, F-18, MiG-29, SU-27 and others. This would be done somewhat differently however, making their designs lie between the Iroquois concept and the pure turbofan. The F-119 for the F-22 shares with the Iroquois the descriptor "low-bypass turbojet" although for some reason fashion has now decided to call all these later engines turbofans.

The Iroquois does not appear, contrary to popular "Arrowhead" belief, to have been the first jet engine to use the annular combustor. The ATAR engines, developed in France by Hermann Oestrich, were already employing the annular combustor and were flying in the Mystere II by the mid 1950s. Indeed Oestrich's World War II design, the BMW 003 engine, used an annular combustor. Similar to the American "Operation Paperclip," Oestrich's team had been "liberated" by the French authorities from German internment camps at the end of World War II and secreted away to develop the ATAR engines. One of the resultant engines, the ATAR 101, was producing the same dry thrust as the TR-5 Orenda engine in the same timescale. On the Iroquois design Orenda borrowed Oestrich's brilliance, and that of another German engineer (Gerhard Neuman, discussed later), and turned both concepts into functioning engines that exemplified the student exceeding the master. Oestrich's ATAR annular-flow designs were producing, by 1957, less than half the thrust of the similarly sized PS-13 at the time.

The Iroquois, unlike the earlier TR-5 Orenda, employed an annular combustor. All other engines, aside from the already noted BMW and ATAR exceptions, fed the pressurized air from the compressor section into cylindrical-shaped cans or flame-tubes arranged radially around the engine, right behind the final compressor stator section. Orenda chose to dispense with separate cans and made the entire combustion area one connected "doughnut." All modern jet engines use annular combustors yet many that followed the ATAR and Iroquois designs used the "cannular" design, something of a hybrid between the pure can design and the annular arrangement. These tended to be heavier, use more fuel, and make more smoke (smoke of course being a very bad thing for stealth). The annular concept promised to overcome these problems provided they could make the design resistant to a combustor flameout.

In case of just such a contingency the Orenda engineers developed, and patented, the first oxygen re-light system. While they were the first, they would certainly not be the last to use this concept. This innovation would prove very advantageous for high-altitude flight where there is little oxygen, and where, as a result, the engine demands a very high amount of airflow to be rammed into the intake. A flow disruption, such as a compressor stall, or combustor flameout, would severely limit the re-light potential in such a flight condition since any flow disruption would

result in dead air stagnating in the intake. To be at high altitude and speed when this happens is not conducive to mission success or safety.

Every major design concept used on the PS-13 was cutting-edge, yet probably only the transonic compressor, hot-streak ignition for the first fully variable afterburner, use of only two bearing assemblies for a two-shaft design, the variable stator stage between the LP and HP sections of the compressor and the bypass concept were entirely original. The materials required to achieve all of these marvels in a package weighing less than the (less powerful) competing designs were far from mundane however. The PS-13 was designed to add a leap in metallurgy to the mix. Titanium, the strongest metallic element in its pure form, was found capable of enduring temperatures above that of alloys of aluminum and stainless steel while standing up to repeated cycles of heating and cooling. Better yet, it was found, if properly alloyed and treated, to maintain its strength at high temperature, and considering the heat and radial stretching loads on spinning turbine blades, this made titanium very attractive. Largely based on this property of strength per-pound at high temperature Orenda tried to design the Iroquois as a titanium engine. Their choice of titanium, in addition to all the other world-beating technologies Orenda decided to toss into the mix, was an extra gamble. While their other gambles would be proven valid in this and later engines, the use of titanium in certain areas would prove catastrophic.

By Black Friday the Iroquois 2 was reasonably reliably producing between 16,000 and 18,000 pounds of dry thrust in flight (limiting it to about 20,000 with afterburner) and was thus slightly short of the design goals due to vibration and mounting flexibility problems which were interrelated. In other words, they had a difficult time telling if the engine was causing the limitation or Canadair's housing. This thrust level was about the same as the Pratt & Whitney J-75 output at the time since this engine was also just emerging from development. Unfortunately the B-47 could not simulate high speeds to increase ram effect limiting the quality of the data.

This was still a better thrust to weight and thrust to diameter performance than any engine in its class yet the engine clearly needed another year in which to be perfected. Had the PS-13 been flying in the Arrow in late 1958 or early 1959, even at those low thrust figures, the Arrow would have demonstrated radically improved performance by being over two tons lighter with about 30 percent additional thrust. New speed and altitude records were a foregone conclusion! They were projecting the twenty-first Arrow Mk. 2 to meet the full 19,250/26,000 lb specification which would have given the Arrow Mk. 2 44 percent more thrust than the Arrow Mk. 1. In this book are performance curves for what the Mk. 2 Arrow was projected to do at design thrust and they are very impressive even against modern fighters. For one thing they were predicting it to be capable of pulling 6G at 50,000 ft. The author believes this performance is yet to be achieved by any aircraft in service. The F-22 Raptor is to pull 5G at 40,000 ft and this number is above any known previous aircraft in this role. At only 600 more pounds of thrust (as related by Avro to the RCAF in their proposal for the Arrow 3) Avro was projecting Mach 3 as a combat speed for an Iroquois 3 powered Arrow variant.

Even with the J-75 powered Mk. 1, had Avro really wanted to set a speed record, they probably could have done it. American jets like the F-106 Delta Dart, F-4 Phantom, F-15 "Streak Eagle" and others set their records being stripped down and equipped with up-rated engines, engines that were in all likelihood scrapped after the record runs due to excessive turbine inlet temperatures on their record runs. The CF-105 Mark 1 nearly set a record being considerably overweight with the instrumentation pack, heavy engines and ballast, and was apparently not even at full throttle. Indeed more than one ex-Avroite states that they were categorically forbidden by Crawford Gordon from breaking the speed record with the J-75 engine. With the PS-13 the Arrow would have been hard to cancel since it would have been the highest performing interceptor anywhere in the world, without question. Indeed it already was with the J-75 when all performance aspects are weighed in combination. Even so, at the de-rated rpm of the 1957 100 hr. endurance test the PS-13 developed high enough numbers to promise to make PS-13, and the CF-105, category leading products for the foreseeable future. Cabinet documents state the CF-105 was cancelled a month early, however, to save 10 million dollars.

Motive Force, a brief history of the PS-13

Orenda still had two of the best axial-flow aerodynamicists in house in the persons of Harry Keast and Burt Avery when in April of 1952 Charles Grinyer joined Orenda and quickly rose first to Chief Engineer, then to Vice President Engineering and Chief Engineer. The Iroquois or Project

Study 13 really seems to have been masterminded by Harry Keast, with many of the more radical ideas to be introduced on this engine coming from him. In an interesting anecdote from *Shutting Down the National Dream,* Keast's old employer and inventor of the turbojet engine and the afterburner, Sir Frank Whittle, paid a visit and viewed one of the Orendas in the test cell. When he asked Keast if it was an axial flow, Keast's affirmative reply generated the whispered response, "Traitor!"

Grinyer had been involved in many engine development programs in the UK including the Bristol Phoebus and Orpheus jets, and notably, the Olympus turbojet for the Vulcan B.2, Canberra B.2 and later used in the TSR-2 and Concorde. Grinyer had personally been responsible for the official "type test" certifications of ten engines and not one had failed to pass on the very first try. In those days this was an unheard-of feat. Considering the Olympus is still one of the highest performing turbojets of its diameter, this says a great deal about Iroquois potential under his guidance.

Project Study 13 began as a strictly private venture funded by the company whereas most undertakings of even less sophistication and technological effort elsewhere in the world were usually specified and subsidized by government, often through the military. Indeed every high-performance turbojet the author is familiar with began life this way. In the fall of 1953 Harry Keast and others from Orenda presented their design to the Hawker Siddeley Group Design Council for a two-spool high-technology turbojet weighing only 4,500 lbs and providing 20,000 lbs of dry thrust while moving a mass flow of between 280 and 300 lbs of air per second. Right around this time the thirsty single-spool de Havilland Gyron was producing a record *wet* thrust, on the test stand, of around 25,000 pounds in afterburner. The Bristol Olympus was also approaching this figure in development. Both were old technology in many respects compared to the Iroquois and both had weight or size and efficiency disadvantages compared to the engine Orenda was embarking on. That Hawker Siddeley was willing to invest money in this engine speaks volumes about the potential they saw for it.

At the time of the Iroquois design layout of course, the TR-5 Orenda was one of the highest performing military turbojets in the world. It was an axial flow design, however still used can-type combustors. Burt Scott, Orenda test-cell engineer, related to the author in his Irish brogue that the reason the TR-5 was such a world beater was

Orenda PS-13 Iroquois 2

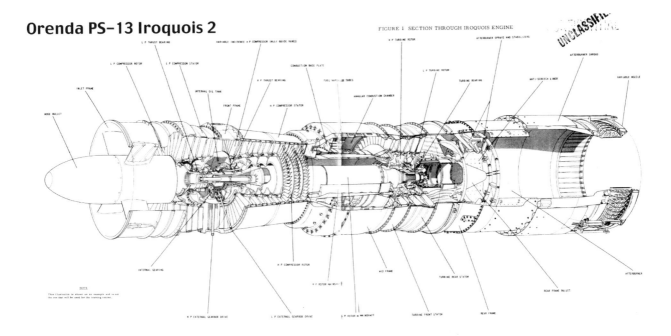

FIGURE 1 SECTION THROUGH IROQUOIS ENGINE

because Avro Gas Turbines (later renamed after their excellent Orenda engine) was the first to develop an efficient fuel control system. Up to this time one had to handle the engine throttles (and sometimes other engine controls at the same time) on turbojets very gingerly to avoid causing compressor surges, stalls and/or combustor flame-outs. Of course the last thing a pilot wants in combat is to have to move the throttle delicately while watching the jet pipe temperature threaten his aircraft while a hostile is doing the same thing! While the Orenda was a leading design structurally and aerodynamically, it was its flight manageability and relative immunity to stalls and flame-outs which truly established the Orenda as a leading engine. "We figured it out first," says Scott, to this day with a mixture of relief and elation.

Once A.V. Roe rejected designing another 10,000 lb + thrust class engine in favour of a radical design of double this dry-thrust (in a package of roughly the same diameter), design advanced to the point where a proposal was put before the government and RCAF. In December of 1953 A.V. Roe Canada was authorized by the Hawker Siddeley Group Design Council and the parent company to purchase three ingots of titanium. On 13 January 1954, the company gave Orenda authorization to construct three Iroquois Mk. 1 development engines as a private venture and allocated a maximum 3.5 million dollars of company money for the task. They audaciously planned to have a working engine running under test in twelve short months. This new design was very close in physical size and weight to

the TR-9 Wakunda design, yet was so advanced that it was designed to nearly double the output.

Meanwhile the basic concept behind the Iroquois was unique and has never been discussed to any serious degree in any other publication on the subject. Perhaps the reason for this is because the conceptual difference was very subtle.

Most engine theory describes the intake-compression-power-exhaust cycle of a piston or turbojet engine and goes on to point out the advantages of high compression in allowing more fuel to be burned (more completely) in a smaller volume, thus allowing a smaller engine to do more work. As achieved by the turbojet engineers of the day and since, they have tended to try to compress the air as much as they could with the mechanical designs of the day and then burn as much fuel as possible in this compressed volume. In other words they tried to get as much of the air they were moving through the engines to burn as possible. Since the high compression pre-heats the air considerably before combustion, turbine inlet temperatures reach very high levels on a high compression turbojet. One method, seemingly employed on engines for the B-52 and other aircraft, of cooling the combustion and thus reducing the turbine inlet temperatures was to actually put *too* much fuel into the air-fuel mixture and allow the extra fuel to cool the combustion. This band-aid solution to a materials and cooling technology problem made for a lot of pollution and poor fuel economy. (This rich-burning technique is also employed by automobile racers.) The Orenda designers however designed the engine to move as much air as it could and burn relatively less of it as completely as they could. They designed it to move more air, faster by having less machinery in the way of the mass flow, and "working" the air less as it went by. In effect, the Iroquois 2 and Iroquois 3 high altitude engines were using theories combining the benefits of the turbofan with the high speed abilities of the turbojet. Turbojets have a speed advantage over the turbofan due to their accelerating the whole mass of air more. The Iroquois was an even higher speed turbojet because it accelerated it the same amount, but slowed it down less to start with. This thinking promised magnificent dividends, given the freedom to perform.

It has also been discussed that running a turbojet on a stationary (static) test-stand is entirely different than running the same engine at 50,000 feet and Mach 2. Ram effect and the compression done in the intakes of aircraft, such as the Arrow, raised the temperature of the air in *front* of the compressor section of the engines to around 500 degrees and pressures of about 45 pounds per square inch. Since air density at 50,000 ft would give an ambient pressure of about 3.5 lbs per square inch, one can see that the Arrow intake was expected to achieve (in the Mk. 3 version at 45 psi) a compression ratio of about 12 to 1 all by itself. When the Iroquois added an 8 to 1 ratio to this, one can see that it actually was a very high compression engine, when running at speed in an aircraft similar to the Arrow. Higher compression engines had to take less air, decelerate and compress it more, and then burn as much fuel with it as possible to keep turbine inlet temperatures at bay. Orenda simply decided to burn only a portion of the air moving through the engine while using the rest for cooling. Since they did not run a deliberately rich fuel mixture, the actual flame temperatures were higher and combustion was more complete, leading to less pollution and very good fuel efficiency.

One hurdle encountered at the beginning of construction was contamination in the titanium ingots themselves. They contained hydrogen impurities which made the titanium brittle in use and resulted in parts exhibiting much lower strength and other attributes than what the material was selected for in the first place. Orenda developed a purification procedure where the titanium was placed in an autoclave which heated the metal under vacuum and drew out the hydrogen. Special tools of extreme hardness such as diamond-tipped drills and cutting tools were developed as were special welding and forming techniques. These lessons would largely be learned all over

again several years later by Lockheed during development of the A-12/YF-12A/SR-71 Blackbird.

Incredibly Orenda exceeded its lofty goal of having an Iroquois running in 12 months by 39 days. This was an incredible performance for a jet engine design. For an engine as exotic as the Iroquois it was utterly astounding. On 5 December 1954 the first Iroquois sprang to life in the Orenda test cell. This occurred as a rather nervous Charles Grinyer was de-planing in Ottawa before giving a presentation to government officials on the engine. Apparently this was about the time that the RCAF was promoting the Iroquois as a powerplant for their "Arrow Weapons System" and replacement for the just cancelled Curtiss-Wright J-67. Even though the Orenda engineers had to remove all the accessory covers around the compressor section to get enough air to light-off, Grinyer and his boys felt mightily justified.

During the first serious run a problem was encountered that would be a headache for the design team right to the cancellation date. At 6,000 RPM a vibration was encountered that threatened to destroy the test engine. In other words, the main rotating drum/shaft was flexing and encountering heat expansion to extremes which the outer casing was not capable of matching by virtue of a lack of stiffness in the rotating core, and the lack of a correct coefficient of expansion in the outer case. Harmonics could aggravate matters to the point of catastrophic failure. Asymmetrical friction, caused by a discovered oil leak, was found to be the main cause of the phenomenon on this run. Once the leak was corrected, the engine performed much better allowing the engineers to concentrate on perfecting the engine's aerodynamics.

As mentioned, titanium was seen as the strongest and lightest material available for the Iroquois. Thus the compressor blades, stators and case were all made of titanium. Early on titanium's rather poor heat dissipation, and relatively high rate of thermal expansion were discovered. These two characteristics, discovered in the West largely by the then leader in titanium use, A.V. Roe Canada, actually aggravated the problem of keeping the case and center shaft assemblies expanding at the same rate. It was strong and light but would still flex. If it would flex, the rotating discs and blades would hit the stationary "overhung" stator blade assemblies. It was found that the Iroquois 1 (and 2) would rub discs under certain conditions and cause unbalancing friction and heat in these areas plus possible engine disintegration. Titanium will burn under some conditions and at least one Iroquois Mk. 1 engine was lost in this way. The combination of titanium's poor heat dissipation, high rate of thermal expansion and flammability was threatening the program. At the same time Pratt & Whitney were trying to put titanium compressor blades into their J-75. They failed. They tried again in a few years and succeeded while Orenda set out to design the Iroquois 2 for service using the lessons learned from the prototype engine.

Inco developed a new nickel alloy blade material (the now well known Inconel) which was substituted in some hot sections. Other high-tech steel and titanium alloys were substituted in the compressor section. These substitutions went a long way towards eliminating the problem. These changes cost about 300 lbs in engine weight. Even so the Iroquois would soon produce a dry thrust to weight ratio only exceeded by the Olympus 593 developed for the Concorde about a decade later. To develop the Olympus, Bristol Aircraft Engines had received an Iroquois example in 1961 and made good use of the technology.

Vibration was a problem that would prove more difficult to eliminate. Orenda found that aligning the front bearings in the vertical plane would help alleviate the flex problem (they were originally spaced some distance apart). Once the material changes and bearing modifications were completed, testing and development progressed rapidly. As early as June 1956 the Iroquois was in the test cell undergoing its first 50-hour PFRT (Pre-Flight Rating Test). Charles Grinyer himself explained (taken from Greig Stewart's *Shutting Down the National Dream*) the demands of the PFRTs, in this case referring to the final 150-hr type test for certification:

> The test itself commences with a performance curve, and a given number of accelerations. The endurance part consists of 15 ten-hour periods, some of which cannot be run without a ten-hour interval, whilst others must have less than two hours between them. Total accelerations must exceed 100. No stop is permitted in this period, without the penalty of re-running that period. The thrust levels vary in the periods, and very complete records are taken.

> The test is completed by another performance curve. It is not usual to expect approval if the performance has decreased by more than three percent. Only limited service is permitted, and this has to be specified before the test starts. The engine is stripped down and parts examined for wear or failure. Dimensional checks are made, and the parts again checked to the drawings. The Test is thought to represent about 400 hours of military flying.

In other words, an initial run is done with many accelerations and decelerations normally encountered in demanding flying conditions to establish the thrust, temperature characteristics and general functional norms for the engine in brand-new condition.

It is then subjected to 15-hour non-stop runs at various altitude and temperature conditions with "throttle-slams" being many of the acceleration/deceleration criteria to test the engine's resistance to compressor stalls and surges, during which time it must not encounter a flame-out. These tests are done after long cool down periods simulating a cold-start, and short ones representing hot-starts. On some tests the engine is deliberately "flamed-out" to test its re-light characteristics at various altitudes and temperatures. Finally a final performance curve is done to make sure the engine's output has not declined by more than 3 percent.

The final portion is a very rigorous check to make sure all the engine components are still in "like new" condition.

The Iroquois passed the first 50 hr. test without difficulty, producing 19,350 lbs of dry thrust. Mr. Grinyer's reputation emerged unscathed. This was done at a reduced rpm where the engine didn't suffer from vibration problems and was therefore reliable. This de-rated *dry* thrust performance was equal to the emerging J-75 engine's full *afterburning* performance as installed in the Arrow Mk. 1! Obviously this was a very impressive performance on this

A J-75 engine by Pratt & Whitney, one of the most powerful engines in the world at the time, but very heavy.
(Aircraft Engines of the World)

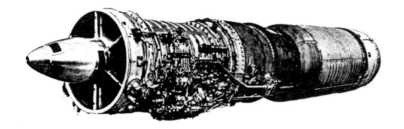

One of Osterich's ATAR engines. All were similar sized designs that were very light and used the annular combustor which Osterich's team had originated in Germany with the BMW jet engine effort. ATARs for the Mirage III and IV were almost identical in size to the Iroquois, yet the Iroquois made double the power.
(Aircraft Engines of the World)

early endurance test. More than one Orenda test cell engineer has confided to the author that Iroquois tests were done at up to 25,000 pounds *dry* thrust which is very close to the much later Pratt & Whitney F-100's (for the F15A and F-16A) full *afterburning* output!

Milberry's *Pratt & Whitney Canada Story* discusses J-75s for the Arrow. In relating the experiences of John N. "Tony" Clark, P&WC's J-75-Arrow representative, he writes (page 104):

> While Pratt & Whitney America [P&WA] was providing flight-test engines to Avro, it had wider goals. Here was a chance to test the J75 twinned in one aircraft and to observe the results of installations and operations and make on-going improvements. Tony Clark adds: 'The Arrow held promise as a lucrative project for us. We knew what Orenda was up against in pouring millions into a powerful new engine. Though we felt confident that Ottawa would keep the Arrow going, the Iroquois could be dropped at any moment. We had the J75 ready to fill the vacuum should that occur.'

Milberry continues (page 105): "A P&WC memo of August 8, 1958, noted that the J75 'equals or exceeds the performance of the Iroquois except under supersonic cruise'." A caption to a photo of the Arrow mistakenly states: "... the Arrow was powered by a pair of P&WA J75s each rated at 17,200 pounds of thrust (24,500 in afterburner)."

In reality the J-75s Avro received were very early P-3 models with 30 percent less thrust than the J-75s described in the passage above. The higher figures were actually for the developed J-75 that powered the F-106 and Republic F-105 Thunderchief, and by 1958 they weren't producing 17,200 pounds reliably. Their rating at this time was more in the order of 16,000 pounds dry thrust. When P&WC generated the August 1958 memo, the Iroquois was running at between 16,000 and 18,000 pounds dry thrust in the air. Orenda felt they would be reliable at that rating in the Arrow airframe. Thus, at that time, the *developed* J-75 was approaching the undeveloped Iroquois in thrust. The

P&WC memo is no doubt accurate in their comparison, yet to use the exception "except under supersonic cruise" and not explain it is misleading. The Iroquois was *designed to be a supersonic engine.* The corollary of the above comparison is that the undeveloped PS-13, a low-compressor ratio engine, was meeting the performance of the developed J-75 *in the J-75's peak performance regime* (lower speed and lower altitude where higher compressor ratios are advantageous). The Iroquois also had a far better thrust to weight ratio.

On 27 July 1957, the first 100-hour PFRT was carried out successfully at a marginally reduced thrust of 18,750 pounds. Apparently Orenda still felt more work was needed to achieve certification at full thrust. The final 150-hour type test at full design thrust was delayed by Charles Grinyer until August 1959 since he felt there were a few more bugs to iron out to guarantee that the engine would perform flawlessly and be ready for mass production. (Unfortunately the project was terminated before this date.) Orenda felt they could produce a reliable Iroquois 2 by this time, meeting the world record-breaking thrusts of the 1956 50-hour pre-flight rating test. This is the 19,250 lbt dry, and 26,000 lbt wet quoted in the CF-105 Mk. 2 specification.

In real terms, the ATAR 09K and J-79 were 10,000 lb thrust-class engines but are included to show the current state of the art at the time. While they were both only slightly smaller in diameter than the Iroquois, they were only moving about half the mass flow. The ATAR 09 was developed from the ATAR 101 used in the first Mirage IIIs, the Mystere and Vautour. No wonder the French tried to purchase up to 300 Iroquois engines to power their Mirage IVB bomber. When the Iroquois was cancelled they then tried the Pratt & Whitney J-75 and ended up cancelling the version of the aircraft... from lack of thrust to weight or politics? Some have suggested the Mirage III might have obtained the Iroquois. If it had (and the Iroquois would practically slide right in based upon nearly identical installed diameter and length), it would have made the Mirage III by far the highest performance light-fighter of the

Iroquois versus Contemporaries

	PS-13 Mk. 2	Olympus 300	J-75	J-79	ATAR 09K
Dry Thrust	18,750 lbs	20,000 lbs	16,100 lbs	10,900 lbs	10,500 lbs
Wet Thrust	26,800 lbs	no afterburner	24,500 lbs	17,000 lbs	15,000 lbs
Wet-Dry Ratio	1.43-1	no afterburner	1.52-1	1.56-1	1.43-1
Diameter/Length	42"/231"	42"/151"	43"/259"	38.3"/208"	40"/234"
Frontal Area (FA)	9.6 sq ft	9.6 sq ft	10.1 sq ft	8.0 sq ft	8.7 sq ft
Dry Thrust to FA	**1953-1**	**2080-1**	1600-1	1360-1	1600 lbt/sq ft
Wet Thrust to FA	**2790-1**	no afterburner	**2425-1**	2125-1	1724-1
Mass Flow (lb/sec)	**300 (est)**	**270 (est)**	265 lb/sec	169 lb/sec	159 lb/sec
Weight	4,800 lbs	3,800 lbs no AB	5,960 lbs	3,700 lbs	3,275 lbs
Compression Ratio	8-11	2-1 (est)	12-1	12.9-1	6-1
Shaft	2	2	2	2	1
Compressor Rotors	3+7	8+7	8+7	10+7	9
Turbine Rotors	3	2	3	3	2
Thrust -Weight Dry	**3.9-1**	**3.8-1**	2.7-1	3.0-1	3.2 lbt/lb
Thrust-Weight Wet	**5.43-1**	no AB	4.1-1	**4.6-1**	4.5 lbt/lb
Year of figures	1957	1957	1958	1958	1959
Fuel Consumption Dry	.85 lb/lbt/hr	**.75 lbs/lbt/hr**	**.79 lb/lbt/hr**	.86 lb/lbt/hr	1.04 lb/lbt/hr
Fuel Consumption Wet	**1.85 lb/lbt/hr**	no AB	2.20 lb/lbt/hr	**1.94 lb/lbt/hr**	2.15 lb/lbt/hr
Aircraft	CF-105Mk 2	Vulcan B.2	F-106-F-105	B-58/F-4/F-104	Mirage 3&4

Notes: The above Iroquois figures are from the July PFRT while the rest are from *Aircraft Engines of the World*. With the exception of the Iroquois, the above numbers are for developed engines as they actually flew. Only the Iroquois figures above are those of an early test engine under development. The best and second best of class figures are bolded for easier comparison. The Olympus 300 was lighter but this was due to its lack of an afterburner, which considerably skews the dry thrust to weight figure in its favour. The Iroquois mass-flow above is estimated at 300 lbs/sec while Orenda expected 350. This underestimation is considered reasonable since it was producing 18,750 lbt dry rather than the sought 23,000 lbs.

era and even, in all likelihood, to this day. It would have supercruised (without afterburner) at about Mach 1.6, and would have had excellent fuel efficiency as a result.

The J-79 was an interesting design and, with the Iroquois, one of the first engines to use variable pitch stator blades in the compressor section. Although it didn't really set the world on fire in terms of thrust to size or weight, it was one of the first to allow the pilot to handle the throttle forcibly and with confidence. Good handling was due in part to the variable-pitch stator blades which adjusted the airflow to the engine rpm. It was thus efficient and "user-friendly" over the lower rpm ranges. It would sacrifice maximum dry thrust however, due to play in the mechanisms, and this is borne out by its fairly low maximum thrust to size ratios.

The variable pitch stators owed their design to one Gerhard Neuman. Neuman had emigrated on a mechanic's apprenticeship to Hong Kong in 1939 from Germany. When the war in the Pacific heated up he found himself fixing aircraft for the AVN "Flying Tigers" in China and was thus working against his homeland's Japanese allies! He would later be instrumental in repairing the crashed Japanese Zero fighter abandoned in the Aleutians and subsequently tested against every major US fighter design. This was instrumental in learning to fight the extremely manoeuverable and reliable Zero by "fighting the engine" of the more powerful US designs. These tests also demonstrated that American fighters were comparatively very complex, heavy and also very unreliable! The title of Neuman's fascinating autobiography says it all; *Herman the German: Enemy Alien U.S. Army Master Sergeant #10500000*. Neuman was also behind the variable-stator J-93 discussed later. The J-79 would provide reliable power for both the F-4 Phantom and the B-58 Hustler.

The proportionally similar yet relatively under-powered F-106/J-75 package set an absolute speed record in December of 1959. It wasn't advertised of course that this was a "ringer;" a specially lightened and tuned aircraft/engine combination. An F-4 would be similarly prepared and set a new record soon after using the comparatively feeble (by Iroquois standards) J-79 in an aircraft not *that* much smaller and lighter than the Arrow. All in all, at the time, the J-75 was the Iroquois' only serious competitor in the afterburning turbojet category yet was much heavier and moved considerably less mass flow through a slightly larger diameter. In the key areas, even at the reduced rpm/thrust levels, the Iroquois clearly outshone all others in terms of thrust to size, thrust to weight, and fuel economy.

Judging by photos of the engine in extreme temperature test-cell conditions at the Nobel cold weather research establishment, the PS-13 engine was not coddled on the test stands. Others were conducted at high temperature. Such thermal extremes across the length of the engine (compressor frigid, rear section glowing hot) clearly validated the progress in materials and design. Later F-106 northern-basing tests however, showed the Delta Dart and J-75 to be problematic in arctic conditions with cold weather aggravating the fuel starvation problems.

By 1957 the 42 inch two-spool, axial-flow, annular combustor, free-floating 2-combination bearing, 30 percent less compressor-complex Iroquois was producing thrust figures that would not be matched in the same dimensional size in the air until seven years later by the TSR-2 using the Bristol Siddeley (by this time Bristol Aero Engines and Armstrong-Siddeley Motors had merged) Olympus afterburning variant. Had the US developed the J-67 afterburning version of the British Olympus, they might have had the TSR.2 engine much sooner. But then, had this happened, the Iroquois would likely never have been developed. Contrary to the diplomatic and political assurances of the US that they were interested in standardizing equipment for the defence of the West on the best products, despite where they came from, clearly the passage in 1954 of the "Buy American Act" contradicted these assertions. The Buy American Act also includes a clause stating essentially that if any other country were to discriminate against American goods, trade sanctions would be applied.

Worse still, they were not interested in licensed production of the best foreign products within the United States. Curtiss-Wright Aero Engines had tried to develop the Olympus as the afterburning J-67 and had had the contract cancelled early in the development phase. Later they would be discouraged from doing the same with the Iroquois. Of course dependence upon a foreign power for crucial defence equipment makes a nation militarily, industrially, diplomatically, politically and economically dependent on that foreign power. The J-75 engine, reputedly designed from the monstrous J-57, is virtually identical in basic configuration to the Olympus used in the TSR.2 and proposed as the Curtiss Wright J-67. One might-wonder how much of the J-75 program was "inspired" by the Olympus J-67 development program. In fairness to Pratt & Whitney it should be noted that their J-57 for its day was a very impressive design. It was an axial-flow engine and the first the author knows of to employ the two-shaft concept.

In many other publications on Avro and Orenda, it is pointed out that a mysterious set of "toothpick" turbine blades had arrived at Avro by Black Friday. These appear to have been for the Mk. 3 version of the Iroquois. This version is described in brief in the 27 October 1958 Preliminary Proposal to the RCAF and government for the Arrow Mark 3. The Iroquois 3 is described as having a slightly enlarged bell-mouth (allowing more mass-flow) and a shorter hot section. The combustion section was to be shortened by about six inches while the turbine rotors and stators were also shortened, using blades of a narrower chord than those of the Iroquois 1 and 2. This would have made the engine lighter and more powerful while improving the mechanical properties that were troubling the engine. A shorter distance between bearings and lower rotating mass and improved materials were the keys to achieving this. As mentioned earlier, turbine inlet temperatures were and are a major limiting factor in jet engine design. High speeds, high compression and low pollution all result in high temperatures just behind the combustion area of the engine where temperatures are nearly white-hot. By reducing the chord of the turbine rotor and stator blades by about one third overall, the Orenda engineers also reduced the heat expansion and mass of this end of the engine by about 30 percent.

Considering that an early Iroquois, with the smaller bell-mouth, had recorded 25,000 pounds of thrust *dry,* on the test stand, one might assume that the figure of 23,000 pounds dry thrust for the Mark 3 was very conservative. Even so, Orenda was only proclaiming 19,850 pounds of dry thrust for the Iroquois 3 as of October 1958. This was done to ensure that the figures Orenda was quoting were entirely realistic. Again A.V. Roe was being very conservative in their estimates. The table below gives the figures Orenda was projecting for a developed version of the Iroquois 2, as

	PS-13 Mk 2	Olympus 320	J-93	J-58	TF-30
Dry Thrust	23,000 lbs	23,000 lbs	24,000 lbs	24,000 lbs	11,500 lbs
Wet Thrust	30,000 lbs	34,000 lbs	32,000 lbs	32,000 lbs	19,000 lbs
Wet-Dry Ratio	1.43-1	1.48-1	1.33-1	1.33-1	1.65-1
Diameter/length	45"/231"	42"/320"	52.5"/237"	50"/180"	38"/178"
Frontal Area (FA)	9.6 sq ft	9.6 sq ft	15 sq ft	13.1 sq ft	7.9 sq ft
Dry Thrust to FA	**2400 lbt/sq ft**	**2400 lbt/sq ft**	1750 lbt/sq ft	1740 lbt/sq ft	1456 lbt/sq ft
Wet Thrust to FA	**3125 lbt/sq ft**	**3541 lbt/sq ft**	2133 lbt/sq ft	2443 lbt/sq ft	2405 lbt/sq ft
Weight	4300 lbs	6000 lbs	5200 lbs	6500 lbs	3200 lbs
Compression Ratio	8-11	2-1 est.	8-1	6-1	2-1 (turbofan)
Shaft Number	2	2	2	1	2
Compressor Rotors	**3+7**	8+7	**5+3**	8	3+7+7
Turbine Rotors	3	**2**	**2**	**2**	4
Thrust -Weight Dry	**5.35 lbt/lb**	3.8 lbt/lb	**4.6 lbt/lb**	3.7-1	3.6-1
Thrust-Weight Wet	**6.97 lbt/lb**	5.7 lbt/lb	**6.15 lbt/lb**	4.9 lbt/lb	5.93-1
Year of figures	1961 est.	1965	1964	1964	1965?
Fuel Consumption Dry	**.75 lb/lbt/hr**	**.75 lb/lbt/hr**	.86 lb/lbt/hr	.8 lb/lbt/hr	.85 lb/lbt/h
Fuel Consumption Wet	**1.8 lb/lbt/hr**	2.0 lb/lbt/hr	1.94 lb/lbt/hr	**1.9 lb/lbt/hr**	2.0 lb/lbt/h
Aircraft	CF-105 Mk 2	TSR.2	XB-70	A-12/SR-71	F-111/F-14

Note: All figures are taken from Paul Wilkinson's unfortunately out of print *Aircraft Engines of the World* publication.

published in the *Aircraft Engines of the World* 1959 edition. The engine was rated the "world's best" in the publication for that year.

Other than the Iroquois, in the table above the TSR.2's afterburning Olympus and the Valkeyrie's J-93 really stand out. Once the PS-13 was cancelled, the Olympus was clearly the world's best by 1965 in terms of dry or wet-thrust per given frontal area and in fuel economy. It, like all the others, had some severe teething problems, and due to the cannular combustor, initially made a lot of smoke. Thrust to diameter, thrust to weight and fuel efficiency are everything in aircraft propulsion. None of the above engines met the values produced by the PS-13 in any of these critical areas, save the Olympus in thrust to diameter. Both the J-58 and J-93 were much larger in terms of frontal area, had lower thrust to weight wet or dry. As far as complexi-

ty is concerned, the only rivals to the earlier Iroquois were the J-93 and J-58. it is interesting that the J-93 was designed for operation at speeds up to Mach 3 yet shares the Iroquois 2's compressor ratio, suggesting Avro's Mach 3 expectations were reasonable.

As for the J-93, it was an awe-inspiring effort and the author does not know if it was cancelled simply because the XB-70 was, or if the design had critical flaws.

By the time it flew, the J-58 was already an antiquated single shaft design, and relied on a 44 percent larger hole area by which to achieve its thrust. It never made anything near 44 percent more thrust as its frontal area would indicate it should, provided it was as efficient. The J-58 used a cannular combustor and single shaft design like the ATAR in a much larger diameter engine. It added bypass tubes similar in concept to the earlier PS-13.

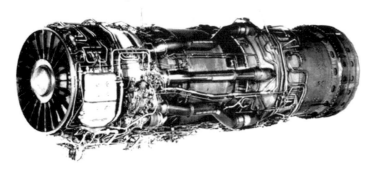

The Pratt & Whitney J-58: Power for the Blackbird (courtesy Aircraft Engine Design.com)

The Pratt & Whitney TF-30, power for the F-14A Tomcat and F-111 "Aardvark." *(Aircraft Engines of the World)*

Looking at the TF-30, other than the obvious fact this still later engine was not a leader in any critical performance regime, one can see that the F-111 and F-14A Tomcat certainly weren't at the cutting edge of thrust and weight. In the Tomcat at least, the TF-30 was so prone to compressor stalls and flame-outs that a pilot could simply *not* handle the throttle with confidence in a manner required under the demands of real combat flying. This last criticism is repeated in most histories of the F-111 and F-14. How many intrepid F-14 crew members lost their lives in peacetime due to this engine's problems will never be known.

The Iroquois produced other simply startling performance achievements. During its 50 hour test it went from idle to full military (dry) thrust in 2.8 seconds. Idle to full afterburner, with the engine howling up to full military thrust, then afterburner light-off and final nozzle "turkey-feather" arrangement was an astounding 4.5 seconds! I mentioned these times to CF-18 Hornet pilots in 1991 and they simply scoffed, refusing to believe that this 35-year-old design was capable of matching the performance of the Hornet's General Electric F-404 turbojet. The phenomenal but much smaller F-404, known for very fast spool-up times, blasts from idle to full afterburner in a well-advertised 3-odd seconds under ideal conditions. The author has sat in a Hornet in less than ICAO standard conditions and noted much longer times. Again, the F-404 engine shares an almost identical aerodynamic arrangement to the Iroquois but only produces 10,000 lbs dry thrust. Its spool-up time is greatly assisted by its small diameter (less rotating inertia) and computerized fuel control system. The well advertised number of sensor inputs by which the F-404 engine accom-

plishes this performance are virtually identical to those used by the much earlier Iroquois engine's air data computer. By contrast the infamous TF-30 engine used in the F-14A Tomcat and F-111 would normally flame-out if the throttle was handled in such a way as to try to duplicate this rate of acceleration.

At the time of the Arrow cancellation on 20 February 1959, the Iroquois had accumulated 7,000 hours of testing both in flight (on the B-47 test-bed aircraft) and in the test cells on 13 engines (unlucky PS-13?). The Canadair off-thrust center housing on the B-47 did not allow the Iroquois to be operated with afterburner in flight due to asymmetric thrust. Even at de-rated rpm and without burner the Iroquois was so powerful the aircraft had to be put into a climb with all the bomber's standard engines throttled to idle except the two on the outer wing opposing the turning moment applied by the single Iroquois. The outer engine had to be operated at full thrust to keep the big jet under control. Quite a testament to *power* when the six engine B-47 had to be climbed with four engines at idle to absorb the thrust of the Iroquois without afterburner! Quite a testament to the abilities of the test pilot Mike Cooper-Slipper in getting around the limitations of a poorly designed engine pod as best he could. Again one must wonder about an Iroquois powered B-52.

Arrow Mk. 2 RL-206, the first of the Mk. 2 Iroquois-engined versions, was inside the plant on February 20th with one Iroquois engine installed and another on a dolly beside it awaiting a fuel control component. This last detail was provided during conversation between the author and an Avro employee on the engine installation team. Would it have been ready to fly in March? The engine installation team-leader believes the engine was ready. Jim Floyd, Mike Cooper-Slipper and others say it wasn't. It seems the engine people thought it was and the airframe men didn't. On the other hand, the engine people would have had the best information on how severe the B-47 nacelle flex was. Earlier planning documents from Avro said that during March of 1959 RL-206 would do 25 hours of ground running to test the installation after which the engines would be removed, stripped and inspected. Jim Floyd says that he had no doubt the Iroquois would be perfected with time. It is profoundly sad that the Iroquois was denied a fruitful marriage with the Arrow airframe. We will never know what progeny this union might have produced.

Iroquois versus turbojets from the 1970s

	PS-13 Mk 2	Olympus 593	PW F-100	GE F-110	GE F-404
Dry Thrust	23,000 lbs	30,000 lbs	14,590lbs	17,260 lbs	10,500 lbs
Wet Thrust	30,000 lbs	35,000 lbs	23,770 lbs	28,980 lbs	16,000 lbs
Wet-Dry Ratio	1.43-1	1.17-1	1.62-1	1.68-1	1.52-1
Diameter/length	42"/231"	47.8"/138"	40" (est)/208"	40" (est)/182"	30" (est)/159"
Frontal Area (FA)	9.6 sq ft	12.5 sq ft	8.7 sq ft	8.7 sq ft	4.3 sq ft
Mass Flow	**350 lb/sec**	**440 lb/sec**	225 lb/sec est	250 lb/sec est	150 lb/sec est
Dry Thrust to FA	**2400 lbt/sq ft**	**2400 lbt/sq ft**	1670 lbt/sq ft	1983 lbt/sq ft	**2441 lbt/sq ft**
Wet Thrust to FA	3125 lbt/sq ft	2800 lbt/sq ft	2732 lbt/sq ft	**3330 lbt/sq ft**	**3720 lbt/sq ft**
Weight	4400 lbs	5000 lbs	3700 lbs	4000 lbs	2200 lbs
Compression Ratio	8-1	12-1	25-1	25-1 est	N/A
Shaft Number	2	2	2	2	2
Compressor Rotors	3+7	8+7	3+10	3+9	3+7
Turbine		2	4	3	2
Thrust -Weight Dry	**5.23 lbt/lb**	**6.0 lbt/lb**	3.94-1	4.31-1	4.77-1
Thrust-Weight Wet	6.81 lbt/lb	7.0 lbt/lb	6.42-1	**7.14-1**	**7.27-1**
Year of figures	1961 est	1969	1972	1975?	1974
Fuel Consumption Dry	.75 lb/lbt/hr	.75 lb/lbt/hr	.75 lb/lbt/hr est	.75 lb/lbt/hr est	N/A
Fuel Consumption Wet	1.8 lb/lbt/hr	2.0 lb/lbt/hr	2.0 lb/lbt/hr	2.0 lb/lbt/hr	N/A
Aircraft	CF-105	Concorde	F-15/F-16	F-15/F-16	F-18

Notes: Iroquois and Olympus figures taken from *Aircraft Engines of the World*, figures for the F-100, F-110 and F-404 from *Air International* Vol 47, No 2 Aug. 1994. One change from these published figures is the weight for the Olympus 593. The author has added 500 lbs to the weight of the engine since the figures quoted in the reference did not include the variable/thrust reversing nozzle and rear duct section since these were made separately (by Dassault) and were considered part of the airframe. When one considers that this engine was 5.8" larger in diameter than the TSR.2 Olympus version, the weight handicap applied is probably quite conservative. Inlet diameter and frontal area calculations of the US engines are based upon the author's best guess since only the maximum diameters of the engines were available during research.

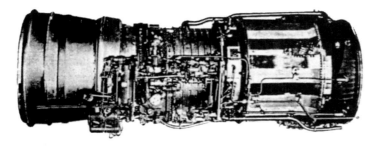

The Olympus 593 for the Concorde. It is so short because the afterburner and rear ducting was constructed separately as part of the airframe rather than the engine. It is still one of the most powerful engines for its size in the world. (*Aircraft Engines of the World*)

In the above table the Olympus, first certified by one Charles Grinyer, again clearly stands out, this time with a significantly enlarged frontal opening. Even so its performance is incredible to the point of again raising the question *why* the US cancelled development of the J-67 license-built afterburning Olympus variant and/or failed to license produce the TSR.2 version (not to mention the PS-13!) One must question how seriously those in power in the US really took the Cold War when this engine was beating the competition (sans PS-13) by a good margin right from 1957. On the other hand, the J-75 looked a great deal like a J-57 updated to the Olympus (or J-67) arrangement.

The F-100 and F-110, very similar in design one to the other, developed the bypass concept of the Iroquois by building in a bypass duct around the circumference of the engine behind the LP compressor sections. They were actually fairly high bypass ratio designs meaning their performance drops off somewhat at the higher supersonic speeds

The Boeing B-47 modified as an Iroquois flying test-bed. The Canadair installation wasn't particularly effective. Flying the aircraft to absorb as much as possible of the Iroquois' thrust demanded a lot of the test pilot, Mike Cooper-Slipper, and crew.
(Hugh McKechnie & Avro Canada)

compared to a low-bypass turbojet like the Iroquois. The relatively high amount of compressor air bled off around these engines and the F-404 helps cooling and provides extra oxygen to allow a rather high afterburner augmentation level while assisting mass flow. This high-bypass concept made these engines a bridge between the pure turbojet and the turbofan. Considering the complexity, these engines were very light yet still failed, 15 years later, to match the Iroquois dry thrust to weight ratios and only beat the wet thrust to weight by their high afterburner augmentation ratio. The F-100 was also given very relaxed standards on its PFRT since it was deemed "essential for National Security" since the F-15 Eagle had to have this engine. Every six hours the engine was allowed to be stopped and have heat-critical parts changed! This last testimony was taken from a magazine article written by an American military officer and engine specialist, involved with this engine's military service.

The GE F-404 was nearly identical to the Iroquois in design only much smaller, and employed the bypass duct rather than the shroud of the PS-13, and tubes of the J-58. From the figures in the table above this engine was very competitive pound for pound and inch for inch with the almost 20 year earlier Iroquois. Indeed one might consider it a miniature Iroquois. It would be very interesting to know how much the Iroquois design influenced this excellent engine considering the layout, thrust to diameter and spool-up times. This engine also began development not too long after the Iroquois program was terminated. Apparently the F-404 began as the GE-1 "new core technology" engine around 1964.

Meanwhile the Russian Lyulka AF-31F for the SU-27 bears more than a passing similarity to the P&W F-100. Whether this is a case of "engineers who ask the same questions get the same answers" or a case of industrial

espionage is left to the reader to decide. Notwithstanding, later developed versions of both the P&W F-100 and the GE F-110 would match the performance of the Lyulka AF-31 and all would be incredible performers. So equipped, the SU-27 and derivative designs (SU-35 etc) are long-range interceptors to be feared. Today, they display similar performance to the CF-105 Mk. 2 of forty-plus years earlier but not when they have weapons and fuel tanks "hanging in the breeze."

The Canadian government would prove self-defeating in their vision for the Iroquois, while A.V. Roe Ltd. would, in retrospect, prove justified in their confidence. Rolls-Royce would, in the end, actually gain from the cancellation when they gained Bristol-Siddeley aircraft engines and their Olympus 593, an engine that had been redesigned (as the Olympus 320 for the TSR.2) to incorporate some Iroquois technologies.

The Ultimate Iroquois?

So far we have compared the Iroquois specifications, realistically projected for 1960/61, with later engines. This of course fails to consider the probable development of the Iroquois after this date. As we know the Iroquois 3 had an enlarged bell-mouth as did the Olympus 593 version produced for the Concorde. Some improvement could be gained by an increase in compression ratio from the modest 8-1 of the PS-13 Mk. 2 however, and Avro documents show they were working on a high compression version for lower altitude use. Since the Iroquois 2 matched the Olympus' mass flow and diameter, it is assumed in the table below that the enlarged developed Mk. 4 Iroquois would equal the mass flow per square foot of frontal area. It likely could have been increased far above these figures based upon a mass flow significantly above that of the Pratt & Whitney F-119.

In the following table, the phenomenal F-119 continues to validate the "less is more" concept of compressor and stator section design. It is the first two-shaft engine to use *less* compressor sections than the PS-13 and yet produce comparable thrust to size dry, and with afterburning. From the table it is clear the aerodynamic capabilities of the, at the time, radical concept of employing only 3 low pressure and 7 high pressure compressor stages was borne out not only by the "mini-Iroquois" F-404, but is also being exploited by the F-119. This engine seems to be the "best of all-worlds" design comprising the thrust to weight of the F-404, the turbine simplicity of the Olympus and the compressor simplicity (minus one!) of the Iroquois. It certainly has a few tricks of its own however. All the compressor blades are molded integrally with the rotor, a concept that could have saved Orenda some headaches. The stator (non rotating) blades in the turbine section were also eliminated by making the LP and HP turbine rotate in opposite directions, thus making the LP turbine do double duty as both the LP rotor, and the LP stator. The contract for the development of the F-119, itself based in large measure upon earlier designs, was worth $1.4 billion as of 1994. It is unknown if this engine has gone over budget. If history is any guide it has, and significantly.

	PS-13 Mk. 3	Olympus 593	P&W F-119	GE F-404	Lyulka AL-31F
Type	Turbojet (TJ)	TJ	bypass TJ	bypass TJ	bypass TJ
Dry Thrust	28,300 lbs	30,000 lbs	24,000 lbs	10,500 lbs	17,857 lbs
Wet Thrust	40,500 lbs	35,000 lbs	37,000 lbs	16,000 lbs	27,560 lbs
Wet-Dry Ratio	1.43-1	1.17-1	1.54-1	1.52-1	1.54-1
Diameter/length	45"/231"	47.8"/138"	42" (est)/208"	30" (est)/159"	41" (est)/195"
Frontal Area (FA)	11.8 sq ft	12.5 sq ft	9.6 sq ft	4.3 sq ft	9 sq ft
Mass Flow	**400 lb/sec**	**440 lb/sec**	280 lb/sec	140 lb/sec	280 lb/sec (est)
Dry Thrust to FA	2400 lbt/sq ft	2400 lbt/sq ft	**2500 lbt/sq ft**	**2441 lbt/sq ft**	1984 lbt/sq ft (est)
Wet Thrust to FA	3432 lbt/sq ft	2800 lbt/sq ft	**3850 lbt/sq ft**	**3720 lbt/sq ft**	3062 lbt/sq ft (est)
Weight	4500 lbs	4800 lbs	3700 lbs (est)	2200 lbs	3373 lbs
Compression Ratio	21-1	12-1	25-1	27-1 (est)	23-1
Shaft Number	2	2	2	2	2
Compressor Rotors	3+7	8+7	3+6	3+7	4+9
Turbine Rotors	3	2	2	2	3
Thrust -Weight Dry	6.28 lbt/lb	**6.6 lbt/lb**	**6.43-1**	4.77-1	5.21-1
Thrust-Weight Wet	**9.0 lbt/lb**	7.8 lbt/lb	**9.45-1**	7.27-1	8.17-1
Year of figures	1975 (est)	1968	1992?	1974	1985?
Fuel Consumption Dry	.75 lb/lbt/hr	.75 lbs/lbt/hr	N/A	N/A	N/A
Fuel Consumption Wet	1.8 lb/lbt/hr	1.5 lb/lbt/hr (est)	N/A	N/A	N/A
Aircraft	Avro SST?	Concorde	F-22	F-18/F-20	SU-27

Notes: The figures for the F-119 are estimated from a number of sources, especially Bill Sweetman's book *The F-22 Raptor*. The 1994 *Air International* article mentioned earlier is the source for data on the Lyulka and F-404 engines while the figures for the Iroquois are informed estimates based on characteristics of the Iroquois 2 and Olympus. The author has not adjusted the weight of the Iroquois 3 since it had a lighter turbine section but larger afterburner and front bell-housing which would tend to cancel each other out. Orenda however, considered that any engine would be lightened considerably once it proved itself in service. Mass flow and thrust figures for the Mk. 3 are based upon the fact that the Iroquois 2, under test and as projected, matched the developed Olympus and this assumption has been extended to the larger Mk. 3.

While the above developed Iroquois isn't the clear leader against engines of the 1980s and 1990s, it is still competitive and approaches a very magic number in jet engine design: the 10 pounds of thrust per pound of engine weight. Would Orenda have achieved or exceeded these figures? They had the basic running hardware and aerodynamic/structural design to do so in 1957. Every design aspect of the Iroquois has been proven valid in subsequent engines. The assumptions in the above tables on the speculative Iroquois variants are all in line with directly comparable engines and the only assumptions used are from figures that the Iroquois is known to have demonstrated on the test stand. Orenda's designers had already proven their design leadership by way of the Orenda engine. Compared to the reasonably similar F-119 for the F-22, Orenda had a 30 year head start by which to achieve this performance. It really does appear that Orenda was set to move out in front in turbojet design, and stay there.

Up to cancellation, about $147 million had been spent on the Iroquois. Considering that cars, for example, cost about 10 times as much today as in 1959, the expenses of the Iroquois and F-119 (estimated at $1.4 billion) are comparable. What is not comparable however is the fact that the Iroquois was a radical original design and did not benefit much from earlier programs as the P&W F-119 did, certainly from the F-100, and also from all previous engines including the Iroquois itself. The F-119 will still be well worthy of accolades, if and when it enters service in the F-22 Raptor. Advertised figures for the F-22 nevertheless show it to be designed for less than Mach 2.2 by virtue of the extreme compressor ratio, the selection of a fixed geometry intake and materials used in the airframe. Its very high compression ratio means that the F-22's top speed may also be limited by turbine inlet temperatures, the very reason the Iroquois 2 had a comparatively low 8 to 1 compressor ratio designed into it: to allow the Arrow to fly higher and faster than anything in the sky! It is difficult to comprehend what might have moved Diefenbaker to consider abandoning the present day equivalent of 1.4 billion dollars' worth of engine development. Shortly after Black Friday, Ontario's Premier Leslie Frost tried to persuade the Diefenbaker government to put in the three remaining million to see the Iroquois 2 certified. Frost tried to do this for employment and to help preserve Ontario's tax base, not to mention that of Canada. Some question A.V. Roe Canada's refusal to finish the engine, yet the company didn't own the engine, and it was the owner who abandoned it.

The F-22 also seems to have performance figures associated which may be the first realistic appraisal of a front line US interceptors' "real world" performance. Performance figures for the F-4 and F-15 have been largely taken out of context since they are only achievable by an airframe with no external stores and little internal fuel. Streak Eagle and the other previous USAF and USN "ringer" record attempt performance figures are often quoted as maximum performance figures for *service* aircraft. Other maximum performance figures are for clean (unarmed and un-tanked) planes. Canadian Hornet pilots, for example, report that the

F-15 does not perform nearly to the comparative level promised by published performance figures as compared to the F-18. British performance estimates, also extended to the CF-105 (and further handicapped by the RCAF), are conservative by comparison, but are much more realistic in terms of what could be expected in actual service. In terms of thrust and drag the F-22 aircraft/engine combination is capable of at least Mach 3. It was demonstrated, in the YF-22 pre-production examples, (one of which crashed), to be capable of cruising at Mach 1.58 at altitude without afterburner. It was also shown to be capable of supersonic cruise speeds at sea level without afterburner. So was the CF-105 with the de-rated Iroquois 2 some 30 years earlier. Indeed hand plotted performance curves compiled by Jan Zurakowski in the Mark 1 Arrow demonstrate that it was probably capable of Mach 1.1 at sea level with the J-75's! The aircraft might have been able, but the low wing loading would have made this a very rough trip for the crew at this height and speed.

Meanwhile Avro and the RCAF had only proceeded with the CF-105 and Iroquois designs since they promised a considerable improvement over the J-75/F-106 design *specifications*. When the F-102 and F-106 were dramatically failing to meet their less demanding requirements, this was kept quite secret although it was impossible to hide the fact that the barely supersonic F-102 was supposed to "be" the F-106. When the CF-105 Mk. 2 and Iroquois figures were also degraded and progress slightly delayed for reasons of prudence by A.V. Roe management, the government was livid and took the tack that nothing Avro had said, now said, or would say was the truth! What Jim Floyd feared (as he put it in a memo to Avro management), was that Avro's prudent, conservative and often interim figures were compared to the "clean and dry" specifications for a "massaged" F-106, liberally presented all over Convair brochures, not the loaded "real world" performance of a service aircraft/engine. Of course these facts were, as much as possible, kept *top secret* supposedly for reasons of Cold War secrecy. The Soviets however had excellent intelligence services and analysts. In fact a paper by Vladislav M. Zubok, in the archives of the American National Security Agency, and available through the CIA website, titled "Spy vs. Spy: The KGB vs. the CIA," makes it clear that the Soviets always had a good picture of what was going on in the United States. The technology was often available in the engineering and scientific journals long before it caught the interest of the American establishment!

Airborne Arrow. The first flight take-off.
(The Orenda newsletter)

ENGINE RUNS WERE CONDUCTED on the pre-production Arrow Mk. 1 on 18 January 1958. Also in January 1958, taxi trials at speeds of up to 100 knots were done. Drag chute deployment proved unreliable so some modifications were introduced. On these tests Zura found that idle thrust from the de-rated J-75s was sufficient to maintain a taxi speed of between 25 and 50 knots. Heat-sensitive paint was applied to the engine bays to observe temperature characteristics during these runs. During these taxi-trials the brakes were found to be inadequate under emergency conditions and new units were developed. The nose-gear door was found to have the potential to cause crosswind-landing weather-cocking (making the nose move sideways in the direction of any crosswind) and was modified to close after gear extension.

During this period the weapons pack was ground tested by conducting repeated extensions and retractions to test the doors and missile struts. With the Falcon missiles, extension, door closure and firing were designed to be accomplished in less than one second. "Quite a trick," as Jim Floyd stated in 2001, a trick apparently accomplished during tests. Dummy-missile firings into sandbags were conducted in an effort to determine the wear characteristics of the launch rails.

CHAPTER SEVEN

The Arrow Soars Aloft

Better than projected.

Standing room only! Avroites stand shoulder to shoulder breathlessly awaiting a glimpse of the fruit of their labours on its maiden voyage. Some historians have questioned whether the cancellation of the Arrow was such a tragedy to the employees. This photo speaks for itself. (Jim Floyd collection)

For three weeks in February RL-201 was on jack-stands in the flight-test hangar undergoing intensive flight-control system checks. These were the "last chance" checks to convince Zurakowski that the radical, computer controlled, synthetic flight control system would actually work "as advertised." The flight-control development rig, already described, that had been developed into a simulator was not quite right on the simulator side. Other works have mentioned that Zurakowski and Potocki had quite low survival times in the simulator—in the order of seconds in the dynamically unstable regions under simulation. Zura elected to fly the jet anyway, believing it "looked right" and having faith in the engineers and designers. Obviously he wanted to make very sure that the actual prototype's systems were working perfectly, under every

flight performance regime they could simulate in the hangar while attached to the computers. (This anecdote came from a letter from Jim Floyd to Dobson, responding to a rumour Dobson had heard, that the Arrow had flown in February 1958!)

On 25 March 1958, the bird was ready to fly. RL-201 had been scheduled to fly on the previous Saturday but an all-too-common (to sophisticated aircraft) hydraulic leak had scrubbed the mission. Once it was ready, the plant loudspeakers blared an invitation for non-essential personnel to leave their posts and witness the making of history. The plant emptied in seconds! Zura's diminutive form marched smartly around the big delta while he conducted the pre-flight inspection. He then climbed the ladder, completed his strap-in and helmet connections and began the cockpit check. Long seconds later the switches were flicked, throttles adjusted and the big J-75s began their slow moan, ignitors snapping, as the engines spooled-up to light-off rpm. After a brief roar they quickly settled down to idle revs. Zura scanned the instruments for rpm, exhaust gas temperatures, hydraulic pressures and other signs of life, while working the stick and rudder and watching for correct movement of the control surfaces. "RL-201, taxi 3-2!" was the characteristically crisp request for taxi clearance. On reply the brakes were released, throttles quickly cycled to about 75 percent then back to idle and the big jet sprang eagerly forward. A fast stab at the rudder pedals indicated nose-wheel steering function but Zura apparently found differential braking to be more precise with the wide-track landing gear as he swung the nose around and entered the taxi-way. Final checks were mouthed along the route to Malton's longest stretch, runway 3-2. The gleaming white wedge serenely paused at the hold position while the CF-100 and F-86 chase jets clambered down the runway. It must have appeared to be an act of almost arrogant confidence as the big delta leisurely turned its high-pointed nose down the runway to follow. Zura moved the throttles to full military thrust. The engines responded to the command by howling their eagerness while the test-pilot flicked experienced eyes

across the panels and the engine note went from a low moan to a hissing bellow. Zura's mind considered wind speed, crosswind component, engine rpm, exhaust gas temperature, altimeter setting, magnetic versus gyro-compass alignment and a score of other factors. As a signal of his approval two small flight-booted feet on the brakes relented to the insistence and Zura's body was snapped to attention by the force of 25,000 lbs of jet propulsion. Eyes flicked from airspeed to rapidly blurring runway center-line as he pushed the throttle past the detents and into full afterburner. Two tightly spaced slaps in the back acknowledged their cooperation. At 100 knots indicated air speed (IAS) the stick was progressively pulled backwards. The nose began to rise as control authority increased. At 120 knots the nose-wheel left the tarmac. By 170 knots the main gear legs had completely extended and then wheels left terra firma ... the Arrow was aloft!

There was no time for pondering the moment however as the Arrow was now thundering hungrily for both more altitude and speed! As the airspeed zoomed upwards and the runway disappeared under the nose, a gloved hand, probably a bit too slowly, backed off the throttles and selected "gear-up". Having the confidence to select gear retraction on a first flight was and is still somewhat unusual.

Landing number one.   (Avro Canada)

Once RL-201 was airborne, the then state-of-the-art Orenda-powered fighters closed in to check for proper gear retraction and to have a general look-over of the aircraft. Externally, all appeared as it should despite Zura's cockpit indication of incomplete nose-gear door closure (this annoying yet minor glitch would rear its head on subsequent occasions). The throttles were nudged forward slightly to give an airspeed of 250 knots. At 11,000 feet a general handling assessment was conducted with the fly-by-wire system in emergency mode. A half-hour of flight time passed and the aircraft was returned to the landing circuit. A faster than projected approach was made for the sake of safety with the aircraft touching down smartly at 160 knots. The drag-chute streamed "as advertised" and the aircraft came to taxi speed less than halfway down the runway. Zura only required light braking to slow to taxi speed well within the hard-top available. On the way back to the shacks Zura was heard to exuberantly shout over the radio: "*Wonderful* stuff!"

Once the Arrow had stopped, the engines spiralled down and Zura climbed out. He was immediately accosted by a jubilant horde. Zurakowski was instantly hoisted shoulder-high and paraded around the tarmac! The first flight snag sheet was framed since it revealed only the failure of two tiny microswitches in the nose gear bay! Zura's comments included the statement that the aircraft behaved "within expectations," with his one gripe being the lack of a clock by which to check the time! Perhaps this is an indication of how time fails to progress in a linear fashion when flying something out of this world!

Statistically speaking, the second flight of the Arrow, less than a week later, roughly doubled the performance of the first flight. Speeds up to 400 knots were demonstrated at altitudes up to 30,000 feet. The aircraft was turned at past 60 degrees of bank at 2.5 G. Again the nose-wheel door microswitches malfunctioned and did not indicate full closure. Two short days later the Arrow spread its supersonic wings and broke Mach 1.1 at 40,000 feet before throttling back. On its third flight the Arrow had, for all intents and purposes, met the top performance of the F-102 without even breaking a sweat. On the return fly-past from this record-breaking flight Zura began something that would become his trademark during Arrow testing. "Zorching" over the runway at modest speed he pulled the nose up... higher... still higher... then impossibly high to the vertical with full afterburner thrust ripping attentive eardrums. The gleaming delta pulled up into a vertical climb and almost disappeared from sight. This manoeuvre became a symbol of the confidence of the company and pilot in the performance and potential of their products. It was certainly an analogy of what they expected the project's future to bring not only to Avro but also the Canadian people, and perhaps the people of the Free World. (In the fall of 1958 the British magazine *Aviation Studies* stated that "Canada owes it to the free world to put into production the Arrow aircraft, the most advanced interceptor in the Western world.") The Iroquois-engined Mk. 2 would have been able to accelerate while climbing vertically and carrying a useful load. The developed Iroquois promised this performance at close to gross take-off weight.

Most of the remaining development flying of the Arrow was devoted to exploring the various flight regimes of the aircraft in an effort to obtain data with which to refine the fly-by-wire and artificial stability programming and to validate the mechanical design. Stability tests, stress, temperature effects and other variables were quantified and assessed against projections. They found no "show-stopper" design deficiencies, unlike the CF-105's competitors. Zuuring in his *Arrow Scrapbook* complains about a very low flying rate, among so many other things, for the CF-105 program. The fact is, however, that money was very tight for the Arrow project and flying is quite expensive, even if one only considers that some 2000+ gallons of fuel are burned. Further to this, even the Mk. 1 had cleared 95 percent of the RCAF specification within eight months with no real problems having been found with the airframe. Indeed in a letter from Sir Thomas Pike, then head of RAF Fighter Command, to Jim Floyd regarding Jim's attempt to save some Arrows by having the British acquire the flying examples for SST research, Pike acknowledges that the flying Arrows had demonstrated remarkable reliability and serviceability. For an aircraft of the technology and complexity of the Arrow that was high praise indeed.

Regarding the flying development method at Avro, they employed their brain and computer power to the maximum by outfitting the flying Arrows with as much equipment as they could carry to measure and evaluate the huge amount of data being generated on every flight. There was a gargantuan amount of test data to analyze from the multitude of onboard and ground telemetry equipment. This kind of low flying rate with a multitude of onboard sensors, followed by careful analysis of data, flight-control systems

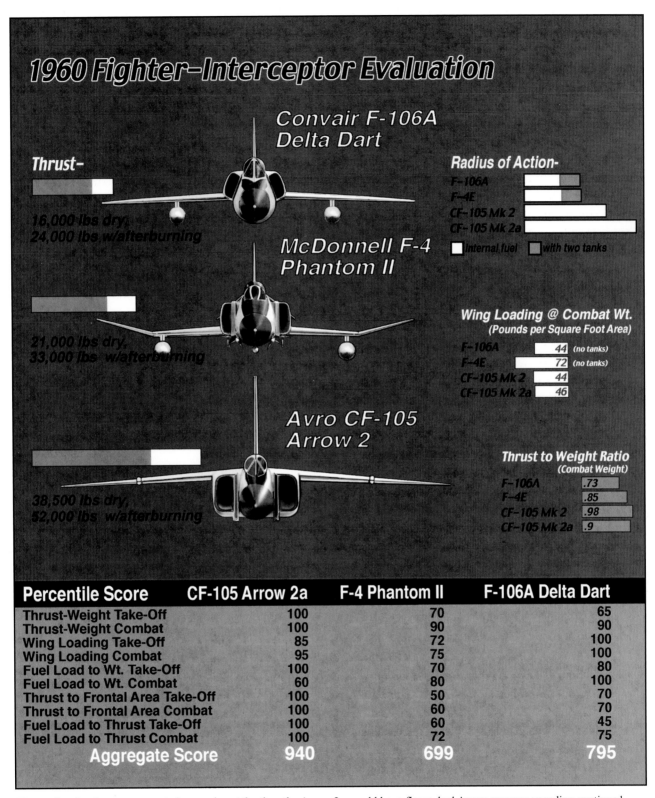

1960 Fighter–Interceptor Evaluation

Convair F-106A Delta Dart

Thrust–

16,000 lbs dry,
24,000 lbs w/afterburning

McDonnell F-4 Phantom II

21,000 lbs dry,
33,000 lbs w/afterburning

Avro CF-105 Arrow 2

38,500 lbs dry,
52,000 lbs w/afterburning

Radius of Action–

F-106A
F-4E
CF-105 Mk 2
CF-105 Mk 2a

☐ Internal fuel   ☐ with two tanks

Wing Loading @ Combat Wt.
(Pounds per Square Foot Area)

F-106A	44 (no tanks)
F-4E	72 (no tanks)
CF-105 Mk 2	44
CF-105 Mk 2a	46

Thrust to Weight Ratio
(Combat Weight)

F-106A	.73
F-4E	.85
CF-105 Mk 2	.98
CF-105 Mk 2a	.9

Percentile Score	CF-105 Arrow 2a	F-4 Phantom II	F-106A Delta Dart
Thrust-Weight Take-Off	100	70	65
Thrust-Weight Combat	100	90	90
Wing Loading Take-Off	85	72	100
Wing Loading Combat	95	75	100
Fuel Load to Wt. Take-Off	100	70	80
Fuel Load to Wt. Combat	60	80	100
Thrust to Frontal Area Take-Off	100	50	70
Thrust to Frontal Area Combat	100	60	70
Fuel Load to Thrust Take-Off	100	60	45
Fuel Load to Thrust Combat	100	72	75
Aggregate Score	**940**	**699**	**795**

Top performing interceptors entering service at the time the Arrow 2a would have flown, had Arrow program spending continued. The relative performance of each aircraft is assessed, with a score of 100% going to the top performer in each category. Interesting that the Arrow scores highest in both thrust to weight and thrust to frontal area (at both take-off and combat weights) considering it had 3 times the range of the other aircraft, and thus required an enormous internal fuel load. (calculations and images by R.L. Whitcomb)

Arrow test pilots (l to r): Wladyslaw "Spud" Potocki, Peter Cope, Jack Woodman (RCAF) and Janusz Zurakowski. Potocki would also test fly the challenging Avrocar and later test fly at North American Aviation, while Woodman would go to Lockheed to test fly the L-1011 jumbo-jet. (via Jim Floyd)

and other refinements is now the standard procedure in aircraft development. The USAF system at the time was more akin to taking the first prototype and "flying it till it breaks" while the development of the F-22 has taken over *10 years* of flying!

By August 1958, the second Arrow prototype was flying and broke the sound barrier on only its second flight. RL-202 flew twice on August 26th and once on August 27th and again two flights were completed on the 28th. The interceptor reached speeds of between Mach 1.5 and 1.7 on each of these flights. This was an outstanding achievement for an aircraft just entering testing and renders Zuuring's point irrelevant. It's an even more astounding feat considering the experience of the XF-92/YF-102/YF-106. Five Mach 1.5+ flights in three

days on one airframe is an *excellent* serviceability record for current developed supersonic designs in routine service.

Pilot duties on these flights were shared by both Zura and W.O. "Spud" Potocki, a World War II Polish Spitfire comrade of Zura's and former British RAE Test Pilot, and Peter Cope. Cope, according to *Shutting Down the National Dream,* had joined the RAF in 1941 and after the war had flown at Armstrong-Whitworth as a test-pilot on the Meteor fighter and Lincoln bomber. He came to A.V. Roe Canada in 1951 and made over 1900 test flights in CF-100s. Due to his combat experience his major tasks on the CF-100 program were related to armament development. He stayed with Avro until 1961, then went to Boeing for, as Stewart wrote; "A long career associated with the

747." Jack Woodman of the RCAF flew the Arrow to validate Avro's claims independently for the RCAF. On 14 September 1958, RL-202 reached Mach 1.86—this being the highest speed reached by Zura while test flying the Arrow.

In interviews, both Floyd and Zurakowski lamented the lack of publicity Potocki receives today regarding the Arrow. Zurakowski related that during one test flight of the first Avro Vulcan prototype an in-flight emergency occurred that threatened to destroy the aircraft. Although Potocki was only the co-pilot on this flight, apparently it was his coolness under pressure and fast thinking that saved the aircraft—to Dobson's eternal gratitude. Zura also mentioned that during World War II, Potocki really stood out among the Polish pilots under his command. He went on to test-fly the exceptionally challenging Avrocar, Frost's flying saucer, and then to North American Aviation. He lost an eye at NAA in an accident and, apparently, ended his working days managing a small motel.

On September 22nd RL-203 flew for the first time and "went super" on its maiden flight reaching Mach 1.2. This event and those above showed the confidence both the test flight planning section and the test pilots had in the design.

Even in landing configuration and speeds, with the gear down and airbrakes extended, the Arrow could be handled well and landed safely on one engine without afterburner. If the burner was cycled on and off to help maintain airspeed or attitude, the flight control system would automatically and instantly compensate for the tendency to swing from the extra thrust, without the pilot noticing any changes. On one flight the Arrow was climbed at an attitude of 60 degrees in full afterburner when Potocki "chopped" one engine. No more than one degree of sideslip registered. This was a very demanding test of the fly-by-wire system in the performance region where the aircraft was dynamically unstable. The system passed with flying colours.

In actual fact the design exceeded its projections in most ways and, due to Avro engineers having overestimated the aircraft's drag, largely met OR 1-1/63 while being about 44 percent underpowered relative to a developed Mk. 2 with the Iroquois. With the de-rated J-75's this plane was also overweight due to the weight of this engine, ballast in the nose to compensate for the shift in the center of gravity, and a very heavy instrumentation/telemetry pack.

Snipers

As shown in Zuuring's *Arrow Scrapbook* (the reproduced documents make an interesting read, although this author disagrees with most of his conclusions) the NAE, RCAF and Defence Research Board ganged up and descended upon NACA (sans Avro) in the US to "Discuss Aerodynamic Problems of Avro CF-105 Aircraft." Zuuring says this visit was not known to Jim Floyd but it most certainly became an understandable thorn in his side considering the permanent damage done by the unknowing critics. One of the engineers (Lukasiewicz) recently endeavored to support his claims on television, even though his statements were disproven *most* dramatically through actual flying in 1958. These critics claimed the Arrow would have twice the supersonic drag Avro estimated, disparaged the delta-wing concept, slammed the "fly-by-wire" flight control system, the synthetic stability system, the negative camber of the wing among other things.

Later appraisals, once Floyd, Chamberlin and others (with the RCAF, DRB and NAE along) had made a remedial trip to NACA, validated their design with the exception of NACA's still estimating supersonic drag to be about 10 percent higher than Avro's estimate. This was probably just erring on the side of caution and in fact a later British examination of the drag coefficient would echo NACA's. (That assessment proved about 30 percent too high, suggesting Avro's aerodynamics were superior to NACA's and the British experts'.) Despite the lukewarm vindication, the RCAF and the government had the jitters. As late as January 1958 the RCAF was sending letters to Avro complaining about performance degradation of the aircraft before it had even flown. This was based upon their padded drag figures and truly minor (by contemporary standards) increases in the aircraft's weight.

They were assuming, based upon the opinions of others, that the performance of the Mk. 2 would be below the performance requirements of OR 1-1/63. In fact, again in late December 1957 and early 1958, the government critics were taking Avro to task because Avro had lowered *slightly* their estimates for the Mk. 2, bringing their aerodynamic drag coefficient more into line with what the British and Americans estimated, perhaps to deflect criticism that they were being unrealistic and inflexible! Avro, thus in Performance Report 12 of December 1957, estimated the Mk. 2 to be .15 G short of its combat specification at Mach 1.5 but fully meeting the 2 G requirement at

Arrow RL-203 in late 1958. This aircraft is in the interim day-glo paint scheme and was the only Arrow with the Red Ensign on the tail. (Avro Canada)

an even higher speed (Mach 1.8). Floyd and Chamberlin, however, had already erred on the side of caution in their drag estimates, figures that the others had simply further inflated and then used to criticize Avro. Furthermore, Avro was chastised for optimising the Iroquois for Mach 2 flight, rather than the Mach 1.5 required by OR 1-1/63. In reality the engine-airframe combination functioned better at Mach 1.5 with the engine optimized for Mach 2. They were upset because Avro was clearly ignoring the drag estimates from the RCAF and trying to produce an aircraft and engine that would greatly exceed the specification and therefore be able to remain in service longer. In fact the Arrow performed better at Mach 2 than it did at Mach 1.5 due to better intake ram effect and the fact that more speed was necessary to achieve very high altitude with a supersonic aircraft. Mach 1.8 was optimal with the fixed intake. Why the RCAF would criticize Avro for building an aircraft that would exceed its specifications and remain in service longer is an interesting question.

There are several such letters from various specialists in the RCAF. All of the criticisms centered around deviations in

Avro's performance reports following the 1955 estimates. The criticisms grew to be pretty universal by the end of 1957 and this no doubt was a major cause of the oft repeated opinion that the Liberals were going to cancel the program after the 1957 election. In 1955 Avro had estimated the performance of the Arrow 2 (with Iroquois) as follows (from the January 1955 British evaluation titled "Evaluation of the CF.105 as an All Weather Fighter for the RAF":

Maximum speed of Mach 1.9 at 50,000 feet.

Combat speed of Mach 1.5 at 50,000 feet at 1.84 G without bleeding energy.

Time to 50,000 feet of 4.1 minutes.

500 foot per minute (fpm) climb ceiling of 62,000 feet (i.e.; able to climb at 500 fpm from this height)

400 nm radius on the high-speed mission

630 nm radius on the low-speed mission

[Ferry range is not given, but estimated at 1500 nm]

Impressive figures, ones that encouraged an RAF offer to purchase 200 Arrows, as is detailed in Chapter Ten. The worst Avro performance estimates got (circa December 1957 with Performance Report 12) seemed to be approximately:

Maximum speed unchanged at Mach 1.9

Combat speed of Mach 1.5 at 50,000 feet at
  1.6 G [G loading estimated]

500 fpm climb ceiling of 58,000 feet.

264 nm radius on the high-speed mission

408 nm radius on the low-speed mission

Ferry range of 1254 nm

An enormous amount of bad "ink" was generated over these lowered estimates. In one letter Footit personally accused Floyd of mismanagement, and repeatedly came to the stunning conclusion that Avro was mismanaging the program. It is interesting that in one of Footit's letters he accuses Avro of having covered up various facts. He later had to acknowledge that Avro *had* properly informed the RCAF of the changes in the performance estimates, and that he simply hadn't seen them! One can see that Avro was in a very difficult position. If they stuck to their original (higher) estimates, they would be accused of being incompetent in the face of all the other "expert" opinion and, thus, the rest of their estimates would be "treated with reserve" as the government agents so often recommended. If they revised their estimates to match the NACA and RAF estimates, they would show a performance degradation that would also endanger the program. Those must have been very trying days.

Then the unimaginable happened: an interceptor in development flying *greatly exceeded* the manufacturer's own estimates. Incredibly, the manufacturer was Avro, and the interceptor was the Arrow. On Remembrance Day 1958, with Potocki at the helm, the second Arrow, RL-202, achieved the maximum speed of the Arrow program ... at least the maximum recorded speed. In a flight of 1.25 hours the jet reached a corrected speed of Mach 1.96 *while climbing through 50,000 feet, accelerating, and while only in intermediate afterburner* (some say the correction factor was incorrect and the true airspeed was Mach 1.98 but the point is largely irrelevant). The long duration of a maximum speed run such as this underscores the range potential of the aircraft when compared to aircraft such as the F-18. At any rate, the 44 percent underpowered Mk. 1 was very near the top speed of the fastest US aircraft, such as the very short-range and low-payload F-104 Starfighter.

The Mk. 1 was also 3.5 tons overweight. Speed records for the Mk. 2, even with an undeveloped Iroquois 2, were clearly a foregone conclusion.

Unfortunately, this flight was followed by a landing accident where all four tires blew and the aircraft left the runway and tore off one main gear. Rather than being ecstatic that their new interceptor was shaping up to exceed their requirements, the RCAF took Avro to task in the most severe way. They blamed pilot error and Avro management for this accident. Later Zura would point out the full-down position of the elevators as they were when he saw them after the aircraft stopped and succeed in clearing Potocki's name by suggesting a flight control system malfunction on landing that did not allow full weight on the main wheels when the brakes were applied. Photos taken of the landing by teenage trespassers (another source says spies) were later confiscated and developed. These photos do not show the elevators being in the down position. During the landing run the Arrow was known to land very lightly with touchdown being almost indiscernible on a good approach. Potocki admitted this landing was "hot" (fast) which would exaggerate this effect and possibly lead to the aircraft "ballooning" back into the air, reducing greatly the runway remaining for landing. From personal experience the author knows it is customary to give the brakes a little "tap" just after touchdown to make sure they are working. It is at least possible that Potocki locked up the main wheels while there was little weight on them. Such a theory would vindicate the aircraft's fly-by-wire system while unfortunately tarnishing Potocki's reputation. Of course after such an exhilarating high-mach flight, one which he had every reason to believe might save the project, Potocki can be excused somewhat for having his own internal clock running faster than normal standard time and thus accelerating both the landing speed and his point of brake application.

This flight, despite the ignominious finish, more than vindicated Avro's *original* supersonic drag figures. This Mk. 1 aircraft had exceeded Avro's own maximum speed estimates for the powerful Mk. 2. The author has met several ex-Avroites who stated that the Arrow, to their elation, actually came in some 20 percent below Avro's *own* estimates in drag! This appears to be due to the then largely unknown exhaust plume effects which may have "filled in" the Sears-Haack or area-rule shape behind the aircraft. Some of the drag reduction may also have had to do with exceptional skin smoothness due to the milled, rather than unrolled sheet-metal, wing skins. Whatever the reason, as this flight proved, the Arrow was quite suddenly coming very close to meeting the RCAF requirements even with de-rated J-75s.

All other arguments and wrangling about ASTRA, the Iroquois, range and expense are quite simply rendered irrelevant by this one fact. Range projections by the RCAF were based upon their own drag numbers, with some other strange handicaps thrown into the mix. The original specification was 2G at Mach 1.5 and 50,000 feet. The best that the nearest US competitor (the F-106) could achieve was about 1.5G at 35,000 ft and Mach 1.5. This US competitor was using the same engine as the Arrow 1 but with 15 percent more output due to its being a more developed version. Development of the Iroquois was not necessary to meet OR 1-1/63. Development of ASTRA was not required. Development of the Sparrow 2D missile was not required. The plane did what was promised and contracted to do right off the boards with significantly deficient thrust and *no* painful development. Any objections after this date about expense or effectiveness were and are complete nonsense. Any money spent on the airframe, ASTRA, the Iroquois or the Sparrow up to this point was already water under the bridge. It is also generally neglected that the rather late addition of ASTRA/Sparrow to the program, followed by first an acceleration, then a slowdown in the program were admitted by the RCAF to be the most significant factors in *Avro's* cost overruns—RCA and Canadair ASTRA/Sparrow's massively more severe overruns aside. It is difficult to support some of the RCAF and government criticisms of *Avro* management in view of these facts. Another factor in *airframe* cost overruns at the very end

was the requirement to switch *back* to the MA-1/Falcon/Genie systems. When Avro asked in early 1959 for an additional $40 million to accomplish this and finish the job, despite having already tabled a fixed price offer of $3.75 million dollars per *complete in all respects* aircraft, the government had the excuse it wanted. Avro, again, got the blame.

Much commentary critical of Avro, had been generated then and since about the fact that the Arrow was originally supposed to have entered service in late 1959. Considering ASTRA was not added to the development until mid-1956, and since the RCAF had mitigated for a development slowdown as a result, one can again see that Avro's project management is not at fault. The Arrow Mk. 1, flying in March 1958, would have largely satisfied the requirement with off-the-shelf radar and weapons. Even with the Hughes MA-1 system it still would have been far superior to anything else in the sky for years. The Canadian government could have received what it paid for on time for their accepted schedule and for a price similar to what a single, cancelled engine in the US cost their taxpayers. Furthermore, Avro, due to successfully pre-designing the Arrow and implementing the Cook-Craigie method, was ready to produce up to 1,000 Arrows, the limit for the already extant hard-tooling. Indeed, 97 percent of the parts for the first 37 were already on hand. Over 50 percent for the first 100 were also in the plant, or, alternatively, to provide lifetime spares for the 37 on contract.

The only conclusion possible is that there were factors behind the scenes that were forcing the government to cancel the Arrow.

An Arrow Mark 4. The wing pods did triple duty as fuel tanks, ramjets and landing gear bays. (image by R.L. Whitcomb)

THE USAF LRIX (Long Range Interceptor-Experimental) project design was begun on 6 October 1955 with North American Aviation (NAA) receiving a contract to produce two prototypes on 6 June 1957. North American designated the aircraft the F-108 "Rapier". At this time Dr. Courtland Perkins was the USAF chief scientist and, according to Campagna's *Storms of Controversy*, and *The UFO Files* had been consulting with Avro on their flying saucer designs. There can be little doubt that Perkins was operating in the interests of both the USAF foreign technology branch and also, directly or indirectly the CIA in his research, while undoubtedly being at a focal point for the technological decisions pertaining to their LRIX project. In an interview with Campagna while he was preparing *Storms*, Floyd stated that Perkins also discussed the LRIX program and requested information on the Arrow as to its suitability to the specification. As related in *Storms*, Perkins, also contacted, denied having had anything to do with the Arrow *"then or*

CHAPTER EIGHT

The Contenders

USAF or CIA Arrows?

North American Aviation's F-108 Rapier

Image of the F-108 derived from a photo of the mockup. There are fins on the undersides of the wings. It was more than slightly Arrow-similar and included a high-temperature canopy. It would be interesting to know exactly what kind of performance North American Aviation was promising for this aircraft as of the cancellation in late 1959.

now." This author has subsequently spoken to Jim Floyd and received documents to prove that Perkins was keenly interested in the Arrow and other Avro projects. In the first document, dated 6 March 1957, Floyd wrote Perkins and the following line makes his interest clear:

> I know that you want to see the enclosed data as early as possible.
>
> The attachments include the briefing charts on the Arrow, which I used on your recent visit, and also some data on the L/D max [maximum lift to drag ratio; an important aerodynamic statistic], which we discussed....
>
> I will send you, some time next week, a write-up on the philosophy of synthetic stability on the Arrow.

A possible reason for Perkins' reluctance to acknowledge, even late in life, discussing the Arrow is due to the fact that Jim Floyd and Fred Smye took Perkins aside during one of his visits and "pumped" him for the LRIX specification, which he spilled!

In a "memorandum to file" on the visit of Perkins to Avro of 18 July 1957 (dated 29 July 1957), Jim Floyd included the following:

> Dr. Perkins said that his interest and feelings on the Arrow at present ran something like this. U.S.A.F. have let out a contract for a design study on a L.R.I. [Long Range Interceptor] with North American, and are embarking on a complete and major weapon system program with associated engine, missiles, fire control system, etc., in much the same manner as the R.C.A.F. embarked on the Arrow complete weapon system.

In view, however, of the figures which are coming out of the design study, both in aircraft weight, which is around 110,000 lbs., and the situation on dollars for defence, the project appears to be losing a great deal of support, and he went so far as to say that he felt it might be discarded in the not too distant future.

Considering the US government had only let the contract to NAA in June of that year, it seems odd of Perkins to suggest it might be cancelled so quickly. In reality he seemed to be looking to Avro for information on the Arrow's potential, since it is quite reasonable to assume Avro had achieved a breakthrough in performance with the Arrow, hence Perkins' desire for the L/D max and other critical data.

Jim Floyd's "memorandum to file" continues:

> Since the Arrow comes closer to the requirement than anything they have seen at the present time, he felt that we should keep the U.S.A.F. constantly aware of our progress on the aircraft so that in the event of a cancellation of the L.R.I., there would be a good chance that they would become vitally interested in the Arrow, especially around that time. The L.R.I. basic requirement is for the interceptor to be scrambled on the receipt of DEW Line information, fly out to the 250 nautical miles radius, loiter for one hour with very high search capability, and then be able to proceed at Mach 3 for a distance of another 325 nautical miles. On encountering the target, 10 minutes combat is required, at 1.2 'g', at 70,000', at Mach 3.

This passage is significant in that it demonstrates a maximum speed for the LRIX of around Mach 3, while it

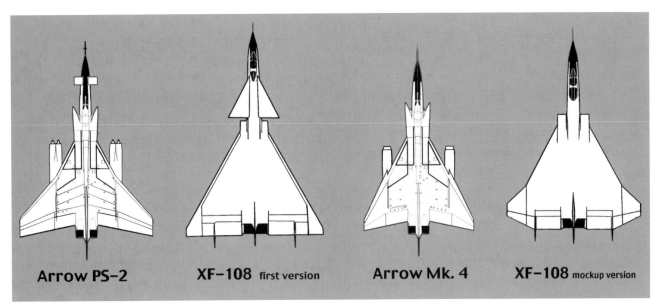

Arrow PS-2   **XF-108** first version   **Arrow Mk. 4**   **XF-108** mockup version

The PS-2 was proposed in June 1957, the Mk. 4 in late 1957. The XF-108 mockup was completed in January 1959.
(image by R.L. Whitcomb)

was publicly advertised as being capable of Mach 5, as we shall see. Most published commentaries on the LRIX also suggest the radius of action was to be 1000 miles. Above we see it was 575 nm with a one hour loiter on a CAP (Combat Air Patrol) profile. To continue:

> On the basis of the previous visit to Dr. Perkins by Messrs Lindley and Chamberlin [John Frost, involved in the Mach 3 flying saucer design for the Pentagon, was also along for this visit] we had a look at the Arrow in this role and, while it is not possible to stretch the aircraft in its present config-uration to meet this requirement, if re-fuelling was permissible during the loiter period, we could achieve the complete mission, provided that we made certain modifications to the aircraft, such as variable intakes, insulated skins, optimized Iroquois, etc. Dr. Perkins said that there was no mention of re-fuelling in the requirement, and North American had done all their studies assum-ing that this would not be permissible. However, he felt that it was well worth talking about and asked us to write up a note for him on our philosophy on the possibilities of using the Arrow with re-fuelling for this particular mission.

Few American aircraft, other than bombers, had this capability at the time. All front-line USAF fighters and reconnaissance aircraft designed after this time would use in flight re-fuelling and *many* aircraft in the US and Britain would be retrofitted to include it. As of the date of the Avro

communication with Perkins on aerial re-fuelling, the con-cept was still experimental as far as high-performance jet aircraft went. Of course it was the Englishman Sir Alan Cobham who had invented and proven the technique and had demonstrated it with Avro Lancasters during the Berlin Airlift.

The last description of the modifications Floyd felt would be required to meet the LRIX specification with an Arrow version are attributes that the Mk. 3 Arrow, already in the preliminary design phases, would feature. Floyd's opinion that the Arrow couldn't be stretched to meet the entire LRIX specification is interesting in view of the sim-ilarities between the Arrow and F-108. Mario Pesando actually wrote that, given the 100,000 pound limit they understood the LRIX contract to include, that he doubted if Avro, "or anyone else" could meet *all* the requirements.

Initially, the F-108 had been conceived as a long-range escort fighter for a future Mach 3 SAC bomber which NAA would produce as the XB-70 Valkyrie in the mid-1960s. The LRIX was to be powered by the impressive GE J-93 turbojet, an engine comparable in thrust to the Iroquois, but much larger in diameter and somewhat heavier. This of course would give the Arrow the advantage in size, weight, range and drag, all other factors being equal. Perhaps to make up the difference, a special chemical fuel (or Zip Fuel) program was begun to improve the output of the GE J-93 engines. Something like $200 million US was spent on the chemical "borane" fuel (Zip fuel) project without it being adopted, just as a lot of money would be spent at the same time in trying to develop practical hydrogen propulsion for Lockheed and the CIA's secret CL-400 "Project Suntan" spyplane. Meanwhile development of the Arrow airframe and production line, including design, tooling and work on eight aircraft up to first flight cost only $111 million. The J-93 first ran in September 1958 and produced 27,200 lbt in afterburner using JP-6, a high-energy fuel.

Interestingly, one of "Zip" fuel's problems related to the formation of a problematic "boron sludge" in the aft sections of engines and exhaust nozzles. The Iroquois afterburner was tested with this fuel and found to be resistant to this formation. One problem with very-high-altitude flight is the low air density and oxygen content which causes first the afterburner, then the engine to flame-out. Avro was looking at tri-ethyl aluminum as a fuel additive, and this product, according to Curtiss-Wright Aero Engines

who had developed it for their ramjets, would burn at an air pressure as low as one quarter psi.

The F-108 was also to carry the Hughes AN/ASG-18 long-range, pulse-Doppler radar and fire control system and the GAR-9 (later re-designated the AIM-47) missile, developed from the Hughes Falcon. The GAR-9 was a long-range missile very similar in appearance to the later Phoenix for the F-14. The ASG-18 radar shared the same huge 38 inch radar dish size as ASTRA, and was begun about a year later.

The Rapier design went through a couple of configurations, the first of which looked much like a mini-XB-70 Valkyrie. NAA was designing the XB-70 at about the same time. The design actually chosen for the mock-up, ready by January 1959, was very similar to the Arrow, especially the Arrow PS-2 variant, using a "cranked arrow" wing and small fins at mid-span on the wings. The PS-2 Arrow was

CF−105 Arrow PS−2
116,650 lbs total thrust at 40,000 feet.
Take−off weight: approx. 110,000 lbs

F−108 Rapier, initial design
60,000 lbs total thrust at 40,000 feet.
Take−off weight: approx. 110,000 lbs

(image by R.L. Whitcomb)

proposed in September 1957. The Rapier was also a high-wing delta design with the intakes, weapons bay, engines and crew arrangements using the same arrangements as the CF-105. When it came to Perkins and what he received from Avro, Floyd mentioned in a note in 2001 that "We bared our soul and gave him everything he asked for!"

The Rapier was cancelled in September 1959, barely after the Arrow production line and flying aircraft had been reduced to scrap. The reasons given were the same ones used by politicians then and since to justify cancelling the Arrow, and other promising programs: ICBMs were the new threat, ICBMs were cheaper for offence, anti-aircraft missiles were cheaper for defence and high-altitude interceptors were vulnerable and thus obsolete. Development of the YF-12A, production of the F-15 and future production of the YF-22 all put the lie to this statement. Something everyone seems to overlook in declaring an interceptor vulnerable to missiles is the simple fact that they generally operate over friendly territory!

The author's suspicion that the F-108 was largely a propaganda piece, designed to cast doubt on not only the future potential of the Arrow but of British designs, is based in part on the extraordinarily long time between contract award and mock-up completion. Usually the mock-up is ready *before* the contract is given to produce the first flying example but in this case over a year and a half separated the two events. When these steps occurred they did so in reverse order. One may say the program was a serious one based upon the amount of money spent on the chemical fuel aspect, however this technology was not developed exclusively for the F-108 by any means.

Further to the "propaganda" view of the F-108 was the length of time during which it was advertised far and wide as having an entry into service of about 1963, and a performance of *Mach 5!!* Bill Gunston, British aviation historian *par excellence* mentioned the F-108 while covering the Arrow's first flight for *Flight* magazine:

Arrow—A World Leading Interceptor by Avro Aircraft

The CF-105 was "the biggest, most powerful and potentially the fastest fighter that the world has yet seen."

We in Britain have nothing like it. Two years ago we curtailed the development of a machine which would have begun to approach it—the so called "thin-wing Javelin"—and have since relied implicitly on a superb electronic defence environment and rel-

atively small weapons such as the English Electric P.1B and Thunderbird and the Bristol Bloodhound [a light, short range Mach 2 capable fighter and ground/sea based air defence missile with an associated ground control/radar infrastructure].

Even the USA has nothing like the Arrow; yet in that country the development of manned interceptors is by no means dead. North American Aviation hold a development contract from the US Air Force in respect of Weapons System 202A, which enjoys a development priority equalled by only one other USAF aeroplane. The vehicle for this weapons system will be the F-108, a chemical-fuel aircraft intended to reach at least Mach 5—a scarcely credible figure.

Considered solely as a weapon system, the chief raison d'etre of the Arrow is to be found in the enormous extent of the area which it is designed to defend. Including her numerous water areas Canada covers no less than 3,737,923 square miles, and is thus much larger than Europe or the USA. During the past five years the electronic defence systems of North America have improved out of all recognition, and there exists today a formidable barrier of long-range radars and fighter bases all controlled from a single unified HQ in the state of Colorado, USA. Yet this "infrastructure" is of no value unless the means exist to intercept and destroy any raiding bomber which might be encountered.

In the above passage Gunston mentions the cancellation of the Thin Wing Javelin, an aircraft that "would have begun to approach" the performance of the Arrow. He obviously couldn't have known that the Arrow had superceded the TWJ as the Hawker Siddeley Group's submission to the British all-weather interceptor specification. The aircraft that he refers to as having been "cancelled" was indeed the Arrow, the same plane he was now reviewing! Gunston then refers to the F-108 performance projection of Mach 5 as being "scarcely credible." From Floyd's documents, sited above, we know he was right on that count.

So why were the Americans pushing the obvious exaggeration of Mach 5 performance? It is hard to escape the conclusion that the F-108, serious program or otherwise, was being exploited to the maximum by US intelligence agencies to suggest all the programs under way in the UK, Canada, and elsewhere would be obsolete as they were entering service.

Avro's other delta-interceptor: the Avro 720 turbojet plus rocket fighter prototype, almost complete when cancelled by Duncan Sandys in early 1957. Using the Armstrong-Siddeley "Viper" turbojet and also their "Screamer" high-test peroxide and kerosene fuelled rocket motor, the 720 promised excellent performance for a point-defence fighter. Saunders-Roe was competing for this contract with their SR.53 demonstrator, to be followed (but for cancellation) by the P.177 service redesign. The 720's plain delta wing would have undergone modification. (Avro UK via Derek Wood)

Meanwhile, the F-108 was directly comparable to the Arrow. NAA designed the F-108 as a mainly stainless steel aircraft. Avro UK had developed a puddle-brazed honeycomb stainless steel sandwich material in the early fifties for the Avro 720 rocket/turbojet interceptor and the Avro 730 strike-reconnaissance platform. Before this they had perfected aluminum alloy honeycomb sandwich material for a low level, transonic strike bomber; an aircraft bearing the same configuration as Boeing's new "Sonic-Cruiser." Both materials were used on the Convair B-58 and later on the NAA XB-70 and one would assume they were applied to the F-108 as well. Even using this material, the XB-70 was overweight and this was a factor in its cancellation. One of the 100 Avro engineers who went to NAA after Black Friday and worked on the Valkyrie described the weight problem to the author in 1996. He stated simply that the Avro engineers arrived "too late to save it." He claimed the design was so far along that to change it would have resulted in a major redesign, something NAA didn't have time or money for. This fellow states it was simply too heavy and had other problems as well. Of course this suggests, relatively speaking, that the F-108 would have been similarly overweight. Based on its larger, heavier engines and from the drawings shown, considerably larger frontal area than the Arrow, one might feel safe in the assumption that the Arrow would have outperformed it by a fair margin, pro-

vided they replaced the intakes with a variable type and took steps to handle the kinetic heating at Mach 3.

The Mach 3+ Arrow 3

Avro's secret "Preliminary Proposal for Arrow 3" was released by Avro's Projects Research Group on 27 October 1958, although other documents show the version was conceived over a year earlier. If Cabinet minutes are any guide, in government circles this visionary aircraft was never disclosed and the preliminary proposal was never heard of again. It was never mentioned to Cabinet but then nothing (aside from vague allusions to the Arrow 2 appearing to be set to "meet" its specification) relating to the Arrow's potential was divulged in Cabinet. Avro's secret proposal diverges from latter-day book and article descriptions of the Arrow 3 in that the proposed combat speed is stated as Mach 3 rather than Mach 2.5.

For a Mach 2.5+ airframe, the most difficult problem to overcome was that of structural (kinetic) heating, due to air/skin friction, which made any conventional light-alloy aircraft vulnerable at these speeds since it would weaken and distort. Even if a light-alloy structure could be made to retain its strength at the high temperatures of Mach 2.5+ flight, cycling the materials through the heat and stress extremes encountered when flying across such a wide range of stressing temperatures often resulted in the struc-

An Arrow Mk. 3. (artist Paul McDonell)

ture becoming continually weaker. While steel and other alloys were known to be capable of absorbing such thermal and loading variables, their usage in an airframe in peace of aluminum alloys carried a stiff weight (and thus thrust speed and altitude) price.

Structural hot-soak leading-edge temperatures of 564 degrees Farenheit were expected by Avro at Mach 3 Arrow. Detailed testing and analysis indicated that not all the structure would have to be made from heavy materials if the aircraft was not expected to hot-soak at Mach 3 for a prolonged period. While titanium and steel were possible for leading edges and other areas, Avro felt they needed to retain aluminum (albeit a new high-temperature aluminum) for the majority of the structure simply from a weight perspective. At the time some researchers in structures for these kinds of speeds were insisting on designing the entire structure to withstand the maximum temperatures. The Lockheed Skunk Works thermodynamic experts, ably led by Ben Rich, chose this uncompromising approach for the

A-12/YF-12/SR-71 right around this time. Others were proposing they simply insulate a conventional structure; Avro decided to apply both of the above concepts. They had, by this early date, decided on a hybrid approach to the problem rather than banking on one technology alone.

The basic Arrow 3, at take-off weight, was projected to be almost 17,000 pounds heavier than the Mk. 2. An extra 10,000 pounds of internal fuel was responsible for the majority of this weight gain with a total fuel load of 28,738 pounds being specified. This extra fuel was carried by using more of the empty wing structure, filling some of the fin with fuel, and in a redesigned central fuselage sub-assembly. The construction technology of these and some other sections was an impressive technological advance Avro termed "sculptured skins." These "skins" were actually billets of the new aluminum alloy X2020-T6 that were machined to include much of the structural members with them being "sculpted" out of the billet and joined in a sophisticated way to the similarly sculpted for-

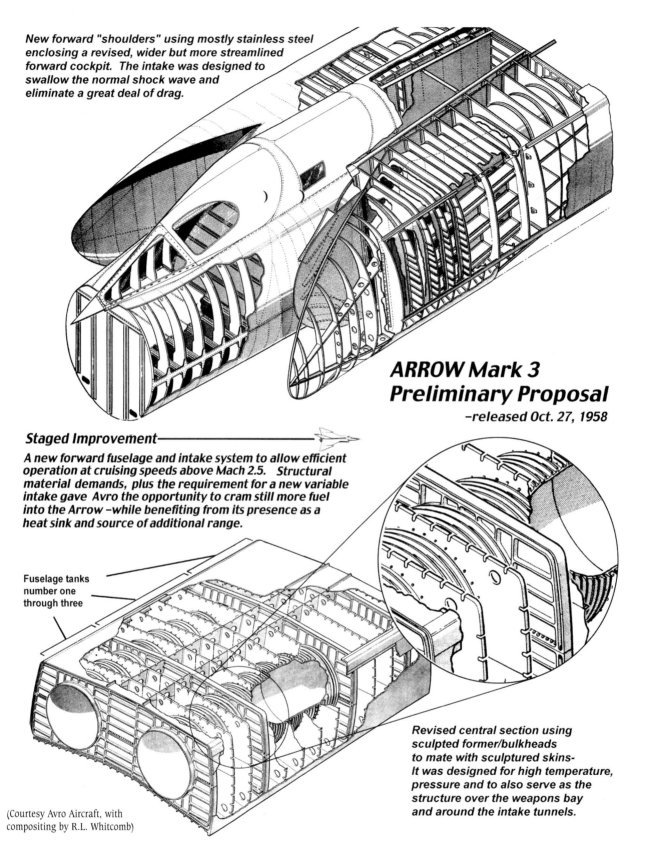

New forward "shoulders" using mostly stainless steel enclosing a revised, wider but more streamlined forward cockpit. The intake was designed to swallow the normal shock wave and eliminate a great deal of drag.

ARROW Mark 3
Preliminary Proposal
−released Oct. 27, 1958

Staged Improvement

A new forward fuselage and intake system to allow efficient operation at cruising speeds above Mach 2.5. Structural material demands, plus the requirement for a new variable intake gave Avro the opportunity to cram still more fuel into the Arrow −while benefiting from its presence as a heat sink and source of additional range.

Fuselage tanks number one through three

Revised central section using sculpted former/bulkheads to mate with sculptured skins- It was designed for high temperature, pressure and to also serve as the structure over the weapons bay and around the intake tunnels.

(Courtesy Avro Aircraft, with compositing by R.L. Whitcomb)

mers beneath. Again, Avro's growing usage of computerized production equipment (CNC machining) made this possible and efficient. The central fuselage area, over the armament bay and surrounding the intake ducts, was to be completely filled with fuel by application of these techniques along with Avro's sealant technologies.

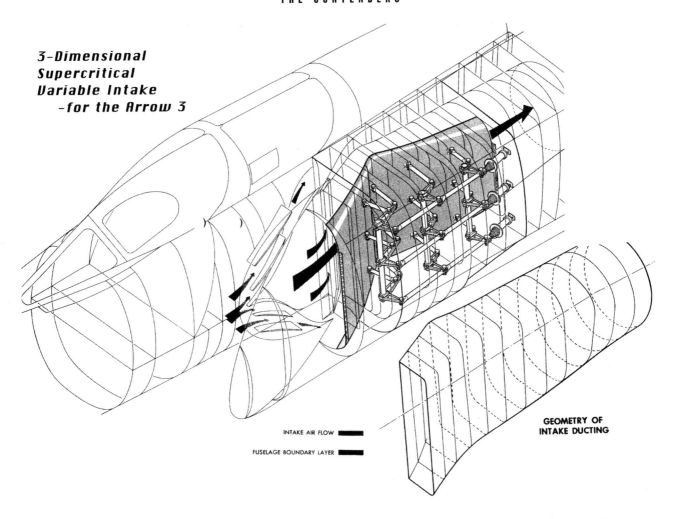

3-Dimensional Supercritical Variable Intake –for the Arrow 3

INTAKE AIR FLOW ▪▪▪▪

FUSELAGE BOUNDARY LAYER ▪▪▪▪

GEOMETRY OF INTAKE DUCTING

Interesting high-temperature aluminum alloys were looked at with Avro proposing X2020-T6 alloy for the structure instead of the 75ST used for the Arrow 2. This appeared to promise acceptable characteristics up to about 350 degrees F. This is about 100 degrees higher than specifications for normal light-alloys in use at the time and since which would have, by itself, allowed a sustained speed of around Mach 2.4. Avro's metallurgical department had done thermal stressing tests on X2020-T6, and 2024-T81, finding the former superior by over 10 percent. North American, at this time into the development of the X-15 hypersonic rocket plane, (designed for up to Mach 7, which it almost reached) had chosen 2024-T6 for cooler areas of the structure. In areas facing extreme kinetic heating, such as the leading edges, stainless steel and/or titanium were specified while other surfaces would employ a combination of any of these materials and/or an advanced honeycomb-composite insulation Avro was developing. It had things in common with the evolving ablative "paints" used on missile nose-cones, and with the later heatshields for Mercury and Gemini. Jim Floyd relates that he wasn't

entirely satisfied with the external insulation scheme specified to go over top of some of the external surfaces of the Mk. 3 as a second skin. Bearing Floyd's concerns about external insulation panels in mind, it is interesting to note that the Space Shuttle uses a conventional light-alloy structure and relies on external insulation to keep the *extreme* structural temperatures under control on re-entry! Gunston's *Faster Than Sound,* published in 1992, shows diagrams of presumably modern external insulation for spaceplanes that can in no way be considered as advanced as Avro's evolving method as it stood in 1958. The SR-71, as most aviation enthusiasts are aware, uses mostly titanium for structure and skin and represents the opposite approach to that of the shuttle. Lockheed's uncompromising approach was commendable perhaps, but heavy and was probably not required for components far from the engines and leading-edges and around the fuel tanks. As of Black Friday, Avro's leading-edge insulation scheme seemed to comprise of an almost foil thin, titanium skin epoxy and heat pressure-bonded to a fibreglass or even carbon-fibre honeycomb core. The core was filled with an

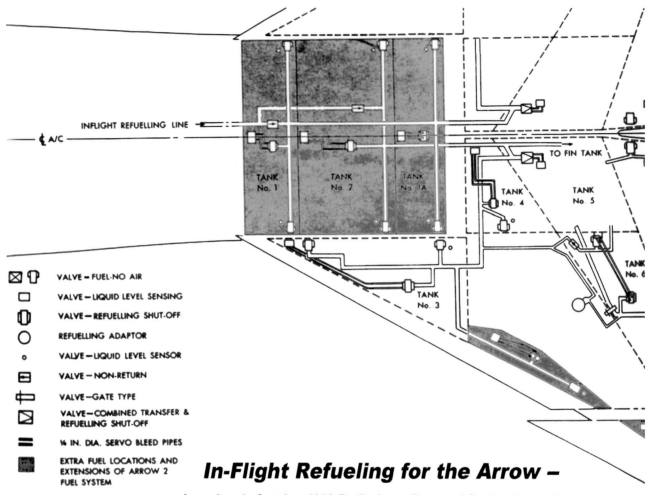

⊠	𝓣	VALVE – FUEL-NO AIR
□		VALVE – LIQUID LEVEL SENSING
𝟎		VALVE – REFUELLING SHUT-OFF
○		REFUELLING ADAPTOR
∘		VALVE – LIQUID LEVEL SENSOR
⊟		VALVE – NON-RETURN
⊕		VALVE – GATE TYPE
⊠		VALVE – COMBINED TRANSFER & REFUELLING SHUT-OFF
═		¼ IN. DIA. SERVO BLEED PIPES
▦		EXTRA FUEL LOCATIONS AND EXTENSIONS OF ARROW 2 FUEL SYSTEM

In-Flight Refueling for the Arrow –

- from Avro's October 1958 Preliminary Proposal for the Arrow Mark 3

The fuel system illustrated assumes an in-flight refueling requirement for the Arrow 3. A vertical rising probe located ahead of the pilot's canopy is proposed for this system since the increased fuselage nose width dictated by the new intakes gives space for a probe and feed pipe running aft into the fuel system as shown.

insulating fibre-glass micro-balloon filled epoxy resin. This arrangement also added structural strength, something the Mark 4 required. Avro's thinking was obviously a mixed approach and as such was sound in concept. (Avro Eng from DH Art)

The Mk. 3 Intake

As mentioned, the original (Mk .1 and Mk. 2) Arrow intake was fixed and limited to a maximum speed of at least Mach 2.3, a very high figure for a fixed geometry intake. During the flight testing of the Arrow it was found, to the joy of the design team, that they had erred consid-

erably on the side of caution when estimating the supersonic drag of the airframe.

This is interesting since a great deal of political trouble had been caused when the NAE, DRB and RCAF had gone to NACA Langley to discuss "Aerodynamic Problems of Avro CF-105 Aircraft." The Avro team had, in the NAE's opinion, underestimated the supersonic drag of the airframe by one-half. It seems likely they were basing their projections simply on the unhappy results of the YF-102 Delta Dagger first prototype. Indeed, AVM Easton wrote a memo to the NAE referring to their simple, mathematical, proportional, enlargement of the F-102's characteristics as a base whereupon to predict the performance of the Arrow, calling their method a "dangerous assumption."

It appears that Avro Canada may have also taught NACA (later the National Aeronautics and Space Administration—NASA) something about estimating drag for such aircraft. At the time there was a controversy over whether Avro should close the intake ducts on its wind-tunnel models or leave them open during testing. Avro tried it both ways and found that with the inlets open the drag was much lower in the wind tunnel. To decide which way was more accurate, they compared these results with the drag of the rocket-launched Arrow telemetry models and found that the model's drag was still lower than either wind tunnel method. In an effort to be safe Avro chose to conservatively apply the middle figure, which had been produced in the NACA Langley tunnels with the inlets open. Today this is the standard testing method. Again, Avro was heavily criticized by some of the Canadian government critics, such as John Orr of the DRB, for having had 20-20 foresight.

Avro's conservative drag assumptions meant quite simply that the aircraft would be capable of much higher top speeds and altitudes than had been projected based upon a given amount of thrust. It was quite apparent that the Iroquois-powered version would be capable of much more than Mach 2.3 if the intakes were changed to a variable type. This higher speed would overload the original intake spillage and bypass system and require a better means of managing the shock effects around the intake.

The Avro engineers devised a rounded and forward swept variable intake. (Interestingly, recent NASA internet presentations relating to hypersonic intake design conclude that a forward swept intake, using part of the fuselage as a compression ramp, is the most efficient for hypersonic flight.) For supersonic speeds the intake would have bleed ramps that would move and pinch the airflow, forcing the excess to be bled away thus allowing good pressure recovery in the air going to the engines while minimising spillage. Since the new design was rounded, it is known as a three-dimensional variable intake. The F-15, MiG-29, Concorde and others use what is termed a two-dimensional intake, the two straight-edged dimensions being width and height. The first aircraft to use this progressive concept was the North American A3J Vigilante of around 1958. It has always been known that a three-dimensional design is potentially more efficient since the airflow at the corners of a rectangle becomes distorted. The reasons why

two-dimensional designs are so commonly used is because the mathematical calculations to design them are much simpler, as are the physical challenges posed in their construction. The addition of the "third dimension," or more correctly third *factor* (roundness), exponentially increased the requirement for "number crunching" to predict effects, and in turn predict the amount of inlet variation required across the speed, temperature, air density and power ranges. This appears to be why even the newest hypersonic designs use a two-dimensional intake system, even while all the technical representations take care to explain the difficulties in computer modelling the flow at the speeds and temperatures encountered at hypersonic velocity. This is interesting considering the Cray supercomputers available to NASA and US industry.

I believe anyone truly acquainted with the history of technological progress will point out that the best supercomputer is still a human genius, perhaps backed up by such machines. Avro had one of the best aerodynamicists in the world in the person of Jim Chamberlin, who was ably assisted by Harry Keast and Burt Avery of Orenda. (Avery had worked at Victory Aircraft and, through a scheme initiated at Avro Canada similar to Dobson's special-apprentice scheme, had gone to the University of Toronto for Engineering. He quickly proved himself at Orenda engines and became chief engineer, later replacing the president, Charles Grinyer, when the latter's *second* resignation stood.) Avro also had the world's largest *digital* computer, the IBM 704, to help "crunch the numbers" plus about 30 mathematicians and engineers dedicated to feeding it.

The Arrow Mk. 3 was designed for a Mach 3 *combat speed*, which is faster than any fighter in the world to this day save the ill-fated YF-12A which became the SR-71, and *perhaps* the MiG-25 Foxbat. Considering the discomfort the MiG-25 created in the US military industrial complex, one might ponder their feelings about the Arrow 3, the credible design for which appeared about eight years before the Foxbat flew. In common with the Arrow 3, the A-12/SR-71 family also employed three-dimensional variable intakes using a round movable spike. The Convair B-58 Hustler used the same concept about five years earlier but applied it in an inferior way.

The Mk. 3 intake was designed to swallow the bow (or normal) shock wave making the intake a "supercritical" intake. The only aircraft the author knows of to enter service with a 3-D variable and supercritical intake is the A-12/YF-12A/SR-71.

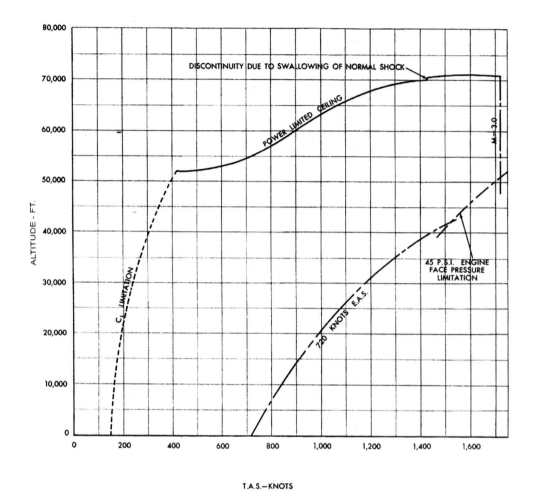

Performance curve from the 1958 Mk. 3 Preliminary Proposal. This astounding curve shows a thrust and performance increase at 70,000 ft and Mach 2.5 and also shows that the Mach 3 "placard speed" is restricted only by an artificial temperature limit, projected due to unknowns in over-all heat-soak structural effects and insulation/materials state of the art. Considering this curve was produced after the true (lower) drag of the Arrow was known from test flight, it should be considered accurate. (Avro Canada via Jim Floyd)

FIG. 19 MAXIMUM LEVEL SPEED AT COMBAT WEIGHT

Avro quoted the combat ceiling at combat weight to be at least 70,500 feet at Mach 3 while still allowing a margin for a 500 feet per minute (fpm) climb. An *anticipated* limitation of the Arrow 2, as pointed out in Avro's Performance Report 13 (before the Arrow flew and revealed her much lower drag coefficient), was due to nearly full up-deflection of the elevators at maximum altitude. The resulting trim-drag was in the order of 5,000 pounds. Evidence that Avro was already thinking of cross-programming the fly-by-wire system to reduce trim drag, and also allow more pitch authority at maximum altitude, by allowing the ailerons to operate as elevators in tandem with the latter, is found in the Mk. 3 proposal. Above 45,000 feet they specified that the Mk. 3's ailerons would be programmed for 5 degrees up deflection. No doubt Avro was watching the flight test data

from the flying Arrows as the means to quantify optimum amounts of aileron trimming at any altitude, and were looking to program them into the Arrow's fly-by-wire system. As Floyd pointed out in his Commonwealth Lecture to the RAeS, programming the flight control system was the most intensive part of the development flying that Avro conducted during the Arrow program, in part because the rest of the aircraft was behaving so well.

Propulsion for the Mk. 3 Arrow was to be the Iroquois Mk. 3. Changes from the Mk. 2 version of the engine included a new combustion section, six inches shorter than that of the Iroquois 2, a new turbine section with much narrower blades (thereby allowing a much shorter turbine section overall) yet with a larger bell-mouth size with correspondingly larger diameter compressor rotors and stator blade sets and structure. To handle the increased mass-flow a larger diameter and slightly longer afterburner section and nozzle assembly was specified. Incredibly, they were only specifying a thrust gain of about 600 pounds, wet or dry, for the Iroquois 3. In reality it would have been *much* higher, especially considering the smaller "hole size" Iroquois 2 had produced 25,000 lbs, without burner, on the test stand.

The intake for the Mark 3 (and later higher-performance Arrow design studies) is especially interesting. The intake Avro proposed was a four-ramp three-dimensional variable concept and was designed to give *no* shock-induced airflow separation on either the ramp surface or the fuselage diverter plate at all supersonic speeds. This was, and is, very advanced thinking and once again Avro's massive computer installations allowed them to design, with confidence, to this radical ideal. This was achieved by very careful computer modelling of the strengths of the triple shock waves produced on the variable ramps at different speeds, while designing the intake to benefit from the bow shock from the aircraft nose. The nose of the Arrow actually became the center "spike" similar to the configuration of the SR-71 Blackbird. The only speeds at which Avro found shock-induced separation *at all* with this intake design were between Mach 1.4 and Mach 1.6, where the disturbed airflow was "bounced" against the fuselage, and bled off between the diverter plate and the fuselage side and spilled overboard. A very narrow "slit" of boundary-layer air was removed on the inside of the intake at the rear of the diverter plate by a knife-edge "razor" bleed and this was supplied to the air-conditioning heat exchangers. Those exchangers, as on all Arrows, exhausted nearly axially (rearward) which is "nearly" perfect. The intake was designed to run at up to 45 psi and thus boosted the compressor ratio of the engine considerably. This explains why the SR-71's engine was designed to give only 6-1 compression and why the Iroquois was also low, at only 8-1.

The most astounding aspect of the intake, however, was the fact that the intake was designed to *swallow* the normal shock wave coming off the nose and use this to both increase thrust and also reduce drag. Absolutely radical thinking. Getting rid of large portions of the normal shock wave would decrease the drag of the airframe considerably since the normal shock "plows" air. Swallowing it actually increased the compression of the air inside the intakes resulting in a *boost* in performance in some regions of the performance envelope, as the per-formance curve above shows. As such it was a "super-critical" intake and was the first of it's kind to the author's knowledge. The first to enter service was that used on the SR-71. For an indication of the drag and efficiency advantages of swallowing the normal shock, one should look to the D-21 reconnaissance drone piggy-backed on the SR-71 for a time. This device swallowed the normal shock with its 3-D intake being at the nose of the drone. In Sweetman's book *Aurora, The Pentagon's Secret Hypersonic Spyplane*, the D-21 is proclaimed to possess a true, yet incredible range of 10-15,000 miles! (The official USAF Museum website, however, lists this range as being "3,500+ miles.") Sweetman was very impressed by this figure and attributed it to the Skunk Works being able to design it for a single design point in terms of speed, altitude and "G" loading. He missed, or didn't acknowledge, the impressive drag and compression advantages of the D-21's "supercritical" intake swallowing the normal shock as applied to the D-21. To be sure, the conservative critics, as in any era or field, would have found the concept ridiculous. Today we know it works.

SUNTANS, Arrows and OXCARTS

In 1957, (coincidentally around the time of presentations to Perkins on what Avro felt a developed Arrow could do), the CIA concluded that their U-2 spyplane would be vulnerable in the near future and that a high-performance successor was required. This was the origin of PROJECT SUNTAN, for a Mach 2.5 cruising spyplane to replace the U-2 and operate at the same altitudes as the U-2; 70,000 feet.

The design chosen, between the Convair and Lockheed proposals, evolved into the Lockheed Skunk Works CL-400, a hydrogen-powered Mach 2.5 cruising long-range aircraft. This design was aerodynamically similar to Lockheed's F-104 Starfighter, but much larger and was equipped with large hydrogen-fuelled turbojets on the wingtips. Construction and development work was done at a secret location in Florida where Pratt & Whitney was also at work on the engines. Aspects of this engine development may have led to the J-58 turbojet used on the SR-71, although most popular sources say the J-58's origin was for a cancelled Navy aircraft. There is probably truth in both. Today US sources claim that "not one word" of the Suntan development leaked to the Soviets up to the latter-day declassification of the vaguest generalities of the development.

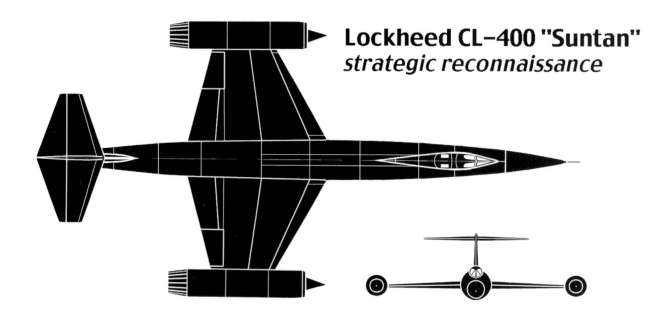

Lockheed CL-400 "Suntan"
strategic reconnaissance

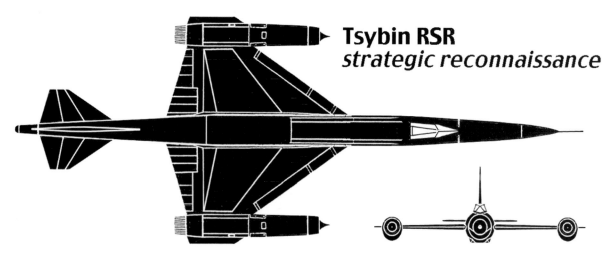

Tsybin RSR
strategic reconnaissance

(image by R.L. Whitcomb)

The Soviets, however, developed a very similar aircraft to the CL-400 Suntan, the Tsybin RSR. The Suntan project was cancelled in 1957 (some say 1958, others 1959), presumably because, although hydrogen fuel has the highest energy by weight, the high-pressure tanks and considerably larger related structure (since hydrogen is less dense and thus occupies more volume for the same amount of stored energy) resulted in a design with less range than a kerosene (jet fuel) version. This was after four prototypes had been built, which suggests that something drastic happened to make them abandon it after such an effort. Considering the effort required to build 4 aircraft, the lack of photographic and other evidence of their existence is almost eerie.

The Soviet RSR, however, used kerosene, and to evade missiles was designed to barrel roll at altitude (around 70,000 feet) and zoom to 137,000 ft. A smaller development version was produced named the NM-1 (Natural Model One) but the entire program was cancelled and the five complete aircraft were ordered reduced to scrap. In an interesting contrast to the common view of Soviet totalitarianism, the workers resisted having the product of their labours treated thus and the authorities allowed the aircraft to be stored for at least three years before they were scrapped without protest. Meanwhile, in Canada the government threatened to send in the Army if Smye did not fully comply with their order for destruction of everything to do with the Arrow.

Perkins had received information from Avro on their evolving ideas for advanced Arrows in July and September of 1957. Of course, at this time Avro's concepts would have been saddled by an exaggerated drag coefficient and would therefore have been conservative by 15-25 percent. The first submission included information on Avro's evolving Mk. 3 Arrow, which Avro felt could do most of the F-108's job with aerial refuelling. In September 1957 Avro passed along information on their Mk. 4 Arrow, and this design would have made the USAF, CIA, Perkins, and probably Kelly Johnson of the Skunk Works gasp! The CL-400 was cancelled around the time of Avro's revelations and wasn't officially replaced with the A-12 until everything to do with the Arrow had been destroyed.

PROJECT OXCART: The Lockheed A-11/A-12/YF-12A/F-12B/SR-71 Blackbirds

Much has been made of this design and even more propaganda swirls around it. In September of 1959, the same month the F-108 was cancelled, the CIA authorised Lockheed to proceed with anti-radar "stealth" studies. This has not been revealed officially until recently. Details of the structural design (such as the shape of the long leading-edge extension, the "chine") and certainly the inward-canted vertical stabilizers are examples of features designed to reduce radar cross-section. This is not mentioned in Ben Rich's *Skunk Works*, a book containing more

than the usual amount of disinformation, no doubt owing to the usual security oaths and corporate "commercial in confidence" restrictions. Rich's book was also vetted by the CIA. The design that emerged was a long delta-winged aircraft with a long leading-edge extension (LEX) or "chine" leading right up to the nose with two large turbojets at mid span. The chine contributed several advantages, usually publicized as being incorporated mainly to improve directional (yaw) stability and increase fuselage capacity. It was certainly also designed to minimize radar reflections. Perhaps its greatest benefit would be to act as a fixed canard to reduce nose "tuck" at supersonic speeds brought about by the normal rearward movement of the center of lift at those velocities. This would reduce supersonic trim drag considerably at high altitudes; one of the main limiting factors of all aircraft operating at such exotic altitudes and speeds.

When the chine is considered as a modified canard, an interesting, earlier design comes to mind, namely the Avro (UK) 730 strike reconnaissance bomber. This design began in 1954, around the time of the CL-400 and X-15 rocket plane projects in the USA. The Avro 730 was designed to meet GOR 330 for an aircraft with a cruise speed of Mach 2.5, an altitude of 60,000 feet by 1000 miles from take-off, and a range of 4000 nm. Very ambitious indeed. The 730 was to use long, side-looking radar emitter/receivers,

The Avro 730 strike-reconnaissance bomber. There were to be four afterburning Armstrong-Siddeley Sapphire turbojets in each engine pod. Construction was to be stainless-steel honeycomb. (image by R.L. Whitcomb)

An SR-71 over Las Vegas. (artist Paul McDonell)

which partially explains the aircraft length—originally about 200 feet but reduced to 159 feet once the aircraft was redesigned for an additional bombing role, using a shorter side-looking radar installation.

The CIA is well known to have an industrial espionage division which, once combined with the Canadian and British generosity with their most advanced technology, assured Lockheed of the best information in the world on advanced aircraft, propulsion and control. Of course they weren't without their own brilliance. Avro projected up to Mach 3 cruise and a 70,000 ft mid-range operational ceiling for the 730. This is, in reality, about the same specification of the Skunk Works' early A-12s in terms of real world cruise and altitude capability. It is not, and was not, intended to reflect the maximum performance of either airframe. The Avro 730 was, of course, cancelled by Duncan Sandys with his notorious 1957 White Paper on defence. The metal mock-up, well along in construction, was cut up and used for scrap bins itself!

The A-12/SR-71 *et al* made extensive use of titanium. It has been pointed out here and in other works, that, at the

time, Avro (or the Hawker Siddeley Group) had the greatest supply channels and most experience in using titanium. The author's research shows that during the 1950s US manufacturers were literally screaming for more titanium. It must have chagrined the US military industrial complex enormously to know Avro had the supply locked down (since much of the then-known natural resources for titanium were in the British Commonwealth), and were years ahead in learning how to use it. Avro Canada relied on Canadian Steel Improvements who liased with Hawker Siddeley's High-Duty Alloys Company, who worked with Avro UK. As Joe Baugher points out in his excellent web article on the A-12/SR-71, Lockheed had to resort to "back channels" to acquire enough titanium for the program, and in fact the majority of it came from the Soviet Union! Clearly Avro was in the way of US strategic vital interests in this regard. Lockheed's difficulties with titanium also make an interesting read since Avro had encountered many of the same problems, and had conquered them, years earlier.

Another OXCART parallel, with the Arrow development, was the use of J-75 engines in the first development aircraft while Lockheed and the CIA were waiting for Pratt & Whitney to perfect the J-58 turbo-afterburner concept. Using the J-73 engine the A-12 had achieved Mach 2.16 and had flown at altitudes up to 60,000 ft. This is solidly Arrow Mk. 1 territory and should tell the reader much about the potential of the CF-105 Mk. 2 and above since the J-58 and Iroquois had similar thrust, although the Iroquois was again smaller and lighter and thus much more efficient. Further, the Mark 1 Arrow's J-75s only produced 12,800 lbs dry thrust while the A-12 was tested using even more developed versions than the F-106 and Thunderchief, at around 17,100 lbs dry thrust.

With the cancellation of the F-108 project a few months after the demise of the Arrow, Lockheed saw an opportunity to secretly field an A-12 version for the interceptor role. They managed to get the USAF involved in October of 1960 and commenced construction of a high-altitude interceptor version: the YF-12A. It is interesting that, a single year after the US *publicly* cancelled their long-range interceptor, they *secretly* commenced design of one with virtually identical performance, only now with aerial re-fuelling. The public cancellation of the F-108 must have made Diefenbaker and Pearkes sleep easier since it, on the surface, vindicated their decision to scrap the Arrow.

Meanwhile, to this day former employees of North American Aviation (designers of the F-108) suggest the F-108 was cancelled to provide funds for the CIA's pet project. General Electric people feel the same way about the amazing J-93's cancellation when viewed against the lower-tech J-58 for the Blackbird. NAA people insist the cockpit for the resulting YF-12A was lifted directly from the F-108. There are photos and drawings of the 108's cockpit to prove this while it is public knowledge that the radar and weapons for the YF-12A came from the Rapier.

In keeping with CIA and related groups' secret agenda, the following passage is quite interesting from Joe Baugher's A-12/SR-71 article:

> With the growing number of A-12s flying out in the western desert, [Area 51 or Groom Lake] the CIA felt that there was a danger that the OXCART project's cover could be blown at any moment. Although the program had gone through development, construction, and a year of flight testing without attracting any public attention, the Department of Defense was experiencing increasing difficulty in concealing its participation in the OXCART program because of the delays and cost

overruns that had increased the rate of expenditures to such an extent that they might ... attract unwanted attention from congressional budget oversight committees.

Three months and seven days after John F. Kennedy was assassinated, his replacement, Lyndon Bains Johnson, publicly acknowledged the existence of the A-12 (which he mistakenly called the A-11). He described the role of this aircraft as "research," with a top speed near Mach 3, and with the capability of operating above 70,000 ft. Previously the cover for the U-2 spyplane had been weather research. Again, it may have fooled some of the voters, but it certainly wouldn't have fooled the Soviets.

The author speculated to some exceptional US aviation contacts that the SR-71 has *always* had a nuclear-strike capability. Another commonly repeated story is that the president reversed the letters in his official introduction of the aircraft, and that it was supposed to be the "RS-71", as in Reconnaissance, Strategic. Strike-Reconnaissance makes ever so much more sense, especially since the ability to jam a 500 lb free-fall nuke *somewhere* in that airframe just seems too tantalizing. On the other hand, Ben Rich, thermodynamics expert (and later head of the Skunk Works) made some interesting remarks after SR-71 retirement. He expressed surprise that the Pentagon had never taken advantage of those two open chine-bays in the SR-71 to house nuclear weapons. Besides the implied possibility, it goes to show what *could* be hidden with internal weapons carriage. And their indication of its original secondary role might be the "A" in its original designators, A-11 and A-12. "A" stands for attack just as "F" stood for fighter and "R" stood for reconnaissance.

The pre-production YF-12A interceptor, in flight test, used the Hughes ASG-18 pulse-Doppler radar with a dish of 38 inches, and the GAR-9 (AIM-47A) missile. The successful (yet later cancelled) AIM-47A evolved into the Phoenix missile used exclusively on the F-14 Tomcat and is thought, in the absence of proof from actual usage, to be a very effective weapon. The Phoenix also made use of the second stage of the earlier AA-N-10 Eagle long-range missile design making the Phoenix something of a hybrid, combining the front and rear ends of two entirely different missiles. Apparently this is the reason for the name Phoenix, since it had "risen from the ashes" of the Eagle and AIM-47A. The Phoenix, by the way, had the same length and span as Sparrow, suggesting the Arrow could have carried at least three internally.

The Eagle was a very long-range, air-to-air missile which the CF-100 Mk. 8 version, rarely heard of, was to use. The 1957-58 concept of using a very stable, yet slow aircraft as a long-range missile launcher was recognized by the US as well. This is exactly the concept the Americans explored with the Douglas "Missileer" aircraft and weapons system of the very early 1960s. The Mk. 8 CF-100 was Avro's response to a 1958 request by NATO for an improved CF-100. Of course no such official request would have been submitted had the CF-100 not been known, even at that late date, to be the most effective all-weather and night interceptor in Europe. According to Shaw's *There Never Was an Arrow* and other documents, this official NATO request was totally ignored by the Diefenbaker government.

The Arrow could have carried the AIM-47As of the Rapier/YF-12A internally. In Avro's proposals for the Arrow Mk. 3 and 4, they noted the requirement for a longer-range radar system and mentioned Hughes' work on a "pulse-Doppler" set. This is assuredly the development that led to the ASG-18 of the F-108 and YF-12A. It appears Avro was looking for either a developed, digital ASTRA 2 set or the Hughes system as an alternate for their high performance Arrow versions. Avro did not expect an acceptable radar or weapon for such a high speed aircraft to be operations ready until 1963-1965 and as such were planning the Mk. 3 and 4 versions to this time table. As we now know, ASTRA 2 was to be fully digital, fully transistorized, and to also include pulse-Doppler.

As tested, the ASG-18 supposedly had a detection range of some 500 miles, while the AIM-47A had a speed of Mach 6 and an interception range of over 100 miles. (Perkins had, however, related to Avro that the Falcon "Z" missile (GAR-9/AIM-47) only had a range of 25 miles.) With such a powerful radar in the sky, the Arrow 3 would have had an airborne radar that was competitive with the ground radars of the DEW line, *and mobile*. Such an impressive airborne surveillance capability would have made the vulnerable DEW, Mid-Canada and Pinetree radar lines, not to mention the entire SAGE concept, obsolete and redundant. The DEW line is still in operation (as the North Warning System) while SAGE is considered a dinosaur—replaced by aircraft relying on the Arrow's autonomous concept of operations. Avro knew from RAF and other demonstrations that SAGE was, as they said, "unworkable" due to its vulnerability to Electronic Countermeasures (ECM) and "carcinatron jamming." (Normal jamming involves flooding the enemy's

radar receiver with a powerful signal across the expected frequencies in hopes of blotting out the return from the enemy's radar transmitter with "noise." This type of jamming is relatively easy to defeat if the system is designed to reject any signal not on the same [or expected] frequency, amplitude and/or pulse-rate of the original signal. Carcinatron jamming is more sophisticated. It "figures out" the frequencies the enemy radar is operating on and introduces a "cancerous" signal, the same as the one being generated by the enemy system, then slowly diverging this signal from the true return. This is done in hopes of misleading the enemy radar into thinking the target is at a slightly different location than it is in reality. This type of jamming is harder to defeat and may not be noticed by the set under such attack, especially if the set is automated as in BOMARC and SAGE.)

According to Baugher's article, 1965 tests with the AN/ASG-18 radar and AIM-47A weapon, as deployed in the YF-12A, were very successful:

> Six out of seven AIM-47 tests resulted in hits, including one fired from an altitude of 75,000 feet and a speed of Mach 3.2 against a target approaching head-on at 1500 ft.

This passage certainly puts the lie to the idea that high-altitude aircraft were more vulnerable than those down low! Indeed in his late 1958 visit to the UK, Floyd was privy to the RAF air defence exercise OPERATION SUNBEAM. This showed that high-altitude interceptors were quite effective against very low targets, and also that Ground Control Intercept (GCI) techniques like SAGE were very vulnerable to ECM and outright destruction. (The American HARM—Home On Radar Missile— itself based on the Sparrow missile's airframe, certainly proved the latter.) Sunbeam proved defensive ground to air missiles were actually useless in the face of the carcinatron and other jamming techniques that the Soviet Union was then known to possess. This exercise and other solid research proved to the RAF, once and for all, that interceptors would be required "for the foreseeable future" and that missiles were no substitute. In fact it proved the missiles' inital purpose; a last-ditch, point defence system to *hopefully* take care of any intruders that got through the defensive interceptor screen. It took some time for this realization to trickle through to the consciousness of the leading politicians in Britain and Canada, for whatever reasons. Clearly however, the United States *never* bought into the missiles-over-interceptors faction even though they profited from the debate.

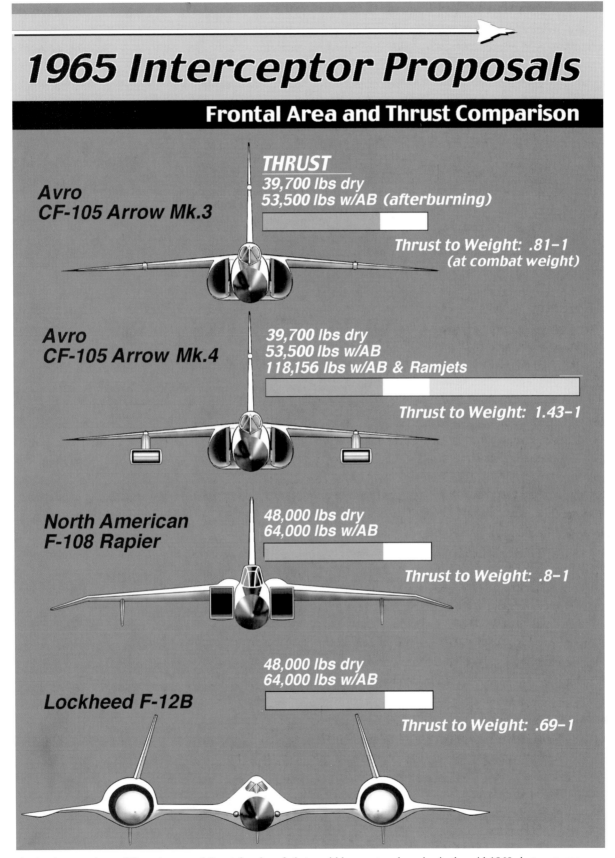

1965 Interceptor Proposals

Frontal Area and Thrust Comparison

**Avro
CF-105 Arrow Mk.3**

THRUST
39,700 lbs dry
53,500 lbs w/AB (afterburning)

Thrust to Weight: .81–1
(at combat weight)

**Avro
CF-105 Arrow Mk.4**

39,700 lbs dry
53,500 lbs w/AB
118,156 lbs w/AB & Ramjets

Thrust to Weight: 1.43–1

**North American
F-108 Rapier**

48,000 lbs dry
64,000 lbs w/AB

Thrust to Weight: .8–1

Lockheed F-12B

48,000 lbs dry
64,000 lbs w/AB

Thrust to Weight: .69–1

A visual comparison of frontal area and thrust for aircraft that could have entered service in the mid-1960s but were cancelled. (by R.L. Whitcomb)

Nothing, really, has approached the Arrow's altitude capabilities in a defensive aircraft other than the YF-12A. On 1 May 1965, the YF-12A compiled a number of records:

- 15/25 km closed course speed record of 1800 knots (Mach 3.13).
- sustained altitude record of 80,258 feet.
- 500 km closed course speed record of 1428 knots (Mach 2.16).
- 1000 km closed course speed record of 1469 knots (Mach 2.23).

These numbers indicate the YF-12A, at that stage of development, was really only capable of *sustaining* an altitude of 80,000 feet, and this height would not likely have been achieved at combat weight. The fact that the shortest closed course speed record was by far the fastest, indicates the YF-12A was vulnerable to Mach heating, despite its titanium construction. The cut back chines (to make way for the radar nose cone) and the nose cone itself probably contributed to some of this limitation although engine turbine inlet temperature was (and still is) also critical. All numbers were solidly in the range of Avro's projections for the Arrow Mk. 3, which Avro stated could have been in squadron service by that time! The Mk. 3 preliminary proposal to the RCAF was finished on 27 October 1958 and Avro was waiting for authority to continue developing this version when the Arrow program was cancelled.

Based on the phenomenal performance of the YF-12A, ASG-18 radar and AIM-47A missile, the USAF requested 93 F-12B interceptors on 14 May 1965. Congress complied and earmarked $90 million towards production for that fiscal year. Strangely, Secretary of Defense, Robert McNamara, refused the funding! He then ordered the tooling for the aircraft destroyed. McNamara pursued another alternative, the mythical "F-106X." This is bizarre behaviour in the extreme when viewed against Convair's performance in the YF-92/F-102/F-106 fiasco. How one can choose tomorrow's "conceivable" aircraft over today's reality (or cancel aircraft in favour of missiles which do not exist) is beyond logic. McNamara also ordered all *existing* (mostly soft) tooling to be destroyed. This had severe ramifications when the Pentagon needed more SR-71s and resulted in older A-12 airframes, substantially different from the SR-71 standard, being cobbled up to produce a few extra Blackbirds.

McNamara's destruction of a decent, existing design in pursuit of his Convair/General Dynamics "wonder-planes,"

the F-106X and F-111 certainly supports theories of the Cold War having been deliberately prolonged by a secret, or perhaps not-so-secret but exceedingly arrogant, government. This opinion is, in part, based on how expensive the F-111 was, how long it took to produce, and on what an under-powered and hard to maintain aircraft it turned out to be. The F-111's use of the notorious and low-powered Pratt & Whitney TF-30 also supports the notion of Pratt & Whitney being the golden boys on the engine side. McNamara went on to head the World Bank. John Foster Dulles, an arch-Cold Warrior, publicly stated (in *Time* magazine when he won "man of the year") that one of his four goals in that position was to "prolong" and extend the Cold War!

Once the F-12B was dead, the CIA retained the exclusive services of the (now named) SR-71 spyplane. It was certainly a success but not without its own problems. Several were lost in development and service, though apparently none due to enemy action.

The fact remains to this day that a Mach 3+, very-high-altitude intruder is virtually impossible to stop. The SR-71 has proven this time and again up to the 1990s. In fact, Lockheed's famous designer Clarence "Kelly" Johnson at one point mentioned that over 1000 missiles had been fired at A-12/SR-71s with none being successful! Experts (such as Bill Sweetman in his work on the Aurora spyplane) now argue that an aircraft of this speed and altitude capability presents a much harder target than even a ballistic missile warhead during re-entry. This is due to the simple fact that a missile nose cone, falling under gravity, follows a predictable trajectory and has an inferior speed and none of the manoeuverability of a high, fast flying aircraft. So much for interceptors being obsolete and missiles being unstoppable. Other stories relate SR-71 pilots watching SAMs (surface to air missiles) slowly climbing up to intercept whereupon a small alteration to the spyplane's flight path would easily put them out of harm's way. This is far from the still-current "consensus" that high altitude aircraft are vulnerable. Obviously a very high-altitude aircraft has an enormous amount of potential energy due to height. Very few missiles can even get to such extremes of altitude.

Many claim the SR-71 is capable of higher speed and altitude than the advertised Mach 3.2 at 80,000 ft. This is no doubt true. However *sustained* speed and altitude are much more important. The SR-71 in fact is quoted as being able to maintain this speed for 48 minutes. Jim Floyd was impressed by this figure, mentioning that it was about twice as long as Avro had achieved in testing of materials

(image circa 1957, courtesy Jim Floyd)

etc. for the Mk. 3. The Mk. 3 was proposed as being able to maintain Mach 3 for 20 minutes. Floyd also pointed out that the Arrow Mark 4 was to use titanium exclusively as the skin material, just like the A-12/SR-71.

The Arrow Mark 4: Mach 3+ Interceptor, Missile Carrier and Strike-Reconnaissance Aircraft

Little has surfaced on this Arrow variant other than information Jim Floyd has provided. As in any active design team, ideas were always being proposed, some not worth the effort, and some brilliant. Avro seemed to take a modular view towards where ideas were directed, specifically, towards satisfying the most stringent demands of particular projects in the UK and US. The LRIX was a major influence, GOR 329 was obviously another, when the Avro 730 was cancelled Avro gave some aspects of this role more consideration, and so on. When that big delta-wing, big weapons bay, big thrust and tiny drag were weighed alongside what could be strapped to the basic aircraft, an incredibly wide variety of tasks could be considered.

The Mk. 3 Arrow, with the external insulation scheme and air-to-air refuelling capability was shown to be an alternative to the F-108. Perkins' comments regarding Avro's feelings that air-to-air refuelling would be a means to achieve the LRIX radius of action requirement of 575 nm, noted that while he was interested in Avro's philos-

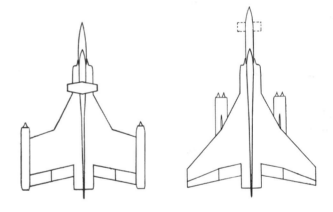

ophy in this respect, the specification didn't mention it, and NAA weren't considering it in their design studies. He also told Avro not to propose a new aircraft for the specification.

Avro began by doing two project studies, to see how the basic Arrow might be adapted. These studies were headed by Mario Pesando of Avro's Project Research Group with the first brochure being released in September 1957. The first one (PS-1 shown at left in the diagram with PS-2 at right) had large ramjets at the wingtips and a trimming canard above the fuselage and just behind the navigator's station, this latter feature being the same as on NAA's first XF-108 proposals. Avro determined that the aircraft would have problems with gear strength, center-of-lift variation and other problems. PS-2 was found to be much more promising. The following is from Pesando's initial investigation.

BASIC MODIFICATIONS OF LONG RANGE ARROW UNDERCARRIAGE

It has been established that the take-off weight of a Long Range Arrow is of the order of 105,000 lb. and it is very unlikely that the present main undercarriage scheme can be developed to cope with these loads. Further the redesign should be capable of a potential take-off weight of much more than the immediate 105,000 lb. requirement.

A plausible solution would be to:

Remove the existing undercarriage and utilize the space for fuel storage.Integrate the main undercarriage with the pylons which support twin ramjets and are located at the transport joints of the inner and outer wing. The bulk of the increased weight would be concentrated at the undercarriage thus keeping the other structural changes to a minimum.

MIXED POWER

A high supersonic performance may be achieved without sacrifice of subsonic capability by the utilization of mixed power plants. This principle when applied to the Avro Arrow results in increased performance at altitude. It is therefore recommended that;

A pair of 36 inch [diameter] ramjets straddle each pylon-undercarriage structure.

INCREASED FUEL

Additional fuel can be carried in:

(1) Ramjet pods 29,200 lb.

(2) Outer wings 6,000 lb.

(3) Former wheel well 2,000 lb.

thus increasing the fuel load to at least 19,438 + 37,200 = 56,638 lb. It is noteworthy that the Long Range Arrow mission profiles to be shown later are based on a 54,600 lb. fuel load and a 105,000 lb take-off weight.

DRAG REDUCTION

A drag estimate of the Avro Arrow 2 showed that at M 2.4, 90,000 ft. altitude and W/P = 250,000 sq. in. the drag components to be:

Profile Drag— 4,080 lb.

Induced Drag— 11,080 lb.

Trim Drag— 6,960 lb., totalling 22,120 lb.

Profile drag is relatively a 'fixed item' and any large improvement of it was unlikely. Therefore the reduction is more probable in the induced and trim drags. Consequently it is recommended that:

A canard be added to provide supersonic trim, 32 sq.ft., L.E. at station O. The wing area be increased from 1225 to 1410 sq.ft. (outer wing increased). The aspect ratio be increased from 2.04 to 2.55.

The preceding three basic modifications would in effect reduce the drag at M 2.5, 90,000 ft. altitude to:

Profile Drag— 4900 lb.

Induced Drag— 6950 lb.

Trim Drag— 1230 lb., totalling 13,080 lb. and reduction of over 9,000 lb.

It should be noted, however, that the subsonic drag, at M = .92, 40,000 ft. and W/P = 22,000, increases approximately from 6,660 to 7,000 lb., a small subsonic penalty to pay for attainment of a 90,000 ft. ceiling.

CANARD

It is intended that the canard be used as an additional trim control at supersonic speeds only.

At subsonic speeds it would be retracted into the 4 ft. nose extension. The aircraft controls in all other respects would function essentially the same. It is felt that the additional canard air loads induced into the fuselage can be adequately catered for by increasing the skin thickness.

WING AREA

The increased wing area may be obtained by utilizing an entirely new outer wing of a lesser sweepback angle. The resulting increased tip chord (from 52.085 to 102 in.) also provides for a much stiffer wing. It is however anticipated that some re-vamping of the aileron and aileron control may be necessary.

The addition of 10 ft. to the existing span increases the aspect ratio from 2.04 to 2.55 thereby resulting in a substantial reduction in induced drag.

This PS-2 version was to use most of the Mk. 3 Arrow including the new materials, center fuselage, insulation scheme etc. and was to be limited to the same Mach 3 top speed strictly for structural and kinetic heating reasons. It certainly had the thrust and drag to achieve *much* higher speeds. Its climb rate, from 40,000 feet with the

LONG RANGE ARROW – Mission # 3 – Low Altitude Toss–Bomb
SUBSONIC CRUISE OUT
INTERNAL FUEL 25,400 LBS, PLUS 29,200 IN RAMJET PODS

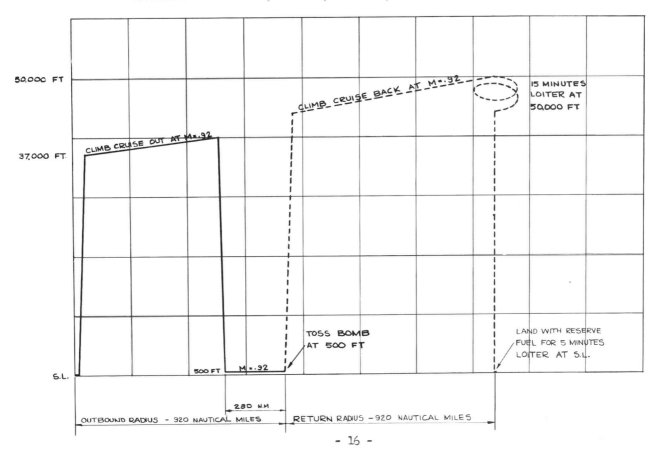

That the Arrow was always looked at as a potentially offensive weapon, and also would have been adaptable to the TSR.2 role is suggested by the "Mission # 3" graph from Pesando's 1957 Long Range Arrow document.

Curtiss-Wright ramjets lit, was an astounding 130,000 fpm and again, these numbers were compiled before the airframe's true (lower) drag numbers were in. In the case of the Mk. 3 Arrow, that difference in drag resulted in a combat speed increase from Mach 2.5 to Mach 3. Again, Avro is proven *conservative* in their estimates. Even so, Avro was estimating that the PS-2 version would be capable of *sustaining* Mach 3 at 85,000 feet while pulling the USAF standard 1.2 G. Its 500 fpm climb ceiling was 90,000 feet.

It would seem that Perkins felt this PS-2 Arrow was too radical a redesign of the basic Arrow airframe and requested a less modified version. Accordingly, Avro developed a less-modified design and this became the Mk. 4 version.

Pesando discussed this less-modified long-range Arrow in a document to Jim Floyd dated 7 November 1957:

In view of the still apparent interest in a longer range version of the Arrow, we have undertaken to simplify the original proposal that we made. You will see that the canard has now been eliminated with a resultant loss of 10,000-15,000 ft. in operating altitude. In other words the aeroplane should be good up to 70,000-75,000 ft. The ramjets have been reduced in size with the corresponding slight reduction in performance which really does not show up because we should limit the aircraft within the Mach 3 and 75,000 ft. boundary. The [only] piece to be added consists of an insert that is placed at the joint between the inner and outer wing panels and it consists of the pylon, undercarriage and ramjets.

We have carried out a check on the longitudinal balance, which appears to be in order. The missions of this particular proposal are fairly close to the original one [described above relating to the PS-2] so that in this brochure we have merely substituted pages of the original one with the necessary weight changes. However, I would like to suggest that for practical discussion purposes, a factor of 95% should be used in all of these figures. [Again, Avro was being conservative, and again these numbers were too low since they were still overestimating the Arrow's drag.]

During one of the [Hawker Siddeley] Design Council meetings, it was mentioned that Perkins of the USAF was alleged to have said that the aircraft to meet the LRI specification should be under 100,000 lb. We obviously cannot do this without resorting to gimmicks such as flight re-fuelling, high energy fuels [Zip fuel] and buddy systems, etc., and I do not think any one else can do it either, within the present state-of-the-art. In other words there is no royal road to achieving this unless there are some major technical break-throughs, and I doubt whether the project can be postponed until these occur.

This version of the Arrow is shown at the beginning of this section. Jim Floyd stated that this aircraft version differed from the basic Mk. 3 airframe by being skinned (perhaps foil-skinned) in titanium. From the arrangement we can see it relied on a slightly more advanced ramjet installation than the PS-2.

Ramjet Pods

Curtiss-Wright seemed to have a genuine respect for British engineering as evidenced by their license production of the Sapphire and attempted license production of the Olympus as the J-67 (and others). They always seemed very prepared to work with Avro Canada, and tried to secure rights to license produce the Orenda Iroquois. This author feels many of that company's problems were brought about by their "foreign affairs" which did not conform to the attitude of the American establishment, as delineated by the Buy American Act.

Curtiss-Wright had also developed ramjets in the United States for the promising (but cancelled) North American Navaho missile project. They had also developed the

propulsion system for the XF-103 which included the J-67 and also ramjets, making the XF-103 a mixed propulsion aircraft. Mario Pesando addressed a letter to Jim Floyd and Bob Lindley on 12 December 1957 which referred to a visit by Curtiss-Wright representatives:

Two Curtiss-Wright representatives, W.J. Mann and B. Nierenberg, visited Avro on Nov. 29, 1957, to discuss the possibility of using their ramjets on the Long Range Arrow. During the course of the meeting it was revealed that Curtiss-Wright have some 34" ramjets, which were produced for the ill-fated Navaho project, available as off-the-shelf items. These units have been paid for by the USAF and, if satisfactory, may be obtained for our use. The meeting was somewhat restricted by Security, i.e. Curtiss-Wright was not cleared to reveal the ramjet information necessary for a detailed design and performance study.

The most interesting thing about the ramjets (other than the fact that the 34 inch version Avro finally settled on produced 16,164 lbt at Mach 2.5 and 40,000 feet), was the fuel carrying system they employed. In short, when they weren't running they were entirely immersed in fuel which the Arrow's main engines would consume before the ramjets were started. From Pesando's letter to Floyd on the subject:

Ramjet Features and Performance

Mr. Nierenberg was able to give some leading particulars of a 35 inch diameter ramjet equipped to carry 1000 lb. of fuel in a collapsible bag in the duct aft of the flameholders. A further supply of about 650 lb. of fuel of which 600 lb. is JP4 is carried in an annular skin tank and in the centerbody, to be burned in the ramjet. The fuel contained in the centerbody is aluminum-tri-ethyl and is pyroforic, i.e. it will spontaneously ignite in a quite tenuous oxygen-containing atmosphere. Its excellent burning characteristics have made possible the burning of a mixture of 15% by weight of this fuel in JP4 at pressures down to 1/4 psi.

While being used as a fuel tank the intake [of the ramjet] is closed off by an umbrella of meshing plates and the exit is plugged by a conical body which is fixed to the centerbody of the ramjet by a long rod. The rear fairing is jettisoned when the tank fuel has been used through breaking the rod by an explosive charge. Presumably the empty bag is either jettisoned before or burned on light up.

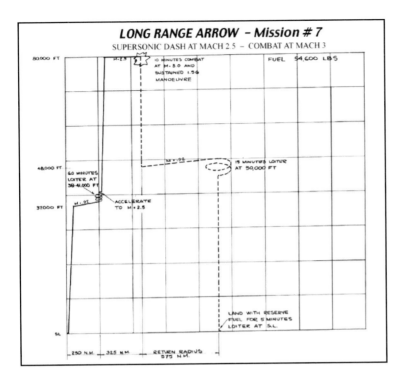

LONG RANGE ARROW – Mission # 7

SUPERSONIC DASH AT MACH 2.5 – COMBAT AT MACH 3

Mission 7 from Avro's Arrow 4 material, given to the RCAF and presumably the USAF as well since this mission is the LRIX Mission. (via Jim Floyd)

The letter went on to describe what the representatives did disclose, and mentioned Avro having supplied Curtiss-Wright with enough information on the Long Range Arrow's specified missions etc. to allow the visitors to compile data that Avro could use for a detailed performance study. On 31 January 1958 Pesando, Rolf Marshall and two other Avro representatives were at Curtiss-Wright's facilities to see what the Americans had come up with. They came away impressed with their ramjet test facilities (capable of simulating Mach 4 at 85,000 feet) and with a source of a new teflon-related seal material called Viton A.

Arrow Mk. 4 -Long Range- Mission NO.7 USAF Long Range Intercept Mission

This mission consists of an economical climb cruise for 250 nautical miles followed by a 60 minute loiter at 38-41,000 ft. The aircraft is then accelerated to Mach 2.5 and climbed to 80,000 ft. at which altitude an approximately 280 nautical miles, Mach 2.5 dash is executed, bringing the out-bound radius to 575 nautical miles. This is followed by 10 minutes combat at 80,000 ft., Mach 3 and sustained 1.5G manoeuvre. The return radius consists of a descent to 48,000 ft. altitude, a Mach .92 climb cruise followed by 15 minutes loiter at 40,000 ft., and a landing with reserve fuel for 5 minutes loiter at sea level. The operational radius of this mission is 575 nautical miles. The deviation of this mission from the [USAF] requirement is dash at Mach 2.5 in lieu of Mach 3, and combat at 80,000 ft. in lieu of 70,000 ft. altitude.

As we can see from the mission 7 information, the Arrow 4 was largely capable of meeting the LRIX specification and was being proposed for just that. (Whether the F-108 was as well is unknown.) This from 1957 so again we know the estimate is exceptionally conservative. Avro projected the ferry range of this aircraft to be 2,540 nm (over 2900 statute miles) which should be considered 15-25 percent conservative due to the high drag coefficient Avro was applying. With aerial re-fueling, this would make the Mk. 4's range comparible to the SR-71. We also know that John Foster Dulles told the Diefenbaker Cabinet in mid-1958 that the US would never buy Arrows. We also know that according to the Truman Statement of Economic Principles, and from American verbal gestures to the NATO allies, that the United States proclaimed they would purchase, for their own use, any weapons systems produced by their allies if the weapons were the best available. To put it mildly, there seems to be a contradiction there. It was a contradiction that helped destroy the Hawker Siddeley Group, Avro Canada and the independent Canadian high technology sector. The evidence also supports the idea that the Arrow 3 and 4 would have outperformed the SR-71 by a considerable margin. The Arrows certainly would have been available before the F-108, the SR-71 and the TSR.2.

CHAPTER NINE

Countdown to Destruction

How the deed was done

IN A DISCUSSION BETWEEN THE US SECRETARY of the Air Force, James Douglas, and the Canadian Ambassador, 30 January 1958, the F-108 is described "very firmly" by the Secretary as something "that they were going ahead with..." He gratuitously added that the F-108 would make the Arrow, in comparison, "look like something which might be picked up in a department store." This discussion is cited in other works as proving the United States was supportive of the Arrow since they offered to buy Canada a couple of squadrons—and let the Canadians operate them! Clearly Douglas was denigrating the Avro project while intelligence estimates available to him indicated an Arrow version, at drag numbers the flying Arrow would prove to be inflated, would prove aerodynamically superior to the F-108. He also would have known that ASTRA 2 was shaping up to give a foreign power the highest-technology radar/fire-control in the world. He would likely also have known about the Mk. 4 proposals (since they were prepared for the USAF), which should have given him further pause.

The response, in diplomatic terms of course, to this charitable offer on the CF-105 Arrow Weapons System, is predictable and was probably counted on, if not by Douglas, then probably by Secretary of State John Foster Dulles, and Director Central Intelligence Allen Welsh Dulles. The Dulles brothers would have had the ability to control the actual intelligence Douglas received since it was their intelligence briefing that greeted the President every morning.

In July of 1958 Pearkes travelled to Washington to meet with US defence officials, John Foster Dulles, the US Secretary of State, and Neil McElroy, the US Defense Secretary. At this meeting Minister of Defence George Pearkes related to the Americans that Canada could afford the Arrow, or Bomarcs and SAGE but not both. On the political level at least, this approach contrasted dramatically compared to the USAF approach regarding their F-108; an aircraft they were "very firmly" going ahead with as of January 1958. This hearty assurance was in contrast to the feelings of Dr. Courtland Perkins and others, that the F-108 weapons system would likely be cancelled. In other words the politicians had put Perkins' rumour, as forwarded to the government by Avro, to rest and thus had already killed one sales approach for Arrows.

We shall see that even by this date Pearkes should have had information showing the F-108 and Arrow to be very competitive aircraft. Considering the fact that the Arrow was known to be the best interceptor available in 1960, and the American's assurances to their allies that they were interested in having NATO standardize on the best weapons, regardless of origin, the Conservatives had several big bargaining chips.

Immediately after Pearkes' visit to the United States, there were top-level meetings between the Canadian politicians and President Eisenhower and Secretary of State Dulles in Canada that decided Canadian air defence policy, with the entire policy being virtually "Made in the USA." Since Diefenbaker and Pearkes had earlier placed the RCAF's Air Defence Command under US direction by joining NORAD, they now found themselves under pressure to alter RCAF equipment to USAF standards. This was used to justify killing the Arrow by the US in their pitches to Canada since they claimed to be going SAGE and insisted they would not purchase Arrows because they were not SAGE compatible. When asked if they would purchase Arrows with MA-1, McElroy and Dulles stated the US would never buy Arrows *period*.

A secret briefing *aide memoire* for Pearkes' 8 July 1958 meeting with John Foster Dulles showed Pearkes revealing that $530 million was being spent on the Arrow project and all its various aspects, with a projected aircraft cost of $5 million each. This is interesting considering that by cancellation (nearly eight months later), only about $300 million had been spent on all aspects of the Arrow weapons system, ASTRA/Sparrow included. The briefing notes also stated that the Arrow and US interceptors operating in Canadian airspace would *require* SAGE and that SAGE would cost $107 million to implement. This proves that by this point Pearkes had accepted SAGE in Canada on behalf of American interests. The Arrow however did *not* require SAGE and at this time was still having ASTRA developed for it. Even the MA-1 system could be adapted to efficient autonomous operations with a few "black boxes" (or the deletion of some) and Avro seemed to feel this was the way to go. Indeed secret internal documents circulated among Avro's top management in September of 1958 saw the SAGE network as being very vulnerable to jamming and outright destruction, and something that

the Arrow should rely upon as little as possible. They still were not comfortable with the progress of ASTRA however and their recommendations against the system at this time, proves the company wasn't trying to sell the government down the river. Indeed, considering what the Iroquois and Arrow represented as complete systems, they were quite competitive even at $5 million each, especially when the sophistication and promised "shelf life" of ASTRA and indeed everything else, were taken into account.

During the bi-lateral meetings Pearkes also complained that half of the Canadian defence budget was being spent on the Air Force. Apparently Dulles and McElroy didn't offer the fact that at the time the US was spending two thirds of its defence budget on its air forces. The US was then spending 10 percent of her GNP on defence, while Canada was then at just over 5 percent GNP. Even with the Arrow program, Canada was getting off relatively cheaply.

According to *Shutting Down the National Dream,* the Americans also objected to the Arrow itself during the July and August meetings. They apparently criticized it as being unable to maintain high supersonic speed for a long enough period. Since the Arrow 2 could maintain Mach 2 (.5 Mach higher than its specification) until it ran out of fuel, the Americans can only have been referring to the Mk. 3 or Mk. 4 specification— the USAF LRIX "mission 7." While the stainless steel NAA F-108's ability to match a ramjet-augmented, titanium-skinned and composite-insulated Arrow 4 is most questionable, the August 1959 cancellation of the F-108 is particularly noticeable. While the Americans seemed to suggest that Canada should buy F-108s, had Canada had a stronger leadership, they would have been demanding to know why the Americans even *started* the F-108 aircraft, ASG-18 radar/fire-control and J-93 engine programs in the first place, given the tone of President Truman's "Statement of Economic Principles." This document suggested they should have "bought into" the Arrow development instead. It probably would have been an easy sell to the allied nations too, since many of them felt somewhat slighted by US considerations.

In an interview with Dr. Reginald Roy on 5 April 1967, Pearkes discussed his ultimate reasoning, and the expert consulted, that supposedly made the difference regarding the Arrow's fate:

> I took chances— we were defenceless against the high powered bomber— we had the old CF-100, it couldn't compete with the modern Russian bomber; we had no supersonic fighter, but the Americans emphasised the fact that they had lots of them. … 'here, we will give facilities for American fighter squadrons to come and be stationed in Canada so that they can get the advantage there, or if not actually stationed in there, when the situation deteriorates they can move forward and operate from Canadian airfields [which certainly neglects the need to respond immediately]. And I had the assurance of the Under Secretary of Defence… he said to me, 'If I was you, I wouldn't put all that money into that aircraft— if you don't want to buy aircraft from us, you may rest assured that we've got lots of them which we can use in the help of the defence of the North American Continent if a crisis comes. And that's what convinced me more than anything else…

It is clear that the Conservatives had, by this time, completely dismissed the strategic problems that had compelled the Canadian government to invite Avro into Canada in the first place—to provide an alternative to foreign systems for national defence, and to ensure Canadian industry maintained a competitive ability in high technology *that could be applied to national goals.* McElroy's offer of free American defence would later be revealed as somewhat disingenuous when, shortly after the Arrow was cancelled, the Americans were insisting Canada either needed to allow USAF permanent basing, or needed to purchase SAGE-compatible (and thus American) interceptors. This advice following Dulles' blanket rejection of Arrows is most interesting considering they were still pushing, hard, the useless Bomarc missile.

Coinciding with the rather one-sided exchange of views in July the Conservatives introduced their Conversion Loan. This was a complicated financial manoeuvre that was essentially a second mortgage on the due-to-be-retired Victory Bonds of World War II. One can be sure that in making their representations to the bankers and investors they were asked why the government of Canada needed all

that money. They were also likely told that they needed to tighten up their spending. Perhaps they were also asked if Canada could afford the nationalistic "luxury" of the Arrow weapons system when "cheap" American interceptors were sitting in the department store window. As Peter C. Newman makes clear in *Renegade in Power*, Diefenbaker wasted on average $400 million a year on unbudgeted, short-term vote buying. His other policies ensured that the Liberal surplus was consumed in no time, and by early 1958 the government was already going deeply into debt. Something needed to be done to "buy" time to right their fiscal ship.

As the Shaw's report said of the Conversion Loan:

> Mr. Diefenbaker had a serious political problem. In a short time, he had gone through the Liberal surplus, and gone deeply into debt. A large addition to this debt was the huge gift paid off to the investment houses, insurance companies and banks, through the conversion loan— a totally unnecessary burden loaded onto the taxpayer. (It has been suggested in the press that this was a return for campaign funds donated for two expensive campaigns; that we have had to pay for being persuaded to vote Conservative…)

McKim and another advertising company were paid handsomely, with public funds, to convince the Canadian public to buy bonds that weren't a good deal for the nation, and which put the government of Canada even more at the mercy of the financial elite. Welcome to Canada Savings Bonds, an excellent method to earn low interest while speculators make high interest from the investors' money, often by depleting companies rather than producing anything useful or advancing technology and civilisation.

In early 1959, about a month after the Arrow cancellation, there was a US Senate sub-committee held to discuss interceptors. During these hearings General Partridge, Commander in Chief of NORAD stated:

> At the present time the Soviets can attack us only with bombers. Our intelligence estimates reveal that they will improve the quality of their bombers and, in a few years, will have a supersonic bomber force. This means that we must not only maintain the defences,… but must also improve them, so we can counteract a supersonic attacking force.

The aim of the North American [Air] Defense Command is to hit an attacker as far away as possible, i.e.; over the Arctic. Bomarcs are useless for this function and are intended only as 'defence in depth' to give the SAC [Strategic Air Command] 'time to get away' and to provide limited 'point defense.' Early Warning Radar Lines can not identify radar signals as intruders, or tell the type of attack, if any.

He added that they needed "the fastest, highest flying, longest-range interceptor available for as long as we can foresee." He also said that, "unfortunately," until the F-108 entered service several years hence, there was in the US "nothing now available except the F-101." Partridge's responsible comments also put the lie to the idea that high altitude interceptors were obsolete.

General White added that the ICBM had not made the manned bomber obsolete since the bomber "can carry multiple nuclear weapons, a much bigger yield and variety, and can be deployed. It has a greater potential for use in limited war."

After cancellation Pearkes would say that the Western provinces were "too far away for Canada to defend." This was apparently said to prepare Canada for US Bomarc sites in the West, which the American politicians offered Canada before Arrow termination and subsequently reneged on after the Arrow and its production line were scrapped.

Pearkes also stated after Arrow cancellation "...the Russians are not continuing the production of any bomber more advanced than... the Bear and Bison." General Nathan Twining, Chief of the American Air Defense Staff, however said "The Russians are now building a new bomber far beyond the capabilities of the Bear and Bison long-range bombers. We do not know what it is yet, but it is an advanced heavy bomber." Intelligence estimates at the time showed between 1,000 and 2,000 Soviet bombers already in existence with the capability of hitting Canada and the US with nuclear weapons. This number may have been slightly optimistic considering the famous CIA over-estimations of the day in order of appearance: 1) the Intelligence Gap (circa 1947 to 1960, 2) the Bomber Gap (circa 1949-1960) and 3) the Missile Gap, (circa 1957-1963). All were excellent methods to increase the paranoia and extremism of American

anti-communist sentiment, and all were especially excellent means of getting the United States and other Western nations further into debt to internationalist bankers. While the bomber gap was exaggerated, the Soviets most certainly did continue to improve their bomber fleets and the Russians, Chinese, Americans and other nations continue to do so today. Canada is putting money into the Joint Strike Fighter, an aircraft optimised more for ground attack than interception. If Canada and Britain purchase the winning Lockheed-Martin version of this aircraft, they will ensure, for another generation, that the United States remains unchallenged in air supremacy—other than by Russia. After being privy to some of the criticisms the Arrow design suffered for poor rearward visibility, it is interesting to note that neither JSF contender offered rearward vision. The Boeing example had a visible engine compressor from the front (looking down the intake duct) which would have been a beacon to radar from the frontal aspect.

Having used the argument that the CF-105 would be obsolete, as it was entering service, as a cancellation justification, when he was pressed on the differences in opinion between his government and the RCAF and USAF over the Soviet bomber threat, Pearkes stated that the CF-100 was good enough. "It will be touch and go as far as combat between the CF-100 and Bear and Bison are concerned, but, as I have pointed out, they have that [sic] aircraft in very limited numbers." It is hard to imagine how 1,000 to 2,000 bombers can be considered a "limited" number. He failed to mention Twining and others' belief that the Soviets were constructing much more advanced bombers, which, in fact, they did.

It is more than interesting that Diefenbaker's Conversion Loan resulted in the government putting the Canadian people back on the hook for another term of wartime Victory Bonds, bonds that were due to be retired as paid off! This was a tactic that the Shaws (*There Never Was an Arrow*) and Peter C. Newman (in *Renegade In Power; The Diefenbaker Years*) seem to agree was a bonanza for the banks holding these bonds. The Shaws go further, alleging that this acceptance of renewed debt by the government was a pay-off for the assistance of an American-dominated financial elite in their election financing, and for influence wherever else they could wield it.

The real target was the Company—the only part of the industry which was doing research, design and development to any extent in Canada; which was helping to build up subsidiary industries, to design and manufacture in Canada everything from highly-specialized electronics equipment, to plastics, machine tools, new metals and alloys, and equipment of every kind.

Jack Woodman recalled "an anti-Arrow campaign" being waged in the media in 1958, coincidental to Pearkes' trip to Washington in July of 1958 to visit Mr. Dulles and others. Again from the Shaw's report of 30 April 1959:

> Since September, a howling lobby has swept the country from coast to coast. It has included, with few exceptions, every newspaper and magazine in the country, and TV and radio programs. The type of attack and reasons behind it are unprecedented in this country....

> Before it had said a word in public, Mr. Diefenbaker labelled Avro a 'lobby', and diverted the public from watching the real lobby swing into action. Because of this mass of propaganda, TV programs, newspaper and magazine editorials, many people have assumed that the decision on the Avro Arrow must have been a correct one. They have ignored the factual articles tucked into the news columns which disproved the attacks, the mis-statements and false conclusions in the editorial columns. They have listened to Mr. Diefenbaker moaning piteously on TV that "no one will ever know the pressure which has been brought to bear on us," but they are not told of the un-answered questions in Parliament, asking him what "these pressures" were, what his policies were, why he has lied, twisted and distorted the facts, and suppressed the most important information, some of which is now being revealed [by Avro].

> They do not know that one newspaper cancelled the daily column of an out-standing writer who tried to tell the facts behind this campaign, and did not carry it again until all reference to the Arrow was dropped. They do not know that every newspaper in the Toronto area, except one, refused to publish letters contradicting only the most obvious lies given out by the Government and press.

Mr. Diefenbaker also claimed, publicly, of course, that "Avro Firings were Needless," that the Company knew that fifty million dollars was available—according to the *Toronto Star*, February 24. [It was an interesting tactic to cancel the CF-105 contract with no notice to Avro then expect Avro to give notice of layoffs. Avro gave notice of those layoffs in September 1958 and again just before cancellation!] In the House of Commons, Mr. Pearson said that he had searched the estimates over the whole period, and could find nothing that allotted this money to A.V. Roe, for any purpose whatever. Even a termination contract has to be negotiated, and is a complicated—and much more costly—process. A lawyer should at least know about contracts. The penalties the Government must pay for termination of the contract would have been sufficient to complete the whole 37 Arrows, and the development and test program.

On 28 August 1958 Pearkes referred his proposal that the CF-105 be cancelled to Cabinet. He then added that SAGE *"had to"* be introduced whether the CF-105 was built or not. Pearkes also mentioned the non-existent F-106C as being comparable in performance to the CF-105 but about half as much money. The Convair/General Dynamics F-106C/D was a radical redesign of the F-106 intended for longer ranges as an (unsuccessful) entry to the LRIX contest that the F-108 had, by this time, already won. The F-106C/D was a "paper airplane" that kept coming back. It seemed to reappear as the F-106X in 1964 and was used by Robert McNamara as justification for the cancellation of the potent F-12B, yet the F-106X was never ordered or developed. The F-106X merely added a canard, two-dimensional, variable intakes, and a variable nozzle to the basic F-106 design. It would have been a much better aircraft yet its range, payload and propulsion possibilities were still relatively limited.

Meanwhile a top secret RCAF brief compared the actual Arrow to the paper F-106C/D specifications and found the Arrow to be far superior. It stated the cost for 100 Arrows, with ASTRA, all tooling, development, production, spares, ground infrastructure, simulators and the like at $8.91

million each. The F-106C/D flyaway cost was $5.59 million. As mentioned, in reality Avro was offering the CF-105 at $3.75 million each before cancellation of the Arrow or F-106C. At the same time Pratt & Whitney Canada was trying to get the Iroquois program cancelled in favour of its US parent's J-75 engine and repeatedly submitted proposals to the RCAF and government. They were rebuffed since the RCAF believed, with good reason, that the Iroquois would be cheaper and more effective.

Third September 1958 Cabinet minutes report on a meeting between Avro's John Plant and Fred Smye, and Finance Minister Donald Fleming and Minister of Defence Pearkes:

> They [Smye and Plant] had stated that the RCAF made a major mistake three years ago by recommending the adoption [development!] of SPARROW and ASTRA. ... Finally, they said that, if the program with their proposed modification [replacement of ASTRA/Sparrow with the MA-1 and Falcon/Genie] were continued, their company would have a reasonable opportunity before the end of 1962 to look for other business. If they found little or none, then Avro would be in real difficulties.

Today there exists plenty of evidence to suggest the government wanted Avro kept in the dark about cancellation to give them no opportunity to mount a public relations campaign, and to ensure the company was in the weakest possible position after Black Friday. The government obviously didn't feel obliged to inform the Canadian people of the secret proposals Avro made for alternative projects to ensure the survival of a company largely funded by the Canadian taxpayer and Canadian and British shareholders! The government was blaming Avro for continuing to concentrate on the single largest development program it had been invited to stake its future on, to meet an *existing* contract for production of 37 flying Arrows with Iroquois engines and their spares. It was high theatre for Diefenbaker to claim Avro had always been told the Arrow might not go into production and that the program was subject to annual review. Avro was keenly aware that the production contract might not be granted. They also had in their hands a signed government contract for production of 37 pre-production Arrows. The Minister of Defence

Production, Raymond O'Hurley, personally guaranteed Charles Grinyer that the Arrow would *not* be cancelled in the fall of 1958, when he knew otherwise! As in the TCA renege on their letter of intent, Avro probably had grounds to sue. Avro also knew the "establishment" would make sure they didn't have a leg to stand on in court. If they were as pugnacious a company as the Conservatives and others actively promoted them to be, they would have sued. Instead they made the only rational business decision left open to them, they laid off the majority of their employees. They did not shrink from the impact that would make. If national defence and economic nationalism meant nothing to the Conservatives, perhaps 30,000 unemployed would! Cabinet documents also reveal that the government knew Arrow cancellation would result in at least 25,000 people being thrown out of work.

Again from the September 3rd minutes:

> Mr. Fleming said that he had pointed out to Messrs. Tory and Smye that their arguments, that of the Falcon missile and Hughes fire control system developed by the United States should be good enough for Canada, could also be used against them in regard to the airframe and engines which they wanted produced in Canada by their own firm. Mr. Smye, in particular, had been very critical of some RCAF decisions and officers.

Smye was no doubt referring to AVM John Easton and probably to W/C Footit. Easton, over the recommendations of Avro, cooler heads in the RCAF, the DRB, and even USAF and British official advice, had pushed through the decision to develop ASTRA/Sparrow. This resulted in, by far, the largest cost overruns of the project along with constant delays. Easton's department also produced a brochure for the government showing the Arrow range to be limited compared to the Bomarc! He was criticized by his colleague, AVM M.M. Hendricks, for applying a six minute "scramble" penalty to the Arrow which it did not deserve, along with adding considerable range to the Bomarc. Easton's department was, in essence, simplifying the mission of the Arrow down to that of a missile. In other words he was presenting it as a "race" between an aircraft on the tarmac and a missile in its silo. For some reason Easton couldn't, or wouldn't consider that Arrows could be kept on rotation and stationed in a Combat Air Patrol (CAP) at the limit of the ground radar (or beyond) with the aircraft's own formidable remaining range adding considerably to that of the ground surveillance. Of course Avro tried to gently point out this operational "credibility gap" but were not successful.

Some of Hendricks' diary notes, published in *Arrow Scrapbook*, are quite revealing. Jim Floyd relates in period documents that the Arrow program was subject to one "agonising reappraisal" after another over the years. (One might wonder the toll of these on Avro management, Crawford Gordon particularly!) During the week of 21 October 1957, (around the time of the Arrow unveiling) it seems the RCAF faced something of a showdown with the Army and Navy. Hendricks relates that the Chief of the Air Staff was called upon at the request of the Army, (which was represented by General Graham) to justify the Arrow program. At this time the DRB presented a "cost per kill" evaluation of the alternative forms of interception. Hendricks found their presentation simplistic and "unsuitable" and seemed to indicate that the RCAF's position, that of agreeing the Arrow could not do *all* of the defensive missiles' job, was a concession to the missile-minded. Hendricks also mentioned that the Bomarc was "very uncertain under countermeasures." Again one can see that the experts, even at the time, had information to show any belief in Bomarc being an effective replacement for interceptors was on shaky ground. Apparently the Chiefs agreed to continue despite the objection of the Army.

It becomes clear from these documents and the Shaws' article that General Guy Simonds was an implacable enemy of the Arrow program. All doubt about that fact can be dispelled with a reading of Simonds "We're wasting millions on an obsolete airforce," an article published in *Maclean's* on 23 June, 1956. Air Chief Marshall Roy Slemon would catch royal hell from the Conservatives for having had the nerve to speak out in support of the Arrow in 1958, after the Conservatives had decided to kill it. In comments published in the October 1958 issue of *Canadian Aviation Industries,* Slemon stated: "Both Britain and the U.S. are developing new advanced interceptors against the 'manned bomber'. They know that Russia is developing very high altitude supersonic bombers and that the first line of defence against the bombers is, and will continue to be, the manned intercep-

tor. The U.S. ... are bringing along the F108 to cope with even faster, heavier bomber threats anticipated years hence." In November Slemon was again speaking in reply to direct questions: "Yes, the manned interceptor would be required for defense for the foreseeable future but no, no interceptor to equal the Avro Arrow will be available for several years."

Diefenbaker was livid when he heard of Slemon's comments, comments made from NORAD HQ in Colorado Springs with NORAD commander General Partridge standing by his side. In the 12 December 1958 minutes his reaction is related: "The Prime Minister said he had been shocked at the statement Air Marshal Slemon had made about the Arrow. It was not a question of whether Slemon's remarks had been misinterpreted or not but whether he should have made a statement of that kind at all." There was a discussion about what kind of action to take against Slemon and he was reprimanded. A written reprimand goes on an officer's file and stays there. If the commander and the deputy commander of NORAD couldn't make those kinds of statements, who could? At least Slemon had commented within his specialty and area of responsibility. Simonds' poisonous article in *Macleans* wasn't related to his specialty at all and he would "troop out" after retirement to repeat his assumptions in the press during the 1958 anti-Arrow media blitz.

Footit had meanwhile shown a propensity for stating in his correspondences that Avro's statements were not to be trusted and routinely characterized their technical estimates as being suspicious. Documents provided by Jim Floyd, regarding discussions between Footit and Avro, show Footit being much more sympathetic however. Footit himself alluded in those documents to "professional jealousy" in existence at other agencies, meaning the DRB, NAE, NRC and probably at Canadair as well. It is hard to reconcile some of what was promulgated under Footit's guidance within RCAF and government circles and what his apparent attitude was in direct dealings with Avro management, engineering at least. Jim Floyd mentioned Footit had a propensity to "blow hot and cold" and that this was puzzling and confusing for the Avro team. On the other hand, Footit felt, according to discussions with Peter Zuuring, that "backing and filling" was the best way to get accurate information. This technique included talking to airframe guys about the engine side, and the engine side about the airframe side, rather than trusting the engineers in their respective specialties. Unionized workers on the shop floor would certainly know little of ongoing improvements and technical theory until the very last stage of their development; i.e., when they were required to physically produce the new parts. What an Orenda worker would know about Arrow flight stability, for example, is most questionable. Footit's tactic brought out petty rivalries between the two sides of the house, and could hardly be considered an optimal method of generating performance or scheduling data. It would be an excellent method of generating *rumours* however.

We have already seen that even NACA had difficulty grasping Avro's advanced aerodynamics. Had NACA's initial 1954 criticism about the delta-wing (and the Arrow) been correct, it seems doubtful that the F-108, SR-71 and XB-70 designs would have adopted it after NACA's stinging criticism of the delta arrangement's range attributes. All the just-mentioned aircraft were to be especially long-range aircraft.

There can be no doubt however that Footit's attitude helped poison the RCAF and government towards Avro. Much later in life, Footit, responding to an invitation to an Arrow reunion, declined in "a very nice letter," according to Floyd, that went on to state that his misgivings about Avro occurred early on and that Avro became the best company with which he had worked. Even if this is the case, the damage had already been done through what the author can only describe as quite unprofessional representations made by someone often lacking the facts and experience to back them up. Footit also recommended Floyd for the Canadian Aeronautical Institute's highest honour, the J.A. McCurdy award, in 1958 while Footit was the president of the CAI. Perhaps Footit was won over by the Avro talents before Black Friday. Nevertheless, Footit and other RCAF officers left several letters on the record condemning Avro for having blown their aerodynamic drag and other projections on the Arrow, and then accusing them of having seemingly lied about it, before the aircraft had even flown!

From the September 3rd meeting between Conservative cabinet ministers and Avro executives, we see Finance Minister Fleming lecturing Avro on weapons suitability while insinuating that Avro was playing games with tax-

payer's money to get the Arrow into production! His implication that there were "good enough" systems available in the US showed both an ignorance of the RCAF requirement, and ignorance in his own portfolio in not realizing the importance to the economy of the high-tech design and production capabilities Avro brought to Canada. Fleming also proved himself ignorant of the sales potential of the Iroquois, if not of the Arrow itself. It was at the time of this statement that the French government announced official intentions to purchase 200-300 Iroquois engines for the Mirage IV supersonic bomber. When they backed out, they did so because, as they announced, they felt the Canadian government was going to cancel both the Iroquois and the Arrow! They then almost bought the J-75, but in the end settled for their own ATAR engines, engines identical in size to the Iroquois, but producing about half the thrust! Finally, Fleming demonstrated his ignorance of the balance of payments problem Canada has always faced. Balance of payments was, quite irresponsibly, also not mentioned in any Cabinet minutes pertaining to purchasing American Arrow replacements.

Prince Bernhard (with sunglasses) of the Netherlands visited Avro twice during the Arrow program, the last time being in May of 1958. Bernhard had founded the Bilderberg Group and later lost the presidency of that body due to allegations of having sought, and accepted bribes during the Lockheed Scandal. (references via www.bilderberg.org, image Avro Canada)

During an Avro/government meeting, Pearkes remarked to his peers that he "felt bound to say that the RCAF had conscientiously made the recommendations they thought would be in the best interests of the defence of Canada." One is left to wonder where Pearkes' confidence in the RCAF was when the two top Air Marshals, Slemon and Campbell, were pointing out at the same time that they needed the Arrow or its (non-existent) equivalent. Pearkes also suggested to his colleagues that the figures on savings mentioned by Mr. Smye should be "treated with reserve." Pearkes scoffed that Smye "Had not been aware, for example, that there were a number of types of Falcon." The Arrow weapons bay had, however, been designed for the radar-guided and the heat-seeking Falcon versions from day one! When the RCAF belatedly chose ASTRA/Sparrow in 1956, the weapons bay had to be re-designed away from the Falcon armament and now was being returned to Avro's original preferences. Pearkes' military background was from the infantry and later high staff positions mostly related to personnel and manning levels. He had on many occasions demonstrated his total ignorance of technology and how it related to the big picture. Worse still, Pearkes repeatedly demonstrated a willingness to be more than "economical with the truth." Technology is everything in time of war. For aircraft and those they protect, it is the determining factor for survival. Unfortunately for the Army and Navy, long range Arrows with anti-shipping, anti-aircraft and air-to-ground missions would make some of their traditional roles redundant as well. On the other hand, their remaining assets would also be better protected.

September 5th Cabinet minutes stated:

If the [Arrow] project were abandoned, arrangements could quite probably be made with the U.S. to purchase [still in the design phase F-] 106Cs [and their nuclear air to air weapons]. The U.S. authorities had also indicated in the last few days that they would be prepared to consider seriously cost-sharing and production sharing of defence equipment. They had also said they would be prepared to relocate northwards some of their proposed Bomarc installations. These Bomarc bases hardly seemed to cover Canada at all.

... Surely the Canadian public would give credit to the government in the long run [for Arrow termination.]

Yes, credit where credit is due. The Conservatives certainly must, in the end, take full credit for what transpired. Incredibly the same document suggests that continuation of the Arrow project would "be playing into Russian hands" since it might prove true Soviet predictions of the ultimate collapse of the western economies! Incredible reasoning on the part of those Conservatives to suggest that the continuation of the one project that was almost single-handedly developing the Canadian high-tech sector (and the brains to support it) would be contributing to the collapse of capitalism! It is even harder to imagine that adoption of what they themselves, the Americans, the British and presumably the Soviets knew would be the most potent interceptor on the planet could be construed as playing into Russian hands! Remember that at this time, and at cancellation time, the Americans were telling Canadian defence specialists that the *only* means the Soviets then had, and for years to come would have, of striking North America was with their bomber fleet of between 1000 and 2000 intercontinental aircraft! It is hard not to conclude that Pearkes was again grasping at straws to try and justify an arrangement that had—in secret—already been agreed to.

September 8th 1958 Cabinet minutes show Pearkes discussing a Canadian option of purchasing Convair F-106Cs along with the possibility of US cost-sharing on the Bomarc. It seems apparent from the progress of American offers that the US was tying Bomarc cost-sharing (American subsidy) to a Canadian purchase of this non-existent Delta Dart version.

On 17 September 1958 Crawford Gordon Jr. informed the government that the USAF was willing to offer the MA-1 (SAGE compatible) fire control system and Falcon missiles to Canada for the Arrow aircraft practically for free. This was after a lightning trip to the USA by Fred Smye, and legal agreements negotiated by John Tory, to secure the alternative systems to ensure his company's product had what it required to be effective. All evidence suggests that the government didn't initiate any fire control and weapons suite replacement plan and seemingly were just hoping the Arrow would die on the vine. In September 21st

Canada's unmanned, one-way nuclear interceptor, the Bomarc. It was very prone to jamming. Those on the ground also only had five minutes from detection of an intruder to decide if it was an enemy aircraft, and to secure authorization to launch a nuclear response. (Via Palmiro Campagna)

Cabinet minutes Pearkes mentioned this offer, while neglecting to inform his colleagues that it was for the SAGE compatible system of the F-106 and gratuitously added that the large cost savings Avro related "appeared to be exaggerated." So Gordon wrote a letter offering to contract on that cost. At $3.75 million each, the complete Arrow 2 was a steal. Single-engine, short-range, questionably-equipped and crewed F-106s are listed at the USAF Museum website as having cost $3.3 million (US) each. Of course the entire XF-92, F-102 and F-106 design and development costs, and those of the J-75, SAGE and MA-1, were not rolled into this American figure as Diefenbaker liked to try to do with Arrow figures.

On 23 September 1958 Diefenbaker stated that the Bomarc could take either a conventional or nuclear warhead. This was simply not true although the United States was supposedly working on this capability. It would have made the Bomarc even less effective considering its utility under jamming was doubtful to start with, as was its accuracy in an un-degraded environment. Diefenbaker stated during the cancellation debate, in Cabinet, that $20 million worth of Bomarcs would give the same coverage to the same area as $780 million worth of Arrows. That was one of the wilder projections thrown around. Of course a nuclear Bomarc could not visually identify, say, an airliner

off course and would just blow it into radioactive dust—as USAF General White affirmed. Nevertheless 3 September 1958 Cabinet minutes stated that they felt 240 one-shot Bomarcs, from four bases, were equivalent to 100 Arrows with eight missiles each, and with a turn-around time of about 10 minutes. The cost of such was listed as $520.3 million. Again, 100 Arrows were finally estimated by the RCAF, with lifetime spare engines and other parts, all the ground infrastructure, simulators, runway improvements, etc. and other expenses as costing about $700 million. The government would have made up *far* more than the difference on taxes alone. They also could have rolled the $107 million for SAGE into the program if they hadn't felt obligated to build the air defence system to American requirements. This cabinet submission also points out that they had become convinced, likely through the influence of LGen Howard Graham (Canadian Army Chief of Staff), AVM Easton and General Foulkes (Chairman Chiefs of Staff committee) that missiles were "at least as effective as a manned fighter, and cheaper" as Pearkes and Foulkes put it. It would be interesting to know where this opinion really originated and for what reason.

The author received Avro's own secret assessment of the Bomarc's utility, dated September of 1958. This prophetic document was circulated to seven of Avro's top engineering staff. Avro concluded the entire SAGE network, including that portion of it optimised for interceptors, was *unworkable* due to vulnerability to jamming. They also concluded that many aspects of the Bomarc system were so vulnerable, especially to carcinogen jamming, that the system was useless if not dangerous. Interestingly the USAF would come to exactly the same conclusions almost immediately after the Arrow program was cancelled. This was during USAF Generals White, Twining and Partridge testimony to the Senate sub-committee as was shown earlier. Even before the Arrow cancellation the RCAF and government had opportunity to hear a similar "consensus" opinion from British RAF and defence experts reversing their official view of defensive missiles vs. autonomous interceptors in the fall of 1958. Earlier it was mentioned that the British RAF, defence specialists and research establishments teamed up to conduct Operation Sunbeam: a test of the overall capabilities of the then-current and projected air defence network.

Cabinet minutes also stated that the "Chiefs of Staff felt that it would be more economical to procure a fully developed interceptor of comparable performance in the U.S." No one mentioned that such an aircraft simply didn't exist. This Chiefs of Staff recommendation was from Foulkes and the Army and Navy Chiefs. Chief of the Air Staff Hugh Campbell and NORAD Deputy Commander in Chief Air Marshal Slemon were *not* of this opinion. In fact Campbell had insisted that, if the Arrow were cancelled, Canada would require equivalent or *superior* aircraft to the Arrow. Even the USAF NORAD CIC General Earl Partridge was obliquely but unmistakably stating, to Congressional hearings, that the US did *not* have an interceptor comparable to the Arrow but would have liked one very much. The professional opinions of these gentlemen, at the height of their careers and expertise, were not admitted to Cabinet.

The government projected that one Bomarc base would cost $120 million to build and equip. Thus, ten disposable, nuclear "squadrons," required to replace the number of CF-100s in service, would cost $1.2 billion. This is hardly equivalent to 100 Arrows which were exaggerated by Pearkes and Diefenbaker to cost $1.2 billion, even while Avro offered a firm price for 100 Arrows of $375 million, radar and weapons included. Of course, when Crawford Gordon met the Diefenbaker Cabinet in September 1958, he pointed out the savings related to adoption of MA-1.

Since each Bomarc squadron would have 60 to 100 missiles, ponder for a moment the radioactive fallout of this quantity of nuclear warheads so close to Quebec City or North Bay, the only places that got Bomarcs. In a memo of 12 January 1959, to the government, Chief of the Air Staff Campbell pointed out that production of 100 CF-105s with engines, spares, ground support equipment, runway improvements and infrastructure would cost Canada $702 million with a maximum single-fiscal-year expenditure of between $162 and $245 million. After Arrow cancellation the government swiftly spent $420 million on short-range, low-level, nuclear-strike Lockheed F-104G Starfighters.

Canada wasn't offered cost sharing on the Bomarc until ten days before Black Friday. Pearkes announced in Cabinet that the US had just agreed to pay $91 million of the cost of Canadian Bomarc bases. By then virtually every government in the West knew the Arrow was dead yet the government of Canada actively conspired to prevent Avro

from learning the news until it was too late. A review of the documents discovered by Campagna, and reproduced by Zuuring, will show this to be true.

On November 11th 1958, the same day Arrow RL-202 was clocked at Mach 1.96-1.98, in a climb, in intermediate afterburner (not full power and still accelerating), Canadian Army General Mackling stated: "We have an Air Force strategically hog tied to the USAF. The RCAF is preparing to give up air-warfare and get right down to earth to fire untested, obsolete U.S. anti-aircraft missiles. It will soon wield no more power than a flock of common barnyard hens." Too bad his boss, General Graham, was against the Arrow as was *his* boss, General Foulkes. It appears to the author that the RCN Chief of Staff was pivotal, yet rational and had enormous pressure applied to him.

The United States of America were going the other direction, *up* and considered they could control the world from space. According to Lyndon Baines Johnson, then US Senate Majority Leader:

> From space the Masters of Infinity would have the power to control the earth's weather, to cause drought and flood, to change the time, raise the level of the sea, divert the Gulf Stream and change temperate climates to frigid. Therefore our national goal, and the goal of all free men must be to win and hold the ultimate position from which total control of the earth may be exercised.

As the Shaws stated regarding the above passage, "Whom the gods would destroy they first make mad." November 25th 1958 Cabinet minutes showed that Pearkes wanted to delete Arrow expenditures from National Defence estimates and was given the green light to do so by Cabinet at this time. The Arrow was secretly killed this day. One would imagine the word was diffused via the "grey-suits old-boys-network" to the other financial barons of the West, secretly of course. All subsequent Cabinet discussions about the Arrow cancellation appear to merely be window dressing for the historical Cabinet minute record. In early March of 1959, just after the Arrow cancellation, Pearkes is on record as having stated (to the public) that the decision to cancel the Arrow was only arrived at a few weeks earlier.

December 22nd, 1958 Cabinet minutes however describe the Arrow cancellation decision as having been *"reached last September"* and took to task NORAD Deputy Air Marshal Slemon's strong public support, with NORAD Commander USAF General Partridge at his side, of the Arrow program. These same minutes mentioned the US Secretary of Defence's comments that the US had decided not to develop any new interceptor aircraft except the F-108. Odd, from this, that the cancellation of the F-106C/D didn't filter through to the consciousness of the Conservatives until early 1959 ... when they were *told.* Again it was wrongly implied that the F-108 was far more advanced than the CF-105 and that this US decision supported the government decision to cancel the Arrow. Even Hendricks' diary notes show they were all convinced that the F-108 would be superior to the Arrow although Avro had the true specifications, courtesy of Dr. Courtland Perkins. Proper intelligence analysis would also have revealed that the F-108 would not be superior to the Arrow. It is hard to imagine how *anyone* was convinced that a bigger and much heavier aircraft than the Arrow, with about the same thrust, would be *superior.* Indeed Avro was reluctant to specify that the Arrow 4, with four additional ramjet engines, titanium skin and insulation, would be able to fully meet the USAF LRIX time at Mach 3 requirements. How the F-108 was to do so without this extra thrust, more weight and stainless steel is incomprehensible. Perhaps this is why it was cancelled once the Arrow and production line were scrap... *it had served its purpose!* Perhaps that is why it is so difficult to find information on the F-108 while information on the SR-71, in service until the 1990s, is now commonplace.

January 10th 1959 Cabinet minutes show Pearkes representing the Arrow program thus: "...the Chiefs of Staff had said there was nothing new to report on the military side that would change its view of the Arrow program." Pearkes neglected to mention that Hugh Campbell and Slemon were for Arrow adoption. Pearkes went on to read economical selections from Campbell's letter pointing this out along with Arrow weapons system cost reductions and improvement in range and performance. By "nothing new" Campbell meant that he still felt the Arrow was the best option, and that the present global military situation still supported his view! Pearkes also mentioned that the price of 100 Arrows had, after cancellation of Astra-Sparrow, dropped almost in half. Pearkes reveals that he now had

the information to know that SAGE was already seen in the USAF as being an inferior concept to the autonomous method when he describes the F-108 as not being designed for SAGE.

In the February 3rd 1959 Cabinet minutes Diefenbaker said Arrow cancellation was a foregone conclusion but that they needed some time to find something to keep Avro employment up. Apparently by February 20th he thought he had it.

A telling clue as to the true source of the Chiefs of Staff recommendations for Arrow cancellation is shown in cabinet minutes of February 4th 1959. Pearkes stated, on the record no less, that he "recommended that development of the CF-105 be discontinued and that the Chiefs of Staff present at an early date the recommendation they *had been requested to make.*" [italics added] This suggests the *true* source of Diefenbaker's house representations and those of his memoirs that "my own Chiefs of Staff didn't want it!" The same document shows Diefenbaker advising his comrades on how to handle the fall-out from the RCAF if they noticed that the 1959 budget didn't include any funds for the Arrow although the decision was not to be taken until March 31st. Diefenbaker advised them to pretend that the budget included funds either for cancellation or "to continue development for a while." Pearkes, much earlier, had recommended they cancel the Arrow and delay a necessary purchase of US interceptors for over a year to let the political fall-out dissipate, which they did. An earlier Cabinet discussion of the Arrow cancellation mentions that it might appear odd that the Chiefs of Staff Committee had reversed its stand on the Arrow. It was mentioned that most of the staff had changed in the meantime, perhaps as a method of deflecting criticism or suspicions about the source of the change of heart. Again, Campbell stood firm in support of the Arrow despite what appears to be more than just an "implied" order.

If one finds it difficult to believe that the Chiefs of Staff would be ordered to make a recommendation with which they did not agree to take pressure off the government, there is further evidence in the Cabinet minutes of 30 June 1959. This was during their debates on who should get the F-104 license-production contract. Cabinet was advised that: "The implication of the views of the Chiefs of Staff was that they would prefer a better aircraft than the

F-104G if more money were available. It would be highly embarrassing if... it became known that the Chiefs of Staff were, on military grounds, in favour of a different and presumably more efficient type of aircraft. *The Chiefs of Staff should be asked to submit a firm recommendation on the F-104G.*" [italics added] The same document points out that the F-104 was selected largely because Lockheed offered to allow Canadian production of components for a German order for 66 Starfighters, rather than due to military factors. A better aircraft, one that could actually carry a bomb load, was the Republic F-105 Thunderchief. The Starfighter's weapons load was minuscule as it had been designed as a lightweight, gun-armed day-fighter.

This of course leads us back to the argument that neither Diefenbaker nor Pearkes ordered the Arrows to be cut up but that it came from Chief of Air Staff Hugh Campbell himself as shown in publically available documents. Jan Zurakowski still believes Diefenbaker was behind the order to cut up the aircraft. The previous testimony from Cabinet itself backs up such a theory of verbal orders being used to duck responsibility. Any former CF officer (such as the author) can relate that, early in training, it is pointed out that there are three kinds of orders; direct orders, indirect orders (those implicit with a job description) and *implied* orders. The government expects all to be obeyed. The first letter from Campbell, where he first recommends destruction of the Arrows, refers to an earlier meeting between Pearkes and himself. The more publicly known letter making this official also refers to Pearkes. It is suggestive of the possibility of Pearkes having verbally ordered Campbell to recommend destruction. Campbell's memorandum also refers to the possibility of the flying Arrows being used as "roadside stands" as a reason to justify the destruction! It is more than difficult to believe that Campbell himself would promote such an absurd notion, especially since they could have been housed in a museum, abandoned wartime hangers or in a multitude of other controlled environments, most of them in the control of the RCAF itself! After all, many military aircraft were stored in secure hangars nationwide and there would soon be lots of nuclear missiles stored in sheds near North Bay and Quebec City! To the author it seems possible, at least, that the "roadside stand" nonsense was a reference Campbell included to secretly poke Pearkes in the chest.

James Dow also finds the cancellation order to be unresolved. He mentions the order came first from Pearkes' department then O'Hurleys. Dow does include the following passage: "A senior air force officer claims he saw a written instruction from the prime minister in the office of a Defence Production official but this has not been verified. ... The order to destroy the Arrows may even have called for the destruction of the order. But wherever the responsibility lies, the wholesale destruction of the Avro Arrow was a reprehensible and mindless act that did a profound disservice to all Canadians and to posterity. It could only have come from someone with an abysmal lack of vision."

Regarding the destruction of everything to do with the Arrow, some have said that it was the custom to destroy design drawings, working lofts and hard tooling, plus prototype aircraft. This is far from the historical case. With most aircraft that were cancelled in the prototype stage, there was no hard tooling to destroy! Tooling, for an aircraft of the sophistication and performance of the Arrow was usually preserved for a few years at least while often in Britain, and almost always in the US, flying prototype examples were kept for museums... that is unless they destroyed themselves during flight-testing. Indeed at about that time the Convair B-58 Hustler was in flight test and 7 of 30 of the aircraft built for this purpose were lost in testing. Others mention various offers to have the flying Mk. 1s taken on by the NAE and/or the British as proving the sincerity of the government in allowing for some to be preserved. A solid look at *who* was actually proposing that the British take on Arrows, and the haste with which the destruction order followed from O'Hurley's office shows that the government was not at all sincere and in fact threatened to send in the Army to ensure not a single Arrow escaped the torches and axes.

Again it was Jim Floyd, among others, sending letters to Sir Thomas Pike, Sir Roy Dobson, Sir George Gardiner and others pleading to have them take the Arrows as research vehicles for the SST program, rather than allowing them to "be ground into dust." Some have suggested the Arrow just didn't have the range to do the ferry flight to Britain. Absurd. It seems clear that the Canadian government told the British not to even ask. The former made it very clear that no Arrows would ever leave Canada and said so. From

The Convair B-58 Hustler. It had about half the dry thrust to weight ratio of the Arrow 2 at take-off. A catastrophic outer engine failure is said to result in aircraft break-up. The original order of over 200 was cut in half and the aircraft only served for about ten years. It was considered, contrary to the assertions of so many experts, to be relatively immune to interception and SAMs during its short career (1960-1971) due to fairly high altitude and speed. (USAF)

Avro Arrow, The Story of the Avro Arrow From Its Evolution to Its Extinction:

> General Electric announced that they would like to use the Arrows [likely to develop the J-93 engine) and were prepared to pay a substantial price for them, including purchase of spares, in a straight commercial deal, but the Canadian Government turned them down.

> The U.K. approached the Canadian Government about acquiring the Arrows. They were told not to pursue the matter, for if they did, the Canadian Government would be in the embarrassing position of having to say an official "No!"… no Arrow would ever leave Canada.

Red Herrings Spawn: Defence Development and Production Sharing

So how was the Canadian government finally induced to abandon the Arrow program? Seemingly, through disinformation from all directions including naïve Canadians who were willing to take US opinions at face value, self-interested Canadians working for US aerospace firms in Canada, jealous Canadians working at the NAE, DRB and others, plus tactical statements by US politicians and others. There can be little doubt that the CIA was heavily involved and had a strategic plan to deal with not only Avro Canada, but British aviation as well. Anyone familiar with aviation history will know that the European Airbus company has been a target of more than just Boeing in the United States. In the 1950s the Hawker Siddeley Group was the biggest competition to American manufacturers. In the 1940s they were the biggest, period.

Defence Production Sharing was the most publicly palatable and saleable red herring, however. Evidence exists to suggest that Diefenbaker and Pearkes were offered, before Black Friday, a production sharing arrangement where they would get an order for Canadair "radar-picket" aircraft in exchange for purchasing (never built) F-106Cs. E.K. Shaw in *There Never Was an Arrow* also mentions the F-106 as being an option in a defence production sharing deal. The radar-picket aircraft would refer to an aircraft similar to the then-current Lockheed Constellation derivative EC-121 or perhaps to an anti-submarine warfare type like the Canadair Argus, either derived from the Bristol Brittania. Diefenbaker apparently wanted to then give Avro the contract for the aircraft for the offensive nuclear Strike Reconnaissance role he had inexplicably but obediently taken on for Canada in 1958. Below is the evidence, such as has been made public. On the other hand, it becomes clear that the Conservatives were looking at pretty much *anything* in terms of production sharing, so long as it could be construed as justification for Arrow cancellation.

There was a push on by Pearkes around the time of the Dulles/Eisenhower visit to Canada in mid 1958 to convince Cabinet that the (paper airplane) F-106C was as good as the CF-105. August 28th 1958 cabinet documents stated that they were investigating a "possible alternative interceptor to the CF-105." This shows they knew full well that interceptors were still required.

The same cabinet minutes describe this F-106C as having been represented by the US authorities as being comparable in performance to the CF-105 and that it cost half as much and would be available several months earlier. But, even the F-106A model would not be truly combat ready until 1960, after over a decade of continuous development and when the Conservatives admitted the Arrow could have been entering service. The F-106A meanwhile had flown four years earlier! This shows the absolute desperation of Pearkes to get the Arrow cancelled. They had also described the F-108 as having a range of 1,000 miles, which the Conservatives naively, or deceitfully, took to mean it had a much longer range than the CF-105. As we have seen, Avro's Jim Floyd and Fred Smye got the F-108 specification directly from the USAF Chief Scientist, Dr. Courtland Perkins, and then proposed an Arrow variant to meet it! The Mk. 2a Arrow had very nearly three times the specified combat radius and gained its extra range from added internal fuel stowage capacity and was a minor modification. Of course no Arrow variants above the Mk. 2 were mentioned to Cabinet.

As for the "F-106C instead of Arrows" idea, a telling passage in the minutes mentions that "...to abandon the CF-105 now and undertake to produce the U.S. F-106C, which was physically quite possible, would be a serious political mistake." That is, unless they could get an extra bonus, such as a contract to produce aircraft for the United States to offset the balance of payments problem. This was also the time when Pearkes suggested they delay the purchase of an American plane for at least a year for political considerations. Obviously this delay had nothing to do with military considerations.

September 8th 1958 Cabinet documents also state that they were looking at 68 aircraft as "the minimum if it were decided to purchase U.S. F-106C planes." This figure didn't come from the RCAF who always wanted at least 169 Arrows. It came from the American politicians. Of course the RCAF would require significantly more than 169 F-106Cs for the same defensive capability as this number of Arrows. Since that day Canada accepted the figure of around 60 interceptors as being sufficient for the country.

Today around 60 seem to be sufficient for Canada's NATO, NORAD and UN duties if Canada's current operational CF-18 Hornet strength is a guide.

December 31st 1958 cabinet minutes also refer to a Convair/Canadair defence production sharing bid. "It was pointed out that, if the Convair-Canadair bid were accepted by the United States, the business would go not to Avro but to Canadair in Montreal."

So there it is. The government of Canada was proposing, to the US, to cancel the Arrow in exchange for an aircraft that didn't exist and a small order for relatively low-tech, mostly foreign developed aircraft to be built by a 100 percent American-owned company operating in Canada! Ten days later it was forced into their consciousness that the F-106C had been cancelled. January 10th Cabinet minutes state just that. Diefenbaker later used the F-106C/D cancellation as justification, under questioning by Paul Hellyer, for Arrow cancellation. In justifying the implications of the cancellation of the F-106C, Pearkes stated his belief that the Bomarc could do the job. This is astonishing in light of the fact that in the same document he was stating that the Arrow 2, with a low-speed (but supersonic combat) mission radius of 575 nm, (but related by Pearkes as being only 300 to 500 nm) couldn't defend Canada while the Bomarc, with a range of only 280 nm, could. Since the F-106C had evaporated, Pearkes was finding himself having to continue justification of Arrow cancellation by very tenuous means indeed; Bomarcs only! Everyone "in the know" knew the Bomarc line was only ever intended as a last-ditch line of defence for American SAC bomber and future SAC ICBM bases.

January 28th, 1959 documents show Diefenbaker suggesting that Avro could build the Strike Reconnaissance aircraft for a NATO role that Pearkes had been convinced to accept by John Foster Dulles in April 1958. NATO was, however, requesting up-graded CF-100s from Canada as late as 1958 and had made secret statements that more than suggested they would very much want Arrows for NATO once they were ready! Of course it is a foregone conclusion that NATO would want the best interceptor on the planet once it was in service. Interesting indeed that the US was pressuring Canada to accept an uncharacteristic nuclear attack role for Europe while Europe itself was requesting all-weather interceptors. At any rate, Diefenbaker wondered if Canada could produce the "Blackburn aircraft" for the NATO role. This aircraft was a developed Blackburn Buccaneer (the NA.39) that was never put into service. The original Buccaneer was of about the same performance as the CF-100 so one can see it would have been absolutely crazy to leap backwards and adopt this aircraft. Pearkes pointed out that the Blackburn aircraft wouldn't be ready until at least 1963 but that Avro could build the Grumman Tiger for the same role.

The idea that Diefenbaker really wanted Avro to remain in business and build the NATO strike-recce aircraft if possible seems entirely disingenuous in light of a Defence Production Sharing bid that *was not* present in the Cabinet minutes: an offer by Republic to build the F-105 Thunderchief *with* Iroquois engines. On page 204 of Dow's book is the passage:

One of the contenders was the Republic F-105 Thunderchief, and after discussions with Avro, the Republic Aviation Corporation, an American company, revised its bid to bring it more in line with the spirit of defence production sharing announced by Diefenbaker when he dumped the Arrow. Avro would produce the Thunderchief for the RCAF [with the Iroquois] and the Iroquois would be used for some USAF aircraft. Ontario's premier, Leslie Frost, seemed enthusiastic when *Smye* told him about the plan. He called Diefenbaker to discuss the proposal and then sent his friend, John Basset, to pursue it further with the prime minister. The president of Republic Aviation, Mundy Peel, sent a letter to George Pearkes detailing the new proposal, but when he came to Ottawa to discuss it, he came away empty handed. [italics added]

Again we see it was Smye and Avro who were trying to save the company; the Conservatives seemed intent on doing the opposite. The Iroquois would have replaced the J-75 in the Thunderchief, meaning it would have practically slid right in. It would have given a considerable boost in payload and performance. And Avro might be around today. All the cabinet documents this author has read say nothing of this offer.

Canadair eventually produced the Lockheed F-104 Starfighter for this NATO nuclear strike role even though it had been designed as an interceptor.

It is interesting to read these Cabinet documents and note that Pearkes was continually moving for Arrow cancellation but the Cabinet repeatedly deferred the decision to a later date. Pearkes' reasoning under questioning by the more responsible members of cabinet continually grew more and more nebulous and less connected to NORAD, RCAF and even NATO opinions—even to the extreme of hoisting the petard that continuation would be playing into Russian hands.

Finally, on February 20th Diefenbaker rose in the House:

Mr. Speaker, with the leave of the House I should like to make a somewhat lengthy statement on the subject of one facet of the national defence of Canada. The announcement I wish to make has to do with the decision regarding our air defence which was foreshadowed in the statement made by me to the press on September 23 last. The government has carefully examined and re-examined the probable need for the Arrow aircraft and Iroquois engine known as the CF-105, the development of which has been continued pending a final decision. The conclusion is that the development of the Arrow aircraft and Iroquois engine should be terminated now. Formal notice of termination is being given now to the contractors. ... Although the range of the aircraft has been increased it is still limited.

He then quoted the original figures, given in 1953 for the development of at least 500 Arrows. This was between $1.5 and 2.0 million each. At that time the development program was for *airframes alone!* ASTRA, Sparrow and the Iroquois were *all* added later, and certainly not for free. In reality the airframe costs were unbelievably close to the original estimates, at $3.75 million each including taxes! Diefenbaker chose to roll all facilities, runway and other related costs for equipping the RCAF with Arrows into the cost he disclosed, but not as $780 million but as $7.8 million per aircraft.

February 23rd Cabinet documents, three days after Black Friday, pointed out that the previous hope that Canadair would receive "a large U.S. contract for radar picket aircraft ... seemed to be less and less hopeful in view of the pressure from the aircraft industry the U.S." Apparently the Conservatives hadn't given up on their bid for *some* kind of interceptor for Canadair aircraft. Meanwhile February 14th minutes, only 11 days earlier, stated that "the [US] Secretary of Defence and others in the U.S. administration were well disposed to place such [production sharing] orders." From this one can see that being well disposed to give Canada orders was a far cry from actually delivering orders. The final news of the production sharing agreement having fallen through was, interestingly, delivered three days after Arrow cancellation, and apparently a single day before the Conservatives were to announce their miraculous Defence Development and Production Sharing Agreement with the USA. Some cabinet members were apparently wondering why they didn't announce this deal sooner. The author suggests that Diefenbaker was hoping against hope for a Convair/Canadair (F-106A for a Britannia variant) deal to be finalized so he could relate tangible proof of the deal's success—so long as it didn't include Avro. After Black Friday he had a genuine production-sharing offer that could have preserved Avro and the Iroquois and kept most of the money in Canada. That offer was not mentioned in any Cabinet documents this author has read.

One wonders if they could have also missed the point that such a deal would mean massive profits from both projects for Convair/General Dynamics, and would not provide a development contract for an airframe to Canada since the Canadair aircraft was the already developed license-built Bristol Britannia derivative, the CL-44. They missed the point that the short-term continuation of employment at Canadair would be the only real benefit to

The Canadair Argus. Developed from the British Bristol Britannia, the radial piston engines were found to be more economical than the original turboprops on low-speed, low-level missions patrolling for Soviet submarines.
(Public Archives of Canada)

Canada since Canadair was 100 percent General Dynamics owned, with profits going to the USA. The Diefenbaker government's attitude to this very important consideration of US ownership (and thus balance of payments) was characterized in Cabinet minutes while the strike-recce aircraft choice was being made. They basically admitted that most Canadians wouldn't pick up on this fact of US ownership, and that as such it was an insignificant political consideration in terms of votes. In relating their reasoning for killing the Arrow program however, the Cabinet minutes stated that it would be preferable to cancel the program before the 100 aircraft were built since it would only be temporary employment! That all contracts are temporary employment until the next comes along seemed to escape the reasoning power of the Conservatives. Their power for rationalization was obviously unmatched. Again and again the Diefenbaker government was knowingly basing choices that negatively affected the long-term economic and military independence of Canada upon an agenda that was at odds with their publicly promoted nationalism.

All of it is suggestive of the politicians having secretly agreed to kill not only the Arrow, but Avro itself, for American considerations in Defence Production and Development Sharing. They appear to have also done everything in their power, including agreeing to a contract to put the MA-1 into the Arrow in November of 1958, (when they had already deleted it from the budget and had decided in September to kill it) to keep Avro in the dark about the coming axe. They certainly knew this would make the company more vulnerable to it when the day came. As the Shaws' document puts it:

> It becomes quite clear, in the light of overwhelming evidence, that the Government was deliberately deceiving not only the public, but the Company, and deliberately putting it into an impossible position, in which it could take no action to save itself; so that, whatever course it took, could be used against it. This, of course, has been done with great success since February. However, to create the necessary public opinion to allow this to be done, it was necessary for the Government and press to grossly deceive and mis-inform the public. If they had had a good case for cancelling the Arrow, they

could certainly have allowed the public to be told the facts, and to listen to the evidence of informed authorities. That they could not do so, tells its own story. The normal processes of democracy would have prevented them from carrying out this vindictive and costly blunder.

The contradictory, false and inexcusable statements which Mr. Diefenbaker and Mr. Pearkes have given to the public as justification for this action, imply that they are merely excuses to cover up the real reasons.

In the face of all evidence to the contrary, the people of Canada were told the Arrow was obsolete, a costly failure, and money down the drain. They were told that we couldn't sell it, implying that no one wanted it, and suppressed evidence to the contrary.

They seem to have suppressed RCAF discussion of the Arrow program as well. Zurakowski related in an article his discomfort during a meeting with RCAF staffers to discuss the Arrow and its characteristics in mid 1958. When it came time for questions from the RCAF there were none. When asked why they were so quiet one of them volunteered that they had been ordered not to discuss the Arrow.

The NATO Strike Reconnaissance Aircraft: Whither Avro

It was the view of the Department of Defence Production that it would not be possible to support three major aircraft firms in Canada.

–Raymond O'Hurley, August 13, 1959

Unfortunately, Raymond O'Hurley, Diefenbaker's Minister of Defence Production was accused of having been a "bag-man" for the (sometimes questionably) democratic Quebec government of Maurice Duplessis, and of having been creative with his resume to the Conservative Party of Canada. Some of the protagonists and circumstances are explored both in the Shaws' work and in Newman's *Renegade* in Power. No matter what the truth of the allegations, the results of his policy statement were the destruction of Avro Aircraft, and the precipitous deterioration of A.V. Roe Canada Ltd and large-scale Hawker Siddeley operations in Canada.

From the 13 August 1959 Cabinet minutes, O'Hurley recommends in conclusion that Canadair should be awarded the new RCAF nuclear strike-reconnaissance aircraft contract. Thus, the government of Canada had made it official policy to kill a public company partially owned by Britons; a company that had been intentionally set up to give Canada an independent aviation industry and means of self-defence. In fact, it appears that the Conservatives fully intended to award the contract to Canadair yet felt, for appearances, that they would have to tender the contract *then* choose Canadair. Cabinet minutes for 30 June, 1959 discuss the F-104G contract, with O'Hurley making the recommendation: "[T]hat the airframe contract be allocated to Canadair Limited on an incentive type contract."

A month and a half later, on 13 August, 1959, O'Hurley discussed the tenders he had just received for the F-104G from Avro, de Havilland and Canadair. He mentions the de Havilland bid as being about double the "nearly identical" other two with Avro's bid being $1.3 million lower than Canadair's. He then states that the Avro bid "did not appear realistic." Again the government was accusing Avro of being either dishonest or incompetent. O'Hurley's department had, however, raised the Canadair bid by $3.3 million dollars because it didn't allow for normal inflation in materials and wages. Obviously the professional costing accountants in the Department of Defence Production felt *Canadair's* bid was unrealistic. Apparently Canadair was consulted and firmly stated, perhaps after consulting their oracles, that there would be no increases in either material or labour and the addition was removed. Canadair further sweetened the pot for the government to choose their higher bid for license-building F-104s. They stated that it would reduce plant "overhead" on the other government contracts for the Yukon and Argus with a savings of up to $12.5 million over a five-year period. By the absence of any further discussion of Avro's tender it seems clear that they were not allowed a similar opportunity to improve their bid. The other considerations, which always favoured a Canadair choice, are equally nebulous. It is unknown if the overhead savings materialised. They also appear to have had to develop a bombing radar for the Starfighter which seems to have been an extra expense.

The Finance Minister related the findings of the Treasury Board, that in their opinion a "rebuilding" of Avro would not be in the national "best interest." The web that O'Hurley had spun netted those less enthusiastic politicians with the

Image of one version of the Arrow proposed for GOR 339—eventually almost filled by the TSR. 2 development a generation later. This British strike-recce Arrow variant, using three discardable tanks and the half-scale, supersonic Blue Steel cruise-missile, bore more than a passing similarity to the Arrow Mk. 4, proposed to the USAF. They were to be the same basic aircraft with different interchangeable wing pods, either with ramjets or tanks. The nose is elongated for extra electronics, and to provide better supersonic flow to the intakes. The tank pylons and wing contain the landing gear which was shorter and stronger than that of the Mk. 1. (image by R.L. Whitcomb)

sweeping conclusion that the government was "faced with the decision of not being able to support three aircraft companies." This paragraph finds the aerospace industry in Canada to be over-expanded at the time while quoting the probable future requirement for aircraft and missiles as being insufficient for the sustenance of three companies. Again the sales potential of the Arrow, Iroquois and other Avro projects are completely discounted. Avro knew full well that Britain and Australia, perhaps Germany and potentially other nations, if not the US itself, would in all likelihood eventually buy an Arrow development and the Iroquois engine. (Germany had also expressed interest in the Arrow, pending seeing it in service in the RCAF.)

It is astonishing that the government of Canada was proposing killing off its largest aerospace company—one that was 43 percent Canadian owned. In December 1957 the Air Industries and Transport association had written Diefenbaker: "It has been our experience in the past that the potentialities of the Canadian aircraft industry and its allied companies have not always been appreciated. Lack of an immediate and long-range program will result in a deterioration of the industry's effective operating capacity. We believe the industry at the moment to be in serious jeopardy." When Avro was begun, the government felt it was crucial to the future of the country to stay competitive in aerospace and to have an indigenous *design* and production capability in *all* related technologies. Clearly such nationalistic and long-term economic strategies were completely thrown out the window on 20 February, 1959.

Meanwhile, of course, Canadair had plenty of work going while producing the Argus and Yukon (Britannia derivatives) for the government. Interference on the part of the government to get the Jetliner stopped had materially aided Canadair, her US parent, and the US competition to Avro (Boeing especially). This last government decision to kill Avro did the same. It weakened the Canadian economy while strengthening the American.

Avro was accused, again by O'Hurley, of having made *"no effort in obtaining commercial contracts."* This was quite disingenuous considering solid bids for production of the Jetliner had been stopped by the previous government, while sales of the Iroquois had been halted by their own! A Royal Air Force Arrow purchase had been stopped, perhaps temporarily, by politicians in Britain. Meanwhile Avro had standing contracts for development of flying saucers for the USAF and US Army and were in early stages of work on an SST design for Howard Hughes and TWA. Others made representations to the effect that Avro was leery of doing business in the free market. Considering how much business A.V. Roe Canada was doing in the free market outside of Avro Aircraft, with buses, rail cars, T-34 Mentors for the USAF, steel, coal and even shipbuilding at St. John's Shipbuilding, this rings hollow.

Further in these minutes the government suggested: "The Canadair plant, though owned by a U.S. company, could reasonably be regarded as a Canadian establishment." They added "[Canadair] received no orders from the parent company." Meanwhile Britain had purchased hundreds of Canadair-built and Orenda-powered Sabres for the RAF. As pointed out in Newman's *Renegade in Power*, by 1962 Canada's economy would be performing so poorly that Britain would be lending Canada money with which to prop up Canada's falling dollar. In the 1950s it had been the other way around, with a billion dollars being loaned to the UK. The Conservatives' logic extended to giving the contract to Canadair because it "was fairly busy now" while knowing full well that without this contract, Avro would likely fail. Their apparent conclusion was that this was the favourable choice. Paul Hellyer mentioned in an

e-mail during the summer of 2000 "but then, Diefenbaker could be very vindictive!"

As to Diefenbaker's vindictiveness and tendency towards "loose talk," a telling line is present in the Cabinet minutes from 22 December 1958; "Avro had put on a tremendous publicity campaign and this played right into their hands [regarding Slemon's statements of support]. If the government decided to continue development it would be accused of giving in to a powerful lobby. Pressure was coming in from other sources in Ontario too. *Even if he thought the decision reached last September [to cancel the Arrow] was wrong, he was determined, because of what had happened since, to adhere firmly to it.*" [italics added]

Apparently, for Avro, the penalty for embarrassing Diefenbaker was death. One wonders if C.D. Howe's embarrassment, at the hands of Avro, for having destroyed the Jetliner program resulted in similar vindictiveness. After all, Howe had stated in Parliament (with parliamentary immunity from prosecution) regarding the Jetliner; "There was everything wrong with it! It had to carry sand in the tail to fly!" (he also neglected to mention that test aircraft require ballast to simulate normal center of gravity changes). Avro was just correcting demonstrable errors that threatened their survival, and in their eyes, the survival of Canada itself. One might think that one of the largest publicly-owned companies in Canada would have the right to defend itself against some of the disgracefully unsupported editorials and articles which appeared with stunning regularity beginning in the summer of 1958. The Shaws and many others who were there at the time discuss what appeared to be a media conspiracy. As Jack Woodman related in his paper to the Canadian Aeronautics & Space Institute of 1978:

> The decision to cancel the Arrow program was, in my opinion, very poorly founded. Nothing has happened since 1959 to support that decision as being correct. In fact, just the opposite happened.
>
> Several months before the cancellation announcement, there was a lot of bad publicity in Toronto newspapers about the Arrow. It was like an anti-Arrow campaign was being waged. Retired Army officers and self-proclaimed experts and others, were implying that the day of the manned interceptor was over.

The retired Army officer in question was Simonds, who came back in the press to reiterate his earlier criticisms and belief in missiles above all.

More interesting logic is evident in the Cabinet minutes where A.V. Roe's Orenda engine division is chosen for the F-104 engine contract over Canadian Pratt & Whitney. It was stated that General Electric, producer of the J-79 engine for the Lockheed F-104, would not be comfortable giving Pratt & Whitney Canada the engine since they were *"direct competitors."* Meanwhile, in keeping with their "let Avro die" policy, they let Convair-owned Canadair produce the F-104, developed by Lockheed, a direct competitor to Convair! Never mind that profits from an Avro production of the F-104 would largely stay in Canada and contribute to the Canadian currency in real terms. No mention of Republic Aviation's obvious comfort with the prospect of Avro building their Thunderchief was made. No mention of Republic Aviation's comfort in equipping their plane for USAF service with Iroquois engines was made. On the monetary front, if the Hawker Siddeley Group behaved as they had to date in this respect, 100 percent of the profits would stay in Canada with none going back to the British parent. At the height of the Arrow program the Canadian dollar had peaked at $1.10 US. As for Avro bilking the taxpayer, all the profits from the aviation side were put right back into Avro's *Canadian* aviation facilities.

During the F-104 Starfighter contract decision process, it was admitted that "the bulk of the items for the electronics and fire control were within the capabilities of the Canadian electronics industry and he recommended that they be produced in Canada." One wonders where this knowledge was when the government stated that major components for both the DEW (Distant Early Warning) line and Bomarc would have to be produced in the USA.

Later Cabinet documents prove that Westinghouse Canada and other US owned firms had acquired the means to produce these items from their involvement in ASTRA/Sparrow, under Avro project management. In other words, Lockheed and Convair gained materially from a Canadian taxpayer investment in the development of a Canadian weapons system, managed by a 43 percent Canadian-owned company which had, to date, kept all of the profits in Canada.

Diefenbaker and Pearkes, early in their mandate, had already agreed to NORAD, Bomarc and SAGE, and also to acceptance of a defensive nuclear role the country just didn't need, *plus* a NATO offensive nuclear strike role that the nation would find morally objectionable! Even in some of Avro's documentation they made clear their distaste for an offensive role for the Arrow, while knowing it would be wise to maintain that ability. There is no question the Americans were, as a matter of policy, pushing the NATO allies into acceptance of American nuclear weapons, (under US control), onto their soil. NORAD and SAGE and the Bomarc accomplished just that.

Fallout: Nuclear Repercussions

A memo (first published in *Storms of Controversy*) printed on the letterhead of the US Deputy Secretary of Defense, June 1, 1960, bears reproduction:

MEMORANDUM ON PRODUCTION SHARING PROGRAM—UNITED STATES AND CANADA

The current program dates back to at least 1941 and the Hyde Park Agreement. This agreement provided generally that each would produce in areas of greatest capability. In 1950 a Statement of Principles of Economic Cooperation was issued by the Truman Administration. It advocated, among other things, a coordinated program of requirements, production and procurement; the exchange of technical knowledge and productive skill; the removal of barriers impeding the flow of essential defense goods. In 1950 a DOD Directive on Defense Economic Cooperation with Canada was issued. A Presidentially approved NSC paper, 5822/1, dated 30 December 58, reaffirmed the Statement of Economic Principles and provided for equal consideration to be accorded the business communities of both countries.

Prior to the NSC paper, and following a visit of the President to Canada in July 1958, Canada took the following actions with the understanding that her defense industry depended largely upon the U.S. channeling defense business into Canada: cancelled the CF 105 and related systems contracts; decided to make maximum use of U.S. developed weapons, integrated into NORAD; worked with the U.S. toward a fully integrated continental air defense. [italics added]

The U.S. in turn established a Production/ Development Sharing Program with Canada with the first quarterly meeting in October 1958. Since then, policy obstacles impeding a free flow of business have been modified in a number of areas such as: Buy American Act; duty free entry of defense goods; security requirement; etc. Also, working groups have been set up on programs of mutual interest (for example, BOMARC); cost sharing agreements have been worked out; and possible joint development programs are being explored.

The last quarterly meeting of the Production Sharing Policy Group was held on 25 May. Despite all efforts, over the period 1 January 59 through 31 March 60, Canadian defence business in the United States almost doubled that placed in Canada. Canada is not satisfied with these results, nor do they appear acceptable from our view.

We must: re-emphasize the program of development sharing activities; encourage American industry to subcontract in Canada; and seek out other legitimate techniques to stimulate the program. Canada should be encouraged to energize her industry which has not displayed the necessary aggressiveness.

This paper states that defence production sharing agreements had been in place at least since 1941 and that the 30th December 1958 NSC paper was really just a reaffirmation of Truman's "Statement of Principles of Economic Cooperation." In other words, Diefenbaker's glorious new Defence Production Sharing Agreement was nothing new at all.

This Department of Defence document also mentions the Hyde Park agreement, which was negotiated in large part in a secret meeting between Franklin Roosevelt and MacKenzie King at a rail siding at Ogdensburg New York in 1938. For a clue to F.D.R.'s and the United States' view of Canada at the time Roosevelt declared in 1937 that: "The people of the United States will not stand idly by if the *domination* of Canadian soil is threatened." [italics added]

This was really just a repackaged restatement of the hawkish Monroe Doctrine which stated essentially that Canada was included in US strategic vital interests whether Canada liked it or not, and that the USA would go to war to ensure it remained under US domination. Is it strange then, that Roosevelt used the word "domination" rather than "sovereignty?"

Meanwhile this later memo states openly that the CF-105 and related contracts were cancelled to gain "...the U.S. channeling [of] defense business into Canada." However in all the precedents to Eisenhower's Defense Production Sharing Agreement, it was agreed that the United States should buy from Canada in areas where Canada had greatest capability. (We have used Defence *Development* and Production Sharing in the heading since this is what it was intended to be.) Where Canada had greatest capability in 1958 was most certainly with Avro. A.V. Roe Canada at that time even owned St. John's Shipbuilding, constructors of the RCN's destroyers. That Avro was producing the best interceptor for North America was also known by both sides, since the USAF repeatedly stated it would be the best in its class for at least five years (until the F-108). In other words assurances of this type made over the years could be seen clearly as of 1958 to be nothing more than seductive disinformation. The United States Air Force Secretary James Douglas, accompanied by his top Generals for USAF requirements, had offered to purchase a couple of Arrow squadrons for Canada in early January 1958! Why didn't Diefenbaker jump at this option, or at least pursue it later?

Apparently Pearkes did, when he met Dulles in July 1958 in a last ditch bid to have the US purchase Arrows. He asked at the time that the US purchase two squadrons of Arrows for RCAF operation in Newfoundland, an area with poor long-range radar coverage. Perhaps he was told straight out at this point by Dulles that Canada would see nothing of Defence Production Sharing as long as "that company" was in existence leaking classified information in her aggressive sales efforts. Dulles certainly could have added that US industry would be more than a little reluctant to provide their designs to Avro since their "proprietary" technologies would be given to the British Hawker Siddeley Group, which was competing with these same US industries as was Avro Canada itself. He could have further noted that it was suspicious, Canada asking the financial powers for the Conversion Loan, while they were pouring money, independently, into every system that goes into an interceptor, plus the interceptor itself, when there were "better, cheaper, sooner" American alternatives. These points should not be overlooked, as they have been in large measure in every other work on this subject. Of course, only a few years earlier, Dulles had threatened France over their refusal to join a united European defence force.

There is evidence that the US government was moved, by the secret international incident involving the falling-through of every deal offered as alternatives to the Arrow, to offer a sincere defence production sharing agreement. About a month before US Secretary of Defense Gates tried to corral Canada into accepting a new F-101B for Canadair CL-44 transports contract, the following passage was contained in a letter addressed to Gates' Deputy:

> There are significant related benefits to be realized. As I have previously mentioned, a sensitive political situation has arisen in Canada due to a series of events involving the CF-105 cancellation in favour of BOMARC and SAGE joint procurement with the U.S., followed by [unilateral U.S.] reductions in BOMARC and SAGE super combat centers.

Acting Secretary of the Air Force Charyk neglected to mention the cancellation of the F-106C/D which had been pushed at Canada when the Arrow's fate was being decided upon. He also failed to mention the F-108 cancellation barely after the Arrows and their tooling had been reduced to scrap!

In the end Canada paid $1.5 million for used F-101 Voodoos *plus* took on the expense of maintaining the Pinetree radar line, *and* purchased SAGE and Bomarc! The significant benefits were obviously basing in Canada and a Canada and Britain dependent on the USA for defence, and technology.

A Diplomatic Cold War Chill?

While Avro workers were in the unemployment lines but the aircraft and line were largely intact, the US dramatically scaled back their adoption of the Bomarc missile. Reasons cited were largely in agreement with Avro's secret evaluation of the system against the Arrow. Certainly Generals Partridge and White had made this a central portion of their plea to the April US Senate sub-committee hearings on air defence. This rational defence priority shift was also used as a reason not to deploy Bomarcs into Canada to cover the West. It also made their decision to cancel the Arrow in favour of Bomarcs in the East, seem less supportable. The Diefenbaker government was running out of US-sponsored air defence options.

It has been discussed in the Countdown chapter how the Convair F-106C cancellation may have disrupted a Conservative cancellation agenda. At that time, (in January 1959) Diefenbaker seemed determined to cancel the Arrow, (right or wrong!) but grant Avro their existence through the NATO strike-reconnaissance aircraft contract. Now, without Bomarcs being a credible option, and without the F-106C, the Conservatives knew they would face searching questions on the air defence front.

Even after the F-106C and Bomarc were shown not to be options, the Arrow could have been salvaged. Unfortunately, not long after the Bomarc scale-back was announced, the order for the destruction of drawings, data, the assembly line and extant examples of the Arrow and Iroquois was issued through O'Hurley's office. Some of the "pro-Avro" group speculate that no Arrows were saved for museums because to leave one intact would provide physical evidence that a remarkably inferior aircraft and operational philosophy was guarding the country. They argue that the Conservatives knew, as of the destruction order, that their most credible remaining defence for their policies was to suggest the Arrow and Avro were flawed.

It seems possible that the North American F-108 may even have become the object of a Defence Production Sharing quest. Les Wilkinson spoke with USAF Colonel Daniel C. Murray in 1992 and the findings of this interview were published in Zuk's *Avrocar: Canada's Flying Saucer*. According to Murray:

> One ominous cloud hung over the Avro program from its onset. The United States and Canadian governments were discussing cost sharing and acquisition of the U.S. Air Force F-108 supersonic fighter. During the middle of the Avrocar program, the Canadian government and the United States Air Force had reached an agreement on the F-108 project and the Avro Arrow was cancelled. Is was ironic that the F-108 was also cancelled.

If this testimony is accurate, one can see that the Conservatives may have been somewhat disturbed by the whole air defence issue by this date. With the cancellation of both the F-106C and the F-108, the government was faced with the realisation that they would have to, in the end, accept an aircraft that they themselves had publically acknowledged as being inferior to the Arrow. With the Bomarc having fallen into disrepute, they were also faced with the fact that it would be widely known that an air defence interceptor was *required*.

It is accepted as fact, however, that over the next several years of Conservative rule, defence relations with the United States deteriorated drastically. Diefenbaker had also publically done an about-face in his remonstrations over the nuclear question. While as policy went the government had accepted a nuclear air defence missile, nuclear artillery and surface to surface missiles for NATO and were in the throes of awarding a contract for a nuclear strike-reconnaissance aircraft, Diefenbaker himself was proclaiming "*There are no nuclear weapons on Canadian soil.*"

Other sources, such as Kay Shaw, Newman and even the 1991 CF AFIC course, show that under Diefenbaker, the Bomarcs sat in their silos with concrete ballast, while the Honest John (formerly Lacrosse) missile carried sand-ballast. This kind of policy would have, beknownst to the interested governments, have left Canada and approaches to the US vulnerable to air attack, and certain NATO fronts in the ETO vulnerable to surprise ground and air attack as well. Certainly this would not have sat well with many American and European officials and agencies.

Most authors, in discussing these events, fail to see the air weapons acquisition "track record" when providing commentary on Diefenbaker's defence problems, and falling-out with the United States. It at least helps explain Dief's refusal to "nuke-up" as he had agreed with the United States authorities. During the Cuban Missile Crisis; however things came to a head with the new US president, John F. Kennedy.

Many books describe the sour relationship between John F. Kennedy and John George Diefenbaker. Some suggest that Diefenbaker carried some animosity towards the United States from earlier events. Logically, one could assume it was over the Arrow and the failure of DPS. One American contact of the author's describes a PBS documentary on the two leaders that suggested that Diefenbaker's 1962 currency devaluation crisis, at the height of the 1962 election campaign and just after, as having been caused by the CIA and US establishment as retaliation for Diefenbaker's failure to respond to the Cuban Missile Crisis. (Walter Lockhart Gordon, Pearson's first minister of finance, points out in *A Political Memoir* how vulnerable to American destabilization the Canadian currency is.) Other sources describe the military steps Canada did take in response to urgent American appeals for increased submarine patrols, and air-defence vigilance (etc.) which were performed on the (perhaps inadequate) authority of RCAF and RCN commanders. Apparently the politicians did not wish to be involved; hardly something the United States would find encouraging.

The Glassco Commission

Due to all of the above Diefenbaker was facing an enormous amount of criticism for defence policies, much of it from the professionals in their areas of expertise: the military commanders themselves. There was also, at the time, a fashionable debate amongst largely civil-servant efficiency experts (such as Robert McNamara in the US) over "new" management philosophies and how the military might be changed to a more efficient model. The investigation and recommendations based on this kind of restructuring were given as reasons for the constitution of the Glassco Commission by the Conservatives in 1963.

Findings of this commission, delivered after the Liberals were returned to office, not surprisingly, envisioned a new structure to the military. It recommended disbandment of the separate services and an administrative and supply centralisation of control, under tighter civilian (political) control. What is surprising, however, is one change to the National Defence Act (NDA) that the Glassco Commission recommended. While Diefenbaker's "Bill of Rights" grandly stated that being Canadian gave one the right to speak out against any perceived injustice, the Glassco Commission recommended making it an offense under the NDA for a Canadian Forces member to do just that. This little-known fact is, arguably, responsible for the subsequent lack of professional criticism of government military policy. Meant to protect the nation from take-over by martial interests, it also prevented dissenting leaders from voicing researched opinions contrary to those of the perceived government line.

A McDonnell F-101 Voodoo in 425 Alouette Squadron markings. Rejected as insufficient in 1953, bought in 1960 second hand, politically considered "good enough" until 1983.   (image by R.L. Whitcomb)

When most of the Glassco Commission's recommendations were implemented, in two phases: "Integration" by the Pearson and "Unification" by the Trudeau government, many of the leaders of the Canadian military resigned with strong words. Others stuck around, a few making technically illegal remarks about the Trudeau government's (especially) handling of defense and implementation of Unification. Admiral Boyle would speak out of line several times, understandably since one austerity measure was powering down his patrol destroyers at night to save fuel, but running during the day to keep up appearances! (Peter C. Newman: *True North NOT Strong and Free*)

While some of the logistical, communications and administrative integration was logical and well implemented by Paul Hellyer, the actual disbandment of the separate services has not been followed by any other nation. This is especially true of any nation with fighting services bearing the legacy of the RCAF, RCN and Canadian Army. Moreover, this entailed a breaking of ties, hard fought for

in real terms, between Canadian services and British services. This was an unfortunate result of Diefenbaker's government, one that had pledged to strengthen ties with Britain, with less emphasis on the United States. It is ironic that the agency recommending what was almost a "People's Army" type of defence structure with uniforms to match, was convened when Diefenbaker's US relations were at low-tide. In the end, the Royal Canadian Air Force lost it's "Royal" allusions to Britain, as did the Royal Canadian Navy, while the RCAF faced the added requirement to shift from a rank structure that pre-dated the USAF and mirrored that of the Royal Air Force, to one invented for the US Army.

THIS WAS AN ABSURD ASSERTION by a Canadian government trying to find a way to justify scrapping the Arrow. In those days (at least) no one purchased a fighter aircraft before the country that designed it adopted it in service. The Arrow, however, was almost an exception to this rule. There is documentary evidence that the Arrow had been selected to become Britain's new all-weather fighter in 1956, coincidentally after a trip to Britain by Jim Floyd and others from Avro Canada in December 1955. The same almost re-occurred in 1959 after a fall 1958 visit by Floyd and other Avro representatives. Had the Arrow been produced there is no doubt in the author's mind that the British would have purchased some. The only other aircraft almost purchased under such terms was the F-111, selected by the British after the Arrow, and then their own TSR.2 were cancelled. The F-111 came in so grossly under projections, overbudget and *late* that they dropped it entirely and eventually settled for F-4s! The British would have purchased Arrows over F-4s (the Americans' most-sold aircraft after the F-86 Sabre) virtually without question.

In late December 1955 a team from the RAF, British Air Ministry and Ministry of Supply (MoS) came to Avro to see if the Arrow would meet their requirement for an all-weather fighter. On the surface this visit was to evaluate the Arrow program for the RCAF and Canadian government and that is how it has normally been presented. Up to this time the Hawker Siddeley Group had proposed a Thin Wing Javelin (TWJ) for their Operational Requirement 329, which resulted in the aircraft specification F.155T. They had won the design competition with this aircraft proposal. By this time however, the Arrow was well along in design and the Iroquois had run successfully. Their 50-odd-page report, titled "Evaluation of the Canadian CF-105 as an All Weather Fighter for the RAF," although based upon what would turn out to be an exaggerated supersonic drag coefficient, stated that the Arrow as it stood in 1955/56 held significant performance superiority to the TWJ. As British historian Tony Buttler proclaims in his book *British Secret Projects, Jet Fighter Designs Since 1950*, the CF-105 Arrow actually became the Hawker Siddeley Group's submission for F.155T over the indigenous TWJ aircraft of the same consortium. They even explored permutations such as license producing the Arrow, equipping it with British engines and/or fire-control systems and weapons and other variables. It came out that the Canadian-built Arrow 2 was the optimum choice.

CHAPTER TEN

POLITICS AS USUAL

The British Experience

Arrows for the Royal Air Force

"Nobody wanted to buy the Arrow"

As reproduced in Campagna's *Storms of Controversy*, RCAF Chief of the Air Staff (CAS) Air Marshal Hugh Campbell commissioned a summary of US and UK interest in the Arrow in December 1955, over two years before the Arrow had flown and revealed her true performance potential. In this document the major findings of the above reference are summarized:

The Minister of Supply (UK) requested from the Minister of Trade & Commerce permission for the Director, Royal Aeronautical Establishment and the Deputy Chief of Staff RAF to visit AVRoe to examine the CF 105 aircraft. The team visited AVRoe in Jan 56. The highlights of their report were, general agreement with the aerodynamic calculations; that the electronics system will still be superior to the best British equipment available in the same time period; and included comparative costs for buying 100 aircraft in Canada, manufacturing 100 aircraft in the UK with a UK engine and fire control system.

The report also stated that the use of a British fire control system would downgrade the performance of the aircraft very materially. At this point Avro was still proposing the Arrow with the Hughes MA-1 system, in development for the F-106. The conclusion was that the best course of action would have been to buy 100 CF-105s from Canada, but this was felt by the British team to be unlikely *for financial reasons.*

The real reason for the request by the British to visit Canada and examine the CF-105 have not been revealed before however. In a confidential letter to Sir Roy Dobson dated 19 December 1955, Floyd reported on his visit:

...with regard to the trip itself, I believe that it was well worthwhile for a number of reasons, one of the most important to me being that the discussions with Roy Ewans [one of Hawker Siddeley's top aerodynamicists] and the boys at Woodford [supersonic wind-tunnels], and also with Nicholson [one of the top British government aerodynamic experts] and his experts at the R.A.E., made me more sure than ever that we are really on the right track on the CF-105, especially with regard to the aerodynamic side. While Roy himself may or may not still have certain reservations about the aircraft, the reports which he very kindly obtained for me, of the tests which were done by Bethwaite and Leavy at Woodford on the leading-

edge notch and extension, which were tried on the 707, [Avro UK's delta test-bed for the fabulous Vulcan] tend to confirm what we have been assuming on the CF-105....They were all very keen technically on the CF-105 and considered it to be the most potent weapon in its time scale. I told them that we could fulfil the requirements of their new O.R.329 with more power or the use of an auxiliary rocket and they were more than interested....I strongly recommended to Sir John Baker [head of the British Joint Services office] and to Sir Thomas Pike [then head of RAF Fighter Command] that they team up together and make a visit over to Canada on the Spring, with representatives of the Air Ministry, the Ministry of Supply, and the operators [the RAF] to do a detailed evaluation on the cost of manufacturing in the UK.

The fact that the delegation from the RAE, RAF, and British Ministry of Supply arrived *immediately* after Floyd's visit seems to indicate Floyd was correct when he indicated they were "more than interested!" A similar trip in the fall of 1958 promised a repeat performance, although the Arrow was, by then, *finished* in the eyes of the Diefenbaker Cabinet, who made themselves unavailable for consultations. The Shaws point out six meetings between Avro and the government of Canada in the winter of '58-59 that were cancelled or delegated to junior executives. John Plant of Avro Canada forced Floyd to revoke his invitations to some British authorities, arguing that such "political" arrangements should be left to himself, Smye, and Gordon. Jim provided copies of original letters he wrote to try to save first the Jetliner prototype for a museum (seemingly turned down by John Parkin of the NRC/NAE), and the flying Arrows, declined by the British delicately, although the probability of a behind the scenes "don't even ask!" from the Canadian government is high.

In the RCAF summary of foreign interest (mentioned earlier), despite the earlier British feeling that the financial powers would not allow it, it is noted that the RAF again expressed interest in the Arrow in April and May 1956:

The question of charges for a license to permit the CF 105 to be manufactured in the UK was the subject of a letter from the Deputy Minister DDP [Department of Defence Production] to Sir Roy Dobson. This letter covered royalty payments, provision of components from Malton and the use of drawings, tools, etc., as the basis for a possible licensing agreement.

In a reply to a letter from the RCAF CAS on comparative studies on all-weather aircraft carried out in Canada, Air Marshal Pike stated:

> ...there is no doubt that the CF 105 is a very attractive proposition to the RAF except that it is rather late to meet their requirement date of early 1961, [apparently he was assuming RAF examples would follow production of RCAF interceptors] and even this date could only be achieved by using a British fire control system. This would reduce the capability of the aircraft and is therefore less attractive.

He expresses the opinion that the chances of obtaining the CF 105 for the RAF are rather small.

Meanwhile in discussions with Jim Floyd, Pike and other Air Marshals and leading scientists and engineers in Britain had come to the conclusion that 200 Arrows, in their multi-role Mk. 2 livery, as documented by testing and development up to 1955, "could defend all of Britain, and knew of nothing that would be as good," in the words of Jim Floyd from the December 1955 letter to Dobson.

Clearly many in the RAF still saw the Arrow as the best aircraft for the all-weather interceptor job yet they now obviously knew ASTRA was going to join the development—if the new comments on fire-control system design time scales are a guide. (ASTRA was quasi-officially added to the Arrow program in June of 1956 by C.D. Howe over Avro's objections. Probably some of Avro's objections to the switch to ASTRA [and the British official advice in line with Avro's] were due to the British experts almost universally adoring the Arrow and wanting it as Avro had proposed it, *with* the Hughes MA-1.) A/M Pike was also clearly referring to the estimated date of service of the TWJ when he refers to early 1961. Despite these objections, Floyd insists Pike was a real Arrow booster in Britain and did his best to secure for Britain the best multi-role aircraft in the world. He would, in fact, do so twice.

In Floyd's December '55 letter to Dobson, he mentions having outlined to the British authorities his thoughts on the optimal methods of solving time, balance of payments and other problems that went with Arrow acquisition and license production. Simply, the idea was for Britain to take one squadron of Arrows from Avro, built with the help of the British engineers who would accumulate data to license build them in the UK, while the planners, ground and aircrew personnel got to know the first batch of aircraft through operations. Once the British-built Arrows were being delivered, those who trained on the Canadian Arrows would be in a position to become operational instructors once home in the UK. This scheme would not cause any serious delays in deliveries to the RCAF from Avro in Canada, while also giving the RAF an excellent opportunity to fly the aircraft and develop the various mission profiles and a training syllabus. With the Arrow's truly multi-role versatility the roles would be many—especially since the RAF is both offensive and defensive.

Slipping ASTRA into the equation did nothing for this sales opportunity although once developed Canada, and perhaps Avro, would have been in a position to share the technology with whomever they pleased. Similarly for the aircraft and engine. The ASTRA technology however is something the Americans would have wanted, and something some would have wanted to keep out of the hands of others.

In *Project Cancelled,* Derek Wood (a former editor in chief of Janes Information Group, probably the most respected and comprehensive source of data on military and civil aircraft in the world) points out that in 1956 British manufacturers had gotten wind of a *"super fighter"* development with unprecedented speed, range, altitude and payload capabilities. Of course it was in January of 1956 that the British evaluation team had released their assessment of the Avro Arrow.

Enter Duncan Sandys

Duncan Sandys (pronounced "Sands") was an aristocratic personage who, in the latter stages of World War II,

Duncan Sandys (left) converses with Harvey Smith during a visit to Avro Canada. (Jet Age)

became deeply involved in studies for defence against Germany's V-weapons, the V-1 "Buzz-Bomb" and V-2 Short Range Ballistic Missile. He also married one of Winston Churchill's daughters, although one would doubt ironclad "Winnie" would have approved some of Sandys' policies.

Just over one year after the January 1956 British report had recommended the Arrow over the TWJ (and a resultant official Hawker Siddeley Group substitution of the CF-105 over the TWJ as the Group's entry for F.155T), practically every advanced aircraft program in the UK was summarily cancelled in April 1957. Sandys' reasoning was based on his unshakeable belief that missiles had rendered manned aircraft obsolete. It didn't seem to dawn on him that missiles were much more effective when they were mobile and launched from the air. Missiles certainly have altitude and range limitations when launched from the ground. Perhaps his belief in the value of missiles was due to his earlier work in the missile defence projects, even though it was proven that an interceptor, a Spitfire derivative at that, was the most effective weapon against the V-1. The V-2 or even ICBMs however, could be accounted for using the Arrow as missile-carrier, according to Avro at least. Whatever the case, Sandys' confidence in the ground-launched missile was proven premature and remains so to this day. Other documents prove Foulkes, Pearkes and Easton obviously shared Sandys' obsession with missiles.

One can only imagine the outrage experienced by the flying RAF, who were not yet equipped with decent short-range, air-portable missiles, by this decision to scrap the flying RAF in favour of a nearly nonexistent, immobile, ground missile defence. One must wonder at the hidden powers behind Sandys when he proclaimed that non-existent weapons would defend the United Kingdom, especially considering the British parliament allowed such a colossally destructive measure to pass.

With Sandys' swing of the ax, Pike and Air Chief Marshal (A/C/M) Dermot Boyle had more reason than ever to want the Arrow. Sandys had just cancelled every project except the light point-defence fighter; the English Electric P.1B Lightning (because it was "...unfortunately, too far along to cancel,") and an evolving *specification* for a strike-reconnaissance aircraft to replace the Canberra. Since it was then taking about eight years to develop a new design, something was needed to fill a huge capability gap in the RAF, and soon.

Arrows for the RAF Part Two:
Floyd almost does an encore

Jim Floyd was again in Britain in October of 1958 to deliver the Royal Aeronautical Society's Commonwealth Lecture on the Arrow, and to consult with his peers within the Hawker Siddeley Group and the government research facilities. Floyd recently pointed out to the author that the government had forbidden him from communicating *any* performance figures. He mentioned this as being akin to fighting (for the Arrow and even the company's life) with one hand tied behind his back! Nevertheless, in March 2001 he mentioned secret briefings he gave to appropriately-cleared Britons on the Arrow's suitability for GOR 339 at this time. He says they were "quite surprised" at how well the Arrow stacked up in this seemingly unsuitable role. He also states that Pike and others were fighting, again, to have the RAF adopt the Arrow. By this time the British were once more interested in an all-weather interceptor under a rejuvenated GOR 329 all-weather interceptor specification and again Avro's official submission is conspicuous by its absence in *Project Cancelled*. Of course the Arrow would have suited this purpose precisely, as had been recognized in 1956 when it was selected for this same requirement. In the interim it had proven, through flight test, to have much lower drag than expected.

As Floyd related the British General Operational Requirement (GOR) 339, the aircraft was to be capable of a 1000 nm combat mission while carrying a significant nuclear or conventional device on what is now termed a "Hi-Lo-Lo-Hi" mission at Mach 1.5. In other words, the aircraft was to fly most of the way to the target at 50,000 feet and Mach 1.5, dive to low level and high-subsonic speed for weapons delivery, then conduct an evasive-manoeuvring egress from the target area, again subsonic at low level, climb back to 50,000 feet while accelerating to Mach 1.5 and return to base. Dobson, in February 1958, asked Floyd to do some studies on possible Arrow variants to see if it could go some distance in filling these roles, *years sooner*. Floyd, in cooperation with Chamberlin, Lindow, Lindley and the rest, came up with two options, one being available virtually instantly and able to fulfill the mission with a stand-off missile, and another more modified Arrow that could meet the range requirement in full.

Floyd mentions the Arrow design was being re-examined to incorporate a Side-Looking-Airborne-Radar (SLAR) and an Avro UK half-scale "Blue Steel" Mach 3 ramjet-powered nuclear missile with a range of 250 nm.

Avro thought the basic Arrow 2 could carry this weapon by housing the missile conformally (semi-externally). The design of the weapons bay, with extra center-line space between the intakes above the bay on the Arrow design, supports Avro's assumptions. Available space on the sides of the bay, left open by the stand-off weapon, could have accommodated the SLAR since most SLARs use long, rectangular emitter/receivers.

As it was put to the interested British, the Arrow Mk. 2a, which Avro hoped would follow the first thirty-seven pre-production aircraft, would only require the development of a special armaments pack and perhaps a few relatively insignificant, mission-specialized "black boxes" to become a viable short to medium range, supersonic, strike-reconnaissance vehicle. It would have an operational radius, with full reserves, of 650 nm. With the weapon's additional range, the 1000 nm specification was very nearly met. Avro had also been looking at aerial refuelling for the Arrow at least as early as 1957. As Jim Floyd's initial letter to Dobson reported, a lightly modified Mk. 2a would be deficient in range even if Avro substituted the high-compressor-ratio Iroquois that Orenda was developing as the core of a lower-altitude (and potentially commercial), Iroquois variant while using the jettisonable belly tank. The Mk. 2a of course boasted greatly expanded internal fuel capacity which was still more expandable in future versions. Indeed, at this time Avro was devising the next-generation forward fuselage with the Mach 3 intakes for the Mk. 3 Arrow. This new piece of engineering provided for much greater internal fuel capacity while improving the aerodynamics and thermal characteristics of the aircraft significantly. Floyd had pointed out to all parties at the time that the aircraft, by virtue of its low-wing loading, was not optimal for high-speed, low-level penetration since turbulence against such a high-lift wing would give the crew a very rough ride.

According to Floyd, Pike (then head of RAF Fighter Command and later Air Chief Marshal of the RAF) and Air Chief Marshal Boyle, the Chief of the Air Staff, felt that the Arrow remained the best option considering it would be available much sooner than an entirely new project in the UK, and especially since the aircraft could fill the vacant all-weather long-range interceptor role *and* the strike-reconnaissance role with the same airframe. It seems however, that Bomber Command, while liking the Arrow and keeping it under careful scrutiny, would have preferred an aircraft with the *ultimate* low-level speed and range. If this is the case, their pondering over options cost them dearly in the longer term, especially when the TSR.2 was cancelled, and Britain settled for Phantoms for almost everything.

In 1958-59, the RAF needed something, *anything,* with serious performance to retain much credibility anywhere, except perhaps for the respect the Vulcan's capabilities earned them in the offensive arena, and the emerging Lightning's capability as a point-defence fighter. Since GOR 330 (won by Avro UK's 730) and GOR 329/F.155T (won by Avro Canada's Arrow) had been cancelled, the Arrow, again in the eyes of some of the RAF and British defence establishments, was still the best thing going. Even better, it now came with 20 percent lower drag, and the best digital, transistorized, integrated, fly-by-wire, multi-role systems available (ASTRA-Arrow). Lest there be any doubts, the Arrow's ASTRA system was designed to incorporate ground-mapping radar and the radar altimeter into a serious bombing option. The fact is, with a fully developed ASTRA system, the same aircraft, with the addition of a few very minor "black boxes" in the mission package, could do either mission. But ASTRA was thrown on the scrap heap in September 1958.

To more fully meet the GOR 339 specification, Avro's Project Research Group put together an initial proposal for a more heavily-modified Arrow derivative. This aircraft would have been based on the Mk. 4 design that Avro had been working on with strengthened wing spars (perhaps using stainless or other high-strength steels, thicker wing skins, the center-wing, revised, landing gear arrangement of the Mk. 4 and would carry three external drop tanks. The new, much stronger, main gear would retract into the two wing pods resulting in a much shorter and stronger landing gear able to support the projected take-off weight. The all-up weight would be in the order of 110,000 lbs and in his letter to Dobson, Floyd pointed out that JATO (rocket assist) bottles would be desirable for safety on take-off, then jettisoned once airborne. The weight figure, by the way, is exactly what the TSR.2 would weigh loaded. It seems that they were being quite conservative on range and take-off requirements, but then Avro always was. One would think that this version would be capable of a significantly greater radius than 1000 nm and indeed Avro was quoting potential radii of 1400 nm, depending on the mission profile. Perhaps part of the reasoning behind strapping all that extra fuel on was to bring the wing-loading up to a level that would allow transonic speed on the deck. All the extra stressing metal proposed would help the

structure absorb the punishment while the extra weight of fuel, structure and weapons would increase the wing-loading substantially, making the ride less punishing for the crew. It would still be a very wild ride with the throttles up and the trees big.

One can only assume how non-plussed were those wishing the Arrow would stop popping up its needled nose! They had seen the cancellation of the specification that had resulted in the Hawker Siddeley Group's submission of the Arrow (over their own TWJ), to GOR 329/F.155T yet were again confronted by expert opinion stating it could fill an even more demanding role, while still retaining superlative interceptor abilities. But it was not to be, especially not once the Arrow was cancelled in 1959. After a bizarre series of specification changes and financial problems, the newly formed British Aircraft Corporation (which became British Aerospace in 1977 when a weakened Hawker Siddeley was finally absorbed) was tagged to produce the TSR.2, an aircraft whose repertoire was the opposite in strengths, few as they were, to the CF-105, even while its design was very similar!

The British Aircraft Corporation TSR.2

By 1956 the British were beginning to think about a replacement for the English Electric TSR.1 Canberra. This was a separate development to the GOR 329/F.155T specification for an all-weather interceptor, and the GOR 330 specification for an advanced, long-range, strike-reconnaissance bomber. The Canberra is, to the author's knowledge, the *only* aircraft to remain in front-line service for 50 years and was one of the only foreign aircraft the Americans purchased before the Buy American Act. The Canberra replacement was to be a Mach 1.5 class aircraft capable of carrying a variety of weapons and reconnaissance equipment, low-level high-speed attack, and short field take-off and landing. The GOR 339 narrowed the specification down to a 4-6000 lb operational payload with more emphasis on the low-level recce, penetration, and delivery aspects of the mission. As the TSR.2 would prove, the CF-105 was nearly ideal in all other features aside from the low-level aspect.

The evolving GOR 339 somehow survived Sandys' swing of the axe, perhaps due to outrage generated by cooler heads in the aerospace industry and RAF. The specification did not, however, emerge without seven months of acrimonious debate. GOR 339 was not released to British manufacturers until September 1957 even though designers on both sides of the Atlantic would be anticipating requests to fill such a role. It was in February of 1958 that Jim Floyd responded to a request from Avro UK's Sir Roy Dobson for information on the adaptability of the Arrow to GOR 339. No doubt strike capabilities of the basic Mk. 2 Arrow would have been estimated before this time for the RCAF. By March 1958 it was announced by the British that Avro, Hawkers, Vickers-Armstrong and English Electric had been selected to further develop their design proposals.

In *Project Cancelled,* Wood mentions the British hearing about a "super fighter." If the images in his book are any guide, he was apparently unable to locate drawings or specifications for the Avro submission to GOR 329 *or* GOR 339. While he doesn't discuss either Avro submission, made over two years apart, there is a clue to what aircraft Avro submitted for GOR 339 in the book, when he discusses the changes made to the unsuccessful Hawker submission. Sir Sydney Camm of Hawker had been developing the P.1121 single Olympus-engined aircraft with a ventral inlet (like

The impressive British Aircraft Corporation TSR.2: Built after full provision of Arrow technical, construction and materials information plus a running Iroquois engine. (BAC)

the F-16 and Eurofighter) for the OR 329 (interceptor) specification. When Sandys killed this development, Camm enlarged and revamped the design in an effort to make it applicable to GOR 339 (strike-recce). By June 1957 he had sketched out these improvements including twin-engined versions designated P.1125 and P.1129. According to Wood, "Camm... offered a modified 1129 with certain improvements taken from the Avro design."

When one compares the P.1121 to the final P.1129 design the improvements mentioned were: an additional engine, a 5 degree anhedral being added to the wing along with a sawtooth leading-edge extension, twin side-mounted intakes, an area-ruled fuselage and conformal carriage of a single, large weapon in the belly. All of these were concepts designed into the Arrow although the P.1129 would not have had the interchangeable weapons pack. Thus P.1129 would not have had the flexibility of the Arrow, especially in an air defence role. In light of the evidence already presented it is obvious the aircraft behind the veil is, once again, the Arrow. It had killed the Thin Wing Javelin and was now seemingly about to intercept another brood of British designs! Jim Floyd had worked under Camm for a year in the mid 1930s, and readily professes a real admiration for Sir Sydney.

Again according to Wood, it was about this time (1957) that a rather bold recommendation was made to the British government. The House of Commons Select Committee on Estimates issued a report calling for a forced reduction in the number of British aerospace manufacturers through equally forced amalgamations. Gunston supports this view in *Faster Than Sound*. It was also demanded, in July 1958 according to Wood, that Hawker Siddeley Group members withdraw their various submissions and submit a single aircraft. Apparently Camm's P.1129 was submitted as a result although the chronology Wood uses to support this appears to be backwards in *Project Cancelled*. So did the Arrow submissions to GOR 339 die at this point?

Contrary to GOR 339's early low-altitude optimization, it was modified in late 1958 (as GOR 343) to include *higher* altitude capabilities along with higher speed, longer range and shorter take-off runs with the ability to operate from semi-prepared strips. A further refinement required that the aircraft achieve its 1000 nm radius with only internal fuel. This would have eliminated Arrow derivatives. As Derek Wood put it, the specification "was rapidly becoming the stuff of science fiction."

From the chronology at least, and despite the flack, it still appeared that cooler heads tempered the progress of design selection for the British strike-recce specification. It was not until January 1959, when those in privileged government circles had every reason to believe the Arrow would be cancelled, that some details of the strike-reconnaissance specification were announced in the British House of Commons. Wood mentions that the Treasury people and some senior bureaucrats were pushing for the improved version of the Blackburn Buccaneer for the role, and it was at this time that Diefenbaker was promoting this aircraft to his Cabinet. This aircraft was pushed at Australia by Lord Louis Mountbatten while he was intriguing against the TSR.2, according to Wood and others. In fact the "Buc" was a great transonic STOL aircraft. It would have been a poor strike-reconnaissance aircraft and a pathetic interceptor however. Conversely, members of the RAF, MoS, RAeE, and of course the Hawker Siddeley Group were trying to sell the British politicians the Arrow for this role. It doesn't take a vivid imagination to decide which was the better option!

Oddly, with the January 1959 announcement of the Strike-Reconnaissance contract, it was announced that English Electric had been selected to develop their P.17

design. This political "award" was still somewhat premature as we shall see, leading to the plausibility of the idea that announcing English Electric as the winner was designed to convince the Canadian politicians that the Arrow was out of the running, (and thus not saleable) while also to encouraging Blackburn to join English Electric.

Despite these tactics, it was not until September of that year, when it was clear that the CF-105 was dead, that even the specification was finalized, no doubt due to the RAF resistance itself. When all is said and done, the fact that the TSR.2 was officially begun five months after Black Friday suggests the TSR.2 was the "next best thing" in some influential Royal Air Force circles to the RAF securing multi-role Arrows. This is especially so considering the TSR.2, by virtue of its tiny nose, could not carry any serious air to air radar system while the Arrow 4 could change roles by changing wing pods and armament packs! The TSR.2's high wing loading also meant it could not reach high altitude, and could not turn as well at the heights it could reach. It would have been a devastating aircraft down low however, yet the author would still argue low-level vs. high-altitude utility, especially in the digital age, which the Arrow nearly introduced. Weapons accuracy, at least in those days, was another matter—lower was better. With a nuke however, the pilot might not agree, especially if he was transporting a toss-bomb weapon which is what was initially proposed for the TSR.2.

Again according to Wood and Gunston, in late 1959 another financier-generated caveat was added. This time a requirement was introduced for the contracted company to merge and form a consortium with as many other British manufacturers as possible. This is surprisingly similar to the purported blackmail attempted against Jack Northrop

The British Aircraft Corporation TSR-2 beside a Vickers Valiant. By the time of the TSR-2, Vickers was part of BAC. (BAC)

in an effort to have his company merge with Convair. The dramatic and Arrow-similar cancellation, then destruction, of his promising YB-49 jet-powered flying-wings, in 1949, were alleged to be the retaliation for Northrop's recalcitrance. According to Evan Mayerle, (a history-oriented American aeronautical engineer) a Congressional investigation into this scandal was convened and during testimony Jack Northrop denied having been coerced. Later, near death, he acknowledged that he had lied to Congress with this denial to prevent further shady retaliations, from the same shady operators, against his company.

The Cold War is also awash with cases of American aircraft companies bribing powerful individuals almost on a "cost of doing business" basis. The Lockheed scandal would unseat several officials and politicians. Iran was, apparently, paid significant bribes to acquire the F-14 Tomcat during the Shah's reign, and many other examples, revealed and still hidden, no doubt exist.

The TSR.2 contract was not officially awarded until October 1960 by which time English Electric, Blackburn, Bristol, Hunting and Vickers-Armstrong (which included Supermarine) had reluctantly agreed to amalgamate. In the case of Sir Handley Page, he was so adamant against merger that he carried on alone, with his company being liquidated in 1970. For the Hawker Siddeley Group, the Harrier would eventually emerge, but this stroke of genius seemed to create a requirement of its own due to its amazing abilities.

On the propulsion side, the Iroquois would have been a very attractive engine for the TSR.2, had this aircraft been developed and had Avro not been cut down. The TSR.2's Olympus was also almost a ton heavier than the Iroquois, each as deployed in the TSR.2. Quite simply, the Arrow would have achieved much of the payload requirement of the TSR.2 simply by weight savings in the engine bays. Indeed, after Black Friday, Bristol Aircraft Engines received at least one Iroquois engine. This appears to have occurred in 1961 according to an ex-Orenda engine employee. In the back lot at Orenda was found a complete Iroquois that was, apparently, crated and sent to Bristol. At least three (some Orenda sources say four) other Iroquois engines were, at various times, crated after cancellation for shipment. The author has not found solid proof of this, but believes along with ex-Orenda and ex-Avro personnel that Pratt & Whitney, General Electric, and Rolls-Royce each received a sample engine. This is perfectly in keeping with the Diefenbaker cabinet's policy of freely providing data

and personnel from Avro to the Americans in return for American production-sharing "goodwill." In confirmation of the Orenda employee's testimony to the author from around 1996, it was revealed, shortly before the millenium, that the engine Bristol had received was found in pieces in Britain after examination by Bristol. Other indicators are apparent in the Olympus engine. The engine used in the TSR.2 and Concorde changed from a typical three-bearing design to the central-drum, two-bearing design like the Iroquois. Bristol unfortunately ran into "bell mode" sympathetic vibration problems that delayed development for about a year, mirroring the vibration problems that plagued the Iroquois. This engine also demonstrated that this general arrangement could function, in a significantly more complex and heavy engine, to a standard suitable for civil certification, as evidenced by the 593 version used in Concorde.

Some say the TSR-2 would have flown almost a year earlier (in 1963) but for the decision to change the Olympus engine configuration from the three-bearing conventional shaft design to the two-bearing drum/shaft. Yet the change clearly was considered important to improve the performance of the engine. To develop the Olympus an Avro Vulcan was modified with a huge duct and nacelle on the belly that gave centerline thrust (unlike the B-47 Canadair-built Iroquois flying test-bed installation). During a ground run a bell mode vibration problem caused the Olympus to disintegrate which also caused the Vulcan bomber to explode in a horrific fireball with large chunks of the aircraft raining down over a considerable distance. The closest parallel during Iroquois test-bed flying occurred when the PS-13 threw a compressor blade that punctured the fuselage of the B-47.

Despite its convoluted history and some difficult development problems, the TSR.2 promised an impressive performance. At a take-off weight about 30,000 lbs heavier than the CF-105 Mk. 2, it was capable of a maximum speed of Mach 2.25 at about 40,000 ft. The TSR.2 was better optimized for low level and semi-prepared field operation however. At the time it was felt that operation at very low levels meant better survivability for the aircraft since it was trumpeted at the time that high altitude aircraft were vulnerable to ground air defences such as missiles. The Gulf War experience showed this not to be the case, when one reviews the loss record of the Panavia Tornado in this conflict on behalf of the oil companies. Conversely, the historical invulnerability of the SR-71 proves the same

The plane nobody wanted: The General Dynamics F-111. (NASA Dryden)

thing. Of course, at ultra-low altitude, aircraft are vulnerable to everything from birds to thrown rocks. There is a "cost of doing business" at low level.

Of course as soon as the TSR.2 program got underway, US interests began suggesting that the TSR.2 was far too expensive and would not meet expectations while the General Dynamics (Convair) F-111 would. Furthermore, the F-111 would be much cheaper and available sooner. In retrospect the F-111 would be far less effective than the TSR.2 or Arrow, would come in many times more expensive than promised, and to top things off, would be at least six years late! One might wonder, in light of the facts presented in this book, at the true origin of the American TFX concept that began around 1959, that of designing one aircraft that could do many roles. The fruit of this concept was the General Dynamics (Convair) F-111—as big a failure at Convair as the Cooke-Craigie plan.

As mentioned, the US was trying to sell the F-111 to Britain. They were also trying to sell it to the Australians. According to Wood and the Air International article (see Bibliography), the Australians were pretty much sold on the TSR.2 by 1962 until the new British Chief of the Defence Staff, Lord Mountbattan, arrived shortly thereafter and suggested the TSR.2 program was so full of problems and expense that it would probably not make it into production. To fill the void the Americans swiftly offered the non-existent F-111 promising delivery in 1967 for about $6 million dollars a copy. Mountbattan's influence on the TSR.2 program is detailed in unusually explicit terms for a politician in this comment from Wood's *Project Cancelled*:

In March 1964 Australian Air Minister, Fairbarn, stated that the RAF and BAC were hoping that 100 TSR.2's would be ordered, but that he was doubtful whether this would materialise, "if the present

head of the UK Chiefs of Staff [Mountbattan] remains in authority."

While there were no orders forthcoming from Australia for the TSR.2, despite evidence that suggests they would have wanted it, the TSR.2 program continued for a time. Then the government changed in the UK and Labour was elected. According to Tarpley and Chaitkins in *George Bush: The Unauthorized Biography,* the socialist Labour government of Harold Wilson was elected due to the influence of Victor Rothschild! According to Zubov, James Jesus Angleton (the CIA counterintelligence hawk under Allen Dulles), apparently felt Wilson was a KGB asset! In Chapter 12 it is described how some Avro managers, at least, felt that similar North American banking titans were behind Diefenbaker's early victories. In shades of Pearke's hat in hand visits to the US in April and August 1958, trips that doomed the Arrow, the new British Prime Minister Harold Wilson and 20 top Defence and Aviation ministry officials went to visit President Johnson in December 1964. Derek Wood, at the time a correspondent to the publication *Interavia* wrote:

The industry believes that Prime Minister Wilson, who has no engineering, sales or military background, may have allowed himself to be sold down the river by the US... The outlook in the British industry is extremely gloomy and likely to remain so.

In *Project Cancelled* Wood continues:

Wilson states in his book "The Labour Government 1964-1970. A Personal Record," after American discussions, "It was becoming increasingly clear that all three of the controversial aircraft, HS.681 [a short/vertical take off and landing transport similar in appearance to the recent McDonnell Douglas C-17], P.1154 [an advanced supersonic Harrier also a Hawker Siddeley project], and TSR.2 would go, and be replaced in the main by American purchases.

The HS.681 was one of Hawker Siddeley Aviation's proposals after Black Friday, produced by the Advanced Projects Group working out of Kingston, England. This team was led by Jim Floyd, and included several ex-Avro Canada talents. Time after time in the fifties and sixties, Avro and Hawker Siddeley had won design competitions only to have the rug pulled out from under them by politicians.

In almost mirror image to Diefenbaker's September 1958 run-up to cancellation in Canada, British Prime Minister Wilson rose in the house on February 2nd, 1965 to set the stage for TSR.2 cancellation. Wilson cited development costs already spent and further inflated the cost of the TSR.2. He mentioned a figure of 750 million for development and production of 150 samples. Even at this, once the 150 million already spent on development was removed, the figure for each TSR.2 was 4 million each (roughly 9 million dollars). BAC projections were in the order of 2.5 million apiece. The true figure was probably right in the middle at 3.2 million per. Wilson also, in a method akin to Diefenbaker Cabinet assertions about F-106Cs, prophesied that 300 million could be saved if the F-111 was purchased instead.

Conveniently the US capitalized further by offering the British politicians General Dynamics (Convair) F-111's for a price of around 2.2 million each, with the proviso, as Joe Baugher states in his TSR.2 article "The UK did not have to commit itself to actually buying the F-111." This open-ended, non-contractual, word-of-mouth assurance would prove advantageous for the struggling manufacturer, Convair/General Dynamics, as we shall see.

On April 6th 1965 Prime Minister Wilson rose in the house and cancelled the TSR.2 outright. His Defence Minister, Denis Healey, proclaimed that the government had been extremely reluctant to do so, but that the cost of the TSR.2 program had become an "intolerable burden." He added the remarkable observation that Britain could no longer afford to develop combat aircraft for its own armed forces' exclusive use. (This is again nearly verbatim from the Diefenbaker Cabinet's post Arrow cancellation exhortations, and the aerospace sector reduction-by-hatchet that followed!) Healey went on to state that the UK would purchase a new strike aircraft, the F-111A, since the government had been convinced they could acquire this aircraft for about half the price of the TSR.2. Again this is of the American

"better, cheaper, sooner" genus, a chameleon-like creature that assumes many promising forms, but always disappears like a French "reve chimeric" when it is cornered! In January 1968, (the TSR.2 was to have entered service in 1967), the F-111 was having such incredible development problems, was performing so poorly, and was experiencing such massive cost escalations that the British cancelled their option to purchase it. Far from the 2.2 million figure the British were originally given, the F-111 price, once available about six years late (circa 1973), was now worth about 9 million each with spares and support equipment, according to Wood. That is about 21 million a copy, six times Avro's 1959 price guarantee. This escalation was far higher than inflation, while the Arrow was far more powerful.

According to British web-historian Damien Burke, Healey would later state that getting American support for an International Monetary Fund loan was "not the reason behind the British order for F-111's and the TSR.2 cancellation." As Burke succinctly puts it "A denial from a politician, as the TSR.2 program showed on numerous individual occasions, is not worth the paper they refuse to write it on." This British IMF loan is also surprisingly similar to the July 1958 "Conversion Loan" in Canada.

Meanwhile, according to the Air International article, Australia sold the "better, cheaper, sooner" line, impatiently waited for their F-111's. Rather than getting them as promised in 1967, the first F-111C didn't land in Australia until June of 1973. To appease them in the interim, the US offered in the late 1960s to lease the Australians ancient Boeing B-47's! The reaction of the Australians to the offer to pay for something that was a tactically useless, sitting duck is predictable. Finally in 1970 the US offered to loan them F-4 Phantoms. This was accepted. When the US suggested the Australians buy them in October of 1972, the angry *no* was punctuated by the Aussies swiftly returning six Phantoms to the US in the same month! Australia has since spent well over 500 million in upgrades to the F-111 and is today the only air force still flying them. The British simply purchased F-4 Phantoms and replaced them with Tornados once they were ready.

The actual first delivery of F-111's to Australia in 1973 was a full eight years after the superior, British-produced, TSR.2 was cancelled and eleven years after the Australians had been convinced to choose the American jet product over the TSR.2—a full 15 years after the British government had chosen to produce (at massive expense, with Arrow technology sharing and an Iroquois engine exam-

Performance Curves – *Arrow versus Modern Fighters*

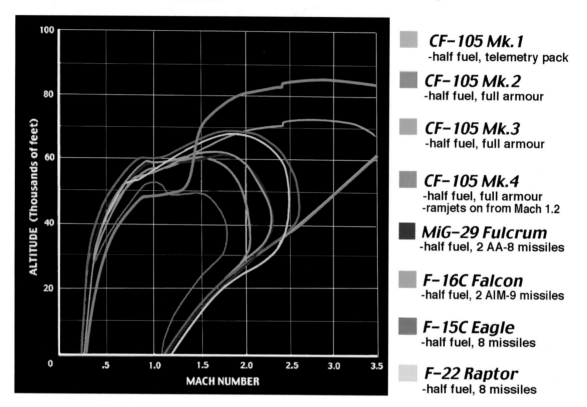

CF–105 Mk.1
-half fuel, telemetry pack

CF–105 Mk.2
-half fuel, full armour

CF–105 Mk.3
-half fuel, full armour

CF–105 Mk.4
-half fuel, full armour
-ramjets on from Mach 1.2

MiG–29 Fulcrum
-half fuel, 2 AA-8 missiles

F–16C Falcon
-half fuel, 2 AIM-9 missiles

F–15C Eagle
-half fuel, 8 missiles

F–22 Raptor
-half fuel, 8 missiles

ple), to develop the TSR.2 in the first place and 17 years after Britain had tried to purchase Arrows! It is also interesting that the F-111 design was, again according to Wood and Gunston, based on the work of Sir Barnes Wallis in England, after the British had been asked by the US to come to NASA and work on his swing-wing, laminar-flow concepts in their facilities!

Meanwhile the F-111 had a terrible development record, just like the F-106, F-102A, YF-102 and XF-92 by the same company. Gunston mentions its flight trials as being perhaps the most troubled in history. Its greatest problem, after the US Navy rejected the aircraft, was weakness in the swing-wing assembly. This caused several fatalities when the aircraft briefly and unsuccessfully entered service in Vietnam. Several were lost despite an absence of enemy action. When the F-111 was finally rendered survivable, the Americans seemed reluctant to release what was by 1971 or so, a state of the art offensive nuclear weapon to the Australians. They first offered them the over 20-year-old, sitting duck, Boeing B-47, and then finally offered them the 13-year-old F-4 Phantom. Australia stuck to their guns however and received F-111's for, as Gunston proclaims, three times the original price.

Arrow Versus the Modern Fighters: Still a World-Beater

The above performance curves are taken from several sources including hand-drawn ones from the Arrow Mk. 1 flight trials. The Mk. 2 and 4 curves are interpolated from specific points given in various documents including information given by Jim Floyd himself. The amazing Mk. 3 curve is direct from the Avro Mk. 3 Preliminary Proposal. The F-22 and F-15 curves are based on curves published in Bill Sweetman's book *The F-22 Raptor* while those of the MiG-29 and F-16 are from *Air International*.

The curves show that even an F-16C Falcon, with the uprated GE F-110 engine (about 29,000 pounds thrust with afterburner vs. 25,000 for the F-16A series) would be inferior to the Arrow Mk. 1 in terms of flight envelope. From the graph one can see that the performance of a fully combat-loaded (and thus longer-range) Arrow Mk. 1 is, where it counts, equal to that of a MiG-29 equipped with no tanks, half-internal fuel and only two small heat-seeking missiles! The curve of the F-15 Eagle is the smallest because it is carrying the largest combat load of any of the aircraft, *externally*. If it had the same combat load as the F-16 and MiG-29, (only two tiny heat-seeking missiles) its curve

The Sukhoi S.37 "Berkut" development fighter. Like the Lockheed-Martin F-22 Raptor it has reverted to internal weapons carriage. It will be capable of un-coupled manoeuvres beyond the Raptor.
(image by Paul McDonell)

would probably be larger than that of the MiG-29, which is about the same as the Arrow Mk. 1. This clearly shows the huge drag penalty external stores invoke. The author has also been privy to performance curves which show the delta Mirage 2000 to be a nasty little knife-fighter at high altitude where lift production and low induced drag are king. Indeed, the Mirage 2000, based upon the mid-1950s Mirage III design, will make a mess of a late 1970s (Convair, renamed General Dynamics) F-16 Falcon at medium to high altitude, this despite the Mirage being comparatively underpowered.

The curve of the Arrow Mk. 3 is very similar to that of the A-12/SR-71. Incredibly, even at only 19,350 lbs dry thrust for the Iroquois 3, it is capable of much greater than Mach 3 speeds, with a limit of Mach 3 being artificially imposed due to aerodynamic heating concerns. The Arrow Mk. 3's curve would be just under that of the SR.71, however, Avro seems to have been extremely conservative in their projections. It is difficult to believe, for example, that the SR-71, with lower thrust to weight and higher wing-loading than the Arrow 3, would be a superior performer yet it is known to be capable of cruising at Mach 3.2 and 80,000 feet—yet the Mk. 3 curve is limited to 70,500 feet.

The TSR.2 curve, were it shown, would be something like that of the Arrow Mk. 1 but with a lower ceiling and slightly faster capability at low level (the bottom right portion of the curves). The Arrow PS-2's curve would be larger than that of the Mk. 4 due to lower wing-loading and the canard which reduced trim drag at high altitude. The PS-2 and Mk. 4 both would have had enough ramjet thrust to put them into near sub-orbital altitudes in a ballistic zoom climb. Imagine *that* with reaction controls (for near-space flight control) *and* the P-13 anti-ICBM missile Avro was proposing for the Arrow! The Lockheed NF-104 altitude-record machines of the time period had rocket-boost and reaction controls. The F-15 carried an anti-satellite missile, Litton's ASAT, with reaction controls for space intercepts of Soviet "moving targets." (Jim Floyd was also involved with Litton for six years in the sixties, although not for the ASAT project but for inertial navigation and similar systems.) The ramjets Avro was proposing were also units that had been proven on the North American Navaho missile. For the missile Avro had been talking to Douglas Aircraft, the company that produced the successful NIKE-ZEUS anti-ICBM missile in the mid-1960s.

(image by R.L. Whitcomb)

A.V. ROE CANADA LTD. had several research and development branches in operation. Under Jim Floyd were the Project Research Group, Special Projects Group and lower-order operations. Rolf Marshall operated an advanced transportation projects group (plus lending his artistic skills for many of the diagrams and renderings of Avro proposals), and produced Avro's monorail concepts. There were, confusingly, two Special Projects Groups at Avro, one not related to the main Engineering Division, run by John Frost for work on his saucer concepts, and another for advanced Arrows, civil transports and SSTs etc. run by Chamberlin. Mario Pesando, however, ran the Project Research Group. A document from Engineering in 1956 describes Floyd's rationale for setting up these groups, especially since most of the engineering of the Arrow was well advanced by this time and they strategically needed to look ahead. This document also goes into some detail in describing materials research, with composites being given special attention at this early date. From this 13 December 1956 Memorandum to File:

Project Research Group will be set up with two main sections, one on research, which would investigate the following :

(a) Nuclear research

(b) Electrogravitics [anti-gravity]

(c) Automation and computation

(d) New and unusual materials such as ceramics, glass products, etc., high temperature studies.

(e) Power plant research, including chemical fuels, etc.

(f) Missiles

The other group would be set up to do project studies on actual aircraft hardware, including :

(a) Military projects

(b) Commercial projects

(c) Economics

(d) General planning of projects

(e) Systems

(f) Special projects, such as Mono-Rail

(g) Their job would also include writing up of a number of brochures for sales discussion purposes.

Initially, Mr. Pesando will take Group One, and Mr. [Rolf] Marshall will take Group Two, which will accomplish the integrating of the present Design Research Group into the new group.

CHAPTER ELEVEN

AVRO Project Research Group

Space Planes and Anti-ICBM Missiles

There is no likelihood man can ever tap the power of the atom.
—Robert Millikan, Nobel Prize for Physics (1923)

Mario Pesando, one of the originals from Victory Aircraft days, had been leading some of the company's studies into hypersonics and space flight phenomena. This operation was run from the office adjacent to Floyd's, with the only access being through the latter's office. This "Initial Projects Office" setup was similar to the "holy of holies" special securiy design office across from Roy Chadwick's at Avro Manchester. (This is where the Lancaster and other secret developments had been conceived.) It is interesting that in the public mind today Jim Chamberlin seems to be the personality from Avro most connected to space. Meanwhile Mario Pesando's Project Research Group, established under Jim Floyd in 1956, took the lead in space systems while Chamberlin's own Special Projects Group looked into civil aircraft design, including SSTs and the high-performance Arrow derivatives already discussed.

Other Avro design efforts produced studies on systems, including:

- a turbine-powered monorail rapid transit system for Toronto (under Rolf Marshall)

- a Ship-Borne Missile for the Royal Canadian Navy in 1955. The RCN later received Sea-Sparrows.

- a vertical take-off, Mach 2, X-wing fighter for the US Navy circa 1956

- the SCIMP (Supersonic cheap interceptor missile) in 1958

- an Infantry Anti-Tank Missile in 1957. The CF later received the wire-guided "Carl Gustav" missile, then the optically-guided TOW missile.

- the Arrow launched P-13 Anti-ICBM Missile in 1957. The only weapon acknowledged as having been developed which shares this concept is the USAF F-15-launched ASAT (anti-satellite) weapon developed in the late 1970s by Litton-Temco-Vought, with Litton presumably the lead contractor.

- Arrow launched solid satellites (solid-state electronics.)

- Gerald Bull would, in the mid 1960s run the HARP [High Altitude Research Project] and would launch functioning "solid" experimental satellites up to 300,000 feet altitude with modified 16-inch caliber naval guns. This program was operated through Montreal's McGill University and many successful launches were completed. Bull apparently found that his electronics, cast inside a resin/filler material, would operate despite their being loaded to 10,000G when the launch charge was detonated. It has recently been disclosed that some of the projectiles launched were testing tri-ethyl aluminum, the pyroforic material Avro was interested in for the ramjet boosted Arrow versions. He later developed similar guns for the Iraqis—at the time when they were considered American allies.)

After Black Friday

- an Orenda designed turbine-powered transport "tractor." This promising truck was built and toured across Canada. This seems to be an ignored technology considering the fact that turbine engines have much higher fuel efficiency potentials than gasoline and diesel.

- the "Bobcat" amphibious all-terrain tracked armored personnel carrier. This was cancelled and CF personnel drove their aluminum-armored Lynx vehicles, all in need of replacement, in Bosnia, much to their peril.

The Anti-ICBM Missile for the Arrow

As has been said, Avro was trying to develop an anti-ICBM missile for the Arrow. Some have suggested to the author that the Arrow Mk. 3 and other proposals including this missile concept were "hatched" by Avro in late 1958 and early 1959 as a thin ploy to have the government reconsider cancelling the program and scattering Avro's brainpower to the winds. The facts show nothing could be further from the truth. Jim Floyd has provided documents on the research and development structure of Avro from 1956. These documents show that advanced Arrows, space systems, nuclear-hydrogen plasma drives, ion thrusters, nozzles and wings and even anti-gravitics were being given attention. This author's research certainly demonstrates that, for example, Pesando and Avro's thinking on an aerospace plane was and still is valid. An alternate chorus to this kind of song describes the anti-ICBM missile as being a desperate gambit to deflect the argument that missiles made manned aircraft obsolete. As is described elsewhere, Avro had plenty of hard data to show that defensive missiles had a *much* lower value in an air defence plan than interceptors.

The P-13, had it and the Arrow been produced, meant a defence system identical in intent to President Ronald Reagan's "Star Wars" system could have been in service in the mid to late 1960s. The missile was to be built for carriage on any of the Arrow versions; however faster and higher altitude variants such as the Mark 3, 4 or PS-2 would have been most effective as missile-carriers and the Mk.4 papers mention this role. ASTRA's capabilities for managing fully-active homing missiles would also have been a boon to the prospects of this total weapons system concept as this suited the Nike guidance system and would

(image by Paul McDonell and R.L. Whitcomb)

add more resistance to jamming and decoys to the total guidance equation. Discussions alluded to in the meeting between Avro management and the government in Pearkes' office on 24 February 1959, and Avro documentation, show that they were looking at adapting the Nike-Zeus system to the Arrow. This would have been interesting since the Nike-Zeus anti-ballistic missile system was judged a success and there are those who suggest it was more effective under counter measures than the system currently in development in the United States to deal with incoming nuclear weapons. To appreciate the size of Nike-Zeus one should realize the early air-launched models were launched on Nike boosters. The P-13 envisioned only the Zeus guidance and warhead portion of the package with a smaller booster.

A large missile radar-seeker head would be linked to the Arrow's radar and computer systems to help guide the missile to an incoming ICBM. Avro did have a lead in some of

A NIKE-ZEUS launch. This missile was designed and deployed to destroy incoming nuclear missiles either in space or the upper reaches of the atmosphere. Jim Floyd calculated that if the seeker assembly and warhead were launched from an Arrow at 50,000 feet or above and Mach 1.5, that the total missile size and weight could be reduced by two-thirds. This payload and performance were within Arrow Mk. 1 capabilities. Launched from a high-performance Arrow such a defensive weapon would gain even better intercept capability, far in excess of the successful ground launched version shown here. (McDonnell Douglas) the control and guidance areas, having used and developed various computer systems, including cutting edge digital technology, for both design work and "black-boxes" for various control and data link applications. The successful fly-by-wire system in the Arrow with its high level of integration allowed it to factor in both flight performance information plus information from radars and other inputs from both onboard and external sources. The Arrow also promised the best performance when operating autonomously rather than as the teeth in a GCI.

In the publication *Flight and Aircraft Engineer* dated February 14, 1958 an article appears titled *Ironclads and Arrows*. The following is especially relevant from this article:

It might be supposed, for example, that in every aspect of employment the anti-missile missile would prove to be very far removed from the manned fighting aeroplane. Yet the possibility is already seen that, in order to achieve its maximum kill potential, the "anti" missile may actually form an alliance with the manned fighter.

The feasibility of this rather bewildering departure has been expounded by Jim Floyd, Avro Aircraft's vice-president engineering, in an address designed to reassure his colleagues "whereas the launching of the Russian sputnik satellites was a very significant event in the annals of aviation, its effect on the Arrow program should be singularly positive." Mr. Floyd considers that even when the ICBM comes along the Arrow interceptor will be one of the most potent weapons in combating it. "If you think about it for a minute," he says, "the normal launching platforms for anti-missile missiles are stationary. The Russians can find out where they are and destroy them. On the other hand, an airborne missile mothership (which could be the Arrow) can be rapidly moved from one place to another carrying an anti-ICBM missile...

It might be imagined that a missile suitable for carrying an anti-missile warhead would prove a formidable load even for the mighty Arrow; but Mr. Floyd had looked into the matter with a "quick, specific calculation" on an ICBM approaching at Mach 10 at 200 miles above the earth. He finds that if an "anti" is launched from an aircraft flying at Mach 1.5 at 60,000 ft, its thrust need only be about one-third of that required for a ground-launched weapon carrying the same size of warhead to a given point in approximately the same time. And dividends would accrue in range and accuracy.

The anti-ICBM project is also discussed in the Engineering Division report to the Avro Management Committee of 5 June 1958:

MISSILES

6. Study of Anti-ICBM Missile

For some time we have considered the possibility of carrying an anti-missile missile on the Arrow, used as a mother ship, to provide a mobile launching platform, giving better mobility, dispersion, etc. Jim Chamberlin has discussed this subject generally with Dr. Abrams, who is most interested in the basic philosophy. Dr. Abrams suggests that we establish a need to know through the RCAF, since quite a bit of data is available which would be very useful to us in our studies. This requires some discussion between the Company, the RCAF, and DRB, and should be followed up as soon as possible.

Jim Floyd mentions the anti-ICBM missile as being under study after his return from Britain in the fall of 1958 in a 7 November letter to J.L. Plant, Avro Aircraft's general manager at the time (Smye had moved up to executive director of A.V. Roe Canada Ltd.). This combination was looking "very promising" according to this confidential document. The properly security cleared British authorities were also advised of the potential of, and work done on, the P-13 anti-ICBM missile. Perhaps this is part of the reason why, again in 1958, some of the leading RAF and aerospace authorities were once more proposing that 200 Arrows could defend Britain and that Britain would be foolish not to acquire Arrows considering their versatility and performance. Indeed in the 17 October 1958 issue of the British publication *Engineering*, an article on the Arrow states:

... it seems a sensible suggestion that the Royal Air force could and should share in the privilege of using what may well prove to be the ultimate in light alloy airplanes.... It might, therefore, in the present circumstances prove sound economically as well as militarily for the Ministry of Supply to announce the interest of this nation in the Avro "Arrow," a machine which the Hawker Siddeley Group has already designed and developed and the first examples of which have been built on production tooling so that supplies would be almost immediately available were an order placed.

It is interesting, in light of recent disclosures, to examine the Arrow anti-ICBM concept regarding the new ABM system the United States is trying to develop and deploy. The United States actually deployed an anti-ICBM system in the mid 1960s called Nike-Zeus before the 1972 ABM treaty with the Soviet Union. An interesting critique is published in a 2000 issue of *Harper's* of the new ABM system by one of the original engineers of the submarine-launched medium-range ballistic missile Trident system. To put it mildly, this writer/engineer found the new system severely wanting compared to even the old Trident (and by extension Nike-Zeus) and the missile's actual performance in testing supports the criticism. This gentleman also seemed to suggest that there was a possibility of the testing being something of a whitewash. It is hard not to come to the conclusion that an Arrow equipped with its own radar and onboard systems integrated with the seeker methods, and decoy rejection systems, of the Nike-Zeus guidance system would have produced a sum that was worth more than the parts of Nike-Zeus alone. Other than space-based particle weapons, a super-high altitude performing interceptor capable of carrying a serious ABM missile still seems like the optimum method of dealing with ICBMs.

By 1958 Avro engineering division documents describe a developing investigation of the next-generation interceptors. By the end of that year they seemed to concude that the Arrow, modified, could handle the sub-orbital intercept. They also concluded that orbitol intercepts and strike abilities would be the "next big step." One of the most interesting proposals was for a winged aerospace-plane, or space-shuttle, which Avro proposed could be developed over a 10-year period. Avro's investigations into all the various propulsion methods, aerodynamic configurations, materials and control systems led them to the conclusion that this method was the most economical method in the long term of deploying payloads and personnel into space. Today's conclusions support them in this regard.

Mario Pesando explored the feasibility of such an "orbital and re-entry ferry vehicle," as he called it in June 1958 when he released the "company-confidential" classified *Space Threshold Vehicle* study brochure. Floyd was quick to point out that these studies, while valid, were very rudimentary compared to what was produced by Hawker Siddeley Aviation's Advanced Projects Group, which he led, later in the early 1960s.

STV-Space Threshold Vehicle

The Space Threshold Vehicle is described in the Engineering Division report of June 5th 1958:

RESEARCH

11. Study of Orbiting Winged Vehicle

It became obvious to us some three or four months ago that it was possible to put a winged vehicle into orbit, and that there was a corridor where normal winged flight was possible between the minimum speed curve, above which it was impossible to sustain lift, and the maximum temperature curve, below which the structure gets too hot. This opens up the possibilities of hypersonic flight with a relatively conventional aircraft of low wing loading (about 20 lb. per square foot), which appears to us to be the easiest way to get a man into the threshold of space and recover him, flying back through the corridor.

We are at present carrying out a study to ascertain the relative merits of the winged vehicle versus boost glide or ballistic techniques. We hope to shortly give a briefing on this and later determine where we should go from there.

The concept has been discussed with John Orr [Director of Engineering at the D.R.B.] and Gord Watson, who expressed a great deal of interest in it, and suggested that they may like to have a joint study carried out between ourselves and DRB.

From the above it is apparent that Avro was well aware of the three types of re-entry vehicles that the United States defense and NASA researchers were working on. Project Mercury, the panic operation of the newly formed NASA to beat the Soviets in getting a man into orbit is a "drag re-entry" approach to the problem. NASA and military documentation regarding Project Mercury show that everyone knew this was the simplest method of lobbing a man into orbit and recovering him, especially with limited rocket boosters. Avro did not like this approach since it promised dangerous re-entry temperatures and had no operational value. After all, the thrust of their orbitol studies was focused on developing an aerospace interceptor/strike aircraft to succeed the Arrow 4's potential. Floyd's research and development budget and manpower were small, but focussed on the future.

The boost-glide concept was actually proposed in 1938 by Sanger and Bredt in Germany and was pondered by the Nazis. The idea was to loft a winged vehicle with low-wing loading via rocket into a ballistic trajectory at extreme altitude. It was felt that the speed of re-entry would allow the glider type vehicle to "skip" off the atmosphere in slowly descending steps and thus be capable of deploying a weapon anywhere on the globe.

Of course the Americans latched onto this concept, along with many of the German scientists, at the close of World War II through Operation Paperclip. Luftwaffe Major

Avro Canada's Space Threshold Vehicle Concept.
(image by R.L. Whitcomb)

General Walter Dornberger had been the commandant of the Peenemunde facility Werner Von Braun and the others had worked on the V-2 and other advanced weaponry. (Peenemude was dealt a heavy setback by a special force, of the RAF's longest-range, fastest and heaviest payload bombers in 1944. This force relied exclusively on Avro Lancasters.) Dornberger was soon running Bell Aerospace in the United States while Von Braun made a name for himself in US Army rocket facilities in Alabama. According to Gunston in *Faster Than Sound,* while at Bell Dornberger and Ehricke worked out a two-stage to orbit system using two delta-configured craft, one serving as a mothership, the other being the manned spaceplane. This project, called BoMi (for bomber-missile) lasted from 1951 to 1955, apparently without bearing fruit. What seemed to replace it was the X-20 Dyna-Soar, a collaboration between Bell Aerospace, Boeing and Martin. It was less demanding using Martin's Titan II missile as the primary launch vehicle. Dyna-Soar was also to be basically un-powered, having only thrusters for station-keeping and limited manoeuvring but no main engine. After Project Mercury got going and promised results, Dyna-Soar, or X-20, was cancelled. It has always seemed odd to the author that the United States persisted with the drag re-entry concepts after Mercury for

Gemini and Apollo and then made the big leap to an aerospace plane, the Shuttle. Dornberger's "Bo-Mi" for example, uses the same concepts as Germany's modern-day aerospace-plane, not surprisingly named Sanger and Sanger D.

From the above it is clear that some believed winged aerospace-planes "flying" out of the atmosphere and into space were viable, and at a very early date. Avro documents show engineering was looking down the road for a project to replace the Arrow once production ended. In those days, the idea of a Commonwealth space program, competitive with American efforts as a means of ensuring the Commonwealth possessed all key technologies and could thus compete economically, was seen as a distinct possibility.

A concept was under study at Avro for a hypersonic plus sub orbital spaceplane design called the Space Threshold Vehicle. This document explored all the main variables and limiting technologies and graphically presented the findings. One of the key findings was that the state-of-the-art presented a corridor into space for a winged vehicle which employed hybrid-propulsion techniques.

STV Aerodynamic Configuration

How Avro was forced to develop a sort of "lifting-body" theory for the Arrow has been discussed. This was due to many factors including the fact that at the time no integrated aerodynamic theory existed to explain all of the delta configuration's characteristics. Avro Canada had benefited from a special Delta wing modelling computer AVRO UK had developed with flight data from the various Avro 707 and Vulcan flight data. Another problem was figuring out how the thin wing would twist under various control-surface deflections, speeds and other factors. A lack of knowledge in any of those areas would not allow the designers to properly design any of them. Since the Arrow was to be a Cook-Craigie production philosophy, Avro's management faced the decision to either invest in the means and the brains to pre-design, or risk the development on a more "intuitive" approach. Using Avro's computer facilities and Chamberlin, Pesando, Floyd and others' brains applied in their specialties allowed Avro to develop aerodynamic theories and methods of problem solving which essentially corresponded to today's three-dimensional fluid dynamic modelling. Using this and other advanced "integrated" methods of design and development, they developed the structural design, using testing at various times in the development to refine the derivatives and thus the aircraft and tooling.

NACA and various other American government agencies, the military especially, were looking hard at a means of overcoming the contradictions between space flight and aerodynamic flight in hopes of eventually producing a more efficient means of getting into orbit. The reasons for wanting such a hypersonic vehicle were described as late as 1993 in the House of Representatives Appropriations Committee Energy and Water Development Subcommittee during the 102nd Congress, 2nd Session, Part 6, pages 1669-1670:

> The need for a Hypervelocity Aircraft-Delivered Weapon derives from the ability of such a system to rapidly deliver, or threaten to deliv-

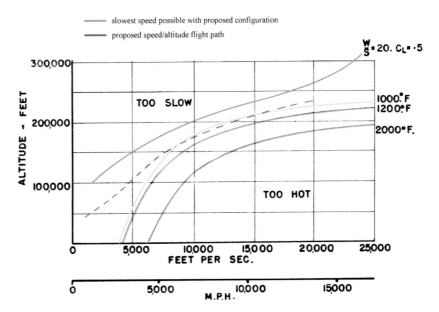

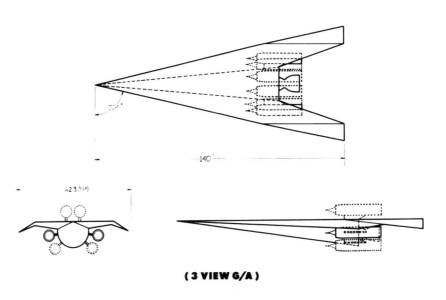

Pesando's STV configuration from the study dated June 1958. The wedge shape on the underside would produce shockwave compression which the winglets would convert to lift. Incredibly, the engine intakes would also benefit from this compression, as does NASA's current round of hypersonic vehicle proposals. (Avro Canada via Jim Floyd)

er, nuclear weapons into a theatre, while maintaining the launch platform well outside potential defenses. Hypersonic velocities enhance defense penetrability and survivability of the weapon and the delivery aircraft against state-of-the-art defenses, while precision guidance can lead to reduced yield requirements, and consequently, collateral damage.

It seems that as late as 1958/59 Avro Canada certainly and a few others felt that Canada and the Commonwealth should have their own independent systems and capacities in these regards, *and* the ability to defend against them. Like the Arrow, this was to be a primarily defensive weapon, but it would retain the ability to be more than slightly offensive as well.

The US saw the same potential and from the *Aerospace Daily* issue of March 1985 the article "DARPA Chief Notes Potential of Supersonic Combustion Ramjet" is enlightening:

[The hypersonic aerospace-plane could] fly up to maybe 150,000 to 200,000 feet, sustain mach 15 plus for a while, slow down and engage an intercontinental bomber or cruise missile carrier at ranges of 1000 nautical miles…

The range mentioned by the DARPA (Defense Advanced Research and Development Agency) seems more than slightly sanitized for public consumption considering that Sanger and Bredt's "interpodal bomber," and the American Bo-Mi, Avro's STV and Dyna-Soar vehicles were designed for ranges of at least half the circumference of the earth (about 12,500 nautical miles).

The problem of developing a spaceplane that would fly most or all of the way from take-off to re-entry under its own power has proven to be extremely complex. On the purely aerodynamic side, it was obvious that a means of getting a high L/D (lift to drag ratio) in a vehicle suitable for hypersonic speeds (and thus of narrow wingspan) was a crucial requirement. Alfred J. Eggers Jr., then an assistant director at NACA's Ames Aeronautical Laboratory, had been pondering methods of improving the L/D performance of hypersonic aircraft. Apparently he was mowing his lawn one day in 1957 and the drone of the machine allowed his mind to wander. He postulated that at high speed, a conical body could be modified in such a way as to benefit from the shockwave produced by the basic shape to create lift. This was the origin of the famous USAF/NASA lifting bodies, so well known from the crash-sequence at the beginning of the TV series, *The Six-Million Dollar Man.* Egger's compression lift theories were the basis of the NAA XB-70 Valkyrie Mach 3 bomber design.

Eggers' compression-lift and lifting-body theories and research, and proposals relating blunt-body re-entry shapes as a means of reducing re-entry temperatures of ballistic-launch vehicles were mentioned in the 21st Wright Brothers Lecture in early 1958. This lecture would appear to have been more of a catalyst for the space race by far than President Kennedy's 1961 challenge to be the first to land a man on the moon. Apparently Avro had some talent present at that lecture taking notes. Interestingly, Eggers' lifting body showed a modified inverted airfoil as the ideal shape—this corresponding crudely to Avro's highly criticized airfoil shape for the Arrow, as well as Whitcomb's later "supercritical" airfoil.

It was compression-lift that the Valkyrie's designers and Avro's Mario Pesando found especially brilliant however. Pesando grasped the concept immediately and did research suggesting Avro could achieve an L/D max of about 6 using a delta-shaped vehicle that employed Eggers' theories. This L/D max is very high, and is shared by the Boeing B-52 which uses swept high-aspect ratio wings to achieve it and therefore its long range. Pesando, Floyd and Chamberlin may have also suspected that the 4-degree anhedral of the Arrow wing actually made it a "compression-lift" aircraft. Interestingly, NASA-Ames' later lifting body work, with Eggers heavily involved, produced the blunt-bodies that only had L/D ratios in the neighbourhood of 1.5-1 while Pesando was looking at 6-1. If the Canadian NAE and DRB had problems following Avro's aerodynamics with the Arrow, they would have been even more at a loss with the STV design. An interesting 2001 NASA-Langley internet discussion of "integrated" versus "waverider" shapes for precisely an STV-type craft is titled *Aerodynamic Performance of Realistic Waverider-Derived Hypersonic Cruise Vehicles* (http://larcpubs.larc.nasa.gov). It concludes that a smoothly blended, integrated design would suffer in terms of potential L/D ratios, and that a waverider style design could provide an L/D max of about 7, with its L/D ratio at a lift coefficient of .05 would be about 6. Pesando quoted exactly those figures for the STV design, which he acknowledged was essentially an "Eggers body."

Materials proposed for the STV from the same selection as envisioned for the Arrow Mk.3. The insulation scheme proposed for the Arrow 3 would have been acceptable for this vehicle, especially considering it was essentially the same as the heat shields used on Mercury and Gemini if left un-covered by a thin titanium skin. Being fibreglass honeycomb with resin filled by microballoons meant it was a light, high temperature, structural material. The core structure of the STV was to be mainly high-temperature steels

The North American XB-70 Valkyrie. It made use of Alfred Eggers' (of NACA-Langley at that time) compression-lift theories which resulted in a good L/D max, thus giving much better range and altitude performance than had been assumed possible previously. (North American via NASA-Dryden)

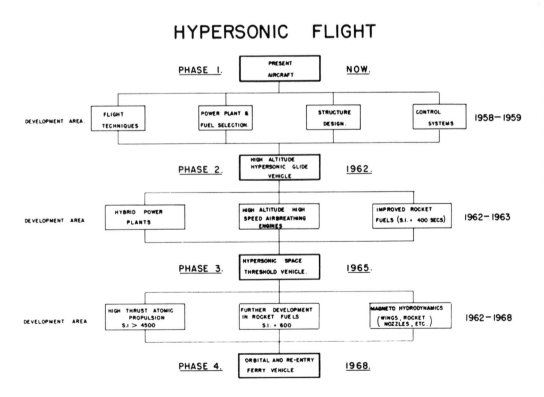

This page from Avro's study postulates a development plan and timeline to produce a winged orbital aero-space-plane and have it ready by 1965. Nuclear/hydrogen-plasma was one of several propulsion technologies proposed for the later version of the vehicle, proposed for 1968. Magneto-hydrodynamics include ion-propulsion, and some are also related to anti-gravity techniques.

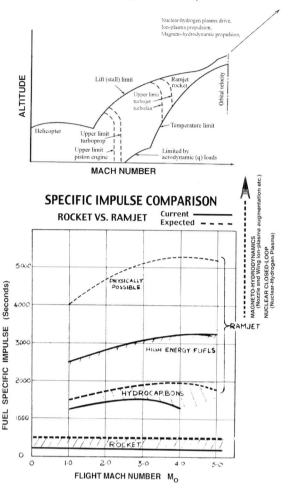

PROPULSION COMPARISON
By Altitude & Speed suitability

Nuclear-hydrogen plasma drive.
Ion-plasma propulsion,
Magneto-hydrodynamic propulsion,

ALTITUDE

Lift (stall) limit

Ramjet
rocket

Upper limit
turbojet
turbofan

Helicopter

Upper limit
turboprop

Temperature limit

Upper limit
piston engine

Limited by
aerodynamic (q) loads

Orbital velocity

MACH NUMBER

SPECIFIC IMPULSE COMPARISON
ROCKET VS. RAMJET

Current ——
Expected - - - -

MAGNETO-HYDRODYNAMICS
(Nozzle and Wing Ion-plasma augmentation etc.)

NUCLEAR CLOSED-LOOP
(Nuclear-Hydrogen Plasma)

FUEL SPECIFIC IMPULSE (Seconds)

5000

PHYSICALLY
POSSIBLE

4000

RAMJET

3000

HIGH ENERGY FUELS

2000

HYDROCARBONS

1000

ROCKET

0

0   1.0   2.0   3.0   4.0   5.0

FLIGHT MACH NUMBER M$_0$

These graphs show the suitability of various modes of propulsion to different speeds and altitudes. The second graph is from Pesando's STV study, with references to the specific impulses of advanced propulsion added by the author. Pesando's document reveals Avro's startling familiarity with almost all the currently-debated advanced propulsion technologies and problems. (First graph courtesy Jack Mattingly & aircraftenginedesign.com)

with titanium alloys in the skin and structure where required. Pesando felt that Avro could produce a vehicle with a take-off to landing weight ratio of 4-1. In other words, 75 percent of the vehicle weight would be devoted to fuel, consumables (oxygen etc) and payload using mostly known materials and construction techniques.

NASA's Dryden Flight Research Center website (http://www.dfrc.nasa.gov) shows an interesting graph which plots L/D ratios against range for several configurations of hypersonic and ballistic re-entry shapes. It shows the L/D ratio of the blunt-bodies coinciding with that of the Space Shuttle at a relatively poor 1.0-1.5 range. This restricted their re-entry glide ranges to the order of

600-1,500 miles. The ballistic "capsule" shapes were even less suitable, which is why they heat so much on re-entry. This also explains why the shuttle needs such a heavy tile insulation scheme; the steeper the descent, the higher the heating penalty.

The shape shown with the best range performance however, is the X-24B, which was the X-24A blunt-body redesigned as a sharp body like the STV. This shape is shown to have an L/D max of about 2.5-3.0 which shows it is about one half the L/D ratio of 6, which is what Pesando thought the STV could have. This low L/D ratio for the X-24B would have two causes, the most important being that it didn't employ Eggers' compression lift, and the second that it was an adaptation of a design intended for another purpose. As mentioned above, NASA is now of the same opinion regarding a similar waverider hypersonic body, as perhaps they have been all along. On the other hand, research facilities have been known to disagree within NASA, and the Ames Research Center was the leading proponent of lifting-body hypersonics throughout this period and the 1960s (Avro aside). It is interesting to remember that Ames himself was one of the NACA consultants invited to hear Avro experts Chamberlin, Floyd and Lindley's rebuttal of NACA Langley and the RCAF, DRB and NAE's condemnation of the Arrow's aerodynamics. One might remember that NACA had already criticised both the Arrow's inverted airfoil *and* Delta-wing. That two-day conference was chaired by Hugh Dryden—another NACA leader who would have a research facility named after him. At this time Ames already did.

Pesando's STV document discusses this plan and it is clear that the "present aircraft" in the chart on page 237 is the Arrow. When the Mk.4 Arrow, with the high-temperature materials and ramjets, is examined, the consideration of the Arrow as phase one becomes even more striking given that this aircraft could have zoomed to somewhere around 150,000 to 200,000 feet or higher with a supplementary rocket. In discussing this schedule, Pesando wrote:

Considering a possible time table, it is believed, as shown on the accompanying chart, that using known data and techniques within one year it should be possible to finalize engineering of an interim hypersonic glide vehicle with burn out speeds in excess of 10,000 ft. per second [about 6,000 mph]. Such a vehicle could possibly be built by 1962 and would be considered a research vehicle.

Further development in the areas indicated could, by 1963 at the latest, increase our knowledge and techniques sufficiently to enable us to extend our vehicle concept to velocities approaching orbital speeds. We have, therefore, shown this vehicle as operating by 1965, this vehicle would constitute the long range operational vehicle with ranges of 12,500 miles or greater.

Having this vehicle completed would enable us to immediately begin the utilization of further advances in propulsion methods and magneto-hydrodynamics expected by 1968, to provide us with a winged orbital and re-entry ferry vehicle by the late 1960s.

The importance of phase 3 and 4 vehicles in the military field is of course obvious and this could be one of the objectives expected of such a development program.

Propulsion was the greatest challenge, however, and still is. Phase 2 of the above diagram refers to the STV design as shown in the illustrations. The propulsion for this vehicle was to be hybrid ramjet and rocket units. Pesando's study showed that the ramjets would more than merit the additional complexity of the machine because of their superior specific impulse (amount of thrust per unit of fuel weight) as compared to a rocket. In fact, turbojet engines also have far better specific impulse than rockets. Rockets have merely been known as the simplest and lightest motors available using take-along oxidents into air-less space. Ramjets were found capable of getting the STV to orbital velocit and required no oxygen since the ramjets were air breathing.

Pesando's STV was envisioned as being a single stage to orbit (SSTO) vehicle, the same concept the United States

Mario Pesando. After leaving Avro he went to RCA in the United States and worked on their space projects. He later worked on the Saturn boosters for the Apollo spacecraft. (via Jim Floyd)

tried with the X-30, and that some of the Europeans have been exploring—the British HOTOL design being one of the best. From Pesando's STV study:

> The hypersonic vehicle postulated, takes off on rocket power alone with a full load of oxidizer and sufficient ramjet fuel to enable it to climb to an altitude in excess of 40,000 ft. and maintain flight during airborne fueling proceedings. [The STV concept] is for a hypersonic vehicle which is really an extension of the conventional supersonic airplane. When airborne fueling operations have been completed the aircraft is accelerated to ramjet light up speed and begins its climb and acceleration to higher speeds.

Flight re-fueling is a rather novel approach to the SSTO problem, one that appears to be entirely original and un-copied as of yet.

Nuclear-Hydrogen Plasma and Electrical Propulsion

The final stage of Avro's STV development scheme was to produce an orbital ferry or shuttle. This would have employed new propulsion schemes including nuclear power and magneto-hydrodynamics. Documents from Floyd show that the specific nuclear propulsion system Pesando was considering was a nuclear-hydrogen plasma drive. This is still seen as one of the most powerful "deep space" systems for moving large ships.

Ion, plasma and electrical propulsion methods have been discussed for a very long time and are still being discussed although they are currently acknowledged as being limited to small vehicles and thrusters. Development has occurred although progress is shown to have been far slower than Pesando assumed it would be back in 1958. Although ion plasma engines actually cover a fairly wide range of possible engines, the concept has been around since Robert Goddard postulated briefly on the possibility of electric propulsion in 1906. Nikola Tesla is rumoured to have done work to this end, including discussing a flying saucer design that employed anti-gravity techniques which he is supposed to have claimed he was ready to build in 1929. Hermann Oberth, the father of German rocketry and a flying saucer theorist also discussed electric propulsion in a chapter of his 1928 book *Wege zur Raumschiffahrt*. Sanger also contributed some theories as did Ernst Stuhlinger who, in 1954, introduced the important concept of specific impulse. In 1958 the American Rocketdyne Corporation operated the first ion-engine demonstrator. By 1964 the Russians had the first plasma thrusters in space aboard the Zond-2 satellite.

Today several electric ion propulsion techniques are in space, with NASA and Hughes Aerospace having produced Xenon (rather than hydrogen) gas ion-plasma thrusters for some satellites. The only ion-thrust main engine the United States acknowledges having launched is aboard the Deep Space One (DS-1) research craft; a small scientific craft sent to investigate some of the planets in the solar system. Avro knew in the late 50s what is so widely known today, that this type of engine provides more "specific impulse," due to the fact that the dissociated electrons and protons in the ion plasma are potentially capable of being electrically accelerated to very nearly the speed of light. This means the thrust produced is *much* higher by mass flow of the stream than with a rocket engine, or with a turbo-jet or ramjet engine where the exhaust is merely super or hypersonic.

The above electric ion plasma engines are now referred to as EIP drives. They generally develop low amounts of thrust despite their very high specific impulse. Pesando had been proposing the eventual development of a nuclear-hydrogen plasma drive for the STV's final development phase. This seems to be considered an NTR (Nuclear Thermal Rocket) today although Pesando was looking at various methods of modifying the engine with electrical means. NTRs were projected with specific impulses of about 900 seconds at the time but Pesando seemed to feel (and the graphs in his study support that assumption) that with hydrogen plasma and electrical techniques, the specific impulse could be raised to about 4,500 seconds. The heat of a closed-loop reactor (closed-loop meaning the propellant isn't radiated, or is radiated very little) would heat and ionize hydrogen. Electrical techniques would be used at the nozzle to ensure the plasma beam detaches from the ship and provides propulsion. Pesando seemed to count on technology improving the ramjet to the point of allowing orbit to be achieved with ramjets alone to prevent radiation of earth. It has been theorized for a long time that scramjets (supersonic combustion ramjets) could reach orbital velocity. Today we still seem to be unable to achieve this without the nuclear reactor although pre-heating the hydrogen fuel along hot leading edges to recover more of the energy being expended in a Ramjet seems to offer promise. Pesando was also eyeing ducted-rockets, which are now called ram-rockets. This ducted or ram-rocket concept appears to be very promising for hybrid propulsion techniques, combining possibilities for chemical, air breathing, rocket and electric propulsion, even nuclear techniques, into one multi-function engine design.

Another possibility for the reactor was in making electrical energy for a purely electrical main engine, this being practical due to the high output of a reactor compared to other means of generating electric power such as solar energy. Of course nuclear propulsion for aerospace-planes or any other type of aircraft has been taboo for many years despite the fact that many satellites went up with reactors on board. The Americans and Soviets were never afraid to simply not tell the population what they were doing. *Popular Mechanics* ran an interesting article in late 2000 postulating that a lifting-body nearly saucer-like military shuttle has been in operation for years, using nuclear propulsion, and designed to either remain in orbit with nuclear weapons, or drop nuclear missiles off in orbit for later use.

During the February 24th meeting between the Avro management and the ministers, Avro tried to promote the spaceplane concept as a means of putting satellites in orbit. They were trying to interest the Canadian government in pursuing a development program with Britain and other members of the Commonwealth in a joint space program. Obviously the Space Shuttle of today uses a similar though probably less-advanced concept as Avro's 1958 STV for putting satellites in space although it is designed to a much higher payload capacity and thus requires those massive boosters at launch. This according to Jim Floyd who helped place them after 100 engineers from Avro were employed at North American Rockwell, the company that designed the Shuttle. By 1992 the Shuttle had stopped carrying military payloads for reasons of economics. The Lockheed-Martin "Venture-Star" promised improved costing, however it appears to have been cancelled in March of 2001, again fueling speculation about where the program funds went, and what the technology developed will be used for. In the author's opinion technology development in many areas has stalled, at least in the public domain, since the 1950s.

Avro's 1965 Space Threshold Vehicle appears feasible with Pesando being careful to propose only existing technologies, carefully employed and optimised. The ferry vehicle was extremely ambitious and this author believes that the unexpected problems with scramjets, plus the resistance to nuclear aircraft, might have slowed its development. In the end this writer believes that the STV would have become an orbiter, however it would have been closer in technology to the 1965 phase using propulsion that was further optimised, plus perhaps some of the ion and plasma propulsion techniques. One might suggest that Chamberlin, Lindley and over 25 other ex-Avro engineers *did* prove they could have built such a craft when they took so much responsibility for *Project Mercury* and *Project Gemini*.

DURING THE DESIGN OF THE ARROW, Avro's aerodynamicists made extensive use of NACA wind tunnel facilities to validate and improve the basic Arrow design and to assist in the design of other aircraft and techniques. One of the most sophisticated wind tunnels in the world at the time was the NACA facility in Langley Virginia, run by Dr. Robert Gilruth.

By early 1958 the Americans were already in the throes of trying to decide how to respond to the "space race" due to Sputnik's surprise launching in October of 1957. From March 10th through 12th 1958 the ARDC staged, at the offices of the USAF Ballistic Missile Division in Los Angeles, a "Man in Space" symposium. LGen Donald Putt was at this meeting and suggested a cooperative program teaming the USAF and NACA in a cooperative venture. Putt had been a Jetliner fan and had, in fact, been the one who tried to get $20 million set aside to purchase them for the USAF. Putt had been around Avro a great deal and was later also involved in Frost's saucer programs.

NASA's official history points out that at this time the leaders seemed to be convinced that the way to proceed into orbit was a "quick and dirty" drag re-entry approach using the Thor missile booster with a new second stage flourine/hydrazine section adding an additional 15,000 lbs thrust to the package. NASA's history also states everyone missed the more apparent booster for this concept at this time: Convair Aeronautics' ATLAS ICBM booster.

During June ARPA's "Man in Space Soonest" group had another meeting involving NASA, the USAF, Convair, Lockheed and others for a fresh theoretical discussion and consideration of methodology.

By early 1958 the Eisenhower administration had decided to try to be the first to place a man in orbit and the July passage of the "space bill" paved the way for a major expansion of NACA through the re-assignment of some of the military research and development programs and facilities to the new agency; NASA. Jimmy Dolittle, famous for air racing and the Tokyo bombing raid of 1941, was at this time NACA Chairman. By late July the USAF was trying to derail NASA and requested, through their ARPA group, funds for their "Man in Space Soonest" project described above. They were turned down while NASA got $40 million to start their man in space effort. The USAF however seemed to be very slow learners in this regard and tried again in August and were similarly re-buffed. By this time the USAF Dyna-Soar project was underway and they were allowed to continue development of this somewhat more advanced concept.

CHAPTER TWELVE

AVRO INVADES NASA

Project Mercury

The X-20 Dyna-Soar was to be the USAF's strike-capable X-15 successor. It was a boost-glide vehicle, designed for launch into orbit by a Titan booster. Payload was a second crewman or about 450 lbs of military payload (read "potential nuclear device"). It would have largely followed Dr. Sanger and Dr. Bredt's concepts.   (USAF)

One of the first things that NASA did after its formation was establish a specialized "Space Task Group" with its single mission being to get an American into space. This occurred on November 5th 1958 with 35 individuals comprising the STG. Robert Gilruth from the Langley facility was placed in charge of this group with Maxime Faget from NASA's Pilotless Aircraft Research and Development (PARD) facility as his deputy. Faget had also been pushing for the simplest method, the simple Atlas with a drag re-entry capsule.

Documents show Avro was proposing a drag re-entry vehicle as a possible first step in "their" space program using the Atlas booster and a spherical capsule to measure "G" forces and re-entry heating as of June of 1958. By this time the various former NACA research centers were not of like mind on how to accomplish the objective of getting a man in space *first*. The Virginia-based "Langley Consensus" felt that a simple drag re-entry vehicle on Atlas would do. The Californians at the Ames research center however wanted to use a "lifting body" of blunt profile as a "boost-glide" aircraft, allowing more pilot control. NASA's new "High Speed Aerodynamics" facility simply felt that the limiting factor would be what Atlas could carry and that this should determine what configuration made the cut. As we have seen, Avro Canada wanted to do a proper aerospace-plane from the beginning.

Due to the enormous challenge of putting a man into space, the new NASA administration was hard pressed. They had also inherited the Navy's Vanguard missile program, the Explorer from the Army Ballistic Missile Agency, the USAF's Jet Propulsion Laboratory and an Air Force/North American Rocketdyne study for a 1 million pound thrust rocket booster and a great deal of other assorted projects and facilities. Significantly, the US Army did not relinquish Werner Von Braun's team working out of Huntsville Alabama or any of this group's programs to NASA in the beginning. NASA also gained at least two layers of political bureaucracy thanks to the respective efforts of Lyndon Johnson and Congress. In 1958, spread across America, NASA had $117,000,000 in funding, a considerably lower figure than Avro Canada's operating budget at that time.

By December of 1958 Project Mercury, that would eventually put John Glenn (and others) in orbit, was largely conceived and gaining momentum, bodies and headaches. By February of 1959 McDonnell Aircraft had been awarded the development contract for 20 Mercury capsules. By this time the STG effort was growing exponentially and they were very short of qualified people to run the development effort. Happily for the United States the Diefenbaker government opened up a large talent pool by cancelling the Avro Arrow and not replacing it with anything, not even promises. Considering the "house cleaning" at the end of the Arrow cancellation and rough treatment by the government, many at Avro felt they had been "done-in" and so the talent dispersed.

Incredibly, Cabinet documents from mid-1959 reveal that the Conservatives rather considered the engineers and other talent at A.V. Roe Canada, subsidiary of the British Hawker Siddeley Group, to be their employees rather than the company's. These documents show that the government of Canada saw these brains as a bargaining chip to be used to gain defence production sharing deals with the United States. From the Cabinet minutes it even seems that the fact these people were employees of a private company, many sent over from Britain by the parent company, didn't even enter their consciousness.

It has been written that several United States aeronautical companies were already at the Royal York Hotel in downtown Toronto the day after Black Friday. Other sources insist they were actually tipped off in advance and were there a day before cancellation. The important thing is that many of the brains of Avro left Canada, and a similar grouping of genius capable of turning brilliance in so many areas of advanced technology into hardware has not been seen in this country since. In a letter to Sir Thomas Pike (trying to have Britain take on the flying Arrows) as early as April 1959, Jim Floyd reports that he had already lost 75 percent of his best engineering talent. Jim Chamberlin and Bob Lindley, so crucial to the Arrow and other programs at Avro met with Gilruth in March. By April Chamberlin was working for Gilruth as acting Director of Engineering and Contractual Administration for Gilruth's Space Task Group, a very responsible title. Bob Lindley went to McDonnell and worked on the Gemini capsules. About 30 others joined the American space race either directly at NASA or at some of the subcontractors. In January 1960 Chamberlin was given more staff and made Project Manager. To say he carried the responsibility for Project Mercury would be reasonably accurate although there were several layers of administration above him within the NASA hierarchy. He was still the one responsible for getting the machines designed and built, and would be the one blamed if they didn't function "as advertised."

A Mercury test capsule after recovery. The streaks are from the glass-fibre and filler material vaporising and re-condensing from the extreme heat. A similar heat shield material was proposed earlier for the Arrow 3. (NASA)

The Mercury Control Center. Ex-Avro engineers John Hodge, "Tec" Roberts and Fred Mathews would be pivotal personalities in the tracking and mission control systems first in Virginia then at the Houston Space Center. The system in effect allowed ground-uplink fly-by-wire control of the Mercury spacecraft relying on telemetry and systems reporting from the capsule. In many ways this was an ASTRA-similar integrated approach with human back-up. Project Gemini would reverse the machine-pilot order of priorities and provide a piloted spacecraft with automated data-link guidance assistance. This involved taking the information available through the Mercury ground tracking data-link sites and presenting it to the astronauts better, while designing a spacecraft "fly-by-wire" control system that was much more controllable. (NASA)

Launching of the NASA-designed LJ6 Little Joe rocket on 4 October 1959 took place at Wallops Island, Virginia. This was the first successful launch of an instrumented telemetry and temperature test capsule with a Little Joe booster. The first Mercury test capsules were only what NASA termed "boilerplate" incomplete machines in a stepping-stone kind of low-risk development far removed from any Cook-Craigie approach.

On 9 September 1959, two Atlas missiles were launched, one from each coast of the United States. One of these was being assessed by the military and the Convair builders as America's first ICBM and its flight was judged a failure. The other was for NASA and had a "boilerplate" lash-up of the Mercury capsule strapped to the tip. Fortunately NASA's missile functioned according to the brochure although the payload didn't. The separation and re-orientation of the capsule did not work properly. The capsule, however, did eventually right itself simply due to its center of gravity and aerodynamic design and re-entered the atmosphere, subjecting the heat shield to more punishment than a nominal re-entry. The USAF felt justified enough to proclaim to the world that the Atlas nuclear ICBM was now operational, even though the only two remaining missiles were for training. The heat shield under test was made up of fibre-glass honeycomb with a phenolic resin for strength while the honeycomb was filled with a rubberized material filled with "microballoons." This is exactly the heat shield material Avro had proposed in 1958 for the Mk. 3 Arrow version minus a titanium skin. Interestingly, much of this technology was proprietary to Avro as of 1958, especially regarding the microballoon vulcanizing filler.

Rhesis monkeys were lofted in Mercury development capsules to make certain that the evolving systems would not produce any momentary physiological stresses that a human occupant could not endure. The first American in space would be up-staged by several weeks by the orbit of Yuri Gagarin of the USSR. Alan Shepard and NASA were ready to go at the Space Task Group's Virginia launch center on May 5th, 1961 in a McDonnell capsule tipping a Redstone missile. Atlas had already lifted two capsules by this time and a manned flight was scheduled, yet by mid 1961 they had decided Redstone provided the fastest, safest method for achieving a suborbital hop and gaining the desired experience.

Even before Shepard became the first Westerner in space, Jim Chamberlin was consulting with McDonnell personnel from the Mercury capsule program on a second-generation spacecraft. According to NASA's history of Project Mercury:

In the meantime, James Chamberlin followed his own course. He had arrived in St. Louis (McDonnell) in February, convinced his job was to

At work on the Mercury capsule. Space was tight when replacing an ICBM warhead and expecting to get it into orbit with the Atlas booster. (NASA)

re-design the Mercury capsule from the bottom up. This was a view not widely shared. The common view had it that the Mercury capsule only needed to be improved. Chamberlin felt, and as engineering director of Project Mercury he was surpassingly well qualified to judge, that the Mercury design precluded simple upgrading. The Mercury capsule was merely a first try at a manned spacecraft. It took too long to build, test, check out and launch. The heart of the trouble was Mercury's integrated design, which packed the most equipment into the least space with the smallest weight. This could hardly have been avoided, given the limited weight lifting capacity of the boosters available.

On 17 March 1961, after Shepard's successful flight, there was a meeting of the top STG members to discuss future missions, mostly related to Mercury, and to discuss development of ideas for rendezvous missions in space. Rendezvous was an on-again off-again area of research as was the concept of earth orbit and/or lunar-orbit rendezvous during the debates on how to get a man to the moon.

Chamberlin launched into a largely impromptu blackboard lecture on the program's future, which

he saw as very limited. The trouble with trying anything more ambitious with Mercury than had been planned was that even these relatively modest goals could only be achieved at the expense of the most painstaking and arduous care in testing and check out. This was not a manned spacecraft problem so much as it was a Mercury design problem. Drawing on his experience with fire control and weapons delivery systems for fighter aircraft, Chamberlin sketched a new capsule structure with its equipment located outside the cockpit in self contained modules easy to install and check out. Although Chamberlin focused his remarks on capsule modification, he had obviously given some thought to a suitable mission for the new design. He had, in fact, prepared a brochure dealing with an audacious circumlunar flight for the improved Mercury, which Silverstein looked at and dismissed without comment.

However his boss, Dr. Robert Gilruth, authorized Chamberlin to continue his consultations with McDonnell and Bob Lindley.

The guiding idea shared by Chamberlin and his McDonnell colleagues was "To make a better mechanical design;" capsule parts would be more accessible, leading to "a more reliable, more workable, more practical capsule." The experimental Mercury capsule was to be transformed into an operational spacecraft.

It seems Chamberlin and the other ex-Avroites gave real impetus to progress and problem solving on Mercury. This gave Chamberlin especially heavy sway over the systems design and even the mission(s) of NASA's next-generation spacecraft. Some sources seem to present his influence as having been somewhat resented in some circles, in shades of his and Avro's rocky relationship with the Canadian NAE and others. From NASA's "On the Shoulders of Titans:"

...Chamberlin was moving much more quickly than his colleagues [in early 1961]. Perhaps the greatest defect in his plans was that they assumed the rendezvous technique itself to need no special work, that a few flights would suffice to prove the technique before going on to apply it to larger ends. This was an assumption not widely shared, and both plans were rejected for Mark II, although Chamberlin may well have blazed the trail for rendezvous in Apollo."

John Glenn's "Freedom 7" Mercury-Atlas blasts off on a date with history. After an incident with "fireflies" darting around outside his capsule, re-entry would prove to be a bit dicey. (NASA)

In the beginning NASA was not convinced they needed a bridge between Mercury and the moon mission, which had been under study for years first within the USAF, and later within NASA itself. Considering the broad range of capability gaps between Mercury and what would have to be accomplished for Apollo, one might assume Chamberlin's conviction that they needed a serious middle step to be visionary. Chamberlin later remarked "The sequencing of the escape system was one of the major problem areas in Mercury in all its aspects, its mechanical aspects in the first part of the program, and the electronic aspects later."

Chamberlin also despised the extra weight with the escape rocket tower on Mercury and fought to specify ejection seats for his Mark II capsule, which would evolve into the Gemini spacecraft. It was a daring idea but this went a long way towards making the Gemini vehicle more of a piloted spacecraft than a ground-controlled ballistic device. At this point some of those involved questioned this move since the explosion rate of a hydrogen and oxygen powered rocket would be too fast to allow successful ejection. In other words it wouldn't work fast enough with the Atlas booster. Again Chamberlin was looking down the road to the emerging Martin Titan II booster. This warhead lifter promised two and a half times the payload of the Atlas booster while using a safer and more easily handled hydrazine type propellant system. Martin presented relevant data to NASA in May of 1961.

One of the limitations of the Mercury capsule was its hatch size. It was, to put it mildly, cramped. While designing the ejection system Chamberlin and his McDonnell associates designed a large, overhead clamshell door with forward vision. Apparently Chamberlin specified this door arrangement with extra-vehicular activity in mind, yet wasn't mentioning this widely at the time. As of June 1961, the new Mk II capsule was still a single-man affair. Even so at this point the Space Task Group wasn't sold on the need for such a redesign and merely endorsed a study on a "minimum change" Mercury capsule. Later it would be felt that the astronauts who died on the pad of Apollo 1, may have been able to escape with Gemini's ejection systems rather than the more Mercury-like port of North American's Apollo capsule.

Project Gemini

Chamberlin had already been discussing the possibility of Mercury Mk.2 (later redesignated Project Gemini) achieving the man on the moon objective laid down in challenge form by President Kennedy in May of that year (1961). With the mission adapter package and an orbiting Agena rocket with a single-man lunar lander, Chamberlin was convinced the Gemini spacecraft could accomplish the Apollo mission sooner and at much lower expense. His concept meant the planned torturous development of the Nova-class booster (in the end replaced by the Saturn V), could be reduced by one or two steps. By the end of July 1961, NASA management had accepted the idea of a two-man spacecraft. As "On the Shoulders of Titans" puts it "When August 1961 began, Jim Chamberlin, backed by the Space Task Group and McDonnell Aircraft Corporation, had produced the makings of a post-Mercury manned space flight program." This article describes an August 14th meeting where Chamberlin presented his vision for Mercury Mark II, which became Project Gemini. The program objectives, as he saw them, were:

To prove the vehicle combination through unmanned instrumented launches.

Conduct pilot-manoeuvred elliptical orbits instrumented to investigate the Van Allen belts.

Demonstrate precise ground landings using a controllable "para-glider" system in place of simple parachutes.

A Project Gemini launch using Martin-Marietta's Titan II booster. (NASA-Langley)

One of the single-man lunar lander proposals. In reality it probably made as much sense as the two-man vehicle used for Apollo. Owen Maynard, formerly of Avro Canada, was an important figure in the development of the lunar lander for Apollo and other payload integration tasks. (NASA-Goddard)

Conduct rendezvous and docking in space with other Mark II spacecraft and/or a booster with a Gemini docking adapter launched separately into orbit.

Provide valuable astronaut training in techniques necessary for the lunar mission.

Potentially to conduct lunar orbits by rendezvous with a booster in orbit to leave earth orbit for the moon and thus "accomplish most of the Apollo mission at an earlier date."

NASA and the US government allowed a separate project office to be set up for the new program. This group was also given responsibility for the remaining MERCURY flights yet deleted Chamberlin's sixth objective, that involving lunar orbit. Chamberlin's lunar objectives were further dashed when the Apollo program was established and set up as a separate undertaking. Perhaps in reaction Chamberlin then presented a detailed plan to put a man on the moon using the two-man Gemini with a single-man lunar lander. Most considered his approach too bare-bones, relying on one man staying in the Gemini capsule in orbit over the moon while the second exits the capsule to enter the single-man lander, lands, then launches to rendezvous with the Gemini return vehicle in space. Simplistic or visionary Chamberlin didn't get the opportunity to prove his theory. NASA management ensured all mentions of a lunar landing, and even a circumlunar flight, were deleted from any official statements of the Project Gemini mission objectives.

As "On the Shoulders of Titans" explains:

After cutting circumlunar flight from the Mark II plan, Chamberlin revived the even more daring idea of using the spacecraft in a lunar landing program. The booster was Saturn S-3 and the key technique was a lunar orbit rendezvous. The scheme involved a lunar landing vehicle that was little more than a 680 Kg skeleton, to which a propulsion system and propellants were attached, 3,300-4,400 lbs weight depending on propellants.

When Chamberlin proposed this scheme to Gilruth's senior staff at the start of September 1961, he was the first to offer a concrete plan for manned lunar landing that depended on the technique of rendezvous in lunar orbit although he did not originate the concept.

Space Task Group so far had seen little merit in any form of rendezvous for lunar missions, but it reserved its greatest disdain for the lunar-orbit version.

Two Gemini twins rendezvous in space and prove air is not required for formation flight, nor is pointing in the same direction. (NASA)

Up to this time most scientists, apparently including Werner Von Braun for some time, thought lunar orbit rendezvous was something of a dream to be considered down the road. Clearly, well into 1961, those running the American space program really didn't know how they were going to get a man on the moon. Until the proposals of Chamberlin and others, those running the lunar mission were concentrating on a direct flight to the moon from a single launch of the massive Nova booster Von Braun and others were working on. The Nova booster was even more powerful than the massive Saturn V booster that would carry the Apollo lunar missions into space. Chamberlin's proposal required two launches, one using the Titan S-3 to loft the Gemini capsule with mission adapter and lunar lander, and another, possibly an Atlas with a second Agena stage with propellants to be picked up in orbit by the Gemini package, then used to propel the hardware into lunar orbit. From there the booster would detach, the second crewman would board the lunar lander and depart. After his work on the moon a lunar orbit rendezvous would be accomplished, the lander discarded and the Gemini capsule with its own Centaur or other booster in the adapter package would depart for Earth. It was an elegant plan requiring the least amount of booster thrust. It provided for one more possible abort point as well but added the technical challenge of docking in Earth orbit. Gemini as it was run certainly would make that task routine, along with orbital rendezvous of two lightweight craft.

On the 15th of January, 1962 Dr. Gilruth split the Space Task Group into three project offices— Mercury, Apollo and Gemini— with Chamberlin leaving his position as head of the Space Task Group's engineering division for that of Manager Project Gemini. According to the NASA article:

> GPO [Gemini Project Office] enjoyed a degree of autonomy that permitted Chamberlin to deal directly with McDonnell and Air Force Space Systems Division. He reported directly to MSC (Manned Space Center, the new name of the larger STG umbrella organization in NASA) Director Gilruth, and that was chiefly a matter of keeping Gilruth informed on the status of the project.

At McDonnell Aircraft Corporation Walter Burke was in over-all charge of the company's space activities but it was Bob Lindley, who had left Avro in Britain to come to the Canadian component and had later become the Chief Engineer for the Arrow Weapons System, who was the Engineering Manager for the Gemini spacecraft. Apparently the speed with which Chamberlin and his cohorts came up with a viable mission and equipment design was a major factor in Gemini getting the go-ahead in the new space program, considering the impetus and money Kennedy's challenge had provided. As the NASA article states: "Project Gemini had won approval in late 1961 over several competing rendezvous development proposals because its design was further along than those of its competitors..." Bob Lindley was later interviewed regarding Gemini by Flight International and he remarked on the speed with which Gemini progressed: "Like so much else in Gemini, subcontracting plans were well along before the project received formal sanction."

Gemini at the very beginning got its initial $75 million simply through internal re-allocations within NASA. With rising estimates by the fall of 1962 the Gemini program was seeing yet another grab for control by the USAF, a budget crisis, and failings with the para-glider landing system, under subcontract by North American Aviation. Martin's Titan booster was also providing unexpected headaches. Variations in the thrust of the engines were known to sometimes result in an amplification effect being transmitted up the rocket structure resulting in bouncing, of varying violence, at the tip of the booster. This was termed "pogo" and Titan had it worse than expected. Pogo had also plagued Atlas but the limited systems and control provided by the astronaut, plus careful rocket manufacture and selection made it tolerable with Mercury/Atlas. It was less tolerable in Gemini since the occupants were expected to function as pilots, not as autopilot back-ups.

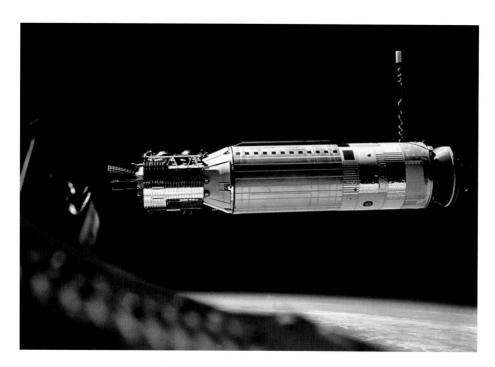

The Lockheed Agena target booster being approached by a Gemini spacecraft.   (NASA)

The upper portions of the Atlas structure had to be beefed up to absorb more of a shock load and this increased weight. Replacement of aluminium oxidizer feed lines helped as did other minor modifications but the lift-off and ride with the Titan was never as smooth as promised. Pogo was reduced to about .6G positive and negative (which still results in 1.2G jolts of varying frequency, certainly enough to rattle one's eyeballs!) which the Air Force felt was adequate. To a certain extent the Air Force dug in its heels and resisted any further improvement on something they were funding as a weapons carrier rather than personnel carrier, with Chamberlin insisting the improvement was not enough. He seemed to be a demanding taskmaster, while he had worked for another with very exacting standards earlier in his career!

Due in part to these problems and a budget draw-out of political origin, the Gemini funding requirement doubled between the summer of 1962 and spring 1963. By this time the typical Avro "get it done yesterday while the bureaucrats catch up" along with the almost "single-man department" approach took its toll. Some were demanding blood and to be sure, Chamberlin was an obvious target. He had moved heaven and earth to get the job done and probably bruised a few egos on the way. He'd also undertaken a crushing burden, guiding both Mercury and Gemini through their formative stages and was thus deserving of a more supervisory role... and right on the heels of designing the best interceptor and multi-role aircraft the world had seen to that date! Jim Chamberlin was relieved of his duties as Manager Project Gemini and became the Senior Engineering Advisor to the Director MSC, Dr. Gilruth himself. As such he became an important behind-the-scenes guiding hand for the Apollo program. However as the NASA article "On the Shoulders of Titans" proclaims:

> But perhaps, in a deeper sense, Chamberlin can be seen as a victim of the way Gemini was created and funded. Approved as something of an afterthought on the American manned space flight program, absent from NASA long-range budget plans, Gemini began on shaky finances.
>
> When Chamberlin left Gemini, an era ended. In the large and complex undertakings of modern high technology, one person can seldom be credited with so large a share in the shaping of a project as Chamberlin deserved for Gemini. Much of the ultimate success of the project had its roots in Chamberlin's brilliance as a designer and engineer.

After an instrumented flight and another with Sam and Miss Sam (two Rhesis monkeys), Gus Grissom and John Young lifted off on the Gemini III mission at the tip of the mighty Titan II on March 23rd, 1965. Orbital altitude was varied using spacecraft thrust under pilot control from about 110 miles to 73 miles in 3 orbits.

The June 3rd-7th 1965 Gemini mission of James A. McDivitt and Edward H. White II accomplished still more objectives. It included the first extravehicular activity (EVA) by a Westerner; White's "space walk" being a 22-minute EVA exercise.

Gemini VIII March 16th 1966, commanded by Neil A. Armstrong with an assist from David R. Scott accomplished the first docking with another space vehicle, an unmanned Lockheed Agena booster stage, adapted for the mission. This was an important step towards putting a man on another celestial body, the moon. This Gemini flight lasted 10 hours, 41 minutes and was marred by a short in the flight control system. This malfunction caused uncontrollable spinning of the craft with divergence increasing in both yaw and roll. The crew undocked and effected the first emergency landing of a manned US space mission.

Gemini X of July 18-21, 1966 was commanded by John W. Young with Michael Collins being his co-pilot. This mission, of 2 days 22 hours' duration not only accomplished docking of the Gemini spacecraft with the Agena booster, but included use of the Agena target vehicle's propulsion systems. The spacecraft also rendezvoused with Gemini VIII which was still in orbit. Collins had 49 minutes of EVA standing in the hatch and 39 minutes of EVA to retrieve an experiment from the Agena stage. In all, 43 orbits were completed in this most ambitious, and successful mission.

Jim Chamberlin and everyone else involved at NASA had proven many technologies and techniques and had made such a multi-aspect mission seem almost routine. Project Gemini, which began later than Apollo and had to finish sooner, was judged a magnificent success, in the end completing many more objectives than the five (minus references to the moon in Chamberlin's sixth objective) originally outlined for the program.

As NASA Director Webb put it before Gemini flew, Gemini had "what I would characterize as the potential for the first workhorse of the Western space world in very much the same way that the DC-3 airplane became a great workhorse of aviation for many, many purposes."

That passage sounds hauntingly similar to one used to describe another craft some of the Canadians at NASA had worked on, the Avro Canada C-102 Jetliner.

Bob Lindley, so deeply involved in the Gemini spacecraft design at McDonnell Douglas, later joined NASA on the Shuttle project, this time working with North American-Rockwell and a myriad of others. Lindley became the Director of Project Management at NASA's Goddard Space Flight Center and still later went to the European Space Agency as a consultant on the "Spacelab" project. His work overseeing Goddard's radical concepts certainly put him in the driver's seat for a number of amazing research ventures!

John Hodge, Fred Matthews and Tec Roberts were crucial to the mission control aspects of Mercury with Hodge being very highly placed within the Space Task Group. Hodge and Chris Kraft were flight controllers on Mercury with Fred Matthews being a back-up controller. Hodge and Kraft would do the honours for Apollo once Matthews left. Hodge and Roberts were key in the design of the Houston space center but Matthews did not want to move to Houston and left to join Mario Pesando at RCA. Owen Maynard was a major factor in the Apollo program with responsibilities for systems integration, especially regarding the lunar lander which was contracted to Grumman Aerospace. Carl Lindow, Arrow project manager, went to Boeing and was the Project Engineer on the Saturn S-1 and S-1B boosters. This involved him with Von Braun and his team. Lindow went on to become the development manager for Boeing's advanced space launch systems, their aerospace-plane concepts and nuclear propulsion work.

Mario Pesando, who had left Avro for RCA to lead their space technology development efforts, ended up working with Boeing on Von Braun's Saturn V boosters, one of which ultimately put a man on the moon.

Frank Brame, Chief of Technical Design on the Arrow served at Boeing for 27 years. He was supervisor of the 737 design studies and was the Chief Project Engineer on systems and avionics for Boeing's SST designs. Up to his retirement in 1988 he was Program Manager on Boeing's renewed SST efforts.

Another ex-Avroite who made a major contribution to the US space program was John Sandford. Born in England, Sandford joined Avro Canada after graduating from the Cranford Institute of Technology in 1957. After serving as an engineer on the Arrow program, Sandford joined the space division of North American/Rockwell in 1962. From *de Havilland, You STOL My Heart*: "One of his major achievements there was leading the winning proposal for the Nasa Space Shuttle Program. He was appointed president and chief executive officer of de Havilland in 1978. While there he oversaw direction of the company during the Dash 8 development and launch into service."

It was under Sandford's direction that the Dash 8 was conceived. His article in the de Havilland book points out the difficulties in producing what would become the best selling commuter aircraft in the world, due to political problems and doubters in the company and other agencies. In 1992 Sandford became managing director of the Rolls-Royce Aerospace Group.

(image by R.L. Whitcomb)

AS DETAILED ELSEWHERE IN THIS WORK, Avro Canada produced a number of jet passenger aircraft designs after the Jetliner flew in 1949. Some of these were very advanced using swept wings and podded engines, as the Boeing 707 would. It is generally not known that Avro was also conducting parametric studies to determine if a supersonic airliner could be engineered to be economically and technologically feasible. As a result Floyd, Chamberlin and others devised several SST designs optimized for slightly different route and economic niches. The painting at left shows what was perhaps the *first* credible SST design in the West.

Jim Floyd pointed out that this Avro Canada SST design was actually produced *for* Howard Hughes and TWA. In the book *Howard Hughes and TWA*, TWA's Chief Engineer and Mr. Hughes' technical advisor, Robert Rummel, acknowledges that the SST designs produced by Avro for TWA were the first credible SST designs he was aware of in the world. Rummel also noted that TWA acquisition of an Avro SST would depend on no further political interference such as was experienced with the Jetliner. Floyd also mentions Howard Hughes' technical and commercial interest in the Jetliner. Hughes was an excellent pilot and also had a strong technical mind. Floyd relates enduring a 13-hour nocturnal marathon at the Beverley Hills Hilton going over blueprints with Hughes. He was impressed and fascinated by the Jetliner, asking questions to determine the engineering rationale for Avro's most minute details.

Robert Rummel in *Howard Hughes and TWA* (Smithsonian Inst. Press, pg. 267):

> I never doubted that Jim Floyd and his team could have produced excellent jet transports well tailored to satisfy TWA's operational requirements, notwithstanding the shadow of possible government interference cast by Minister C.D. Howe's untoward actions in the Jetliner affair. The design of AVRO's Jetliner was superb, and given the freedom to perform, comparable results seemed likely.
>
> During 1958-59, Jim Floyd proposed several supersonic transports for TWA's transatlantic operations—as far as I know, the first supersonic proposal by a responsible, major manufacturer. The first was designed to operate at 900 mph supersonic speeds, the final one was an attractive, extremely sleek, 1,200 mph jet with a double-ogee wing plan-form. It would have been years ahead of anything else.

CHAPTER THIRTEEN

The SST Saga

Canadian Contributions Exposed

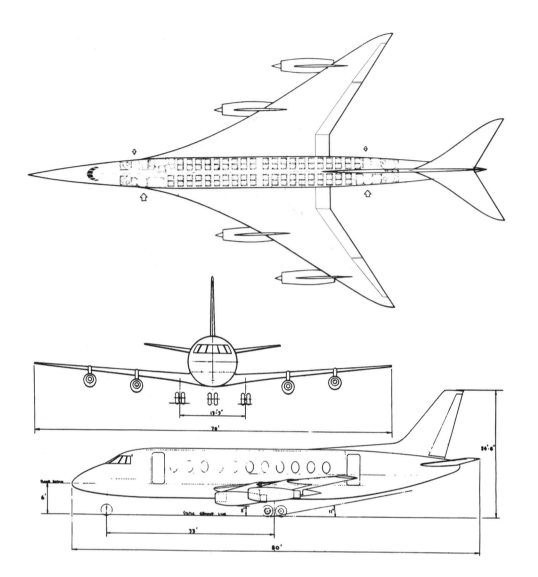

Avro's "Configuration 6" in their SST discussions with TWA.
(courtesy Jim Floyd)

Avro's proposed swept-wing Jetliner development of 1956. SSTs came later.
(courtesy Jim Floyd)

Jim Chamberlin (in the Initial Projects Office) and others in Mario Pesando's Project Research Group (both reporting to Floyd) and had been undertaking continuing parametric studies, exploring configurations over a wide variety of stage lengths, altitude considerations and maximum supersonic cruise speed, analyzing them against various market models. Avro's leadership in supersonics and SST design did not go unnoticed by the rest of the western aviation fraternity and related parties. Floyd for one, had been discussing supersonic technologies regularly with RAeE, the Hawker Siddeley Design Council and British ministry officials.

Crawford Gordon Jr. was found in the office of "Sir Dobbie" just after the Arrow cancellation when he placed a call to Jim Floyd. Dobson and Hawker Siddeley Aviation's (HSA's) Technical Director, Stuart Davies, wanted Floyd on the earliest available plane to discuss the possibility of his

leading Hawker Siddeley Aviation's most prestigious design effort; to produce a winning design for the British SST competition. Floyd refused to go over right away since he was in the US trying to "loan" his top engineers and his loyalties remained with them until the future of Avro was decided. He and others were also somewhat suspicious that the whole SST project could be another political disaster in the making and never get off the ground. Davies reassured Floyd in a personal letter in which he gave the effort a better than 50/50 chance of production if the design was good and Hawker Siddeley behaved as a fully integrated company to satisfy the "establishment."

Davies also pointed out that Floyd would occupy the most important and prestigious position in the rapidly integrating Hawker Siddeley Aviation concern and be entrusted with their most important project. It was something akin to his "dream" job, that of being recognized in the ranks of the "Chief Designers" such as Sir Sydney Camm. Of course in those harried days Floyd and most senior engineers and managers from Avro Canada were being bombarded by lucrative offers from the United States as well. While in the US "loaning" his talent, and after he returned, Floyd had many lucrative offers pour in from American firms but in the end chose to remain with the Hawker Siddeley Group and some of the people he had worked with throughout his already considerable career. He was going to lead a hand-picked team of talent from within the Hawker Siddeley Group and they would produce the first industry-sponsored SST designs in Britain. Once he returned from placing a great many Avro engineers into positions in the US, in hopes of retrieving them if Diefenbaker relented, Floyd then immediately flew to England to take over Hawker Siddeley Aviation's Advanced Projects Group and the design of the Group's entry into the British SST competition.

British studies into supersonic travel had been ongoing at STAC and within the government research establishments since 1956 and nothing had been presented by a British manufacturer by mid 1959. Indeed at the time that Avro was submitting their SST design studies to Rummell and TWA, Convair in the United States was proposing an SST version of their B-58 Hustler bomber! This interesting aircraft development plan depended on USAF acceptance of a stretched B-58 with a front canard but utilising a modified fuselage. Phase two of the transformation called for new main wings which would have had upper and lower tip-fins at about a 45-degree angle making the wing appear like a sideways "Y". Propulsion was to be an advanced engine such as the J-58 for the SR-71 although Convair took an interest in the Iroquois as well. In the end, this two-step process would have produced an almost entirely new aircraft. It was an interesting way to try to get an SST of small capacity and dubious economics into existence.

At the time there was a major competition developing between Britain and the United States over who would deploy the first SST aircraft. Studies had shown the market was relatively small, therefore the first company or nation to build one that was reasonably economical would likely sweep the field. After so many disasters in Britain, and the change of heart regarding industrial nationalism taken by the likes of Duncan Sandys, Britain steeled herself and set out to produce the first SST. The arrival of the Avro boys, doubtless with voluminous data from the Arrow project and

their own SST studies in hand, provided a real kick-start to Britain's SST effort after Avro was destroyed in February of 1959. As Jim Floyd pointed out in a 1990 paper:

> I know that the small team that went with me to the Advanced Projects Group in the UK were highly respected and acknowledged to be among 'the best in the business.'
>
> Five of the senior ex-Avro Canada engineers who had worked with me on the Arrow were in the group, John McCulloch, who had been our UK liaison man on the Arrow, was brought in as chief of administration, Pat McKenzie, structural engineer on the Arrow as our chief of structural design, Colin Marshall, systems designer on the Arrow, was chief of systems design at APG, Ken Cooke, landing gear specialist on the Arrow was put in charge of landing gear design at APG, and Joe Farbridge, also an engineer on the Arrow, was in our tactical analysis team in APG. John Morris, who had been chief of performance on the Arrow, later joined APG in the same capacity.

Peter Sutcliffe was Jim Floyd's deputy at the APG however and had formerly been Avro Manchester's chief aerodynamicist. They all reported to Stuart Davies, the same man that had persuaded Jim Floyd to go to Canada for the Jetliner program and who had persuaded him to come back from Canada as well. But then, they had both worked together back on the Lancaster project and at the Yeadon "think tank" and they held one another in high regard.

The HSA.1000:
Hawker Siddeley Aviation's SST

Originally Hawker Siddeley Aviation had hoped to design to Mach 3 since they understood that Kelly Johnson's "Skunk Works" was working to this specification. The powers at Britain's Supersonic Transport Aircraft Committee or STAC, had settled on a cruise speed requirement for the SST of only Mach 2.2. Perhaps this is as good a sign as any that they were desperate to beat the United States in this field after so many unhappy collaborative ventures. They knew from many sources, the Arrow project included, that Mach 2.2 was achievable with a light-alloy aircraft. The STAC officials felt that many time consuming materials and fabricating headaches would be avoided by this decision.

Jim Floyd's team at HSA's Advanced Products Group produced an extremely advanced aerodynamic and structural design allowing for a Mach 2.2 conventional light-alloy supersonic transport designated the HSA.1000. The

The stunning HSA.1000 supersonic transport design produced by Jim Floyd's Advanced Projects Group at Hawker Siddeley in the UK. It was submitted in December of 1959, only ten months after Black Friday. It featured an integrated or blended wing and fuselage. Mach 2.2 and Mach 2.7 versions were proposed, as were military versions.   (image by R.L. Whitcomb)

knowledge and technology behind this stunning aircraft was based very much on Avro Canada's successful materials and production technology developed for the Arrow program with Arrow flight test validating much of the engineering and aerodynamics. The Royal Aeronautical Establishment had been consulting with many leaders in the aerospace field on the SST during the 1950s in cooperation with STAC and the British manufacturers and had also discussed it at length on more than one occasion with Jim Floyd well before Black Friday. He had been in discussions and exchanges as Avro's engineering representative with the Hawker Siddeley Design Council, with Nicholson at the RAE, and many other British experts on the thinking relating to SSTs, for years by this time.

The basic aerodynamic shape was one of three that had been evolving at Nicholson's RAE for some time. One of these RAF concepts was an interesting M-shaped wing design. Another was a delta "slenderbody" and the third was a gothic-canard-delta that, from the theories expounded in this work, would have been a poor wing design with serious pitch-up and longitudinal stability problems. The APG team decided the slenderbody was the best approach and STAC expected them to demonstrate how it could be engineered. In keeping with Floyd's flair for producing designs that were expandable and adapt-

able, the basic HSA SST structural design was modified to allow a cruise speed of Mach 2.7 and was co-submitted with the Mach 2.2 cruiser. The most important re-engineering was simply in materials substitution with the light-alloy structure of the Mach 2.2 vehicle being replaced by high temperature and strength steel alloys for much of the Mach 2.7 aircraft. Again, the same approach to the same problem as the later Arrow development proposals. A secret military version of the HSA.1000 was also proposed.

This incredible design used a blended fuselage and wing arrangement that, apart from the fin and engines, would have been an ideal stealth shape! It was also an almost perfect hypersonic shape. The passenger compartment was unusual in that it had no windows, this being due to the blended shape and the necessity to put tunnels through the structure for windows in such a design. This un-encumbered structure would mean modification into a supersonic long-range weapons carrier would have been relatively easy. Some attention to stealth would have made it an extremely potent weapon. As a passenger carrier it had strong advantages as well. Boeing and McDonnell Douglas, before their merger, were proposing blended wing subsonic airliners, pointing out their something like 25 percent better efficiency. HSA's shape was

Hawker Siddeley Aviation
HSA.1000 Supersonic Transport
circa December 1959

image by R.L. Whitcomb)

just about ideal for high lift and low drag at high super-sonic velocities meaning that by weight and volume it would have been the most efficient shape for this kind of service, all other things being equal. Television screens were proposed to give the passenger a selection of views and functions that they could never experience at that altitude through conventional side-windows. Some were unable to see the advantages however and the lack of windows seemed to be a "show stopper" for some of the most conservative people involved at the influence level.

Some of the other conservatives at this level of influence were also showing more and more concern over the sonic boom and peoples' reaction to it. At the very beginning of the design work by the Hawker Siddeley Advanced Projects Group on the HSA SST a report was produced showing the sonic-boom theory that everyone had been designing to was wrong. This was produced by John Morris (formerly of Avro Canada) and pointed out that about half the sonic-boom's intensity at cruise altitude for SSTs was due to lift production, with the other (recognized) half being from shape and size. Morris' work proved that the industry and government had underestimated the intensity of the sonic boom by about half at 50-60,000 feet. The Advanced Projects Group at HSA saw this as a factor that would very probably limit SST operations to over-ocean routes and responded accordingly. This group also had plenty of experience in the area of computational fluid dynamics and knew that the way the shockwave was shaped and its intensity could be changed, and the onset delayed, through thoughtful design.

In keeping with the typical political intrusions, the STAC decided in September of 1959 that Hawker Siddeley and Bristol should do joint feasibility studies on the SST specification, for their Mach 2.2 cruiser. Hawker Siddeley ended up agreeing to concentrate on their "integrated" or blended design similar to the concept the RAE had proposed while Bristol would pursue more detailed study of the gothic-delta wing configuration. This aircraft was a high-wing delta with a tube fuselage with six afterburning turbojets in a single nacelle installation on top of the wing. From appearance at least, the Bristol design seemed to be designed more along a "blade element" kind of process, as opposed to a three-dimensional, computational fluid-dynamics way of thinking.

In keeping with whatever forces were guiding the establishment, Bristol (now BAC) was awarded the aircraft development contract and Hawker Siddeley Aviation received cancellation notices. This was at odds with Stuart Davies' logical belief that since English Electric (then forming BAC with Bristol, Blackburn, Vickers and others) had gotten the TSR.2 development while Hawker Siddeley got nothing but cancellation notices, that they should have been able to win the SST contract if they produced a good design. As to whether it was a good design or not, one only has to look at the differences between the Bristol SST design, then the HSA-SST and finally the Concorde actual configuration to discover which was the most promising concept. Either by design or default the HSA conglomerate was weakened to the point where, in 1977, BAC and HSA would merge forming British Aerospace. It really seems from examination of the facts that there was no problem with Hawker Siddeley's engineering ability. As for corporate management it could be argued that Hawker Siddeley had come by its integration options the honest way, they had succeeded in forming alliances with companies and were making the best from the individual parts. BAC would

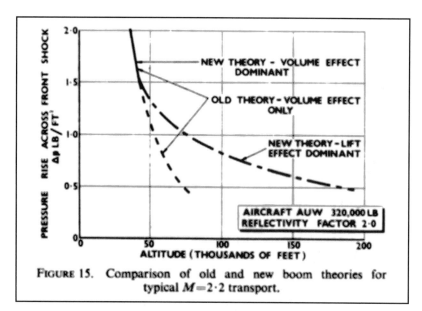

FIGURE 15. Comparison of old and new boom theories for typical $M=2\cdot2$ transport.

This graph, from the September 1961 *Journal of the Royal Aeronautical Society*, demonstrates Britain's defective shock strength theoretical assumptions, based on the work of John Morris. It was part of Jim Floyd's Sixth Chadwick Memorial Lecture titled "Some Current Problems Facing the Aircraft Designer." This paper would later be included in the of the First International Conference on Hypersonic Flight in the 21st Century, held at the University of North Dakota, September 20-23, 1988. Jim Floyd was the guest of honour.

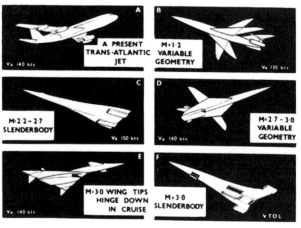

FIGURE 31. Some possible supersonic transport configurations.

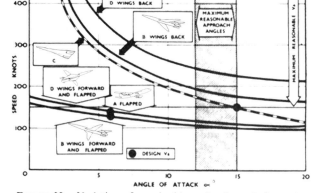

FIGURE 32. Variation of speed with angle of attack for various transport configurations.

The above diagrams, also from Floyd's 1961 RAeS lecture, show the differences in aircraft alpha corresponding to different configurations, and the impact on approach speed. The alpha consideration was important both for pilot visibility on landing, and the intensity of the sonic-boom reaching the ground. It is also an important consideration for supersonic drag. This document noted that a Mach 1.2 variable-geometry aircraft could cruise supersonically without creating a boom. In March 1962 Floyd was awarded the George Taylor (Australia) Gold Medal for "the most valuable paper on Aircraft Design, Manufacture, or Operation," for this lecture. (Journal of the RaeS)

be formed by force of British government will. Whether the people of Britain, the Commonwealth or the world were served or not is open to interpretation.

In an effort to hedge their bets, once Hawker Siddeley was cut out of the development, the British establishment approached first the US then Germany and France to see if they'd join the development effort. France eventually joined after the US refused and Germany seemed largely disinterested. By this time De Gaulle was very concerned about American "colonization" of the skies through a monopoly on airliner production brought about by sales of the Boeing 707.

HSA's Sir Sydney Camm and Bristol's Sir Stanley Hooker would put their heads together to develop a VSTOL (Vertical/Short Take-Off and Landing) aircraft/engine concept. (Bristol's engine side merged with Armstrong Siddeley engines when Bristol aircraft joined BAC.) Hawker Siddeley would gain the phenomenally successful Harrier VSTOL aircraft from their genius not too long afterward. Bristol-Siddeley engines not long after merged with Rolls-Royce. Considering the Harrier's specification was nearly created from the success of the aircraft, one might again say HSA got their rewards the hard way, through effort and ability.

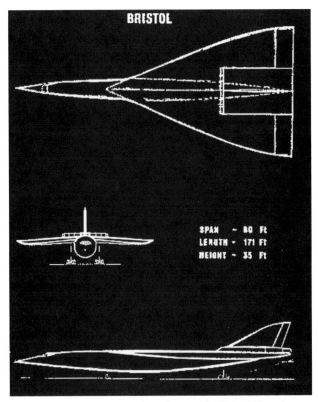

SPAN ~ 80 Ft
LENGTH ~ 171 Ft
HEIGHT ~ 35 Ft

Bristol's SST design was selected over the HSA.1000 and was based on the gothic-delta wing. The Concorde however, is what was actually built.   (via Jim Floyd)

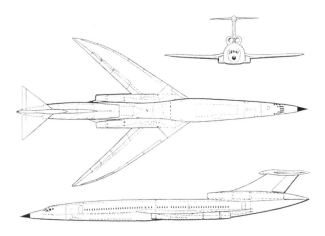

The Hawker Siddeley Aviation Type 1011, a swing-wing supersonic airliner that was designed to travel at Mach 1.15 to 1.2 without creating a sonic boom. Top speed was Mach 1.8 for the military version and about Mach 1.4 for airline economics on the civil variant. The Rockwell (after merging with North American in 1967) B-1B seems to make good use of the theory behind the HSA.1011 and is currently limited to Mach 1.25 at altitude and a sustained Mach .99 on the deck. Boeing appears to have first proposed a transonic airliner around 1971 and is working on their Sonic Cruiser. Some experts expect the configuration of the Sonic Cruiser to change dramatically from that of the first released images due to a predicted yaw-roll coupling problem.   (courtesy Jim Floyd)

By the time of the joint HSA-Bristol SST submission, the French had been exploring a shape using a tube-fuselage and a low, ogival, delta-wing arrangement broadly similar to the HSA-SST and had termed it the "Super Caravelle". In the author's opinion the main differences between the "Super Caravelle", Concorde and HSA-SST was the amount of blending of the wing and fuselage. Concorde is, arguably, more like the HSA.1000 than it is the design that won Bristol (and BAC) the contract.

The HSA.1011 "No-Boom" Airliner

The HSA-APG produced an interesting design for a transonic long-range airliner that would operate at Mach 1.15 to Mach 1.2 without producing a sonic boom when travelling in the stratosphere. This is about 25 percent faster than the 747 which appeared later and which is today still the fastest subsonic jet passenger plane of large capacity. The 747 actually achieves its high cruise speed through better Sears-Haack body conformance by incorporating the upper deck "bulge," something the fuselage shape of the HSA.1011 did in a more sophisticated manner. Meanwhile the only aircraft deployed using the concept of the swing-wing with a well-area-ruled fuselage is the Rockwell B-1 bomber, which hit the drawing boards not too long after the HSA.1011 was proposed. The XB-70 Valkyrie, by the same company, was well along in development by this time but would never be adopted into service. North American also proposed an SST version of the XB-70.

As time would prove, the eventual Concorde design was restricted from operating supersonically over land due to the sonic boom and would have been accepted at few airports due to engine noise on take-off! Jim Floyd and Hawkers had, in reality, anticipated the major cause of the commercial failure of Concorde and provided a solution before Concorde was even designed. This aircraft, the HSA.1011 and a military weapons carrier version of it, were detailed in APG report 1011/104 of June 1961. From the chronology, one can see that once again Floyd and those around him were far out in front and had anticipated the most serious problems for SSTs and designed solutions to them even before the other experts were forced to acknowledge those problems after the fact. Not that Hawker Siddeley Group's experts hadn't tried to warn them: Floyd's Roy Chadwick Memorial Lecture to the RAeS in 1961, titled "Some Current Problems Facing the Aircraft Designer" described these problems precisely.

Artist's impression of the HSA.1011 "no-boom" airliner.   (image by R.L. Whitcomb)

Recently Boeing announced that they had given up on the SST concept, after many attempts, and were concentrating on a blended-wing airliner, and a sonic cruiser. One could say that Jim Floyd and the Hawker Siddeley Aviation APG members can finally feel vindicated with the HSA.1011. Boeing's design is to cruise at "Mach .95 and faster" according to the company which means it is a transonic airliner identical in concept and intent to the HSA.1011. It too relies on very careful application of volume theory (and shock-wave dissipation before it reaches the ground) to allow the aircraft to cruise at or slightly above the speed of sound without creating a sonic boom. From appearances at least this Boeing aircraft appears to offer a lower maximum "no-boom" speed due to poorer Sears-Haack body conformance. The design however is far from completely finalized. If or when it does fly somewhere between 2007 and 2010, it will achieve what the HSA.1011 was slated to do by 1967.

With the award to Bristol's (then BAC) and Sud Aviation in France of the SST development contract, Hawker Siddeley was again left in the cold, and arguably not because their designs were deficient. In terms of government business Hawker Siddeley seemed to have been passed over again, and by the time this switch was in the

works Jim Floyd had already left the company in apparent distaste and in poor health. To have three world-beating designs cancelled was quite enough and the effort and disappointments had taken their toll. His intuition, as evidenced by a dubious letter to Stuart Davies before he took on the HSA-SST design task, was proven correct once again. After the HSA-SST cancellation some of the Advanced Projects Group talents ended up, like their Avro Canada counterparts, employed in the United States. Jim Floyd decided he'd had enough of the big aviation concerns with their obvious vulnerability to political "swings and arrows" as he termed it and started his own firm. While in charge of J.C. Floyd and Associates, Floyd would do in-depth studies into the economics and sonic-boom effects of Concorde. A variable-pitch turbofan engine developed with Dowty-Rotol resulted in a very attractive business jet design that emerged under Floyd's pen. Many other diverse and interesting projects kept this gentleman busy, and at 87 years of age Floyd is still contributing his talents.

Peter Sutcliffe went to Boeing in charge of new product development, a position of monumental responsibility, putting him front and center with Boeing's later SST efforts. John Morris went to Douglas and became a senior company executive on the DC-10 jumbo-jet. Joe Farbridge went to join the ex-Avroites at NASA while Ken Cooke would go to McDonnell Douglas and Colin Marshall ended up at North American-Rockwell. This seemed to be about the time the American SST program really began to gather steam, about three years behind the British as history would prove, and perhaps about five years behind Avro Canada. North American-Rockwell were also into parametric studies for a re-usable space shuttle.

Today the US is still trying to produce an effective airframe shape and materials technology to make the SST profitable and environmentally acceptable. Perhaps we shall see the basic HSA-SST fuselage design again, when it is decided to build a hypersonic passenger transport or a next-generation supersonic bomber. In fact NASA released photos of a Mach 5 transport in the mid 1980s that is very similar to the HSA.1000 except it has two fins and the engines are concentrated in a single central installation on the underside. The evidence of a similar application of hypersonic theory is also apparent on the Aurora spyplane, real or otherwise.

Considering how Avro was generating concepts and products that were decades ahead of what was going on elsewhere, it is no wonder US manufacturers were covetous of Avro engineers. Until Avro closed, the US was being beaten badly in the Space Race by the Soviets. Jim Chamberlin, Arrow aerodynamicist and the brains behind the advanced Arrows and Avro Canada's SSTs, became program manager for the Gemini program and was in a similar position throughout Apollo once he left Avro. Some 30 other Avro brains went to NASA with Chamberlin, most taking management or supervisory

positions. One hundred ex-Avro engineers were taken up by North American Rockwell which produced some extremely high-tech products including the Space Shuttle and B-1B. North American also produced a vast array of space hardware, and were the prime contractor for Apollo.

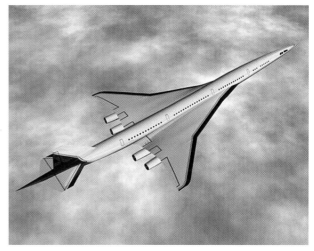

A resurgent Boeing-McDonnell Douglas SST design of the 1990s. Once Boeing acquired McDonnell-Douglas their studies again concluded the economics were just not worth the risk. An integrated design such as that produced by HSA by December 1959 still seems like a more viable design as does the ogival wing rather than the cranked arrow wings of this design and the older Douglas and Lockheed concepts.   (NASA Langley)

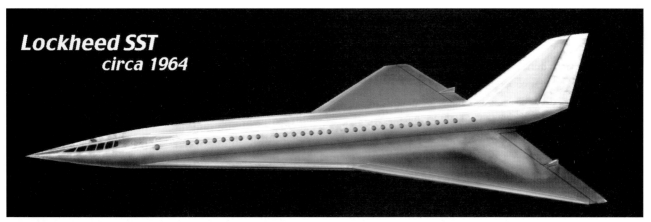

Considering the wide variety of SST configurations released by Douglas, Lockheed North American Aviation, Convair/General Dynamics, NASA and Boeing for their SSTs over the years, one could wonder how serious they really were about the concept in 1959. (image by R.L. Whitcomb)

Epilogue

The Cold War was a perplexing time with more than its share of heroes and villains. It has become clear to the author that it is difficult to remain unemotional about some of the characters and episodes of those times. Some of the questions of governance, hinted at in the text, came as a complete shock during research. In fact, probably 30 percent of the research undertaken for this book has not been included in it. This research involved investigation of the influence of corporate and financial empires on governments. From this a limited view of the sponsors of various political and diplomatic movements, coupled with an investigation of the origins and influences on the major intelligence services and their impact was undertaken.

In view of these factors, aviation has always been a hotbed of intrigue, involving all of the advanced sciences, the military, corporate world, politics and diplomacy. As this work has certainly suggested, there is no end of controversial tales in our aerospace history, which transcend even the Cold War period. A.V. Roe was present almost from the very beginning of aviation.

Postwar, several scandals of note come to mind: the Lockheed scandal warned the public of what could go on in the world of corporate affairs; Israel circumvented de Gaulle's trade embargo that had stopped delivery of Mirage III fighters and acquired the ability to build their own through espionage; Grumman was accused of offering bribes to the Shah's Iran for their decision to acquire a squadron of F-14A Tomcats; the TSR.2 and HS.1154 cancellations created their own heat while the F-111 program did the same; and the promising Israeli Lavi canard-delta fighter was cancelled, apparently in line with US wishes, US support payments being an important subtext.

It has also been suggested that the possibility of weapons system developments, at least those originating outside the USA, was deliberately curtailed.

While this strategy may have been designed to prevent arms proliferation, it also had an impact in reducing nationalism outside the USA, and in strengthening the American industrial base. Arguably, this would make the leading power stronger in face of the Soviet challenge. It would also concentrate economic power in fewer hands, while stifling technological progress, and diplomatic and economic independence, of the other nations.

It was disturbing to find that certain players recurrently appeared at crucial points in the history of the Cold War, as has been shown in this book. Furthermore it has become clear that much of the conventional history of the era was created by the intelligence services. The impact of this on the course of political events is widely demonstrated, as in Sir William Stevenson's book where Intrepid himself declares that part of his reason for exposing the secret war conducted during World War II was to alert Western civilization to the dangers of the intelligence services being co-opted by a powerful private elite. (Foreword, *A Man Called Intrepid*)

Moreover, the question must be raised as to why, in Canada, we have never done an economic impact or other analysis of the consequences of the destruction of the Avro Arrow and Avro Aircraft. Perhaps that in itself demonstrates that there are those who just don't want some disturbing questions answered.

Definition of Terms

Note: No claims are made as to the technical accuracy of the following definitions and descriptions. How they are described here is merely a guide to the author's usage as expressed in this book.

GENERAL AVIATION AND AERODYNAMIC TERMS

ACT: Active Control Technology, where onboard sensors continually monitor external inputs such as gusts, turbulence or unstable conditions and issues corrective control inputs, these inputs resulting in control surface movement without the pilot seeing a corresponding change to his controls.

ACTIVE GUIDANCE: Where guidance of a stand-off device, usually a missile, is accomplished by a continually altered flight plan that is modified via data derived from on-board sensors on the weapon, independent of the launch aircraft. Sensor can be radar, optical imaging on any wavelength of the electro-magnetic spectrum (such as infra-red), sound etc. An Active Guidance Weapon is a "fire-and-forget" missile in military pilot jargon.

AIRFLOW: A stream of moving air or the appearance thereof around a body moving through still air. Vector direction of this flow is called the free-stream.

AoA, or ALPHA: The angle of attack of the wing or aircraft aerodynamic centerline. The angle measured between the free air stream (free-stream) and the aircraft mean chord line or aircraft aerodynamic centerline. Not to be confused with angle of incidence, which is the angular difference between the mean chord line and the aircraft fuselage aerodynamic centerline. Pitching the nose up increases AoA, or Alpha.

AREA RULE: The aerodynamic theory where the total volume progression from nose to tail of an aircraft is considered and modified to correspond to a smooth shape of specific profile for particular optimum cruise speeds. This theory is especially important for transonic drag and aircraft stability at transonic and supersonic speeds. Theory and application concepts usually credited to Dr. Richard Whitcomb of NACA-Langley circa 1953.

ASPECT RATIO: Ratio of the span of a wing to its chord. A high aspect ratio wing is slender and very wide, as on a glider and is known to have less induced drag than a low aspect ratio wing. Supersonic speeds add limitations and changes to this generalization.

BOOST-GLIDE: Aerospace vehicle with no main engine that is boosted to exo-atmospheric or orbital velocity before gliding back to earth.

BOUNDARY LAYER: Layer of relatively slow-moving and turbulent air that is drawn along with an aircraft due to viscosity adhesion on the skin. Thickness varies from nearly zero on the nose of an aircraft to several inches or more at the rear of an aircraft. Supersonic shock-waves can cause separation.

BOW WAVE: The main shock-wave proceeding from the front tip of a body at supersonic speed. Additional protrusions of sufficient volume generate additional shock-waves which generally should be kept within the Shock Cone behind and limited by the Bow Wave.

CENTER OF GRAVITY: The point on a body where vector of weight and mass effects is centered. The center of pressure is normally designed to be located close to, but slightly behind, the center of gravity on a positively stable (in pitch), aircraft.

CENTER OF PRESSURE: Also known as Center of Lift, it is the point on an aircraft where the aerodynamic lifting forces, provided by the main wing, are located. This point moves aft at supersonic speed on a body, which poses design challenges for the aircraft builder. Center of Pressure movement and rapid fluctuations in early designs caused many crashes and design headaches.

CONTROL EFFECTIVENESS: The ability of a control surface to effect a change in an aircraft's attitude on any axis (longitudinal=roll, lateral=pitch, vertical=yaw) at a given speed and configuration.

DELTA-WING: Triangular planform for a wing, i.e.: the wing is triangular-shaped when looking down on the aircraft.

DRAG: Sum vector total of all aerodynamic forces resisting an aircraft's movement through the air, usually expressed in pounds. Overcome by thrust.

DYNAMIC STABILITY: Tendency of a body to move about any axis in response to an oscillatory (wave) motion. An oscillatory motion (such as a gust causing a pitch up, followed by a pitch down due to positive static stability about that axis) can continue indefinitely in a neutrally dynamically stable aircraft. With negative dynamic stability about that axis, the oscillations would grow causing loss of control and/or structural failure... unless compensated for by Active Control Technology (ACT) or the pilot.

FLY-BY-WIRE (FBW): Pilot inputs to affect the flight performance are electrical signals rather than mechanical and/or hydraulic. An electronic flight control computer converts those electrical inputs into hydraulic actuation to physically move the flight control surfaces.

HOT-SOAKING: The effect of travelling at high supersonic speed for extended periods where a large proportion of the aircraft approaches the leading edge kinetic heating temperature from skin friction. The maximum leading edge kinetic heating temperature is also known as stagnation temperature.

HYPERSONIC: The body of aerodynamic theory and application relating to speeds of around 5 times the speed of sound in air. Hypersonic aerodynamic effects begin to appear around Mach 3.

HYPERVELOCITY: The speed range after hypersonic velocity, i.e.; 12 times the speed of sound in air or faster. Generally achievable only at sub-orbital altitudes and in space.

KINETIC HEATING: Effect of air molecules creating heat as they slide over a surface, and each other, between near-zero velocity (stagnation) at the leading edges of a craft and the free-stream airflow. Has long been a limiting factor for supersonic and hypersonic flight.

L/D RATIO: The ratio of total lift to total drag for an aircraft or aerospace-plane at a given performance state. L/D ratio normally drops on a given body at supersonic speed.

LEX: Leading Edge Extension. An extension added to some portion of the wing leading edge to control airflow effects over the wing. (Eg. the saw-tooth on the F-8, F-4 and CF-105.)

MACH NUMBER: Speed relative to the local speed of sound (varies with altitude) expressed as a ratio in decimal form: Mach .5 is half the speed of sound.

MAGNETO-HYDRODYNAMICS (MHD): The branch of science dealing with the tendency of an ionized gas to move under an electrical or magnetic field; has applications in anti-gravitics, aerodynamics, propulsion, material cutting, fabricating and other areas.

NORMAL SHOCK: Shockwave perpendicular (at 90 degrees) to direction of travel of a body at exactly Mach 1. Not present at subsonic speeds and becomes an Oblique Shock at speeds above Mach 1. Airflow behind a Normal Shock is subsonic.

PITCH: Angle of Attack, AoA or Alpha. Elevators, canards, elevons etc. are used to modify an aircraft's Alpha.

PITCH RATE: The manoeuvrability of a craft in terms of how many degrees per second it can change its alpha.

PLASMA: Superheated, ionized (usually by electrical arc) gas. Can be induced to move under electrical or magnetic influence.

RADAR: Radio Detection And Ranging, where a radio signal is generated and transmitted and a radio receiver of particular design listens for an echo of that signal being reflected off an object. Used with great effect by the British in the Battle of Britain to detect attacking Luftwaffe aircraft. The basis of weather detection and aircraft detection, tracking and guidance. Similar microwave generators are used to cook food.

ROLL RATE: The rate, expressed in degrees per second, at which an aircraft can rotate about its longitudinal (fore-aft) axis. Ailerons are used induce and stop roll and make corrections about the longitudinal axis.

RE-ENTRY: Return flight from space or orbit or sub-orbit. Usually associated with extreme kinetic heating although this varies in intensity with the L/D ratio of a body.

SEMI-ACTIVE GUIDANCE: Usually defined in relation to a radar-guided stand-off device such as an air-to-air missile. Guidance or aiming of weapon is altered in its flight by a signal received from the launching aircraft. Can be applied to all, or a portion of a weapon's flight.

STATIC STABILITY: Tendency of a body to move about any axis in response to a disturbance on any axis. Positive longitudinal static stability means an aircraft will return to its previous alpha after being disturbed by a minor gust, turbulence etc. Negative longitudinal stability means an aircraft, if caused to pitch up or down by a gust or turbulence, will continue to pitch up or down at an increasing rate. Neutral longitudinal static stability means an aircraft, when caused to pitch, will continue to pitch at the same rate. The same definitions are applied to tendencies about the yaw and roll axis, although positive yaw stability is normally sought through aerodynamic or electronic means.

SEMI-SPAN: Distance from aircraft centerline to a wingtip.

SHOCK WAVE: The region of compressed air reflected from a body at supersonic speed. Airflow in this region is compressing, behind this region it is expanding. When fully developed at speeds above Mach 1 there are two waves emanating from the body of the vehicle, a compression and an expansion wave, which join some distance from the vehicle. If this wave does not dissipate before reaching the ground, a large pressure disturbance is created which is known as the "sonic boom."

SLENDER DELTA: Delta of low aspect ratio where the root length (cord) is greater than the semi-span.

STAND OFF DISTANCE OR RANGE: The distance that a launch aircraft can be separated from a target due to the additional range of a weapon or surveillance device. Subsonic or supersonic cruise missiles, air-to-air missiles or glide bombs are Stand Off Weapons.

STRATOSPHERE: Region of altitudes above the Troposphere and below the Ionosphere, up to approximately 80,000 feet. Temperatures are relatively constant with altitude while oxygen content drops quickly as altitude increases.

T/C: The Thickness to Chord ratio. Structural thickness of a wing at its maximum camber (thickness point) to the fore-aft length of a wing. A wing with a low T/C ratio will appear very thin from the front. Wings with high T/C ratios are unsuitable for high supersonic and hypersonic speeds.

THRUST: The reactive force of a fluid jet against its containing medium.

TRAPEZOIDAL-WING: A wing design with a generally rectangular, un-swept planform. Can have a high aspect ratio (as on a glider) or a low one as on a supersonic fighter like the F-104 Starfighter.

TRANSONIC: The region of speed between about Mach .8 and 1.2 where there is subsonic and supersonic flow on the same body. Can result in changes in vehicle stability and trim. Difficulties understanding supersonic aerodynamics caused many problems for designers and pilots trying to accelerate a craft through this region to free-stream supersonic velocity.

TRIM: Aerodynamic term to describe how the control surfaces and aircraft are configured in pitch etc. for level flight at a particular speed.

TROPOSPHERE: The range in altitude from sea-level to approximately 36,000 feet where weather occurs. Temperatures progress linearly, decreasing with altitude. Piston engines are normally most efficient at the bottom of the troposphere while jet engines are most efficient at the top of it, right next to the Stratosphere.

VORTEX: A localized spiral of low-pressure, energized air caused by pressure effects around an aerodynamic shape.

YAW: A condition in flight, measured in degrees, where the longitudinal (fore-aft) axis of the aircraft is not parallel to the free-stream. Vertical stabilizers (fins) are used to provide stability and rudders are the control surface used to modify the yaw-angle.

PROPULSION TERMS

AFTERBURNER: Also known as augmentation or reheat, i.e.: augmented turbojet or turbofan with reheat. Extra fuel is injected into the exhaust efflux behind the power turbines of jet engines to produce extra thrust. Potential thrust gain is limited by the amount of oxygen in the stream, with hi-bypass or turbofan engines having higher potential augmentation ratios than pure turbojets.

AIR-BREATHING: An engine type that derives its oxidant from the atmosphere such as piston-engines, turbojets, ramjets, scramjets. Rockets and some variable-cycle engines operate for all or part of their flight using carried oxidant (eg. liquid oxygen) thus being non-airbreathing. Electrical propulsion (ion, electro-static, plasma-jet etc.) is non-air-breathing technology.

BLEED-AIR: High energy (speed, pressure and/or temperature) air removed from a stream either to provide mechanical force for turbine-driven generators, fuel pumps, hydraulic pumps, cooling air, oxygenated air for combustion, or additional mass flow for thrust. Usually derived from the compressor section of a turbojet engine; if so it can be a drain or boost to thrust depending on how it is used. Some engine compressors are designed to blow off a great quantity of additional compressor capacity at some speeds to reduce stress and heat at the inner core of the engine while providing cooling air for additional combustion, or for thrust augmentation at the nozzle by expansion out a suitable ramp. The Orenda PS-13 Iroquois and the Pratt & Whitney J-58 for the Blackbird are in this class of engine as are bypass turbojets like the General Electric F-404 for the F-18 Hornet.

BOOSTER: Engine or vehicle designed specifically to bring a vehicle or payload up to operating velocity. Examples include rockets used to hoist payloads into orbit, or turbojet powered craft to carry a ramjet powered vehicle up to ramjet light-off and subsequent separation velocity, i.e.; Germany's Sanger atmospheric launch vehicle.

CONVERGENT-DIVERGENT NOZZLE: The exhaust nozzle of a turbojet, turbofan, ramjet etc. where the air is accelerated to supersonic velocity at the convergent throat of the nozzle, then allowed to expand (and accelerate if supersonic) out the divergent exit cone or ramp of the nozzle. Increases thrust if controlled properly. Modern nozzles are fully variable for different speeds and thrust levels, afterburner operation etc.

DUCTED ROCKET: Also known as a Ram-Rocket. A rocket engine located within a ramjet duct where, once at sufficient speed, the compressed stream of oxygenated air in the ramjet duct is passed through the efflux of the rocket engine and burned with extra propellant to reduce oxidant storage requirements and provide additional thrust. Has a much better specific impulse than a pure rocket at speeds between about Mach 1.5 and hypersonic.

OXIDANT: That part of the chemical equation for a heat engine required to oxidize (burn) propellant to create heat, expansion and power. Can be derived from the airstream or carried within a craft. If chemical propulsion such as this is applied in space, oxidants must be carried on board the vehicle for a rocket engine. This creates structural, size, weight and other problems.

PISTON ENGINE: An engine that includes a plug which oscillates up and down inside a cylinder, translating expansion force from combustion into mechanical motion. Air is drawn into the cylinder as the plug (piston) moves down, the openings are closed and the crankshaft, attached to the piston via a connecting rod, forces the piston back up the cylinder compressing the air. Fuel contained in the air is ignited at the top of the piston's stroke and drives the piston down again, providing energy to run itself and for work. There are many types and configurations and they are capable of operating on several fuel types.

PLASMA-JET: A moving jet or stream of superheated ionized gas. Can be used to cut materials or for propulsion. Ionization techniques to ionize air in front of leading edges of craft have theoretical propulsive and kinetic-heating reduction potentials. These effects are under the area of Magneto-Hydrodynamic-Propulsion.

PROPELLANT: That part of the chemicals required for a heat engine that is oxidized in the combustion process for heat, expansion and power. May comprise over 1/2 an aircraft's take-off weight.

RAMJET: An aircraft engine relying on ram-effect at high speed to accomplish the compression (before burning) of air before fuel is added and ignited. Stream velocity through the combustion section is subsonic as on jet engines. Must be accelerated to light-off speed by some other force, such as gravity, rocket-boost, turbojet power, linear-induction motors etc.

RAM-ROCKET: See Ducted Rocket.

ROCKET: A simple vehicle that burns stored oxidant and stored propellant (fuel) in a chamber before expelling it out a convergent-divergent nozzle to produce thrust. Relatively efficient at any speed however air-breathing engines are more efficient in the Troposphere and Stratosphere at their design speeds.

SCRAMJET: Ramjet where combustion is accomplished with a stream-velocity that is supersonic, i.e.;Supersonic Combustion Ramjet. Efficient above Mach 6.

SPECIFIC FUEL CONSUMPTION (SFC): Measurement of propulsive efficiency expressed as pounds of fuel burned for pounds of thrust gained, over an hour's time, eg: the Bristol Olympus turbojet engine had an SFC of .75 lbt/lb/hr (three-quarters of a pound of fuel per pound of thrust per hour) without afterburner augmentation which was considered quite good.

SUPERCHARGING: Method of providing additional air for combustion in a piston engine using a mechanically-driven compressor. It could also be considered a mechanical "pre-compressor" since it augments the effect of the compression stroke of the engine.

TURBINE: Mechanical device used to derive mechanical force (rotary) from a fluid (liquid or gas) stream. In a turbine, or jet-engine expanding gases from combustion moving at high velocity encounter one or more turbine discs, rotating on a central shaft and with airfoil shaped curved blades, like fan blades, these derive aerodynamic lift from the exhaust stream and use it to drive another set of fan blades upstream of the combustors. These compressor discs (with similarly shaped blades to those of the power turbine and driven by the latter) draw air into the engine and each succeeding section of compressor blades increases the pressure, and thus temperature, of the air entering the combustors. Here it is mixed with fuel and ignited to expand out the jet-pipe and develop thrust. Excess energy taken from the turbine section to run the compressor section, plus generators, pumps and auxiliary turbines, or for cooling, reduce the speed and temperature of the gas exiting the nozzle and thus reduce thrust correspondingly. Afterburners, using a ring of injectors and flame-holders just behind the power turbine in a turbojet, "reheat" the stream and provide extra thrust, however this method of thrust augmentation is relatively inefficient in terms of fuel required, i.e.; they have a higher specific fuel consumption (SFC).

TURBOCHARGING: Using the energy (heat and velocity) remaining in the exhaust stream of a piston engine to supercharge the intake air. The exhaust is used to drive a turbine while a secondary compressor, usually centrifugal for the sake of complexity, pre-compresses the air before the compression stroke of a piston engine.

TURBOFAN: An air-breathing engine, similar to a turbojet, where a portion of the air drawn into the engine bypasses the combustors and is used for additional thrust. This by-pass air can also be burned in an afterburner for even more thrust gain. Efficient from zero up to approximately Mach 2.

TURBOJET: An air-breathing engine in which air is compressed by a rotating ribbed disc (in a centrifugal compressor type) or succeeding stages of fan blades (in an axial-flow compressor type) before being burned and expended past further fan (turbine) blades that drive the compressor stages. Compressor section, which takes power from the exhaust stream and thus can limit thrust, is used to compress more oxidant (the oxygen content in air) into a smaller space (the combustor) for burning with propellant (fuel) for stream expansion which creates thrust. Efficient from zero to about Mach 3.2 and operates on a number of oxidant/propellant combinations.

TURBO-RAMJET: An air-breathing engine consisting of a turbojet mounted within a ramjet duct. At slow speeds thrust is provided by the turbojet—with or without normal afterburner augmentation. At supersonic speeds the afterburner nozzles inject additional fuel as the ramjet duct pressures increase and inject fresh air into the afterburner stream for additional combustion and thrust. Variations are diverting ram-compressed air through the afterburner core or using separate ramjet-only combustors within the sealed, annular duct.

TURBOROCKET: A variable-cycle engine such as the RB.545 that operates as an air-breathing turbojet at slow speeds, changing to rocket propulsion at hypersonic speed for exo-atmospheric use.

VARIABLE-CYCLE ENGINE: An engine that operates as one type of engine for a portion of the vehicle's performance regime, and then changes to a different mode of operation for higher speed portions of its flight. Examples include turbo-ramjets, ducted-rockets, turbo-rockets etc.

Bibliography

Aerospace Plane Technology: Research and Development Efforts in Europe. Washington: United States General Accounting Office, 1991.

Baglow, Bob. *Canucks Unlimited: Royal Canadian Air Force CF-100 Squadrons and Aircraft, 1952-1963.* Ottawa: Canuck Publications, 1985.

Bingham, Victor. *Halifax — Second to None. The Handley Page Halifax.* Shrewsbury: Airlife Publishing Ltd., 1986.

Bowyer, Charles. *Supermarine Spitfire.* London: Bison Books, 1980.

Brooks, Courtney G., James M. Grimwood and Loyd S. Swenson Jr. *Chariots for Apollo: A History of Manned Lunar Spacecraft.* Washington: NASA Science and Technology Information Division, 1979.

Butler, Tony. *British Secret Projects, Jet Fighters Since 1950.* Specialty Publishers & Wholesalers, 2000.

Campagna, Palmiro. *Storms of Controversy: the Secret Avro Arrow Files Revealed.* Toronto: Stoddart Publishing Co. Ltd., 1992, 1997.

_____. *The UFO Files: The Canadian Connection Exposed.* Toronto: Stoddart Publishing Co. Ltd.,1997.

Corso, LCol (ret'd) Philip J. *The Day After Roswell.* Pocket Books, 1997.

Cuthbertson, Brian. *Canadian Military Independence in the Age of the Superpowers.* Toronto: Fitzhenry & Whiteside, 1977.

Deighton, Len. *Blood, Tears and Folly. An Objective Look at World War II.* 2nd Edition. London: Pimlico, 1995.

Dow, James. *The Arrow.* 2nd edition. Toronto: James Lorimer & Company, 1997.

Ethell, Jeffrey L, Robert Grinsell, Roger Freeman, David A. Anderton, Frederick A. Johnsen, Bill Sweetman, Alex Vanags-Baginskis and Robert C. Mikesh. *The Great Book of World War II Airplanes.* Tokyo: Zokeisha Publications Ltd., 1994.

Floyd, Jim. *The Avro Canada C-102 Jetliner.* Erin: Boston Mills Press, 1986.

Francillon, Rene. *Boeing 707: Pioneer Jetliner.* Osceola: Motorbooks International, 1999.

Goodspeed, D.J. *A History of the Defence Research Board of Canada.* Ottawa; Queen's Printer, 1958.

Gordon, Walter Lockhart. *A Choice For Canada.* Toronto: McClelland & Stewart Ltd., 1965.

_____. *A Political Memoir.* Toronto: McClelland & Stewart Ltd., 1977.

Griffin, Des. *Descent Into Slavery.* Emissary Publications, 1980.

Griffin, G. Edward. *The Creature From Jeckyll Island: A Second Look at the Federal Reserve.* 3rd Ed., American Media, 1998

Gunston, Bill, editor. *Chronicle of Aviation.* London: Chronicle Communications Ltd., 1992.

_____. *Faster Than Sound.* Somerset: Patrick Stephens Limited, 1992.

_____. *Stingers; The McDonnell Douglas F/A-18 Hornet.* New York: Mallard Press, 1990.

Hacker, Barton C., and James M. Grimwood. *On the Shoulders of Titans: A History of Project Gemini.* Washington: NASA Science and Technology Information Division, 1977.

Hallion, Richard. *On The Frontier.* [Part of NASA history series] Washington: US Government Printing Office, nd .

Hasek, John. *The Disarming of Canada.* Toronto: Key Porter Books, 1987.

Hastings, Stephen. *The Murder of TSR.2.* London: Macdonald & Co., 1966.

Keating and Pratt, *Canada, NATO and the Bomb.* Edmonton: Hurtig Publishing, 1988.

Kostenuk, Samuel, and John Griffin. *RCAF Squadron Histories and Aircraft 1924-1968.* Toronto: Hakkert & Company, 1977.

Milberry, Larry. *Aviation in Canada.* Toronto: McGraw-Hill Ryerson Ltd., 1979.

_____. *The Avro CF-100.* Toronto: CANAV Books, 1981.

_____. *The Canadair DC-4M North Star.* Toronto: CANAV Books, 1982.

_____. *The Canadair Sabre.* Toronto: CANAV Books, 1986.

_____. *The Pratt & Whitney Canada Story.* Toronto: CANAV Books, 1989.

Miller, Jay. *Convair B-58 Hustler: The World's First Supersonic Bomber.* Aerofax Midland Publishing Ltd. 1998.

Minifie, James M. *Peacemaker or Powdermonkey: Canada's Role in a Revolutionary World.* Toronto: McClelland & Stewart Ltd., 1960.

Morton, Desmond. *A Military History of Canada.* Edmonton: Hurtig Publishers Ltd., 1985.

Mullins, Eustace C.. *Secrets of the Federal Reserve.* Bankers Research Institute, 1991.

Nesbit, Roy Conyers. *An Illustrated History of the RAF.* 7th Ed., Surrey: CLB Publishing, 1990.

Newman, Peter C. *Distemper of Our Times.* 2nd ed. Toronto: McClelland and Stewart, 1978.

_____. *Renegade in Power: The Diefenbaker Years.* Toronto: McClelland and Stewart Ltd., 1985.

_____. *True North NOT Strong and Free.* Toronto: McClelland & Stewart Ltd., 1983.

Organ, Richard, Ron Page, Don Watson, and Les Wilkinson. *Arrow.* Erin: Boston Mills Press, 1980.

Peden, Murray. *Fall of an Arrow.* Toronto: Stoddart Publishing Co. Ltd., 1987.

Porter, Gerald. *In Retreat: The Canadian Forces in the Trudeau Years.* Beneau & Greeberg.

Quigley, Carroll. *Tragedy and Hope: History of the World in Our Time.* Gsg & Associates, 1975.

Regehr, Ernie. *Arms Canada: The Deadly Business of Military Exports.* Toronto: Lorimer, 1987.

Rich, Ben. *Skunk Works: A Personal Memoir of My Years at Lockheed.* Boston: Little, Brown & Co. 1996.

Shaw, E.K. *There Never Was an Arrow.* Toronto: Steel Rail Educational Publishing, 1979.

Scutts, Jerry. *Hurricane In Action*. Carrollton: Squadron/Signal Publications Inc., 1986.

Statistics Canada. *Quarterly Estimates of the Canadian Balance of International Payments, System of National Accounts*. Ottawa: The Queen's Printer, 1953 (pub.# 67-001).

Statistics Canada *Quarterly Estimates of the Canadian Balance of International Payments*, Ottawa: The Queen's Printer, 1974 (pub.# 67-001P).

Stewart, Greig. *Shutting Down the National Dream: A.V. Roe and the Tragedy of the Avro Arrow*. Scarborough: McGraw-Hill Ryerson Ltd., 1988.
_____. *Arrow Through the Heart*. Toronto: McGraw-Hill Ryerson, 1998.

Sweetman, Bill. *Aurora: The Pentagon's Secret Hypersonic Spyplane*. Osceola: Motorbooks International, 1993.

Taylor, John R., editor. *The Lore of Flight*. New York: Crescent Books, 1978.

Trubshaw, Brian. *Concorde, The Untold Story*. Buckram: Suton Publishing, 2000.

Wilkinson, Paul H. *Aircraft Engines of the World*. (publisher unknown, various years).

Wood, Derek. *Project Cancelled. The Disaster of Britain's Abandoned Aircraft Projects*. London: Janes Publishing Limited, 1986.

Wood, Derek, editor. *Janes All the World's Aircraft*. London: Janes Publishing Limited, various years.

Zuk, Bill. *Avrocar: Canada's Flying Saucer: The Story of Avro Canada's Secret Projects*. Toronto: The Boston Mills Press, 2001.

Zuuring, Peter. *The Arrow Scrapbook. Rebuilding a Dream and a Nation*. Dalkeith: Arrow Alliance Press, 1999.

Periodicals and Papers

Avro Newsmagazine: Special [Arrow] First Flight Issue. unattributed. (Malton: Avro Aircraft Ltd., April 1958).

The Avro Organization. Toronto: A.V. Roe Canada Ltd., 1955.

Braybook, Roy. "Fighting Falcon V Fulcrum." *Air International* Vol.47, No.2. (Stamford: Key Publishing, 1994).

Dallyn, Gordon M,.editor. Special Canadian aviation issue. *Canadian Geographical Journal*. (November 1953).

Diefenbaker Cabinet Minutes, National Archives: 28 August, 1958 pages 6-11; 3 September, 1958 pages 2-5; 5 September, 1958 pages 16-18; 8 September, 1958 pages 6-7; 21 September 1958 pages 4, 9-11; 22 September, 1958 pages 2-3; 25 November, 1958 page 7; 22 December, 1958 page 7; 31 December, 1958 pages 3-4; 10 January, 1959 pages 8-9; 28 January, 1959 page 6; 3 February, 1959 pages 3-4; 4 February, 1959 pages 3-4; 14 February, 1959 pages 3-5; 17 February, 1959 pages 4-5; 19 February, 1959 page 2; 23 February, 1959 pages 2-4; 30 June, 1959 pages 2-4 (shows that Canadair was selected for F-104G before tender process); 2 July, 1959 page 2; 7 July, 1959 page 5; 13 August, 1959 pages 3-4; 14 August, 1959 pages 4-6; 5 September, 1959 pages 11-13.

Unknown. "Disc Shaped Vehicles Studied For Potential as Orbital Aircraft." *Aviation Week & Space Technology* (June 1960).

Floyd, Jim. "The Avro Story." *Canadian Aviation* 50th Anniversary issue (1978).

"Gloster's Grim Reaper." unattributed, *Wingspan,* (September/October, 1986) on Zurakowski and his aerobatics.

Harasymchuk, Ted, editor. *Pre-Flight* various issues. (Toronto: Aerospace Heritage Foundation of Canada).

Harding, Richard. "Say no to 'sissypolitik'." *The Toronto Star* (28 August, 2001).

Henton, Darcy. "Avro Arrow: Right Stuff at the Wrong Time." *The Toronto Star* (27 March 1988).

Isinger, Russell and Donald C. Story. "The Plane Truth: The Avro Canada CF-105 Arrow Program." *The Diefenbaker Legacy, Canadian Politics, Law and Society Since 1957*. (Regina: University of Saskatchewan, 1998).

Javits, Jacob. (US Senator). Entry into Congressional Record re: Bilderberg Group,11 April 1964.

McDowell, Donald R. "Five Years in a Phantom." *Vietnam Chronicles, Air War Over Vietnam*. (Canoga Park: Challenge Publications Inc., 1991).

Michaels, Christopher. "Beyond the Horizon: A Test Pilot's Look At The Lockheed A-12/SR-71, From Mach 3 Plus To The Frontiers Of Space!" *Airpower*. (Granada Hills: Sentry Books, 1993).

Norris, Geoffrey. "The Impossible Pilot." *Jet Adventure: Airmen Today and Tomorrow*. (London: Phoenix House Ltd., 1962).

Onley, David. "Zura Zaps Academics." *Aerospace Heritage Foundation of Canada Newsletter* Vol.1 No.1 (April 1990).

The Orenda (Arrow first flight edition). Malton: Orenda Engines Ltd. (March, 1958).

Postol, Theodore A. "The Star Wars Conspiracy." *Harpers Magazine* (August 2000).

Richardson, Doug. "Burning Desire for Power." *Air International* (Stamford: Key Publishing, 1994) review of current and future turbofans and turbojets.

Rogers, Don. Speech and video presentation to Ontario Society of Professional Engineers, 2001.

Scott, William B. "Space Based Radar Pushed as Anti-Terrorist Weapon" *Aviation Week & Space Technology* (April 1995).

Woodman, Jack. "Flying the Avro Arrow." Speech presented to Canadian Aeronautics and Space Institute, 16 May, 1978.

Young, Scott. *Jet Age: The Way Up. An account of the 10-year history of A.V. Roe Canada Limited*. Toronto: A.V. Roe Canada Ltd., 1955.

Zurakowski, Janusz. "Test Flying the Arrow and Other High Speed Jet Aircraft." *The Canadian Aviation Historical Society Journal*. (Ottawa) Vol. 17 No.4 (Winter 1979) introduction by Don Rogers.

Web Articles

"Allison J35-A-35A Turbojet Engine."(http://www.wpafb.af.mil/museum/engines/eng46.htm), 2001.

"Arrow Decisions" [Pearkes re: cancellation reasons 1967] (http://collections.ic.gc.ca/uvic/pearkes/plv5/parrow.html), 2000.

"AWG-9 Weapon Control System.". (http://www.novia.net/~tomcat/AWG9.html), 2000.

"B-58 Hustler." (http://www.afa.org/magazine/gallery/b58.html), 1999.

Baugher, Joe. "Convair YF-102" (http://home.att.net/~jbaugher/f102_7.html), 1999.
_____. "Convair F-106A Delta Dart." (http://home.att.net/~jbaugher/f106_1.html),1999.

_____. "General Dynamics F-111A." (http://home.att.net/~jbaugher/f111_1.html), 1999.

_____. "Grumman F-14 Tomcat." (http://home.att.net/~jbaugher/f14.html), 2000.

_____. "Lockheed YF-12A." (http://home.att.net/~jbaugher/f12.html), 2000.

_____. "McDonnell F-4E Phantom II," (http://home.att.net/~jbaugher/ff4_3.html), 1999.

_____. "McDonnell F-15A Eagle." (http://home.att.net/~jbaugher/f15_6.html), 2000.

_____. "McDonnell F-15C Eagle." (http://home.att.net/~jbaugher/f15_8.html), 2000.

_____. "McDonnell YF4H-1 Phantom II." (http://home.att.net/~jbaugher/f4_1.html), 1999.

_____. "Republic XF-103." (http://home.att.net/~jbaugher/f103.html), 1999.

"Convair B-58A 'Hustler.'"(http://www.wpafb.af.mil/museum/modern_flight/mf33.htm), 2001.

"Convair B-58A 'Hustler.'" (http://www.wpafb.af.mil/museum/research/bombers/b5/b5-36.htm), 2001.

"General Dynamics F-111A." (http://wpafb.af.mil/museum/modern_flight/mf51.htm), 1999.

"General Dynamics F-111A." (http://intecon.com/museum/aircraft/f111.html), 1999.

"General Electric J79 Turbojet Engine" (http://www.wpafb.af.mil/museum/engines/j79.htm), 2001.

"General Electric J47 Turbojet Engine." (http://www.wpafb.af.mil/museum/engines/eng49.htm), 2001.

Gustin, Emmanuel. "BAC TSR.2." (http://www.csd.uwo.ca/~pettypi/elevon/baugher_other/tsr2.html), 1999.

"Hughes AIM-4F Super Falcon." (http://www.wpafb.af.mil/museum/arm/arm10.htm), 1999.

"Lockheed D-21B Unmanned Aerial Vehicle (UAV)" (http://www.wpafb.af.mil/museum/annex/an11.htm), 2001.

Mattingly, Jack. Various information and diagrams from his Aircraft Engine Design website (http://www.aircraftenginedesign.com).

"McDonnell Douglas Air-2A 'Genie' Rocket." (http://www.wpafb.af.mil/museum/arm/arm16.htm) 1999.

"North American XF-108A "Rapier"" (http://www.wpafb.af.mil/museum/research/fighter/f108.htm), 2000.

"Pratt & Whitney J57 Turbojet." (http://www.wpafb.af.mil/museum/engines/eng54.htm), 2001.

"Pratt & Whitney J58 Turbojet Engine." (http://www.wpafb.af.mil/museum/engines/eng55.htm), 2001.

"Project Suntan." (http://www.aemann.demon.co.uk/suntan.htm), 1999.

"Republic XF-103." (http://www.wpafb.af.mil/museum/research/fighter/f103.htm), 2000.

"'Satellite Killer' LTV Air-Launched Anti-Satellite Missile." (http://www.wpafb.af.mil/museum/space_flight/sf14.htm), 2001.

various NASA articles and documents from http://www.nasa.gov, http://www.arc.nasa.gov, www.hq.nasa.gov.

various. http://www.bilderberg.org.

From the Jim Floyd collection

"An Additional Use For The 'Arrow'." *Engineering* Vol. 206, No.5360. October 1958.

Baker, Sir John W. Letter to Mr. Crawford Gordon from British Joint Services Mission in Washington D.C. thanking him for briefings (during BJSM team visit to Avro) by Grinyer, Frost and Floyd, 23 October 1954.

"Canada's Gift to NASA, The Maple Leaf in Orbit." Heirloom Books. Vol. V, *Wayfarers: Canadian Achievers.* Mississauga: Heirloom Publishing, 1996, pp. 340-345.

Cohen, J. "Comparison of Arrow 2 and Bomarc in the Air Defense of Eastern Canada." Secret Avro Technical Department document, September 1958.

Floyd, J.C. "The Canadian Approach to All-Weather Interceptor Development" Paper presented at the Fourteenth British Commonwealth Lecture. *Journal of the Royal Aeronautical Society.* (December 1958).

Floyd, J.C. "Some Current Problems Facing the Aircraft Designer." *Journal of the Royal Aeronautical Society* (September 1961).

Floyd papers. "The Aftermath." June 1992.

Floyd papers. "Aide-memoire on Transonic Transport — Project 1011."

Floyd papers. Avro Engineering. "Proposal: CF-105 Design and Development Program." Ad-15, Issue 2. Secret Avro Brochure for the RCAF, June 1955.

Floyd papers. Confidential letter to Sir Roy Dobson on his December 1955 visit to the UK, 19 December 1955.

Floyd papers. Early sketch of possible Arrow 4 configuration (undated).

Floyd papers. Engineering Division report to Avro Management Committee "Suggested Projects For Study, Other Than Those Presently On Contract." (advanced Arrows, missiles, SSTs, anti-gravitics, nuclear and plasma propulsion etc.), 5 June 1958.

Floyd papers. "Estimated Arrow Development Potential." 28 March 1989.

Floyd papers. Letter to Air Chief Marshal Sir Thomas Pike re: disposition of flying Arrows after Black Friday, 2 April 1959.

Floyd papers. Letter to Dr. Courtland Perkins, USAF Chief Scientist, regarding Arrow L/D max and other aerodynamic data which was enclosed with the letter, 6 March 1957.

Floyd papers. Letter to G.L. Humphrey (Avro UK-Canada liaison) regarding Floyd's autumn 1958 visit to the UK, 20 November 1958.

Floyd papers. Letter to J.A.R. Kay, General Manager A.V. Roe Manchester re: visit to UK, results of "Operation Sunbeam" interceptors vs. missiles tests and 1/2 scale Blue Steel for an RAF Arrow, 10 November 1958.

Floyd papers. Letter to Mr. J.L. Orr, Director Engineering DRB regarding DRB critiques of Avro wind-tunnel methods (open intakes vs. closed.), 30 August 1957.

Floyd papers. Letter to John H. Parkin, Director NAE, regarding the NAE taking the Jetliner for research, rather than it being destroyed, 29 June 1956.

Floyd papers. Letter to Sir George Gardner regarding the possibility of Britain receiving some of the flying Arrows for SST research, 2 April 1959.

Floyd papers. Letter to Sir Roy Dobson regarding suitability of Arrow for GOR. 339 (TSR.2 spec.), 19 February 1958.

Floyd papers. Memorandum to File, February 1959, subject: Visit to West Coast Aircraft Companies, 4 March 1959.

Floyd papers. Memorandum to File (on possible post-Black Friday) projects for Avro, 11 March 1959.

Floyd papers. Memorandum to file regarding lack of historical accuracy, unsupported revisionism, and anti-Avro bias of Canadian historians, 10 December 1994.

Floyd papers. "Notes on Arrow Project." Paper answering frequently asked questions, 10 February 1989.

Floyd papers. "Notes on Discussions With G/C Footit." Confidential letter to Fred T. Smye, 28 June 1957.

Floyd papers. "Note on visit of Dr. Courtland Perkins, Chief Scientist, U.S.A.F., July 18/57" Memorandum to File, 29 July 1957.

Floyd papers. Private and Confidential letter to J.L. Plant (Avro Aircraft President) regarding Floyd's concerns on charges to the RCAF for Arrow Mk. 2A modifications, 9 July 1958.

Floyd papers. "Reflections on the Arrow." Undated.

Floyd papers. "Reflections on the Manchester/Lancaster period at Avro Manchester." Paper written for Stuart Davies, 22 May 1990.

Floyd papers. "SST to Concord to Concorde, A look back at some of the untold history of the birth of Concorde." unpublished, 1990.

Floyd papers. Strictly Confidential letter to J.L. Plant titled "The Arrow Controversy" detailing the British reaction to his visit to the UK in October 1958, 7 November 1958.

Floyd papers. "Subject: Project Research Group" Memorandum to File, 13 December 1956.

Floyd papers. "Suggested Policy on CF-105." Confidential letter to Harvey Smith regarding Cook-Craigie production philosophy, 11 December 1953.

Floyd papers. Text of speech for CF-100 reunion, January 2000.

"Ironclads and Arrows…" *Flight and Aircraft Engineer* Vol.73, No.2560 (14 February 1958).

"James C. Floyd: Putting Canada at the Forefront of Aerospace Technology." Heirloom Books. Vol. V, *Wayfarers: Canadian Achievers.* Mississauga: Heirloom Publishing, 1996, pp. 18-23.

Pesando, Mario A. Letter to Jim Floyd, "Discussions on Ramjets With Curtiss-Wright at Woodridge, N.J., January 31, 1958." 10 February 1958.

Pesando, Mario A. "Long Range Arrow" Secret Avro Project Research Group publication on the Arrow PS-2 and Mk. 4, September 1957.

_____. Letter to Jim Floyd, "Modified Long Range Arrow." 7 November 1957.

_____. Letter to Jim Floyd and Bob Lindley, "Curtiss-Wright Ramjets." 12 December 1957.

Petterson, G.H. "Preliminary Proposal for Arrow 3," Secret Avro Technical Department document, October 1958.

Pike, Sir Thomas G. Letter to Jim Floyd regarding possibility of UK acquiring the flying Arrows, 7 April 1959.

Rummel, Robert W., VP Planning and Research, Trans World Airlines. Letter to Jim Floyd re: Concorde sonic boom and route analysis, 5 December 1966.

Shaw, Bill U. "Arrow 2A Zero Length Launch Investigation." Secret Avro Technical Department document, October 1958.

Shaw, G and E.K. Shaw. Untitled report to undisclosed recipients on what was behind the Arrow cancellation. Conclusions were that it was done on behalf of American political and economic interests and that the real target was the company, not the Arrow. This document formed the basis of E.K. Shaw's "There Never Was an Arrow," 30 April 1959.

Interviews

In many cases below additional correspondence, telephone discussions and email exchanges have taken place. Scores of others, not mentioned below, have gladly taken time to share their recollections and material.

Jim Floyd (Sept 1 1996, July 14 2001, Sept 3 2001, Oct 22 2001, Nov 21, 2001)

Janusz Zurakowski (April 12 1996, Oct 27 1997)

Fred Matthews (Oct 27 1997, Mar 12 1998)

Les Wilkinson (July 14 1996, May 3 1997)

Ron Page (June 10 2000)

Mrs. Jack Woodman (Oct 20 1997)

Bert Scott

Wilf Farrance (May 2 1996)

Chris Cooper-Slipper (Sept 1 1997)

Palmiro Campagna (Aug 20 1997, telephone interviews Sept 12 2000, Nov 10 2000)

Paul Hellyer (Sept 24 2000, Sept 31 2000, Nov 22 2000)

Don Rogers (Aug 18 1997, June 10 2001, Nov 21 2001)

Index

Aircraft & Systems Index

Note: Aircraft are listed in order of development